DEEP STATE

ALSO BY JAMES B. STEWART

Tangled Webs: How False Statements Are Undermining America:
From Martha Stewart to Bernie Madoff

Disney War: The Battle for the Magic Kingdom

Heart of a Soldier:
A Story of Love, Heroism, and September 11th

Blind Eye: The Terrifying Story of a Doctor
Who Got Away with Murder

Blood Sport:
The President and His Adversaries

Den of Thieves

The Prosecutors: Inside the Offices of the Government's
Most Powerful Lawyers

The Partners:
Inside America's Most Powerful Law Firms

DEEP STATE

TRUMP, THE FBI, AND THE RULE OF LAW

James B. Stewart

PENGUIN PRESS

New York

2019

PENGUIN PRESS
An imprint of Penguin Random House LLC
penguinrandomhouse.com

ISBN 9780525559108 (hardcover)
ISBN 9780525559115 (ebook)

Printed in the United States of America
1   3   5   7   9   10   8   6   4   2

Designed by Amanda Dewey

"Patriotism is supporting your country all the time, and your government when it deserves it."

—MARK TWAIN *(Tweeted by Donald J. Trump, January 29, 2014)*

CONTENTS

DEEP STATE

INTRODUCTION

Given his towering stature, the six-foot, eight-inch, fifty-six-year-old James Comey, director of the Federal Bureau of Investigation, cut a striking figure in the Los Angeles FBI field office's command center room. At the back, a bank of television monitors kept agents and employees apprised of the latest news developments around the globe that might impact them at any moment, from natural disasters to terrorist attacks.

Dozens of employees—mostly custodial and communications staff (Comey had already met in person with everyone with a desk or office)—were sitting in rapt attention as he began his talk about the FBI's new, shorter, simpler mission statement. It was about 2:15 p.m. on May 9, 2017.

It's hard to exaggerate the importance of a field visit to the FBI's rank and file, especially one from Jim (as everyone knew him, though hardly anyone ever called him that, using "Sir" or "Director" instead). When Comey replaced the much-revered and exacting Robert Mueller as director in 2013, four years earlier, he'd aimed to bring greater warmth and a sense of camaraderie to the position and to an organization long dominated by authoritarian directors (all white males) who'd run it like a quasi-military organization.

The FBI was still disproportionately white and male, and politically conservative, for that matter, a state of affairs that was one of the reasons why Comey was in Los Angeles. That evening he was going to speak to more than seven hundred minority candidates for the bureau as part of a diversity recruiting event. Comey had flown in that morning on one of the Justice Department's two Gulfstream G550 private jets, a perquisite of the FBI director (the attorney general has the use of the other).

When he arrived at the Los Angeles office that afternoon, Comey went from floor to floor and desk to desk, doing his best to greet and shake hands with each employee, as he did on every field visit. "Tell me your story" was one of his favorite conversational gambits, one that invariably drew revealing details and he thought helped establish a personal bond with employees. Comey deployed a natural charm, a genuine curiosity about the people who worked for the bureau, and a disarming manner that sometimes belied his keen intellect and demanding standards. Perhaps more than anything, he oozed rectitude, a quality that was both inspiring and, at times, intimidating.

The resulting loyalty, respect, and devotion from the vast majority of the rank and file had stood him in good stead over the past year, which had been one of the most difficult and controversial since the bureau was founded in 1908. In July 2015, Comey and the FBI had been thrust into a highly public investigation of Hillary Clinton, the future Democratic presidential nominee, on her use of a private email server. Comey's decision to inform Congress that the investigation had been reopened—three months after announcing that Clinton wouldn't be charged with a crime, and just days before the election—was seen by many as tilting the election to Donald J. Trump.

That controversial decision had already been overshadowed by far more serious allegations concerning Trump's ties to Russia. Unknown to the public, that investigation had begun well before the election, meaning that Comey and the FBI were scrutinizing both parties' nominees for president at the same time, something without precedent in American history. It was a role Comey neither sought nor relished, later saying the possibility that he'd influenced the outcome of the election made him "nauseous."

Unlike the highly public Clinton proceedings, the Trump-Russia affair was shrouded in the bureau's traditional investigative secrecy. Although there was widespread reporting and discussion of Russian attempts to interfere in the 2016 presidential election, and it was common knowledge that Vladimir Putin had favored Trump over Clinton, it was only on January 10, 2017, that *BuzzFeed News* published a controversial "dossier" depicting scandalous ties between Trump and Russia, and it wasn't until March 20, in an appearance before the House Intelligence Committee, that Comey had publicly confirmed the existence of a formal FBI investigation into possible collusion between the Trump campaign and Russia. Even then, he declined to say whether Trump himself was one of the individuals the FBI was examining. Comey's refusal to clear him had infuriated Trump, because it left open the distinct possibility that he was a subject of the investigation.

By the time of his trip to Los Angeles, it was no secret, least of all to Comey himself, that his relationship with Trump was tense at best. Many were surprised that Trump had kept him on as FBI director, even though his ten-year term had nearly seven years remaining. Their personalities and characters were pretty much polar opposites. If Comey embodied rectitude, Trump would have to be described as louche, given his crude comments, propensity to exaggerate, indifference to factual accuracy, preening vanity, and friends and associates of dubious character. Comey found it hard to be in the same room with the man.

That wasn't necessarily a bad thing. Comey didn't want to be Trump's friend or part of any White House inner circle. While his relationship with President Barack Obama had been cordial, their personal interactions had been infrequent.

There was much to be said for an FBI director keeping his distance from the president. The FBI director might have been a presidential appointee who reported to the attorney general, but the position had a long tradition of independence, solidified by the lengthy ten-year term.

As Comey began his speech in Los Angeles, he wasn't the least bit worried about his job. Only one FBI director had ever been fired—William Sessions, by Bill Clinton in 1993, early in his first term, and only after the attorney general at the time, Janet Reno, asked for his resignation in the midst of a scandal involving the director's alleged misuse of government resources for personal purposes. Sessions (no relation to Jeff Sessions, Trump's first attorney general) had hotly denied the charges and refused to resign, forcing Clinton to remove him. In his stead, Clinton named a former FBI agent of unimpeachable integrity, Louis Freeh, who within weeks of his appointment was investigating Bill and Hillary Clinton's role in the Whitewater affair, the first of a series of scandals that culminated with Monica Lewinsky and Paula Jones. Clinton would surely have liked to fire Freeh—and their relationship was tense—but he was too politically astute to do so.

For similar reasons, the more Russian interference was in the news, the more secure Comey's job seemed, because for Trump to fire Comey would look like interference in an independent investigation, perhaps even obstruction of justice. Richard Nixon had famously found a way to rid himself of special prosecutor Archibald Cox, his nemesis in the Watergate affair, in the mistaken belief it would quell the investigation. Instead, it had raised the public's ire and cost him the presidency. Surely that lesson wasn't lost on Trump and his advisers.

Comey was also getting along fine with the new attorney general, the former Alabama senator Jeff Sessions, who was Comey's immediate boss at the Department of Justice. Comey had seen Sessions just the day before leaving for his trip to Los Angeles, and the meeting was perfectly cordial.

Comey was eager to talk about the new mission statement, which he'd personally labored over. It replaced a lengthy paragraph with numerous independent clauses with just twelve easily memorized words: to "protect the American people and uphold the Constitution of the United States." In its brevity, it underscored that the FBI's mission was to protect the American people, not any one person, not even the president of the United States. It was the essence of government by the people and for the people, subject to the rule of law.

As he began his talk, he got through the mission statement and said he hoped they'd refer to it often, repeat it, and . . .

On one of the television screens at the back of the room, he saw a caption, in large capital letters, next to the Fox News logo:

JAMES COMEY RESIGNS

As his voice trailed off, others followed his gaze to the screens at the back of the room. "That's pretty funny," Comey said, laughing nervously. He figured someone in the office had rigged the announcement as a prank. He wondered how they'd managed to pull it off.

More people turned in their chairs.

They saw new captions, on three different channels at the same time, all with the same message. On CNN it was

Breaking News: TRUMP FIRES FBI DIRECTOR COMEY

Comey realized it wasn't a joke.

IN WASHINGTON, D.C., Deputy Director Andrew McCabe was presiding over the FBI's daily "wrap" meeting, a summation of the day's developments, in his seventh-floor conference room in the fortresslike J. Edgar Hoover FBI headquarters on Pennsylvania Avenue, when his secretary interrupted. Attorney General Sessions wanted to see him immediately at his office at the Justice Department.

McCabe, aged forty-nine, and slightly graying, was lean from years of triathlon competitions. It was highly unusual for an attorney general to request an in-person meeting with an FBI director, let alone the deputy. A few people at the meeting wondered if McCabe was about to be fired. McCabe had weathered a barrage of criticism after the media reported that his wife had waged an unsuccessful race as a Democratic candidate for state senate in Virginia and had taken money from a prominent Clinton supporter (even though McCabe himself, a lifelong Republican, had complied with the bureau's ethics guidelines).

McCabe handed the meeting over to David Bowdich, the associate deputy director. McCabe and another agent, acting as his security detail, walked across Pennsylvania Avenue to the sprawling, neoclassical Robert F. Kennedy Building, the Justice Department headquarters named for President John F. Kennedy's brother Bobby—the kind of "loyal" attorney general, Trump often said, he wished he had.

In contrast to the large but relatively austere FBI director's office, the attorney general's office has an elaborate entrance flanked by murals and portraits of previous attorneys general, elegant swag draperies, and gold-upholstered antique furniture. The office suite has its own bedroom and bathroom and comes with a chef and private dining room across a hallway.

McCabe waited for about ten minutes and then was ushered into Sessions's inner office. The seventy-year-old, white-haired Jefferson Beauregard Sessions III, a name redolent of the antebellum South, spoke with a distinct southern accent. He was an early and vocal supporter of candidate Donald Trump at a time when few senators took Trump seriously or wanted to be identified with him. Sessions was an ardent backer of many Trump policies, especially hard-line conservative positions on immigration and border security. Sessions had nonetheless alienated the president early in his tenure by removing himself from any involvement in the Russia investigation, handing oversight and control to his deputy attorney general, Rod Rosenstein.

As McCabe walked in, Sessions stood in front of his desk with his suit jacket on, flanked by Rosenstein and two staff members. They were also standing and wearing their suit jackets, conferring an air of grave formality that made McCabe apprehensive.

"Thanks for coming over," Sessions said, unfailingly polite. Then he got to the point: "I don't know if you've heard, but we've had to fire the director of the FBI."

As McCabe's mind raced, time seemed to stop. Ever the career FBI agent, he was determined to reveal nothing, to show no emotion.

"No, I hadn't heard," McCabe said.

Sessions said McCabe would need to serve as the bureau's acting head until another interim director or replacement was named. McCabe readily agreed, saying he'd do anything necessary to ease the transition and assist his replacement. Unknowingly echoing Comey's remarks a continent away, he grasped for the words of the FBI's new mission statement, pledging to his Justice Department superiors that he'd do his utmost to protect the American people and uphold the Constitution. He felt an awesome responsibility had just been placed on his shoulders at a potentially perilous moment.

Sessions thanked him and asked if he had any questions.

Of course he did, starting with "Why?"

But all he said was he'd need to make some kind of announcement to the bureau's employees.

"No," Rosenstein interjected. They all had to wait for guidance and a statement from the White House.

"I have to say something internally," McCabe replied.

"Don't do anything until you hear from us," Rosenstein insisted. "Do not say anything about this to anyone, not even your wife, until we get back to you."

The meeting ended, and McCabe walked out. Mobile news crews had already massed outside the building.

BOWDICH WAS STILL speaking in the conference room when someone opened the door: "The director's been fired." A TV was tuned to CNN just outside the room. Wolf Blitzer looked grave. Outside the White House, CNN's senior White House correspondent Jeff Zeleny read a brief statement from the White House press secretary, Sean Spicer:

> Today, President Donald J. Trump informed FBI Director James Comey that he has been terminated and removed from office. President Trump acted based on the clear recommendations of both Deputy Attorney General Rod Rosenstein and Attorney General Jeff Sessions.
>
> "The FBI is one of the Nation's most cherished and respected

institutions and today will mark a new beginning for our crown jewel of law enforcement," said President Trump.

A search for a new permanent FBI Director will begin immediately.

Spicer himself was nowhere to be seen (as the cameras rolled, he and some of his staff were spotted among some bushes near the White House, trying to avoid the horde of reporters that quickly gathered).

Michael Kortan, the FBI's assistant director for public affairs, hurried to his office to draft a statement from the bureau.

Still at the Justice Department, unaware of the White House statement, McCabe called his special counsel, Lisa Page, despite the gag order. He had to tell someone. As the lawyer whose job was to advise and protect McCabe, Page had become his closest confidante. She managed to juggle an intense workload while raising two young children. McCabe admired her outspokenness and candor.

"The director has been fired," McCabe told her.

Page said they'd already seen the news on television. (So much for the secrecy Rosenstein had seemed so intent on, McCabe thought.) She said Kortan was working on a statement. "You've got to stop him," McCabe said. Any statement had to come from the attorney general. Page thought that was preposterous; they had to say something to the rank and file, all of whom now knew what had happened and were reacting with varying degrees of shock. McCabe said he understood but was adamant: no announcement.

McCabe got back to his office about 6:00 p.m. The wrap group participants had regrouped in the conference room and were waiting expectantly. McCabe told them what he knew, which wasn't much. He tried to be calm and reassuring in his first moments as acting director. Together they'd take things one step at a time. They'd get through the next hour, and then the next, and the next day. They'd figure it out.

Just then Comey's secretary arrived with a thick manila envelope. It had come from the White House that day, hand delivered and addressed to Comey. No one had opened it.

McCabe did. Inside were a memo from Rosenstein and a cover letter to Trump from Sessions. And there was the actual letter from Trump firing the director. Saying he'd received the attached letters from Rosenstein and Sessions, "I have accepted their recommendation and you are hereby removed from office, effective immediately," the letter read.

> *While I greatly appreciate you informing me, on three separate occasions, that I am not under investigation, I nevertheless concur with the judgment of the Department of Justice that you are not able to effectively lead the bureau.*

That was odd, McCabe thought. Why would Trump publicly link the firing to whether he was or was not under investigation?

> *It is essential that we find new leadership for the FBI that restores public trust and confidence in its vital law enforcement function.*

The letter was signed in Trump's unmistakable, bold, vertical handwriting.

McCabe's secretary interrupted again. The White House was calling, asking that he be at the Oval Office at 6:30 p.m.

STILL AT THE FBI field office in Los Angeles, Comey had managed to finish his brief remarks and then shook hands with scores of shocked and bewildered employees as he moved through the audience.

Once outside, he fielded calls on his cell phone as the news spread. In his first call, he told his wife he still wasn't sure if it were true. He was trying to learn more. It seemed so bizarre that he'd found out from news reports and had still received no official word.

He took a call from John F. Kelly, the former U.S. Marine Corps four-star general and now the director of Homeland Security. Kelly told Comey he hadn't been consulted. He said he felt sickened by Trump's decision to fire him and wanted to quit in protest. He didn't want to work for someone so dishonorable. Comey urged Kelly to stay. The country needed people like him, Comey insisted, perhaps now more than ever.

Comey's secretary in Washington was finally able to scan and email the contents of the White House envelope, and he saw the president's language firing him. It made him feel "sick to my stomach and slightly dazed," as he later put it.

As he left the office, he tried to reassure employees waiting outside, some in tears. It broke his heart to leave them, he said, but the FBI was bigger and stronger than any one person.

Part of him wanted to attend that evening's diversity recruiting event, even as a private citizen. But he realized his appearance would likely cause a media frenzy and prove a distraction.

He suddenly had no job and no professional obligations. The notion was oddly liberating. He'd always wanted to rent a convertible and drive across the country, and now perhaps he could. He quickly dismissed the notion, but wondered, how was he going to get home?

He called McCabe as McCabe was about to leave for the White House. McCabe was surprised at how unruffled Comey sounded. "What did you do now?" McCabe asked.

Comey laughed. "I must have really hosed something up."

McCabe said he didn't see why Comey shouldn't fly back on the FBI plane, given that the crew would be returning anyway. He said he'd check with the bureau's lawyers.

JAMES BAKER, the FBI's general counsel, had just landed at Washington's Reagan National Airport that evening on a flight from Miami. As he and his fellow passengers turned on their cell phones after the three-hour flight, a chorus of buzzing news alerts filled the plane. Then he overheard people saying, "Oh, my God, Trump fired James Comey."

Unanswered emails had piled up on his phone. "Where the hell are you?" "Please come to the office ASAP." Baker went straight to FBI headquarters, still dressed in jeans and a T-shirt. Everyone had gathered in the chief of staff's office to watch CNN, which was providing nonstop coverage of Comey's drive to the airport. News helicopters were follow-ing his SUV, as if Comey were O. J. Simpson. McCabe already had a pressing legal issue for Baker: As a former government employee, could Comey return on the FBI plane? After some fast research, Baker ruled he could.

Although it was getting late, many lights on the seventh floor were still lit. By contrast, the director's office and adjoining suite—normally the bustling center of activity, especially in emergencies—were dark and empty. To Baker, it felt as if someone had died.

IF MCCABE'S CONFIDANTE was Lisa Page, hers was Peter Strzok. The two communicated constantly, most often by text message, which over the pe-riod from August 2015 until the messages abruptly stopped in June 2017, numbered in the tens of thousands.

Few outside the FBI knew anything about Strzok, which was how he preferred it. But at the moment Comey was fired, Strzok was arguably the single most important agent in the bureau: he was the lead or co-lead in-vestigator for both the Clinton email investigation and the Russian inter-ference in the presidential election, a testament to the extraordinary confidence his superiors placed in him.

Since joining the FBI in 1996 after serving as an army field artillery officer, Strzok had emerged as one of the bureau's top espionage and coun-terintelligence officers, someone who could be trusted with the most sen-sitive cases. It was Strzok who had located a rental car used by three of the September 11 terrorists. He embodied the clean-cut, fit ethos of the bu-reau, coupled with a keen intelligence and soft-spoken manner that belied a tough investigator.

No one was more steeped in the details of the Russia investigation than Strzok. Deeply suspicious of Russian intentions, Strzok considered Russia the greatest global threat to American security, implacably hostile to the democracy and freedom America stood for. Even the possibility that Russia had penetrated an American presidential campaign was a threat of the gravest magnitude.

Over the previous months, even as Comey reassured Trump that he wasn't personally the subject of the investigation, Strzok had wavered over whether Trump should be. He knew that to open an official case file on the president of the United States should only be undertaken in extraordinary circumstances. Not that it was his decision to make. All the top FBI officials had discussed it, and ultimately it had been Comey's decision not to do it.

But Trump's decision to fire Comey had now put him over the edge. At 8:40 p.m., he texted Page: "We need to open the case we've been waiting on now while Andy is acting."

He meant while McCabe was acting director—a state of affairs that might not last long. The whole thing was so sensitive that, even using secure FBI-issued cell phones, he didn't mention any names—just "the case we've been waiting on."

Page, of course, knew what case he meant—the president of the United States, Donald J. Trump.

THUS WERE JOINED in unprecedented and potentially mortal combat two vital institutions of American democracy: the presidency and the Federal Bureau of Investigation, the investigative arm of the Department of Justice.

On the president's side were not just the vast powers of his office, which include the right to name and dismiss the attorney general, his top deputies, and the FBI director, but also his ability to communicate, to shape opinion, to attack, and to defend, especially through direct social media like Twitter—an art Trump had embraced with an abandon and virtuosity never before seen in American politics.

Far from ending Trump's travails with law enforcement, as Trump had hoped and expected, his decision to fire Comey led directly to the appointment of Robert Mueller as an independent special counsel and caused the FBI to open a formal investigation into the president himself. Two years later, by mid-2019, seven people had pleaded guilty and twenty-seven had been indicted as a result of Mueller's investigation, including

Michael Cohen, Trump's personal lawyer and fixer; Paul Manafort, his campaign chair; and Roger Stone, a campaign adviser.

What began as a Russia probe had expanded into many facets of Trump's personal and business empires, with Trump himself squarely at the center. The investigation—with the attendant possibility that a combative and controversial president might be impeached, eventually indicted, and, if convicted, serve time in jail—became a national obsession further dividing an already bitterly polarized electorate.

Trump found himself beset on all sides by what he branded the "Deep State"—career bureaucrats and law enforcement officials concerned only with protecting their own power, even at the cost of undermining the democratic process, by bringing down a president who, however distasteful and threatening they might find him, had been duly elected by voters and the Electoral College pursuant to the Constitution. At the center of this supposedly dark conspiracy were Comey, McCabe, Page, and Strzok, whom Trump reviled obsessively in a stream of tweets.

With a near-constant flow of Twitter messages repeatedly decrying "Fake News" and the "Witch Hunt" of the Russia investigation, cheered on by his base of political supporters and a chorus of like-minded media figures, Trump and his allies set about exposing, attacking, and ultimately destroying this purported Deep State. In doing so, they provided a coherent and powerful narrative that they hoped would undermine any conclusions by Mueller or other investigators and reduced the contest to one of raw power. Richard Nixon, the last president to meddle in a federal investigation of himself, had never managed such a feat.

This intensely combative strategy came naturally to Trump, because he'd been locked in some kind of combat for virtually his entire career. Early on, advised by lawyers who urged him to cooperate rather than attack Mueller and his team, an uncharacteristically subdued Trump was on public display. That changed when he replaced them with the far more aggressive and outspoken Rudolph Giuliani, the former U.S. attorney and New York City mayor, who from the start described the investigation as "illegitimate" and spent as much time on cable news outlets attacking law enforcement as he did proclaiming Trump's innocence.

On March 22, 2019, Mueller delivered his hotly anticipated and voluminous report to William Barr, Trump's choice to succeed the battered
Jeff Sessions as attorney general, whom Trump had forced out the previous year. Barr, who'd already been attorney general for two years under
President George H. W. Bush, had sent a letter to Trump the prior year
criticizing Mueller's obstruction of justice investigation of Trump as "fa-
tally misconceived."

Two days later, in a four-page letter to congressional leaders summarizing Mueller's report, Barr wrote that the "investigation did not establish
that members of the Trump Campaign conspired or coordinated with
the Russian government," which seemed to exonerate Trump. But on the
separate question of whether Trump's dealings with the FBI, Justice Department, and Mueller team—including his firing of Comey—amounted
to obstruction of justice, Barr reported that Mueller reached no conclusion on those "difficult issues" of law and fact. "The Special Counsel
states that 'while this report does not conclude that the President committed a crime, it also does not exonerate him.'"

Nonetheless, Barr informed Congress that he and Deputy Attorney
General Rod Rosenstein had concluded that the evidence "is not sufficient to establish that the President committed an obstruction-of-justice
offense," and hence no charges would be brought.

Trump was quick to declare total victory, telling reporters that Sunday
as he boarded Air Force One for Mar-a-Lago that the report was "complete and total exoneration."

And even though he'd just been vindicated, he took another jab at law
enforcement: "This was an illegal takedown that failed."

Other presidents might well have declared victory and called it a day.
Not Trump. In the ensuing weeks, his thirst for vengeance against those
who had investigated him seemed only to grow. "It was an illegal investigation," Trump reiterated two weeks later, stressing that it might even
have been criminal. "Everything about it was crooked—every single thing
about it. There were dirty cops. These were bad people."

On April 10, Barr told Congress that he'd be scrutinizing the FBI's
handling of the Russia probe, and specifically whether anyone there had

spied on the Trump campaign. "I think spying did occur," Barr told legislators. "I think spying on a political campaign is a big deal."

With Barr at the helm, the Trump investigation had come full circle, with the vast resources of the Department of Justice now poised to be turned against the FBI that had so vexed Trump, and specifically Comey, McCabe, Strzok, and Page—now branded by Trump as the "dirty cops."

With Trump fanning the flames, and his loyal and passionate base egging him on, the battle will no doubt rage through the next presidential campaign and beyond.

At the same time, in their quest for total victory Trump and his allies risk undermining America's long tradition of independent law enforcement and, at the broadest level, the very notion that the United States has a government of laws, not men—that no man is above the law. That concept is the foundation of the American Constitution and dates at least to the Magna Carta of 1215, when King John was forced to acknowledge the primacy of English law over royal writ.

In this epic battle, there can only be winners and losers, to invoke a distinctly Trumpian view of the world. There is no room for compromise. But there is plenty of room for collateral damage. The reputations of both sides have already been harmed, perhaps irrevocably, and at potentially great cost to American democracy and its institutions.

Trump and the people and institutions he views as his enemies inspire great passion. Perceptions and judgments have hardened on both sides of the political divide, often based on suspicion, assumptions, and inferences.

How have we reached this juncture? Does Trump's insistence on an antidemocratic Deep State have merit? Or is it a cynical and destructive effort to mask his own potentially illegal conduct by casting aspersions on the character and motives of those investigating him? Do his attacks on the FBI and the Justice Department and his attempts to undermine their investigation of him amount to legitimate criticism, or are they obstruction of justice—the very question that Mueller failed to answer?

ONE

"NOBODY GETS OUT ALIVE"

T he Caucus Room restaurant on Ninth Street N.W. in Washington, D.C., has always billed itself as a "nonpartisan" restaurant, if such a thing is possible in the nation's capital. Perhaps bipartisan would be a better description: it was partly owned by a prominent Democrat (the power lobbyist Tommy Boggs) and a Republican (the Republican National Committee chair Haley Barbour).

Its somewhat clubby atmosphere, wood-paneled walls, and steak-and-American fare made it the ideal venue for the studiously nonpartisan FBI director, Robert Mueller, and the former deputy attorney general James Comey when the two met there for lunch in the spring of 2011.

It had been nearly ten years since the horrific terrorist attack on the World Trade Center had transformed the FBI from a sometimes overly methodical organization focused on crimes that had already occurred into a potent antiterrorist and counterintelligence organization that tried to anticipate and prevent them. Mueller had taken up his post just a week before 9/11, and he and Comey, who was then at the Justice Department, had met twice daily for the so-called threat briefing, a rundown on every conceivable terrorist threat, until Comey left the Justice Department in 2005.

Mueller's office had recently called Comey to suggest a lunch with the director the next time Comey was in D.C. Comey was now living in Connecticut, working for one of the world's most prominent and successful hedge funds, Bridgewater Associates. After years of almost uninterrupted government service, he was finally making some money (his annual salary at Bridgewater was $6.6 million in 2012, according to his financial disclosures), more than enough to put his five children through college.

Before joining the Justice Department, Comey had been the U.S. attorney in Manhattan and before that had worked as a federal prosecutor. Rudolph Giuliani had hired him as a young assistant in 1987, when the future New York City mayor was seizing headlines and magazine covers and cracking down on Ivan Boesky and other Wall Street criminals.

Comey and Mueller hadn't seen each other for several years, and Mueller was now nearing the end of the FBI director's ten-year tenure. "Who's going to replace you?" Comey asked, mostly out of idle curiosity. (Mueller couldn't be renominated; Congress had restricted the FBI director's term to ten years.)

"You know, maybe you should," Mueller replied.

Comey wasn't sure he was serious. "Why would I want to do that, when I was already your supervisor?"

"When was that?"

"When I was deputy attorney general, you reported to me," Comey reminded him.

"Noooo . . . ," Mueller answered, drawing out the one syllable.

"Yes, you did," Comey said. He drew an organization chart on the paper table cover, with a dotted line connecting the FBI to its superiors at the Department of Justice.

"Well, maybe on paper, but this is a much better job," Mueller said, smiling. "You should consider it."

Comey was flattered, but firmly declined. He wasn't about to move his family again after disrupting their lives and moving them to Connecticut.

That didn't stop the press from speculating that Comey might succeed Mueller (also mentioned were Comey's good friend Patrick Fitzgerald, the U.S. attorney in Chicago, and Raymond W. Kelly, New York City's police commissioner).

Attorney General Eric Holder told *The New York Times* that President Obama basically wanted a clone of Mueller, whom the president described as "the gold standard." In May, Obama said he'd seek Congress's approval to extend Mueller's tenure by two years, through the 2012 presidential election.

Comey wasn't exactly a clone of Mueller: Robert Swan Mueller III came from a far more affluent background, born in New York City in 1944 into the East Coast establishment. His father captained a navy submarine chaser in World War II before becoming a successful DuPont executive and stressed the importance of honor, principle, and public service to his son. As Mueller told the author Garrett Graff, "You did not shade or even consider shading with him" when it came to the truth. Mueller followed his father to St. Paul's for boarding school and then Princeton, where he played varsity lacrosse.

By contrast, Comey's grandfather was a patrolman in Yonkers, New York. His father sold oilcans to gas station operators and later scouted gas station locations for an oil company. Money was tight. After the family moved to suburban Allendale, New Jersey, when Comey was in fifth grade, he was bullied and felt like an outsider at his new school.

When he was a senior in high school, an armed intruder broke into their house while he and his younger brother were home alone. The man held them at gunpoint while ransacking closets and drawers and then locked them in a bathroom. The boys managed to escape through a window, only to be captured again outdoors. Fortunately, the sounds attracted a neighbor and his dog, and Comey fled back into the house and called the police.

The gunman was never found, and the terrifying incident haunted Comey for years. But his survival instilled an appreciation for what mattered in life—not wealth or recognition, but "standing for something. Making a difference," as he later put it.

In this regard, he and Mueller were closely aligned. In what Mueller has repeatedly described as a formative experience in his life, a lacrosse teammate, David Hackett, a year older than Mueller and someone he admired intensely, volunteered to serve in the U.S. Marines following graduation. Hackett was killed in Vietnam in 1967 during a heroic effort to rescue fellow marines trapped by an ambush, which only intensified Mueller's resolve to follow his example by enlisting.

Mueller underwent intensive training in Ranger School and was deployed to Vietnam in 1968. Even in the jungle, he shaved every day and made his bed. He was wounded by a gunshot to the thigh; after recovering, he returned to combat duty before being transferred to the Pentagon. He received numerous awards, including a Purple Heart and a Bronze Star.

"Perhaps because I did survive Vietnam, I have always felt compelled to contribute," Mueller told Graff, much as Comey's brush with death inspired a similar ambition.

For both men, the importance of integrity has been a recurring theme. As Mueller told graduates of the College of William & Mary, Comey's alma mater, in 2013, "As the saying goes, 'If you have integrity, nothing else matters. And if you don't have integrity, nothing else matters.'"

He continued, "The FBI's motto is Fidelity, Bravery, and Integrity. For the men and women of the Bureau, uncompromising integrity—both personal and institutional—is the core value."

That Mueller himself had tried to recruit Comey to run the FBI spoke to the deep bonds they'd forged while Comey was at the Justice Department. They weren't especially friends and never socialized together (it wasn't clear to Comey that Mueller socialized with anyone apart from his family). But they shared something deeper, something Mueller had witnessed firsthand at the bedside of an ailing attorney general, John Ashcroft. It was the same quality that Comey had almost instantly perceived in Mueller, and why it was Mueller whom Comey had summoned to Ashcroft's hospital room on a fateful night seven years earlier.

Nothing had done more to solidify Comey's reputation for a willingness to do what he believed was the right thing pursuant to the law, no matter what the political consequences, than his swift and decisive actions as acting attorney general in March 2004, less than three years after the 9/11 terrorist attacks had led to a drastic revision of antiterrorist tactics, including warrantless government surveillance of the phone and email records of countless U.S. citizens.

Comey was U.S. attorney in Manhattan soon after the attacks, and he'd often walked by the ruins, watching firefighters and cleanup crews hard at work under dangerous conditions. He knew the importance of the government's antiterrorist efforts. At the same time, he understood the importance of civil liberties.

After Comey was appointed by President George W. Bush as deputy attorney general in 2003, Justice Department lawyers convinced him that the National Security Agency's surveillance program, code-named Stellar Wind, had no lawful justification. It plainly violated a law passed by Congress that strictly limited electronic surveillance within the United States. Jack Goldsmith, who headed the department's Office of Legal Counsel, called Stellar Wind "the biggest legal mess I'd seen in my life."

The program was so sensitive that it had to be renewed every forty-five days, with the latest deadline, March 11, fast approaching. Even though it had routinely been authorized, Comey concluded that the program had to be stopped, or at least substantially modified, to comply with existing law.

On March 1, Comey discussed his concerns with Mueller, someone cleared to discuss top secret national security information and in whom he had developed a deep sense of trust. In Mueller, Comey had found a kindred spirit, someone whose reverence for the law—the primacy of the law—matched his own.

At his confirmation hearings to become deputy attorney general, Comey had been asked how he would handle politically sensitive or controversial investigations. Comey had responded, "I don't care about politics. I don't care about expediency. I don't care about friendship. I care about doing the right thing. And I would never be part of something that I believe to be fundamentally wrong. I mean, obviously we all make policy judgments where people disagree, but I will do the right thing."

Comey's wife, Patrice, had taped that excerpt to their refrigerator door.

Not caring about politics didn't mean that Comey held no political views. He'd been a lifelong registered Republican, he'd been appointed by a Republican president, and he'd donated to John McCain's and Mitt

Romney's presidential campaigns (though he never publicly revealed how he voted).

Mueller had made similar statements on numerous occasions. As he said in a speech to the American Civil Liberties Union—a frequent critic of the FBI generally and Mueller in particular—in 2003, "Like those before us, we will be judged by future generations on how we react to this crisis. And by that, I mean not just whether we win the war on terrorism, because I believe we will, but also whether, as we fight that war, we safeguard for our citizens the very liberties for which we are fighting."

As Comey saw it, Mueller's "whole life was about doing things the right way." Mueller was immediately sympathetic to Comey's concerns.

Comey briefed Ashcroft on the same issues on March 4 over lunch in Ashcroft's office. Ashcroft agreed the program needed to be fixed before it could be extended. But that afternoon Ashcroft collapsed in pain, suffering from acute pancreatitis, and was rushed to George Washington University Hospital, where he was placed in intensive care. Comey was named acting attorney general and was now responsible for approving any extension of Stellar Wind.

Comey's position had stirred intense opposition within the White House, especially among defense hawks like Vice President Dick Cheney and his allies, who seemed determined to keep the program intact and operational at any cost. In one discussion at the White House, Cheney had looked directly at Comey and said, "Thousands of people are going to die because of what you are doing."

On the evening of March 10, Ashcroft's chief of staff called Comey to report that President Bush had just called Ashcroft's hospital room, where his wife, Janet, told the president he was too ill to speak; he'd just had emergency gallbladder surgery. In that case, Bush told her, he'd send the White House counsel, Alberto Gonzales, and his chief of staff, Andrew Card, to the hospital room to discuss a matter of vital national security.

Everyone knew what that must be about—the extension of Stellar Wind. Bush was doing an end run around Comey.

Comey told his driver to get him to George Washington University Hospital as fast as possible, and the two raced through Washington traffic with emergency lights flashing. While still in the car, Comey called Mueller, who was at a restaurant with his family. Comey wanted Mueller there as a witness.

Comey reached Ashcroft's room before the White House delegation. Janet Ashcroft was holding her husband's limp hand. His skin looked gray, and he didn't seem to recognize Comey. Comey nonetheless told him what was happening and why he was there.

Outside the room were half a dozen FBI agents, there to protect Ashcroft. Comey suddenly worried that the White House might have him forcefully ejected. He called Mueller, still en route to the hospital, and asked him to tell his agents that Comey should not leave the room under any circumstances. Comey handed the phone over to one of the agents, and Mueller spoke to him. When he finished, the agent assured Comey, "You will not leave that room, sir. This is our scene."

Card and Gonzales arrived soon after, with Gonzales holding a manila envelope.

If the pair were surprised to see Comey and other Justice Department lawyers already assembled, they didn't show it. "How are you, General?" Card greeted Ashcroft.

"Not well," Ashcroft answered.

Card said they were there to discuss a vital national security program. It was essential that it be continued.

Ashcroft managed to push himself up onto his elbows. Clearly angry, he said he'd been misled about the program and, now that he understood it, had serious concerns about its legal justification. He paused, his breathing labored. "But that doesn't matter now, because I'm not the attorney general." His hand shaking, he pointed to Comey. "He's the attorney general."

There was silence. Then Gonzales said, "Be well," and he and Card left without looking in Comey's direction.

Mueller arrived a few minutes later, at 7:40 p.m. He found Ashcroft "feeble," "barely articulate," and "clearly stressed," according to his notes. Comey briefed him on what had happened.

Mueller leaned over to speak closely to Ashcroft. "In every man's life there comes a time when the good Lord tests him," he said. "You passed your test tonight."

Comey's heart was racing, and he felt slightly dizzy. But Mueller's words made clear, as Comey later expressed it, that "the law had held."

Comey was so deeply moved he felt like crying.

THE NEXT DAY, Comey learned the White House planned to go ahead with Stellar Wind over the objections of the Justice Department, notwithstanding the aborted visit to Ashcroft's hospital room. Instead of the attorney general, it would be authorized by the White House counsel. Comey didn't believe that people should threaten to resign to get their way. If things became intolerable, if asked to do something they believed was wrong, they should simply resign.

So that night, Comey drafted a resignation letter. So did a slew of Justice Department lawyers involved in the situation. Mueller, too, told Comey he was prepared to resign. It would likely be a mass exodus unseen since the Watergate era—and a political disaster for a president launching a reelection campaign.

The next morning, Comey joined Mueller for an antiterrorism briefing at FBI headquarters, and then the two went to the White House for their regular threat briefing with the president. Afterward, President Bush asked to speak to Comey alone.

Comey didn't always agree with him, but he liked Bush. He wanted him to succeed. He told him he couldn't find a legal justification for the NSA surveillance program. Bush countered that it was he as president who determined the law for the executive branch. "Only I can say what the Justice Department can certify as lawful," Comey responded, and quoting Martin Luther, the father of the Reformation, cast his position as a matter of deep conviction and principle: "Here I stand. I can do no other."

Comey thought he might be overstepping when he added, "The American people are going to freak out when they find out what we've been doing."

Bush seemed irritated by the suggestion. "Let me worry about that," he said.

Bush seemed oblivious to the impending wave of resignations by the Justice Department leadership, including the FBI director. Comey didn't want to threaten to quit himself, but he thought Bush needed some warning. "You should know that Bob Mueller is going to resign this morning."

"Thank you for telling me that."

Mueller was waiting when Comey left the West Wing. Moments later, a Secret Service agent said the president wanted to see him, too, and he went back upstairs.

Ten minutes later, Mueller returned, and he and Comey got into the FBI director's black armored SUV. Mueller told Comey that he'd confirmed to the president that he couldn't continue as director if the White House ignored the Justice Department's legal objections. "Tell Jim to do what needs to be done to get this to a place where Justice is comfortable," Bush had responded.

Comey and his team worked all weekend to modify the surveillance program, submitting the results on Sunday night. Two days later, White House lawyers responded with what amounted to a curt dismissal. Exasperated, Comey pulled out his letter of resignation.

But he never sent it. Comey didn't know what happened inside the White House, but that week, when Bush signed an order extending Stellar Wind, it incorporated all the changes Comey and his team had asked for.

PRESIDENT BUSH WAS reelected in November 2004, and after his inauguration he replaced Ashcroft, who had fully recovered from his surgery, with his loyal White House counsel, Alberto Gonzales—one of Comey's principal nemeses in the Stellar Wind affair.

Over the past year, Comey had become increasingly dismayed at White House attempts to insert political loyalists into the Justice Department hierarchy and undermine the independence of the department, no doubt partly to fend off the kind of principled opposition Comey had mounted. Like many presidents, Bush seemed to want someone running the department whose first loyalty was to the president rather than to the Constitution or rule of law. Politicizing the department by installing loyalists, in Comey's judgment, was invariably a grave mistake. It was the department's independence that protected the executive branch.

Despite their differences, Gonzales had phoned Comey right after his appointment, saying he was looking forward to working with him as deputy attorney general. But Comey didn't have the stomach for more Stellar Wind battles. That spring he announced his resignation and left the department in August 2005, just as Bush's second term became embroiled in controversy.

Comey's warning to President Bush that the American people would "freak out" once they learned the details of the government's domestic surveillance program proved prescient. Over the national security objections of the Bush White House, *The New York Times* broke the story in December that President Bush had approved a broad program of domestic eavesdropping without benefit of court-approved warrants shortly after 9/11, and reported that "some officials familiar with the continuing operation have questioned whether the surveillance has stretched, if not crossed, constitutional limits on legal searches."

A firestorm erupted in the media and Congress, which only intensified after further shocking revelations of torture of al-Qaeda captives by CIA interrogators. Controversy was still raging when Gonzales fired a raft of U.S. attorneys, in what looked like a purge of prosecutors who failed some kind of administration loyalty test. The hallowed independence of the Justice Department seemed under dire threat.

In 2007, the Senate Judiciary Committee launched hearings into the U.S. attorney firings, as well as Justice Department complicity in the surveillance and torture programs. Comey was subpoenaed and testified on May 3 before the House Judiciary Committee and on May 15 before the Senate Judiciary Committee.

Under questioning from the New York senator Charles Schumer, Comey gave a dramatic and detailed account of the Stellar Wind affair and his interactions with Bush, Gonzales, and others at the White House.

While some aspects of the affair had appeared previously in the press, Comey's principled stand, and his and Mueller's threats to quit, were big news.

Gonzales tried to counter Comey's narrative, arguing in testimony and a book that "contrary to Hollywood-style myth, there simply was no confrontation" at Ashcroft's bedside; that extending the Stellar Wind program wasn't on the agenda; that Ashcroft had never pointed his finger at Comey; and that he and Card would never have gone there had they known that Ashcroft had relinquished the powers of the attorney general to Comey.

But later testimony by others in the room, including Mueller, who produced detailed notes of the incident, corroborated Comey's account. Schumer demanded that Gonzales be investigated for perjury and called for his ouster.

Gonzales never recovered politically from the controversies involving the U.S. attorney firings, the torture of prisoners, surveillance, and ultimately his own credibility. Increasingly viewed as a political liability by the White House, he submitted his resignation on August 26, 2007. In accepting it, President Bush complained Gonzales's name had been "dragged through the mud."

Comey's reputation, by contrast, soared to new heights. The notion that he'd defied the Bush administration, and stood up against government spying on its own citizens, gained him national publicity and praise beyond anything he'd done before, even in his highest-profile cases.

When Senator Schumer introduced Comey at the 2007 hearings, he called him "almost a man who needs no introduction." He continued, "As far as I'm concerned, when the Justice Department lost Jim Comey, it lost a towering figure. And I don't say that because he stands 6'8" tall. When Jim left the Department, we lost a public servant of the first order, a man of unimpeachable integrity, honesty, character and independence."

What few were willing to say, at least publicly, is that a man of unimpeachable integrity is not necessarily what a president or any other political figure really wants. Someone who quotes Martin Luther and whose political philosophy was forged while reading the works of the theologian and philosopher Reinhold Niebuhr, as Comey's was, may not be the most reliable political partner.*

Comey's comments about doing the right thing, which his wife so proudly placed on the family refrigerator, struck others as displaying "a near contempt for partisan politics," as Daniel Klaidman wrote in *Newsweek* in 2013. Politics, in this view, requires often messy compromises, even of moral principles.

"There is also an undercurrent of persistent dissent about Comey," Klaidman continued. While conceding they are a minority, albeit a powerful one, his detractors "see a gunslinging prosecutor who is cocksure and possesses an overweening sense of his own righteousness. They contend, further, that Comey took a narrow legal dispute and imbued it with high drama and grave portent in an effort to burnish his reputation. These critics say his actions reflect an unyielding, black-and-white approach to morality."

As a former (unnamed) Bush White House official put it, "Jim has a flair for the dramatic and a desire to be the moral savior of mankind."

This aspect of Comey seemed to become a near obsession with members of the *Wall Street Journal* editorial page, who never missed an opportunity to excoriate Comey for, as they put in a 2013 editorial, "prosecutorial excess and bad judgment." They harshly attacked his role in the Ashcroft affair: "The biggest of Mr. Comey's misjudgments are the ones for which he gets the highest accolades from his media admirers."

The *Journal* editorial page went so far as to compare Comey to Javert, the dogged pursuer of Jean Valjean in Victor Hugo's *Les Misérables*. But such criticism of Comey was drowned out by the chorus of praise, both for his actions at Ashcroft's bedside and more broadly for his efforts to keep government spying and torture within the bounds of the law.

When Mueller's extension as FBI director finally ran out in 2013, Comey's name remained on a short list of candidates to replace him. This time Eric Holder, Obama's attorney general, called Comey himself, ask-

---

* Comey even had a Twitter account using the name Reinhold Neibuhr. After internet sleuths identified it as his, he opened an account using his real name.

ing him to interview for the post. Comey told him he'd sleep on it, but the answer was likely to be no.

Comey was still cool to the idea, but several things had changed since his last discussion with Mueller: after three years at Bridgewater, he was more financially secure. He'd left the firm earlier that year and had recently joined the faculty of Columbia Law School. But his family was still living in Connecticut, and his wife was in graduate school. And surely, with his Republican résumé, he had to be considered a long shot for the post.

Comey told his wife about the call from Holder, and the next morning he found her at the computer studying real estate listings in the Washington area. "This is who you are, this is what you love," she said of the FBI job. "So go down there and do your best."

Comey arrived at the White House for his job interview in May. He'd never met Obama, who was physically leaner and intellectually more focused than Comey had expected. Obama told him that naming an FBI director and nominating Supreme Court justices are the most important personnel decisions a president makes, because their terms extend beyond the president's. He said he felt there was great value in such a long tenure, in part because it helped ensure the FBI's independence. And the FBI director would still be on hand to give Obama's successor as president seasoned advice, something Obama would have appreciated when he was still a new and relatively untested president. What Obama said he wanted most at the FBI was "competence and independence."

By independence, Obama meant he expected not that Comey would have no political views but rather that Comey would never let those views affect an investigation or any other aspect of his work. As Obama put it, "I need to sleep at night knowing the place is well run and the American people protected."

That aligned perfectly with Comey's views, so much so that maybe his Republican credentials wouldn't bother Obama. Mueller, after all, was also a registered Republican. Comey's being a Republican could even be seen as an advantage. If Comey were Obama's choice, no one could accuse the president of naming a partisan loyalist.

Obama invited Comey back to the Oval Office to confirm that he was indeed his choice. "Once you are director we won't be able to talk like this," the president said. A president and the FBI director couldn't be friends and confidants, but needed to keep a distance. The two had a wide-ranging conversation about thorny legal and military issues, like the propriety of drone strikes against suspected terrorists. Comey was impressed by what he considered the suppleness of Obama's mind and his grasp of the issues.

Perhaps Obama was using the occasion to assess Comey one last time. If so, he passed muster. The president announced his appointment on a sunny June 21, 2013, in the Rose Garden, flanked by Mueller and Comey. President Obama began by lavishing praise on Mueller:

> I know that everyone here joins me in saying that you will be remembered as one of the finest directors in the history of the FBI, and one of the most admired public servants of our time. And I have to say just personally not only has it been a pleasure to work with Bob, but I know very few people in public life who have shown more integrity more consistently under more pressure than Bob Mueller.
>
> I think Bob will agree with me when I say that we have the perfect person to carry on this work in Jim Comey—a man who stands very tall for justice and the rule of law.

Obama stressed Comey's experience and character, placing special emphasis on his integrity and independence and citing the Ashcroft incident:

> To know Jim Comey is also to know his fierce independence and his deep integrity. Like Bob, he's that rarity in Washington sometimes— he doesn't care about politics, he only cares about getting the job done. At key moments, when it's mattered most, he joined Bob in standing up for what he believed was right. He was prepared to give up a job he loved rather than be part of something he felt was fundamentally wrong. As Jim has said, "We know that the rule of law sets this nation apart and is its foundation."

Jim understands that in time of crisis, we aren't judged solely by how many plots we disrupt or how many criminals we bring to justice—we're also judged by our commitment to the Constitution that we've sworn to defend, and to the values and civil liberties that we've pledged to protect. And as we've seen in recent days, this work of striking a balance between our security, but also making sure we are maintaining fidelity to those values that we cherish is a constant mission. That's who we are.

Comey breezed through Senate confirmation hearings, attracting praise from both sides of the aisle. He was approved by a vote of 93 to 1; only the maverick Kentucky Republican Rand Paul voted against him.

Comey was sworn in as FBI director on September 4, 2013, twelve years to the day after Mueller's ceremony.

FROM HIS FIRST day as director, Comey put his own more relaxed stamp on the office, a distinct contrast from Mueller's more formal, hierarchical approach. Despite their shared values, Comey was far more extroverted and open than Mueller, who was known inside the bureau as Bob "Say Nothing" Mueller.

Comey gave his attire considerable thought: Mueller had worn a white shirt every day of his twelve-year tenure. Mueller was never seen in public without his suit jacket on. For his first address to the thousands of FBI employees around the world, Comey wore a blue shirt and tie but no jacket, and sat on a stool.

At his first meeting with his senior staff, Comey pushed aside his bulky briefing books, leaned far back in his chair, and "stretched like a big cat," as Andrew McCabe recalled. Comey worried that FBI employees worked too hard under too much stress, which could undermine sound judgment—something essential for people who had been given so much power over the lives of their fellow citizens.

At one of his first staff meetings, Comey began by asking each person to tell everyone something about themselves that would surprise the others—a personal approach that was highly unorthodox at the strait-laced FBI, where most people knew little or nothing about their colleagues' lives outside FBI headquarters. One said he loved Disney characters; another was a passionate fan of abstract art. McCabe disclosed nothing so offbeat, but revealed he'd once been a criminal defense lawyer. The ice was broken.

At subsequent meetings, Comey asked more personal questions, often pegged to the season: What was your favorite Halloween candy as a child? What's your favorite Thanksgiving food? Your favorite holiday gift? Comey didn't care that the questions might come across as childish. He thought children were often more honest and less guarded than adults.

McCabe appreciated Comey's informality and felt his charm; Comey was the kind of person, as McCabe put it, who in conversation would listen so closely you felt "there were only the two of you in the whole world." But most important to McCabe was that Comey shared Mueller's "larger-than-life sense of rectitude." The Ashcroft story had preceded Comey's nomination and arrival.

When Comey took the director's job, McCabe was working in the National Security Division after a career at the bureau that had begun in New York in 1996. A graduate of Duke and Washington University in St. Louis School of Law, McCabe had prominent roles in the FBI's investigation of the 2013 Boston Marathon terrorist bombings and, the year before, the attack on the American consulate in Benghazi, Libya. Then forty-five, he was exceptionally lean (even by the standards of a fitness-crazed FBI) from frequent triathlons; he often biked the thirty-five miles from his Virginia home to FBI headquarters. He wore glasses and kept his slightly graying hair cropped short.

During his first fifteen months as director, Comey visited all fifty-six domestic FBI field offices and a dozen overseas. He rarely wore a suit jacket. He asked his top staff members to abandon theirs, too. He mingled with the staff and often ate lunch in the cafeteria. He encouraged casual conversations and asked for candor from everyone who worked for him. "Tell me what you really think" was a constant request.

The effort met with mixed success. Suit jackets and ties would disappear from staff meetings, only to creep back as weeks passed, until Comey brought the issue up again. However much he talked about openness and transparency—two management attributes he had absorbed when he was at Bridgewater—the near-military hierarchy and deference to authority that were ingrained in the FBI's culture couldn't be changed overnight, if ever.

Still, by 2015 it could safely be said that the transition from Mueller to Comey had been a success, certainly by the most conspicuous measure, which was that there hadn't been another terrorist attack on U.S. soil. That isn't to say there weren't plenty of threats to monitor and investigate, including the rise of ISIS, and controversies, like the FBI's access to private data on cell phones—one of the thorny issues Obama had raised in his talk with Comey.

Still, in his end-of-year message, Comey warned that the FBI couldn't become complacent. "The coming year will be difficult," he wrote. "The threats we face are moving faster and becoming harder to see. The threat from terrorism, in particular, will likely continue to challenge us. But we are up for that challenge. In a way, it is the reason we joined the FBI. We could do easy stuff for better money elsewhere. But who wants that? We get to do hard and good.

"I also think the American people will increasingly look to us as a centering and calming force in a time of anxiety. In the midst of this, our wonderful, sometimes messy, democracy will elect a new president. We, of course, will stay out of politics and remain what the American people count on us to be—competent, honest, and independent.

"Thank you for a year of service and accomplishment. Take a deep breath and hug your families. Hard lies ahead."

Little did he know.

THE FBI HAD already had a taste of how "messy," as Comey put it, American politics had become. To the frustration of many in the FBI, especially McCabe, nothing was more controversial than the bureau's investigation of the Benghazi attacks, which, after painstaking and difficult work in a notoriously inhospitable country, Libya, had resulted in the successful conviction of the militia leader who masterminded the attack. It was Mc-Cabe's first involvement in an intensely politicized affair, seized upon by Republicans eager to lay responsibility for the death of the U.S. ambassador and three others at the feet of President Obama and Secretary of State Hillary Clinton.

The Obama administration had fueled the fires by first claiming, erroneously, that the attack was a spontaneous demonstration triggered by an anti-Muslim video, rather than the planned terrorist assault it turned out to be. But in November, soon after Comey became director, the House Select Committee on Intelligence issued a report after an "exhaustive" investigation largely absolving President Obama, Secretary Clinton, and the intelligence agencies of any misconduct.

That didn't deter conspiracy theorists and their sympathizers in Congress. The South Carolina representative Trey Gowdy made Benghazi a signature issue. House Speaker John Boehner had named him the head of a new select committee to investigate Benghazi even before the Intelligence Committee finished its work. (Gowdy's was the sixth House committee to take on the task, which was all but guaranteed to keep Hillary Clinton on the defensive.)

In July 2014, Gowdy demanded that Clinton produce all her emails related to Benghazi, and his committee subpoenaed the former secretary. State Department lawyers discovered then that Clinton hadn't used government servers for her email correspondence. She had instead used a single private device and a server located in the Clintons' Chappaqua, New York, home. The lawyers did obtain three hundred emails that referenced Benghazi from Clinton's lawyers and turned them over to the committee.

The State Department, now being run by Secretary of State John Kerry, launched a broader investigation and reached out to Clinton as well as other former secretaries of state, asking for the return of all correspondence. Clinton's lawyers reviewed more than sixty thousand emails. They deleted about thirty-two thousand they deemed personal and turned over about thirty thousand to the State Department, which they delivered in twelve boxes.

Two months later, in late February, State Department lawyers disclosed to the House Committee that Clinton hadn't even had a State Department email account, and all her email correspondence as secretary of state had moved through her personal account and the Clinton server.

At this juncture, it was an open secret that Clinton was mounting a campaign for the presidency, the culmination of a decades-long ambition. In that context, the revelation that she was using a private email account and server for her State Department correspondence proved far more significant than anything the committee unearthed about Benghazi. (After two years of work and $7.8 million in expenses, the House committee produced an eight-hundred-page report that essentially reached the same conclusion as had the other investigations, which exonerated Clinton.)

It's not clear House committee members realized at the time what a potential bombshell they had uncovered. No one on the committee made any public statements or drew attention to it. But someone with access to the information clearly realized the implications and leaked it.

On March 2, 2015, just days after the Clinton disclosures to the committee, the *New York Times* reporter Michael S. Schmidt broke the news that "Hillary Clinton used personal email account at State Dept., possibly breaking rules."

The story revealed the startling fact that Clinton had no official State Department account and that her lawyers had reviewed thirty thousand emails before choosing those that, in their view, related to Benghazi. The story raised questions about whether Clinton's failure to archive official communications might have violated various regulations requiring the retention of official records.

Much of that might have been dismissed as technicalities, and the Clinton response, initially, was to brush it off as no big deal. But the revelation hit Clinton in her Achilles' heel. As the *Times* article pointed out, "The revelation about the private email account echoes long-standing criticisms directed at both the former secretary and her husband, former President Bill Clinton, for a lack of transparency and inclination toward secrecy."

Still, there was nothing in the *Times* article to suggest anything criminal about Clinton's use of personal email. The piece noted that the former secretary of state Colin Powell used a personal email account as well as an official one.

Though they'd known for weeks about the issue, Clinton and her entourage seemed ill-prepared for the publicity and compounded the matter by failing to explain why she would have relied only on a personal email account. Her spokesman insisted she had complied with both "the letter and spirit" of the rules, even though it seemed patently obvious she hadn't.

As a public furor grew, fanned by a well-organized anti-Clinton faction that had been honing their tactics at least since the Whitewater and Monica Lewinsky scandals, Clinton answered reporters' questions after a speech at the United Nations originally intended to showcase her record on women's rights but drowned out by the focus on her emails.

"I did not email any classified material to anyone on my email," she said. "There is no classified material. So I'm certainly well aware of the classification requirements and did not send classified material." Whether classified information had been communicated was a far more ominous issue for Clinton than whether she'd deprived the archives of potentially historical material, because disseminating classified information was potentially a crime.

As far as why she did it, "I thought it would be easier to carry just one device for my work and for my personal emails instead of two," she maintained. (At the time, the BlackBerry phone used by Clinton didn't accommodate multiple email accounts.)

This did little to satisfy skeptics, who wasted little time in pointing out that Clinton had been seen publicly juggling multiple devices, including an iPad. And the explanation came too late, days after conspiracy theories were already taking root. As one Clinton staff member told the website *Politico*, "It took eight days to provide a pretty straightforward simple answer. All of us thought, why didn't you give that [answer] a day and a half after?"

The bad publicity did nothing to deter Clinton. A month later, on

April 12, she made official what had been obvious: she was running for president, again. She had few serious challengers. (Bernie Sanders was widely dismissed as a socialist crank.) But ominously, nearly every article about her announcement mentioned the email affair.

By comparison, the field of Republican contenders was packed, with the former Florida governor Jeb Bush seen as the likely front-runner. Donald J. Trump announced his campaign from the marble steps of Trump Tower on June 16. Few took the real estate mogul, self-proclaimed billionaire, and reality TV star all that seriously. The *Times* called his bid an "improbable quest" and his winning the nomination a "remote prospect." *The Washington Post* said he faced "an uphill battle to be taken seriously."

The next day, Loretta Lynch, the U.S. attorney for the Eastern District of New York in Brooklyn, attended a swearing-in ceremony as attorney general, the first African American woman to hold the position. Unlike Eric Holder, whom she replaced, Lynch wasn't a close friend or confidante to Obama. Both she and Comey spoke on June 17 at a packed ceremony in the Great Hall of Justice honoring David Margolis's fifty years in the department.

Margolis, at seventy-five the longest-serving lawyer in the department, was a deputy attorney general who had long served as the conscience of the department and guardian of its independence, under both Democratic and Republican appointees. He bristled at any hint of political interference while often taking the political heat for difficult decisions. He was equally well known for his keen intelligence, garish attire, and sense of humor. Asked once by a congressman how many people worked at the Justice Department, he'd replied, "About 60%."

Comey had spoken at Margolis's fortieth anniversary, too, and this time he dressed up for the occasion, wearing a bold magenta checked shirt, a mismatched striped tie, and a rumpled jacket. While he lampooned Margolis for his sartorial taste and table manners, he said he always threw Margolis the "hairballs," the most vexing problems, and praised him as the guardian of the department's reservoir of public trust.

Meanwhile, the Clinton email affair had attracted the interest of numerous congressional committees overseeing national security, all concerned that classified information might have been transmitted and compromised by Clinton. They referred the issue to the inspector general for the intelligence community, Charles McCullough III. On July 6, he made a formal referral to the FBI, citing the possibility that Clinton had mishandled classified information in violation of federal law.

Four days later, the FBI formally opened a case file on Clinton. Like all FBI investigations, it had a code name: "Midyear Exam." All FBI investigations, by their very nature, are criminal, whether or not they result in any charges.

Most FBI investigations are run out of the bureau's field offices, which in this case would have been Washington, D.C. But some, including investigations of political candidates, are classified as SIM—for "sensitive investigative matter," "because of the possibility of public notoriety," as the FBI operating manual puts it. FBI agents have traditionally referred to these cases as "specials."

Several days later, Randy Coleman, the FBI's assistant director in charge of counterintelligence, called Peter Strzok and asked him to join the Midyear team as one of two lead investigators. Coleman had two basic but potentially inconsistent commands: be thorough and be fast. The investigation needed to be completed well before the next presidential election, which was just sixteen months away.

To be tapped to run Midyear was the ultimate sign that Strzok had earned the trust and confidence of the FBI's top officials, and he was proud to be chosen. Strzok was the product of a military family and Catholic schools. His father was in the U.S. Army Corps of Engineers, and an uncle was a Jesuit missionary serving in East Africa. An army veteran and Georgetown graduate, Strzok had already made a name for himself in counterintelligence operations, especially those involving Russia.

As Edward William "Bill" Priestap, who succeeded Coleman as the FBI's head of counterintelligence in late 2015, described him, Strzok "was considered one of, if not the foremost, counterintelligence expert on the agent end at the FBI."

At the same time, the assignment was daunting: Hillary Clinton was almost certain to be the Democratic nominee. She might well be the next president.

Clinton's use of a private server while secretary of state had already caused a political firestorm. Now, to a degree unprecedented in FBI history, the bureau had been thrust into the middle of it. There would be no easy way out.

"You know you are totally screwed, right?" Comey's deputy director, Mark Giuliano, told him.

"Nobody gets out alive," Comey replied.

TWO

"THE DOORS THAT LED TO HELL"

Less than two weeks after the Clinton email referral, *The New York Times* ran an article titled "Inquiry Sought in Hillary Clinton's Use of Email," though that wasn't the original headline, which had referred to an "investigation," not an "inquiry." And the original article stated explicitly that the investigation was criminal.

The article also cited a State Department memo concluding Clinton had sent or received "hundreds of potentially classified emails" on her personal account, which flatly contradicted Clinton's statement that she had never transmitted classified information on her private email account.

The revelation caused near panic and a strenuous counterattack from Clinton's campaign staff. After the initial story appeared online, they persuaded the *Times* to change the headline and text and append a correction to the effect that the referral was a "security" referral and not a "criminal" referral.

That was nonsense: all FBI investigations are potentially criminal. The referral had resulted in a criminal investigation of Clinton, as the original *Times* article had accurately reported.

Campaign aides might be expected to shade the truth in their eagerness to shield their candidate from unwanted controversy. More troubling to Comey and others at the FBI was the *Times*'s assertion that "the Justice

Department has not decided if it will open an investigation, senior officials said," when one was already under way.

That "senior" unnamed Justice Department officials might be trying to protect Clinton touched a raw nerve with Comey and his FBI colleagues. That the leading Democratic candidate for president and, until recently, secretary of state in the Obama administration was being investigated by Justice Department officials appointed by Obama was an inherent conflict of interest.

There was certainly a case to be made for the appointment of a special counsel, thereby removing the investigation from any political influence. But naming a special counsel was an enormous step, one that risked elevating the importance and visibility of the investigation and damaging Clinton before any evidence of a crime had emerged.

In any event, the decision to name a special counsel was the attorney general's to make, not Comey's. When he raised the possibility with Lynch, she insisted she and others in the department were capable of overseeing a fair and thorough investigation.

Still, the anonymous comment had planted a suspicion within the upper ranks of the FBI that the Obama Justice Department was not all that impartial and, even if it acted independently, had already sent a message that it was in league with the Clinton campaign.

So concerned was Comey that he considered issuing a public statement contradicting the Clinton campaign and confirming the *Times*'s reporting. But doing so would reveal the existence of the investigation, something the FBI is usually loath to do, both to protect the reputations of possibly innocent people and to facilitate the gathering of evidence.

Comey held off. But his suspicions about the impartiality of some Justice Department officials lingered.

FOR STRZOK AND his team of about a dozen FBI agents, the principal technical challenge was retrieving the thousands of emails that Clinton's aides had erased on the grounds they were personal. Two of Clinton's aides, Cheryl Mills and Heather Samuelson, advised by lawyers from Clinton's law firm, Williams & Connolly, had sorted through the vast trove of emails, separating those deemed personal and then ordering them to be erased permanently. Clinton herself didn't participate.

Nonetheless, those missing emails had caused a public furor. That Clinton's aides had been allowed to decide which emails were personal naturally fueled suspicions that if there was anything incriminating, they would have destroyed them.

So investigators needed to see all of the more than thirty thousand missing emails. Even then, their task was not to determine whether the destroyed emails were strictly personal or whether they contained potentially embarrassing information that might have some bearing on Clinton's fitness to be president.

The only question was whether classified information had been transmitted over an insecure network and whether Clinton knew that—a potential violation of the Espionage Act, as well as several other statutes intended to protect classified state secrets. As one FBI agent later put it, it was important that the FBI act "responsibly" and not engage in a fishing expedition "into the lives of the Clintons."

Passed in 1917, just months after the United States entered World War I, when anxiety about German spies and their sympathizers and collaborators was at a fever pitch, the Espionage Act has confounded legal experts for decades. The act has been criticized for being both too specific and overly vague. Probably the most famous cases under the Espionage Act were Julius and Ethel Rosenberg, convicted in 1951 and executed two years later for spying for the Soviet Union.

Not even Clinton's most virulent critics alleged that she was spying for a foreign power. Partly out of concerns over vagueness, over the years courts had erected a high barrier to prosecuting Espionage Act cases. In one ruling, a judge determined that the government had to prove beyond a reasonable doubt that the accused had "reason to believe" classified information "could be used to the injury of the United States or to the advantage of a foreign nation."

That made Clinton's state of mind when she used her personal email a critical element.

One part of the statute, however, seemed to require a lower standard of proof, that Clinton acted not willfully to harm the United States but with "gross negligence": "Whoever, being entrusted with or having lawful possession or control of any document, writing, code book, signal book, sketch, photograph, photographic negative, blueprint, plan, map, model, instrument, appliance, note, or information, relating to the national defense, (1) through gross negligence permits the same to be removed from its proper place of custody or delivered to anyone in violation of his trust, or to be lost, stolen, abstracted, or destroyed . . . Shall be fined under this title or imprisoned not more than ten years, or both."

But what, exactly, constitutes "gross negligence"? Under common law, all crimes require what's called *mens rea*, a guilty state of mind.

Over the summer, the FBI team managed to retrieve 17,448 of the missing emails. Twelve were deemed by the FBI to both be work related and contain confidential information, though there was no smoking gun or other explosive revelation.

Still, there was no doubt that classified information had passed over Clinton's insecure network—the FBI found eight instances of "top secret" and dozens of instances of "secret" information—contrary to Clinton's claims that none had. But it wasn't clear all the supposedly classified information was classified at the time it was sent. Much of it had already appeared in the press.

And all the classified examples came from or were sent to State Department employees with security clearances.

Did Clinton know the information was classified when she sent or received it? Only a few emails had any overt indication—three paragraphs within longer passages were marked with a capital *C* and no further designation. There was nothing to suggest that Clinton used her private email in an effort to harm the national security of the United States. There were no emails warning her that she was at risk of compromising classified information or telling her to stop using her private account for official business.

By September, it was clear to at least one of the Justice Department prosecutors assigned to the case that they needed evidence that would amount to a "game changer" if they were going to charge Clinton with a crime. Comey himself, while he didn't want to prejudge the evidence, was skeptical they'd find what they needed to prove any crime beyond a reasonable doubt, unless, he said, "we could find a smoking-gun email where someone in government told Secretary Clinton not to do what she was doing, or if we could prove she obstructed justice, or if she lied to us in an interview."

OVER THE NEXT few months, Comey fielded repeated questions about the status of what most people assumed was a Clinton email investigation, no matter the protests by the Clinton camp. He knew the questions would arise again in October, at his quarterly press roundtable. So in September, he and other senior FBI officials met with Lynch and her team to suggest he confirm the existence of a Clinton email investigation but decline any further comment.

Lynch felt it was premature to confirm any investigation, even if the referral was public. Many referrals didn't result in investigations, and it was department policy not to comment.

So Lynch suggested Comey "call it a matter."

Why, he asked, would he do that?

"Just call it a matter," she repeated.

As Comey later recalled, the comment made him "queasy," because it aligned the Justice Department and the FBI with the Clinton campaign's contention that there was no investigation, just a "referral." It brought back all the concerns he'd had after the *Times* story. Still, he decided not to say anything at the moment, not wanting to make a semantic issue his first showdown with the still relatively new attorney general, who was his boss.

"Well, you are the Federal Bureau of Matters," George Toscas, a senior Justice Department official, quipped as they left the meeting. The "FBM"— "Federal Bureau of Matters"—became a running joke inside the FBI.*

At the press roundtable, Comey duly followed Lynch's directive. Responding to a question about a Clinton email "investigation," he said, "I

---

* Lynch later testified that Comey must have misunderstood her, because "I didn't direct anyone to use specific phraseology."

am following this very closely, and I get briefed on it regularly. I am confident we have the resources and the personnel assigned to the matter, as we do all our work, so that we are able to do it in a professional, prompt and independent way."

As Comey had suspected, reporters didn't recognize any distinction, routinely referring to the "investigation," even though Comey didn't use the word. Still, Comey remained troubled by Lynch's request. "That concerned me because that language tracked the way the campaign was talking about the FBI's work, and that's concerning," Comey later told the Senate Intelligence Committee.

Comey and others at the FBI were further alarmed in October, when President Obama, in an interview on *60 Minutes*, described Clinton's use of her own email server as a "mistake" that hadn't endangered national security—this while the investigation into both those issues was still in its early stages.

"You know, she made a mistake. She has acknowledged it," Obama told the CBS correspondent Steve Kroft. He added that Republicans had "ginned up" the controversy, and it was "not a situation in which America's national security was endangered."

Comey's concerns were widely shared in the FBI's upper ranks. As Michael Steinbach, one of the top FBI officials assigned to the Clinton case, later put it, the president seemed to be "prejudging the results of an investigation before they really even have been started," something that's "hugely problematic for us."

Republicans in Congress pounced on Obama's remarks. On October 28, forty-four members of the House of Representatives sent a letter to Lynch asking her to name a special counsel, arguing that the president had prejudged the case. The letter stated that a special counsel was warranted to ensure that the investigation was conducted free from undue bias from the White House.

LATE THAT YEAR, the FBI's deputy director, Mark Giuliano, announced he'd be retiring after twenty-eight years with the bureau. To replace him,

Comey tapped McCabe, aged forty-seven, who was already at headquarters as the bureau's assistant director, a largely administrative post. When he announced the decision in January 2016, he called McCabe the "perfect fit" for the job, praising McCabe's "vision, judgment, and ability to communicate."

Still, Comey's choice of McCabe was viewed with skepticism by some veteran agents. McCabe had completed the FBI's demanding training program at the FBI Academy in Quantico, Virginia, and had been in the bureau for nineteen years. He was known and admired for his self-discipline. But McCabe lacked a measure of street credibility. He'd grown up in comfortable, suburban circumstances, the son of a corporate executive. He'd graduated from an elite private school. He hadn't served in the military. His first assignment had been in New York City, and for the rest of his career he'd been in Washington, D.C. He could be reserved and cerebral. To many agents in the field, he was a headquarters kind of guy, someone adept at briefing his superiors, who had in turn rewarded him with promotions and rapid career advancement.

Lisa Page was aware of the undercurrent of criticism but didn't think it was fair. McCabe had named Page his special counsel when she was thirty-six, soon after he was named deputy director. Page was thrilled; she and McCabe had worked closely together while he was assistant director for counterterrorism and then executive assistant director for national security. When McCabe went to the Washington field office, Page took time off to have a second child. She was tall and willowy, with curly dark hair and high cheekbones that hinted at her Armenian ancestry.

Page was born in Los Angeles in 1979 and, as long as she could remember, had dreamed of a career in public service. She attended a specialized high school for law and government until her family moved to Ohio when she was sixteen. After graduating from American University in Washington, D.C., she worked as a paralegal for the Federal Trade Commission to get a taste of what government lawyers do, and she loved it. After three years at the FTC she enrolled in Ohio State's law school to qualify for in-state tuition and lived at home to save money. She gravitated toward criminal law and after graduating joined the Justice Department in

Washington as a prosecutor. She thought of herself as diligent, hard-working, responsible—someone who, all her life, had followed the rules. Law enforcement was a natural fit.

As a lawyer, Page had never served as an FBI agent and was still relatively low ranking on the FBI ladder. But working for the deputy director thrust her into virtually every aspect of the FBI's work, including the most sensitive cases, like Clinton's emails. She was outspoken and opinionated, a quality McCabe encouraged but that led to resentment among some more traditional agents.

Now that he was the bureau's second-ranking official, there were few people in whom McCabe could confide besides Comey, and even then Comey was his boss. So Page often served as his sounding board. She in turn passed on information, even gossip, from throughout the bureau. As in any large bureaucracy, there was a lot of it, most of it of interest only to someone enmeshed in the internal politics.

McCabe and Page were huddled alone in McCabe's office so often that Comey wondered if they might be having an affair, not that it was any of his business; nothing prohibits FBI employees from dating, though those who did were usually discreet.

But Comey dismissed the thought: Page was married with two young children, and McCabe seemed happily married to a physician. Although he couldn't be involved in the campaign, given his job at the FBI, he'd just backed his wife's bid for the Virginia state senate, her first try at elected office.

That the wife of a high-ranking FBI official was running for statewide office, as a Democrat, was an unexpected twist in the McCabe family saga. Jill McCabe was a physician with no political background or experience, but she'd been quoted in a 2014 *Washington Post* article favoring Medicaid expansion under Obamacare. Virginia Democrats, hoping to gain a majority in the next election, were looking for a woman with medical credentials to run for the state legislature, which had led them to Jill McCabe.

Both McCabes went to Richmond to meet with Governor Terry McAuliffe, who'd been elected in 2013 after a long career as a prodigious fund-raiser for Bill and Hillary Clinton. The consummate party insider and networker, he'd served as chair of the Democratic National Committee, chaired Hillary Clinton's failed 2008 presidential campaign, and was on the board of the Clinton Foundation. His loyalty to the Clintons and willingness to advance their interests seemingly knew no bounds.

Generally speaking, all federal employees have the same rights as other citizens to engage in political speech and activity, as long as it doesn't compromise their official duties. There's nothing to prevent a spouse who doesn't work for the federal government from undertaking political activities, including running for office. That Jill McCabe would be running as a Democrat also didn't mean McCabe, too, was a Democrat. Voters in Virginia don't need to register with a party, but McCabe had voted in the Republican primary. He was, in fact, a lifelong Republican.

Even so, and out of an abundance of caution, McCabe notified the FBI's Richmond field office that his wife might run for office and that he'd be meeting with the governor to discuss the prospect. Afterward, as his wife further considered the possibility of a campaign, he explored the ethical propriety of her candidacy with high-level FBI officials in Washington, including General Counsel Jim Baker and the FBI's chief ethics officer, Patrick Kelly.

Under the Hatch Act, which regulates political activity by federal employees, all FBI agents, officials, and employees are entitled to hold political views—it would be odd if they didn't—and to register and vote. They can donate to campaigns and political parties. They are free to express their views and can even display bumper stickers and lawn signs for candidates.

But FBI and Justice Department employees are held to stricter standards. They can't run for office themselves while in the government's employ, work on a campaign, host a political fund-raiser, make a campaign speech, or organize or participate in campaign rallies. Comey went even further. He didn't vote after becoming FBI chief.

In his administrative position, McCabe at the time didn't have any direct responsibility for the Clinton investigation. Of more immediate concern, given his wife's prospective campaign, was an ongoing investigation of McAuliffe and other Virginia officials into potentially illegal fund-raising and violations of the Foreign Agents Registration Act. So after conferring with various FBI officials, McCabe withdrew from any involvement in investigations of Virginia officials.

With that proviso in place, no one at the FBI had any objections to Jill McCabe's campaign. Through his chief of staff, Comey himself gave his blessing, and when McCabe told his wife the news, she made the commitment to run. McCabe himself kept a distance from the campaign while still giving her moral support, which is why that summer he posed for a photo in which he, Jill, and the rest of their family wore "Dr. Jill McCabe for State Senate" T-shirts. McCabe only wore the T-shirt once. But he knew nothing about how she organized or financed her campaign. While Jill was busy with her race, he trained for an Ironman triathlon, which he completed successfully in October. Between that and his FBI job, he had no time for any involvement in her campaign, which was how he wanted it.

The day McCabe and his wife drove home from their meeting with the governor, he warned her that politics could be ugly, and people would say bad things about her. She insisted she wasn't going to be deterred by name-calling.

It never occurred to McCabe that the name-calling would be aimed at him.

ONCE MCCABE WAS named deputy director, he and Page were thrust into the middle of the Midyear Clinton investigation. The FBI team, led by Strzok and analyst Jonathan Moffa, held weekly updates for Comey, McCabe, and other top officials. Over six months into the investigation, nothing had yet emerged to show Clinton knew classified information had been conveyed on an insecure server, let alone that she intended to do that.

That didn't stop some FBI officials from encouraging team members to bring Clinton down, with comments like "You have to get her" and

"We're counting on you." While FBI employees typically said little at work about their political views, everyone assumed the bureau tilted conservative and Republican, especially on issues of law and order.

Given those proclivities, it's not surprising that Bill and Hillary Clinton brought some of those conservative leanings into the open. Neither was popular with the FBI rank and file. Bill had been impeached and his license to practice law suspended for lying under oath in the Monica Lewinsky affair—a felony, for one thing, and a breach of one of the FBI's most fervently held values, which was being truthful.

Many believed President Clinton had set an appalling example to the nation and to future generations that lying under oath would be tolerated, excused, even encouraged and rewarded. The FBI depends on people telling the truth (making a false statement to the FBI is a federal crime). In their view, Bill Clinton had made their work immeasurably more difficult.

As for Hillary Clinton, she hadn't admitted to any crime. But many at the FBI still didn't believe her sworn testimony in the Whitewater affair or her public statements in defense of her husband, and many at the FBI saw her as an enabler of her husband's worst tendencies.

It didn't surprise or even bother Page that high-ranking FBI officials held strong anti-Clinton views. But some comments crossed the line from opinion to advocacy. Jim Baker, the FBI's general counsel, had also heard troubling comments within the bureau, specifically "You guys are finally going to get that bitch" and "We're rooting for you."

Of course, nearly everyone held some political views, especially regarding candidates running for president. Page didn't especially admire either of the Clintons, whom she viewed as no friends of law enforcement. On the other hand, she deemed Trump beyond the pale.

Both she and Strzok were deeply suspicious of Russian intentions, but Trump seemed to revel in what the media dubbed his "bromance" with Russia's Vladimir Putin, long a target of Republican ire.

At his annual news conference, Putin had called Trump "a bright and talented person without any doubt" and "an outstanding and talented personality." He also singled him out as "the absolute leader of the presidential race."

Trump responded, "It is always a great honor to be so nicely complimented by a man so highly respected within his own country and beyond." Trump dismissed allegations Putin had murdered dissidents and journalists. "He's running his country and at least he's a leader, unlike what we have in this country," he said. "I think our country does plenty of killing also."

After Trump called the Texas senator Ted Cruz a "pussy" just a day before the New Hampshire primary, Page texted Strzok, "I'm no prude, but I'm really appalled by this. So you don't have to go looking (in case you hadn't heard), Trump called him the p-word. The man has no dignity or class. He simply cannot be president."

Strzok texted back that Trump was "abysmal. I keep hoping the charade will end and people will just dump him."

That seemed increasingly unlikely. After Trump dominated the so-called Super Tuesday primaries on March 1, the once-improbable Republican candidate had amassed a commanding delegate lead and looked poised to win the nomination, a prospect that prompted a flurry of texts.

"God trump is a loathsome human," Page observed on March 4. "He's awful."

"God Hillary should win 100,000,000–0," Strzok replied.

Page texted again: "Also did you hear him make a comment about the size of his d*ck earlier? This man cannot be president."

Page and Strzok considered these private, even intimate communications. Many more of their texts were explicitly affectionate, even amorous. Unknown then to any of their FBI colleagues, the two had embarked on an affair by the late summer of 2015, when their texting began. The reason they used their FBI-issued phones and texted each other so often—a year and a half later, their texts numbered more than forty thousand messages—was to conceal their relationship from their spouses.

The vast majority of these texts were routine office communications. There were only a few dozen political comments embedded in them, surprisingly few given their shared level of interest in the campaign. Most were responses to news events. Page later testified that "because I was on the Clinton investigation, I actually felt extremely constrained from talking to anyone about politics at all."

Unlike some of those hostile to Clinton, Page and Strzok never expressed any anti-Trump or pro-Clinton sentiments to other colleagues, and both later testified that their political views had no bearing on their professional work. The texts were merely my "personal opinion talking to a friend," Strzok testified, adding that there was a "bright and inviolable line between what you think personally and believe and the conduct of your official business."

THAT SPRING, Justice Department lawyers had completed the survey that Comey had asked for: a spreadsheet that ran to nearly forty pages of every Espionage Act and mishandling of classified information case and investigation. The lawyers could find only one instance where someone was charged with gross negligence under the Espionage Act: a 2004 case against James J. Smith, an FBI agent who worked in counterintelligence, specializing in China. Smith had retired in 2000 after thirty otherwise unblemished years with the bureau.

Smith had carried on a sexual relationship for nearly twenty years with an informant he'd recruited, a Chinese American businesswoman. The government suspected the woman was actually a Chinese double agent. Over the years, she'd allegedly engaged in "unauthorized copying and possession of national defense materials," which she surreptitiously removed from Smith's unlocked briefcase when he visited her home.

The government charged Smith with making a false statement—for failing to disclose his affair with the woman when questioned by the FBI—and two counts of gross negligence under the Espionage Act, for bringing classified documents to her home in an unlocked briefcase.

Though unveiled with much fanfare, the case sputtered to an inconclusive resolution. Smith pleaded guilty only to making a false statement about the affair, so the gross negligence charges were never litigated. He was sentenced to just three months of home confinement and a hundred hours of community service. All charges against the Chinese American woman were dismissed.

Sex and negligence also figured in a highly publicized case against the former four-star general and CIA director David Petraeus. When questioned by the FBI, Petraeus admitted he'd embarked on an affair with Paula Broadwell, author of the highly flattering biography *All In: The Education of General David Petraeus*, published in 2012. But he denied giving her classified information.

Petraeus later admitted that he had given Broadwell access to highly classified materials for her research, had kept the documents in an unlocked drawer at his home, and then had lied about it. The FBI recommended a false statement felony charge, but no Espionage Act charges were ever filed. Petraeus pleaded guilty to one misdemeanor count—removal of classified material concerning foreign relations with the intent to store it at an unauthorized location—and was sentenced to just two years' probation. He also paid a $100,000 fine.

One of the stranger cases under the Espionage Act involved President Clinton's former national security adviser Sandy Berger, who in 2003 took classified national security documents from the National Archives, concealed them in his socks and pants, hid them at a nearby construction site, and later cut some of them into small pieces and destroyed them. He also lied to investigators about all this.

Berger pleaded guilty to a misdemeanor charge of unauthorized removal and retention of classified documents, without ever explaining his bizarre behavior or why he took them in the first place. He also received a slap on the wrist: two years' probation and a hundred hours of community service. When Berger died in 2015 at age seventy, President Obama issued a statement ignoring the offense and hailing Berger as "one of our nation's foremost national security leaders."

Probably the closest case to the Clinton situation was that of John Deutch, former secretary of defense and CIA director in the Clinton administration. Deutch used his unsecured home computer to process "large volumes of highly classified information," much of it labeled "top secret," a CIA investigation concluded. Deutch resigned as CIA director in 1996 and had agreed to plead guilty to a misdemeanor when he was pardoned by Bill Clinton in 2001. Because he was pardoned, the Justice Department never disclosed for what crime he'd agreed to plead guilty, but presumably it was the same misdemeanor as Petraeus's.

The pardon and underlying events seem to have had no impact on the career of Deutch, who subsequently joined the faculty at the Massachusetts Institute of Technology and has served on a bevy of leading corporate boards, including Citigroup and Schlumberger.

These cases suggested that what often started out as Espionage Act investigations involving "gross negligence" ended up with guilty pleas to a misdemeanor. Besides the negligible punishment for such an offense, the government's level of proof seemed to be much lower: "knowing" removal of classified information with "intent to retain" it in an unauthorized location. But because all these cases involved guilty pleas, there were no litigated cases or opinions clarifying the state of mind required or burden of proof.

Justice Department lawyers also looked at a few cases that were investigated but didn't result in any charges or pleas. The most prominent involved Alberto Gonzales, who'd confronted Comey at Ashcroft's bedside. While White House counsel, Gonzales had taken notes about the NSA's top secret surveillance program, including its code name. He kept the notes in a White House safe in an envelope marked "AG-EYES ONLY—TOP SECRET." But when he left to become attorney general, he took the notes with him, failed to place them in a secure location, and acknowledged that he might have taken them home (he said he didn't remember).

Justice Department officials concluded they couldn't prove the requisite intent, which they defined as "criminally reckless." Such lack of provable intent was a common thread in the other cases they didn't charge.

Given the lack of precedent, department lawyers also dug into the history of the act, especially discussions of the phrase "gross negligence." Congressman Andrew Volstead, a Minnesota Republican better known for the Volstead Act that launched Prohibition, testified in 1917 that gross negligence "has to be so gross as almost to suggest deliberate intention." He continued, "This section should be, and probably would be, applied only in those cases where something of real consequence ought to be guarded with extreme care and caution."

These outcomes—none involving any use of a "gross negligence" standard for criminal liability—were hardly a ringing endorsement of the Espionage Act. All the cases involved significant breaches of classified intelligence and evidence of illegal intent, such as lying to cover up the activity.

By the time McCabe became Comey's deputy, on February 1, 2016, nothing more had emerged to suggest that the Clinton case had any of those elements. Notes of a December meeting between FBI officials and George Toscas, the deputy attorney general overseeing the Clinton investigation for the Justice Department, indicate the investigators still didn't "have much on the intent side, right?" and everyone present had agreed.

Prosecutors' notes from a January 2016 meeting concluded, "Don't see prosecutable case at this point."

IN MARCH, the FBI received a document that raised even more questions about Lynch and potential pro-Clinton bias at the Justice Department. Provided by a highly placed informant whose identity remains a closely guarded secret, the document contained what purported to be an analysis by Russian intelligence of an email from Deborah Wasserman Schultz, chair of the Democratic National Committee, to Leonard Benardo, an executive with the Open Society Foundations, founded by the billionaire and Democratic Party donor George Soros. In the email, Wasserman Schultz assured Benardo that Lynch wouldn't let the Clinton investigation get very far, suggesting that Lynch would protect Clinton.

The analysis also suggested that Comey was deliberately dragging out the investigation to keep a cloud over the Clinton campaign as long as possible, thereby helping the Republicans.

That, Comey knew, was utter misinformation; if anything, the opposite was true. And though he didn't doubt that the document actually was a Russian intelligence analysis, the part about Lynch was hearsay piled on hearsay. The analysis didn't include the text of the email from Wasserman Schultz to Benardo; it merely summarized its contents: a conversation in which Lynch had supposedly reassured a Clinton campaign staff member about the limited scope of the email investigation. More fundamentally, other than the comment about "matters," Lynch hadn't betrayed any Clinton bias during the investigation and hadn't done anything to limit the scope of the FBI probe.

Some wondered if it might even be disinformation deliberately planted by the Russians to sow discord. Yet if that were the Russian objective, it had chosen a peculiarly oblique way of going about it. Given that, and the level of specificity, it seemed plausible that there was such an email, even if its contents were largely false.

Comey was already highly sensitive to the issue of potential pro-Clinton bias at the Justice Department. The secret memo triggered a renewed discussion of whether the Justice Department could credibly dispose of the Clinton case or whether a special counsel should be appointed.

In a text to Page that month, Strzok suggested asking Comey's friend Pat Fitzgerald, a tenacious prosecutor whom Comey had recruited to serve as special counsel in a perjury, false statement, and obstruction of justice investigation of I. Lewis "Scooter" Libby, former assistant to George W. Bush and chief of staff for Vice President Richard Cheney. (Libby was convicted on multiple counts.) Page responded enthusiastically, noting "how great he is." (If Strzok and Page were trying to tip the election to Clinton, the last thing they would have wanted was for someone like Fitzgerald to be named special counsel.)

But none of that materialized, and the Russian information languished. The FBI didn't launch a full-scale investigation into the document's contents; they weren't evidence of any crime. Given that the document itself and its source were confidential, it would be classified for the next fifty years. By then, Comey figured, he'd be long gone.

WORRIES ABOUT WHETHER Justice Department officials were biased in favor of Clinton, or whether they might appear to be biased, would have been moot had prosecutors decided to charge Clinton.

But by spring, Comey had pretty much decided the Clinton investigation was unlikely to yield any charges. As he later put it, he knew by then "there was no fricking way that the Department of Justice in a million years was going to prosecute that," given the prior cases he'd reviewed. "There's no way, unless we find something else in May and June, or unless Clinton lied in her interview," which still had to be scheduled.

Not everyone inside the FBI was so confident Clinton shouldn't be charged. Jim Baker, the FBI's general counsel, later said he was "appalled" by how she and her State Department colleagues had handled classified information and said they were "arrogant in terms of their knowledge and understanding of these matters."

As for Clinton's state of mind, Baker thought she should have recognized the sensitive nature of the information she was receiving on an insecure personal email account. It was sufficient to make at least a misdemeanor case that Clinton intended to use her private email account and knew or should have known that confidential information was conveyed on it. Baker said he "debated and argued" with Comey and other Midyear team members over these issues.

There were also frequent complaints from members of the FBI team that Justice Department officials were being overly cautious about the investigation, were trying to arrange friendly, voluntary interviews rather than using subpoenas, and were generally dragging their heels—"slow walking" in FBI parlance—perceptions exacerbated by the fact that so many Justice Department officials were Obama political appointees and that Hillary Clinton might well be their next boss. Justice Department officials, for their part, thought the FBI was being needlessly aggressive, and some suspected anti-Clinton attitudes within the FBI's ranks.

Strzok, the co-lead investigator, took an especially aggressive approach toward Clinton—even as he was sending Page texts disparaging Trump.

In a March message, he described the Justice Department's cautious approach as "death by a thousand cuts." As Strzok later put it, he was "aggravated by the limitations," and "if you add up this delta over a bunch of decisions, all of a sudden it becomes substantive." He often complained to Page, who suggested he compile a list of examples.

These tensions and mutual suspicions came to a head in a tug-of-war over the FBI's demand that Cheryl Mills, the lawyer who helped sort Clinton's emails, produce her laptop computers and agree to be questioned about how she made her decisions, even though that encroached on the attorney-client privilege. Clinton's lawyers fiercely resisted. But Comey was determined to get access to the laptops as well as testimony about the culling process. On this he wasn't going to compromise. He didn't believe the investigation would be credible if it wasn't thorough, especially in light of all the attention given the missing emails and how they'd disappeared.

In April, Huma Abedin and Mills, both Clinton aides and close confidantes, were interviewed by Strzok and other agents. Given their fierce loyalty to Clinton and their skilled legal representation, it came as no surprise that they volunteered nothing of significance. Abedin said she merely transmitted emails from others to Clinton, and it wasn't her place to decide if anything was classified. Mills, even when shown emails containing classified information, said none of it was harmful or even secret, because most of it was simply repeating what had already appeared in the press.

A few days after the Mills interview, on April 12, Comey met with Sally Yates, the deputy attorney general, and Matthew Axelrod, the principal associate deputy attorney general, in Yates's office. The FBI's Rybicki also attended. Comey said it was time to think about winding up the Midyear investigation, although "I'm not done," but his sense was that no charges would be brought. "How do you credibly decline this?" he mused. "And what can you say to people to support the credibility of the work that's been done?" as Comey recalled the conversation. "The more information you are able to supply, the higher the credibility of the investigation and the conclusion. And that especially in a poisonous political atmosphere, where all kinds of nonsense is said, the more you can fill that space with actual facts, the more reliable, believable, credible the conclusion is. People are still going to disagree. They are still going to fight, but at least there will be facts in the public square that show we did this in a good way, thought about it in a good way and here is our reasoning as to why we think there is no there there."

But in the same conversation, Comey increased the pressure to get the laptops and the lawyers' testimony that the Justice Department had been resisting. If that dragged on past the political conventions, when Clinton would be the formal nominee, he said he might well have to recommend the appointment of a special counsel, because Lynch, an Obama appointee, wouldn't be able to credibly exonerate Clinton once she was the nominee.

Yates was startled by the suggestion of a special counsel, especially so late in the investigation. That would only lend credence to the allegations and would cause a political uproar. Axelrod later said he thought Comey's suggestion might be "some sort of gambit to sort of say hey, if you guys don't pick up the pace, right, this is going to get really ugly."

Comey's tactic broke the logjam. Within two weeks, the FBI had the laptops and testimony from the lawyers. But they, too, yielded nothing significant, nothing to suggest that anyone had deliberately tried to destroy incriminating evidence or mislabel State Department communications as personal. (That a few had slipped through the process, out of the thousands they reviewed, could hardly be considered deliberate obfuscation.)

Even Jim Baker, who'd argued that Clinton could be charged, had come around to Comey's view. Baker later said he didn't see enough evidence to establish knowledge or criminal intent and that he had to consider the sheer volume of "communications" coming "at all times, day and night, given the heavy responsibilities that a Secretary of State has." He considered it reasonable for her to rely on others to make sure no classified information was compromised.

In the next few weeks, Comey pondered how best to make a public announcement that the FBI would not recommend charges against Clinton. Ordinarily, the FBI says nothing. It simply conveys a recommendation to the attorney general and Justice Department, which would make a decision to accept the recommendation or not. If the Justice Department declines to prosecute, it typically remains silent as well, so as not to unfairly tarnish the reputation of someone who was investigated but not charged.

Everyone at the Comey-Yates meeting agreed that wasn't an option. The Clinton investigation had been public from the outset, Comey had publicly confirmed it, and Clinton was about to be the Democratic nominee for president. The media was understandably obsessed with the case.

As Ruth Marcus wrote in a column for *The Washington Post* that circulated within the Justice Department, "In the Clinton situation, there has to be a way to provide more information, in a timely way, from a credible source. Senior Justice officials will be mistrusted whatever they say, but what about FBI Director James Comey, who served in the Justice Department under George W. Bush?"

No decision was reached about how to proceed at the meeting with Yates. Axelrod said he had the vague idea that FBI and Justice Department officials would make a joint announcement while standing in front of a patriotic tableau of American flags.

But after the meeting, Comey had what he later called a "crazy idea": What if he, Comey, simply made the announcement, without informing, including, or consulting the attorney general, Yates, or anyone else at Justice?

As Comey described his thinking, "This is a circumstance that has never happened before. We're criminally investigating one of the candidates for president of the United States." He also worried about public perceptions of fairness: "You've got the President who has already said there's no there there. And so all of that creates a situation where how do we get out of this without grievous damage to the institution?" He wanted to demonstrate to the public, or at least fair-minded members of the public, that "things are fair not fixed, and they're done independently."

Comey unveiled his "crazy idea" at a meeting with McCabe, Baker, the general counsel, and his chief of staff, Jim Rybicki, the next day. "What do you think about the prospect of just me doing something solo?" Comey asked.

Some of the air went out of the room. McCabe and Rybicki looked at each other. As McCabe recalled, "The both of us are just kind of like, oh my God, you know? And I, I mean honestly I, I, at first blush I was like, whew, wow, that's, that could go really wrong. Because for, you know, for the obvious reason. It's just so not what we do."

McCabe finally spoke up, warning Comey that going solo would be a "complete departure" from FBI protocol and could set a "potentially dangerous precedent."

Comey said he realized that and agreed that "conventional wisdom" would argue against it. Everyone at the meeting assumed it was just a trial balloon. On the other hand, Comey had never set much store in conventional wisdom.

And there were some who felt the idea very much appealed to Comey's vanity and ego, a quality Comey himself has acknowledged. Making a unilateral announcement on such a controversial topic would thrust him into the national spotlight in a way he hadn't experienced since the incident at Ashcroft's bedside.

Over the following weeks, Comey continued his discussions and tried out the idea with a widening circle of trusted advisers. Baker said he pushed back "aggressively" and tried to "think about how others would think about things." He and Comey considered a range of options, trying, as he put it, "to find some door other than the doors that led to hell."

Chuck Rosenberg, Comey's former chief of staff in what now seemed the tranquil early years of his tenure, worried that what he was proposing was "outside the norm," and wavered over whether it was a good idea. But he also felt Comey was a "compelling and credible public servant" whom the public would trust.

Not even those who thought Comey might be prone to grandstanding questioned his motive, which was to protect the reputation of the FBI for independence and to bolster public confidence in the rule of law, even (and especially) when it was being applied to someone who might well be the next president.

Although he later castigated himself for it, McCabe, too, resolved his initial doubts and came around to Comey's unorthodox view: "Ultimately I was convinced that he was doing what he thought was right and what was right for the case."

IT WASN'T JUST Comey and his FBI advisers who thought he should have a starring role in announcing the results to the American public. The Ashcroft incident had cemented Comey's national reputation for probity, a quality that even Justice Department officials agreed uniquely qualified him for the announcement. When McCabe had lunch with John P. Carlin, head of the national security division at the Justice Department (and former chief of staff for Mueller), Carlin said he felt strongly that Comey should play a "very active and prominent role" in the announcement.

As one of the prosecutors put it, "I wanted Comey up there on a podium. I didn't care whether the AG [Lynch] was sitting next to, standing next to him, or not. But I wanted Comey to make the announcement that the investigation was closed and that in the FBI's viewpoint there was not a prosecutable case." Because "Comey was a Republican, or had a Republican background. He'd been a Republican-appointed U.S. Attorney. He had been a Republican-appointed" deputy attorney general. And "he was widely respected on both sides of the aisle, before this case especially. And I thought that he had the gravitas, that no matter what he did, it was going to be questioned, but that it would be, that there would be an air of legitimacy to what I thought was a legitimate investigation if he made the announcement."

Still, no one at the Justice Department contemplated that Lynch might be cut out altogether. Indeed, some time after their earlier meeting, Yates was dumbfounded when Comey, in a phone call, told her the FBI might not make any recommendation at all, but would simply hand over the facts and let the Justice Department decide. "Jim, I thought we had talked about it the last meeting," and "we were all going to hold hands and jump off the bridge together." Her assumption was "we were all going to stand there together. We were going to announce it together."

With the idea still gestating, Comey began thinking of what he might say. On May 2, he sent an email to McCabe, Baker, and Rybicki, the same group to which he'd already broached the idea. A few days later he expanded the circle to include Strzok, Page, and Priestap.

"I've been trying to imagine what it would look like if I decided to do an FBI only press event to close out our work and hand the matter to DOJ. To help shape our discussions of whether that, or something different, makes sense, I have spent some time crafting what I would say, which follows. In my imagination, I don't see me taking any questions. Here is what it might look like."

The draft was tough on Clinton and in some crucial ways echoed Baker's earlier arguments that she could be charged. The draft stated, "There is evidence to support a conclusion that Secretary Clinton, and others, used the private email server in a manner that was grossly negligent with respect to the handling of classified information." There was evidence that Clinton "should have known that an unclassified system was no place for such an email conversation." There was evidence that Clinton and her aides "were extremely careless in their handling of very sensitive, highly classified information," and "the sheer volume of information that was properly classified as Secret at the time it was discussed" supports "an inference that the participants were grossly negligent in their handling of that information." He concluded, "Although there is evidence of potential violations of the statute proscribing gross negligence in the handling of classified information and of the statute proscribing misdemeanor mishandling, our judgment is that no reasonable prosecutor would bring such a case."

Why would that be? In Comey's view, it came down to the same issues that had troubled investigators from the outset: precedent and intent. As he was preparing his draft, he asked the Justice Department for a chart summarizing every misuse of confidential information case over the past twenty years. George Toscas, the deputy attorney general overseeing

national security, responded on May 23 with the chart, which he summarized in an email:

> *While it is not noted specifically in the chart, the vast majority of the*
> *listed cases involved documents or electronic files with classification*
> *markings on them. The few examples of charged cases where no*
> *markings were present involved photographs taken by the defendant*
> *(e.g., a case involving photos inside sensitive areas of a nuclear*
> *submarine) or handwritten notes where there were clear indications of*
> *knowledge of the sensitive nature of the materials (e.g., a case in which*
> *there was a recording of the defendant speaking about the classified*
> *nature of information in his handwritten notebooks). The "charging/plea*
> *information" column should make it clear, but the mishandling noted in*
> *the chart often occurred in conjunction with other criminal activity,*
> *including espionage, export control violations, and false statements,*
> *among others.*

Notably, there were no "gross negligence" cases on the chart.

As Comey added to his draft, "All the cases prosecuted involved some
combination of: (1) clearly intentional misconduct; (2) vast quantities of
materials exposed in such a way as to support an inference of intentional
misconduct; (3) indications of disloyalty to the United States; or (4)
efforts to obstruct justice. We see none of that here."

Comey deliberately left his conclusion toward the end of the statement, not so much to heighten the drama as to keep the audience listening. It was important to him that they hear and understand his reasoning
before he revealed the outcome.

On May 17, the wider FBI group met to discuss Comey's proposed
statement, and Strzok summarized comments and added more of his own
and Page's. He and Page hadn't written any more texts commenting on
the ongoing primaries or expressing any opposition to Trump since their
flurry of texts in March. Still, given their earlier remarks, it was significant that both Strzok and Page advocated a more aggressive investigative
approach than Comey had proposed.

Strzok, for example, suggested that Comey disclose the exact number of emails that contained classified information at the time the emails were sent in order to "more directly counter the continuous characterization by Hillary Clinton describing the emails involved in this investigation as having been classified after the fact."

An ongoing concern in discussions of the draft was the use of the phrase "grossly negligent" to describe Clinton's behavior, because it mirrored the statutory language of the Espionage Act. That could well cause confusion because why, if she were "grossly negligent," wasn't she being charged?

Comey said he just took the phrase off the top of his head and hadn't focused on the language of the statute. As he described his thinking, he was "trying to find a way to credibly describe what we think she did," and "mere negligence didn't get it because it was not just ordinary sloppiness, it was sloppiness across a multiyear period." He said if he had to do it over again, he wouldn't have used the phrase "grossly negligent," "but I haven't thought of another term since then."

After another round of discussions, Strzok, Page, and Moffa met in Strzok's office on June 6 and used Strzok's computer to delete the "grossly negligent" reference. Instead, the passage now read,

> Although we did not find evidence that Secretary Clinton or her colleagues intended to violate laws governing the handling of classified information, there is evidence that they were extremely careless in their handling of very sensitive, highly classified information.

Some inside the FBI still found this slightly watered-down version to be too harsh on Clinton. Deputy General Counsel Trisha Anderson, for one, urged dropping the reference to "extremely careless" on grounds that it was superfluous and would only raise questions about why her behavior wasn't grossly negligent. But Comey was insistent that "extremely careless" stay in as the best way to characterize Clinton's behavior. Clinton wasn't going to get a complete pass.

All of this, of course, was dependent on Clinton's interview, scheduled for July 2, with Strzok and two other agents doing the questioning. Comey wanted to close the investigation as soon as possible after that, because the nominating conventions were fast approaching. Comey doubted that Clinton would admit wrongdoing or lie. She was a seasoned witness and had a team of top lawyers advising her. Still, anything was possible.

ON JUNE 15, on his newly created website, the secretive hacker known as Guccifer 2.0 emerged into public view: "Hi. This is Guccifer 2.0 and this is me who hacked Democratic National Committee." Guccifer continued in the third person. "Guccifer may have been the first one who penetrated Hillary Clinton's and other Democrats' mail servers. But he certainly wasn't the last. No wonder any other hacker could easily get access to the DNC's servers."

Attached to the email were an assortment of Democratic National Committee documents stolen by Guccifer 2.0, including donor lists, internal memos, and the party's opposition research on Trump. Guccifer claimed he'd had access to the party's server for over a year and had hacked "thousands of files and mails." He said he'd recently turned them over to WikiLeaks.

The FBI had known since April that the party had been hacked, and mounting evidence suggested that Guccifer was an avatar for Russian intelligence officers whose aim was to disrupt the American election. But what galvanized Comey was the revelation that Guccifer, whoever "he" was, had turned his trove over to WikiLeaks.

It now seemed plausible, even likely, that the top secret email that was the subject of the earlier Russian intelligence analysis involving Lynch was among the emails that had been hacked. Far from remaining secret, as Comey had expected, it might now be published by WikiLeaks. Even if its contents were untrue and unfair, the email would cause an uproar and be fodder for accusations that Lynch had fixed the Clinton investigation.

This was exactly what Comey was worrying about—that Americans wouldn't trust Democratic political appointees to resolve the Clinton investigation fairly and objectively.

ON JUNE 27, Loretta Lynch, her husband, and an entourage of Justice Department employees flew to Phoenix for the start of a weeklong tour to highlight community policing efforts. They arrived on the department's private jet at about 7:00 p.m., several hours late.

Lynch and her husband were about to leave the plane when the head of her security detail said, "Former President Clinton is here, and he wants to say hello to you."

"What?" She was taken aback, having had no idea Clinton was even in the vicinity.

Her security detail spoke to someone outside the plane, then said, "Can he come on and say hello to you?"

Lynch was uneasy. She was especially sensitive to appearances given the upcoming elections. She wouldn't allow herself to be photographed with any candidate for office. She was well aware that Bill Clinton was actively campaigning for his wife, who was also the subject of an ongoing criminal investigation by the very agency Lynch ran. But she agreed, assuming she and the former president would shake hands, exchange a few pleasantries, and then leave the plane. It wasn't in her nature to refuse. As one of her staff said, "She's like the most polite, Southern person alive. I don't know in what circumstances she would have said no."

In a matter of "seconds," Lynch recalled, the former president was on the plane. Twenty minutes later, he was still there.

THREE

A SIGHTING ON THE TARMAC

That Lynch thought she could escape an encounter with Bill Clinton with a handshake and a few pleasantries confirmed the fact that she barely knew the garrulous former president.

Clinton talked about his grandchildren. He discussed his golf game in detail, including some rounds he'd just played in Phoenix, where he'd also spoken at a fund-raiser. He discussed the heat (it was 110 degrees). He sprinkled compliments on Lynch, telling her what a great job she was doing as attorney general.

As his monologue continued, with Lynch murmuring little more than occasional pleasantries, Clinton moved Lynch's tote bags off a seat, sat down, and made himself more comfortable, even as Lynch and her husband remained standing. "What brings you to Phoenix?" he asked.

To be polite, Lynch and her husband finally sat down, which seemed only to encourage him. Clinton brought up Brexit and how the press had failed to recognize (as he had) the reaction to globalization and the resulting identity crisis and how Brexit was simply a manifestation of that.

"We've got to get going to the hotel," Lynch said. "And I'm sure you've got somewhere to go."

"Yes," Clinton said, mentioning the next stop on his trip but then moving on to a lengthy discourse on coal miners in West Virginia and "how their problems really stem from policies that were set forth in 1932.

And he talked about those policies for a while," Lynch recalled. "And I said, okay, well."

Waiting impatiently in a van outside were Lynch's staff. As Lynch's deputy chief of staff, Shirlethia Franklin, put it, she was "shocked," and they all "just felt completely blindsided." Lynch's counselor, Uma Amuluru, agreed. The "optics," to put it mildly, "were not great." The longer the encounter went on, the worse it looked.

Amuluru finally got out of the van and headed toward the plane, thinking, "I don't know what's going on up there, but I should at least go up to intervene or help her if she needs help," recognizing that "this is a bad idea." Once on the plane, she stood conspicuously near the group, hoping to break up the conversation. She shook hands with Clinton, who, unfazed, continued talking. But face to face with a former president, she hesitated to interrupt, so she just stared at them a little longer.

Finally Lynch interrupted to say that Amuluru was too polite to say so, but the reason she was standing there was that they had to go.

"Oh, she's mad at me, because I'd been on the plane too long," Clinton said. "And she's come to get you."

"We do have to go," Lynch repeated.

"And then he kept talking about something else," Lynch recalled. After about another five minutes, she stood up and firmly thanked him for coming. After a round of handshakes, he finally left.

Amuluru looked at Lynch. The attorney general, she recalled, looked "gray" and "not pleased."

"That was not great," she said.

"Yeah," Lynch acknowledged.

THAT BILL CLINTON would be so tone-deaf as to initiate an extended private conversation with the attorney general, the very person weighing criminal charges against his wife, just five days before her FBI interview astonished Lynch's staff. Franklin was furious that Lynch's FBI security guard let Clinton on the plane in the first place.

Clinton was defensive when asked about the encounter and said it was a spontaneous, unplanned gesture and he didn't "want her to think I'm afraid to shake hands with her because she's the Attorney General." He did raise with his own chief of staff the issue of how it would look but went ahead anyway because "I thought it would look really crazy" if "I couldn't shake hands with the Attorney General, you know, when she was right there." As for the ongoing email investigation, he never thought it "amounted to much, frankly, so I didn't probably take it as seriously as maybe I might have in this unusual period."

Clinton's and Lynch's recollections of their extended and, at least for Lynch, awkward encounter differ in some details but agree on the central issue: the Midyear investigation never came up, nor was there any mention of Comey, nor any discussion of positions Lynch might look forward to in a Hillary Clinton administration.

Then again, none of those things needed to be mentioned: they were implicit in Clinton's presence. However benign his intent, had Clinton wanted to sabotage his wife's campaign, he would have been hard-pressed to find a more effective means.

(To many, it was reminiscent of Clinton's damaging remarks in 2008 dismissing his wife's loss to Obama in the South Carolina primary, when he noted that Jesse Jackson had won there in 2000 and 2004 before being trounced elsewhere. Those comments caused such an uproar that Hillary apologized, saying her husband never meant to inject race into the campaign. Bill was muzzled, but her campaign never recovered.)

Less than twenty-four hours later, a local ABC reporter in Phoenix, Christopher Sign, received a tip that Lynch and Clinton had been huddled on the attorney general's plane for half an hour. An ABC reporter in Washington contacted Lynch's director of public affairs for comment, which triggered a series of phone calls and some "talking points" for Lynch.

Later that day, Sign asked Lynch about the meeting at her Phoenix press conference and asked if they'd talked about Hillary Clinton and Benghazi.

"No," Lynch replied. "Actually, while I was landing at the airport, I did see President Clinton at the Phoenix airport as I was leaving, and he spoke to myself and my husband on the plane." She said the conversation was "primarily social" and ticked off the topics they'd covered, starting with his grandchildren. "There was no discussion of Benghazi, no discussion of the State Department emails, by way of example."

Justice Department officials were initially relieved that Sign asked no follow-up questions. But after he broke the story on the next morning's news, Fox News ran with it on multiple programs. The Fox host Bill O'Reilly had Sign appear on his show, and Sign said his "jaw dropped" when his source told him Clinton was meeting privately with Lynch on her plane. Soon the Justice Department was fending off a media frenzy, with every major news outlet asking the same question: Why would Lynch meet with Clinton when his wife was under investigation?

As Amy Chozick wrote in *The New York Times*, the encounter "caused a cascading political storm for Mrs. Clinton's campaign; provided fodder for Republicans who have accused the Justice Department of bias in its inquiry into Mrs. Clinton's use of a private email server at the State Department; and even had Mrs. Clinton's allies asking Friday: What was he thinking?

As Melanie Newman, Lynch's head of public affairs, later put it, Lynch "doesn't take mistakes lightly, and she felt like she had made an incredible mistake in judgment by saying yes instead of no, that he could come on the plane."

At FBI headquarters, Comey, McCabe, and other top officials viewed the furor with mounting dismay. Comey forwarded a link to the first Fox News report—"Why Did Bill Clinton and Loretta Lynch Meet at Her Airplane in Phoenix?"

Strzok, who was busy preparing for the climactic Clinton interview, texted Page: "All the airport tarmac articles finally burst out." He said it was "not a big deal, just ASTOUNDINGLY bad optic." So bad that he wondered if the Clinton interview should be postponed, but decided not. As he said in an email to Priestap, "Timing's not ideal in that it falsely adds to those seeking the 'this is all choreographed' narrative. But I don't think it's worth changing. Later won't be better."

For Comey, the tarmac incident and resulting publicity erased any lingering doubts about what he'd earlier considered his "crazy," go-it-alone strategy to end the investigation without consulting Lynch or anyone else at Justice.

As he later put it, the tarmac meeting "made it easy for me" and "tipped the scales."

On June 30, he added a paragraph to his proposed statement that made his unorthodox approach explicit:

> This will be an unusual statement in at least a couple ways. First, I am going to include more detail than I ordinarily would, because I think the American people deserve those details in a case of intense public interest. Second, I have not coordinated or reviewed this statement in any way with the Department of Justice or any other part of the government. They do not know what I am about to say.

The media furor over the tarmac meeting triggered another round of discussions inside the Justice Department about whether Lynch should step aside and hand supervision of the case over to her deputy, Yates. But doing so might only inflame the perception that she and Clinton had discussed something improper, when she insisted she hadn't.

And although Lynch was the ultimate decision maker about whether Clinton would be charged, she had always planned to follow the recommendations of career officials at the department and Comey at the FBI.

Not everyone agreed with this approach. Newman, for one, felt Lynch should step aside, and failing to do so, while at the same time saying she'd accept whatever recommendation she got, risked trying "to have it both ways."

But Newman was overruled, and Lynch decided to stress this element during her talk at the Aspen Ideas Festival moderated by Jonathan Capehart, a *Washington Post* columnist, on July 1, just a day before Clinton's interview. Capehart asked about the tarmac meeting and whether Lynch regretted not kicking Clinton off the plane. "I certainly wouldn't do it again," she said of the former president's visit.

Asked about the resulting appearance of a conflict, she responded, "I completely get that question, and I think it is the question of the day." She said the resolution of the Clinton investigation would be "reviewed by career supervisors in the Department of Justice and in the FBI and by the FBI Director. And then, as is the common process, they present it to me and I fully expect to accept their recommendations." While she wouldn't be formally recusing herself, "I'll be briefed on it and I will be accepting their recommendations."

Comey interpreted this as tacit encouragement to go ahead and make a decision. As Newman had feared, he saw Lynch's position as "neither fish nor fowl" in that she wanted to remain the ultimate decision maker but at the same time accept his recommendation, thereby removing herself (and the Justice Department) from criticism.

With the nominating conventions drawing ever closer, Comey was eager to make the announcement as soon as possible and settled on Tuesday, July 5, the day after the national Independence Day holiday, and just three days after Clinton's interview. He believed it was still possible, though unlikely, that Clinton would say something incriminating. But all planning was geared toward a recommendation that she not be charged. There was no plan B, not even any discussions of the explosive alternative, which might well have ended her campaign.

The plan was that Comey would call Yates at 8:30 a.m., followed by Lynch at 8:35. On July 1, Comey sent Rybicki an email, "What I will say Tuesday on phone." He planned to read from a script to make sure he said nothing of substance about his decision:

> I wanted to let you know that I am doing a press conference this morning announcing the completion of our Midyear investigation and referral of the matter to DOJ. I'm not going to tell you anything about what I will say, for reasons I hope you understand. I think it is very important that I not have coordinated my statement outside the FBI. I'm not going to take questions at the press conference. When it is over, my staff will be available to work with your team.

HILLARY CLINTON ARRIVED at FBI headquarters for her interview on the morning of July 2, 2016, entering through a basement garage. That, plus it being a Saturday of a holiday weekend, enabled her to escape any public attention. Representing the government were Strzok, two FBI agents, and five Justice Department officials. Neither Lynch nor Comey attended, as was customary, given their oversight roles.

Who and how many people would attend had been the subject of much discussion and debate—an absurd amount, in the view of Page, who had to coordinate the various requests and found it "wildly aggravating," as she put it in a text message. Standard procedure was "two and two"—two FBI agents to do the questioning and two prosecutors. Any more risked intimidating the witness and made it difficult for agents to establish a rapport. But given Clinton's celebrity, everyone wanted to pile on, which prompted a text from Page to McCabe: "Hey, you've surely already considered this, but in my view our best reason to hold the line at 2 and 2 is: She might be our next president. The last thing we need is us going in there loaded for bear, when it is not operationally necessary. You think she's going to remember or care that it was more doj than fbi? This is as much about reputational protection as anything." McCabe replied, "Agree. Strongly."

Page's concerns came to naught: ultimately eight government representatives attended (three from the FBI, five from Justice) as well as Clinton's entourage.

As Comey and the Midyear team had assumed, Clinton was obviously well prepared. She was an experienced witness and had endured intense pressure before, notably when Independent Counsel Kenneth Starr asked her about the curious discovery in the White House of Rose Law Firm billing records that had been missing—and subject to a subpoena—for years. In many ways, the email investigation was easier. She and her lawyers knew the relevant laws and cases and thus that her state of mind was a critical element. During her interview she came across as open and credible on most subjects.

It also worked to Clinton's advantage, as one of the agents later put it, that she was basically "technically illiterate." She still used a woefully outdated BlackBerry handset. Even then, her staff printed out emails and documents for her to read. She didn't even have a computer in her State Department office. (Bill Clinton was even worse. Although he sent the first email from the Oval Office in 1994, he had only used it on rare occasions since.)

While she might have known little about how they worked, Clinton did use many different devices—thirteen in all for her two phone numbers and eight while she was secretary of state. Huma Abedin said Clinton often lost track of them once she stopped using them. Another aide, Justin Cooper, said he'd disposed of two by breaking them with a hammer. (Clinton herself, however, never took a hammer to any device.)

Hillary Clinton knew there was a computer server at her home, but knew little about what servers actually did, or what documents might be preserved on them. In this light, it was plausible that she used her private email purely for reasons of convenience—she didn't want to deal with multiple email accounts—rather than to conceal anything, evade security measures, or destroy official records.

On the key state-of-mind issue—whether she knew anything she transmitted was confidential—she stayed firmly with the story that she didn't. The agents showed her numerous emails containing classified information. In every case, she said she didn't believe it was classified and assumed her aides and others wouldn't send her classified information via email.

The agents pressed her on the emails containing the *C*s, meaning "confidential." Clinton said she didn't know what the *C* meant but "speculated it was a reference to paragraphs ranked in alphabetical order," as the agents wrote in their interview summary. Given there was no *A* or *B* in the document, that struck them as far-fetched. The agents asked her about it four or five times, always getting the same answer.

On the other hand, Clinton maintained that she didn't believe that information was confidential (she was mostly right; it was later determined that only one of the three paragraphs marked with a *C* was secret), and nowhere in the document was there any indication that *C* meant "confidential." As one of the agents put it, "I can't sit here and tell you I believed her. I can only tell you, in no particular could we prove that she was being untruthful to us."

On the potentially damaging subject of the thousands of personal emails that had been deleted, Clinton said she had almost nothing to do with the decision. She testified (as her aides had previously) that she "never deleted, nor did she instruct anyone to delete, her email to avoid complying with Federal Records Act, FOIA, or State or FBI requests for information" and that she "trusted her legal team" would comply with any requests to preserve them, according to the interview notes.

When the agents showed her one of the emails that had been deleted as personal but contained official business, she readily agreed that it should have been retained and handed over.

For the FBI, the issue wasn't whether they believed her but whether they could prove beyond a reasonable doubt that she lied. Not only was her state of mind inherently subjective, and thus difficult to prove or disprove, but her demeanor seemed relaxed and confident, something that Strzok and the agents stressed when they briefed Comey on the interview.

The interview lasted three and a half hours. Nothing Clinton said had changed anyone's mind that she should not be charged with a crime.

In theory, of course, she could have been. She had been careless, and classified information had been transmitted on an insecure network. On the other hand, by that standard, half the State Department would have to be charged. There might even have been enough evidence to ask a jury to consider a misdemeanor or gross negligence standard, although the likelihood of conviction seemed remote. Comey wasn't going to recommend prosecuting a case the department was almost sure to lose.

Of course it weighed on everyone involved that Clinton was the presumptive presidential nominee and, based on early polling, the likely next president. She was a former first lady and secretary of state. Had she been charged, with no clear precedent to justify it, a furor was certain to follow, and the damage to the credibility of the FBI would have been incalculable.

As Comey later explained, everyone involved in the investigation ultimately agreed "there isn't anything that anybody could prosecute. My view was the same. Everybody between me and the people who worked this case felt the same way about it. It was not a prosecutable case. The decision there was not a prosecutable case here was not a hard one. The hard one, as I've told you, was how do we communicate about it."

THE FIRST INKLING that something major was afoot reached the Justice Department at 8:08 a.m. on July 5, when a reporter contacted Melanie Newman in the press office. Newman tapped out an email:

> Just heard that the Director is having a press briefing today at 11 a.m. I have not heard anything but have asked for guidance.

The FBI had worked out a carefully choreographed rollout of the news. Comey reached Yates at 8:28 a.m., two minutes ahead of schedule. He stuck to his script and refused to tell Yates the subject of the impending press conference.

Comey reached Lynch in her office shortly after and spoke from the same script. "Can you tell me what your recommendation is going to be?" Lynch asked.

"I can't and I hope someday you'll understand why," Comey replied. "I can't answer any questions. I'm not going to tell you what I'm going to say."

While Comey was still on the phone, Strzok tried to reach George Toscas, but he was traveling. So McCabe sent Toscas an email:

> The Director just informed [Yates] that at 1100 this morning he has convened a press conference to announce the completion of our investigation and the referral to DOJ. He will not tell her what he is going to say. It is important that he not coordinate his statement in any way. He will not take questions at the conference. His next call is to the AG. I wanted you to hear this from me. I understand that this will be troubling to the team and I very much regret that.

Lynch was Comey's boss, and she could have ordered him to stop. So could Yates, as Lynch's deputy. Indeed, one of the reasons Comey didn't want to reveal anything about what he had to say was that he feared they would block him.

But no one at Justice gave that any consideration. Neither Yates nor Lynch thought Comey would go much beyond a brief statement. It never occurred to Lynch that Comey might go into the results of an investigation that, so far as she knew, wasn't even over. After all, Clinton had been interviewed just three days earlier. And all the machinery of a nationally televised press conference had already been set in motion. For the attorney general to block an announcement by the FBI director on a matter of such political significance risked a public relations nightmare.

LIKE MILLIONS OF Americans, Lynch watched Comey's press conference on a television in her office. Yates, joined by Axelrod, watched in her office. "Good morning," Comey began. "I'm here to give you an update on the FBI's investigation of Secretary Clinton's use of a personal e-mail system during her time as Secretary of State."

As Comey continued with a detailed account of what the FBI had done, and what they found, they listened with mounting dismay: "110 e-mails in 52 e-mail chains have been determined by the owning agency to contain classified information at the time they were sent or received. Eight of those chains contained information that was Top Secret at the time they were sent; 36 chains contained Secret information at the time; and eight contained Confidential information, which is the lowest level of classification. Separate from those, about 2,000 additional e-mails were 'up-classified' to make them Confidential; the information in those had not been classified at the time the e-mails were sent."

At one point, Lynch wondered if she could stop him but concluded it was too late, "short of dashing across the street and unplugging something."

And then came the conclusion: "Although we did not find clear evidence that Secretary Clinton or her colleagues intended to violate laws governing the handling of classified information, there is evidence that they were extremely careless in their handling of very sensitive, highly classified information."

Especially damning: "For example, seven e-mail chains concern matters that were classified at the Top Secret/Special Access Program level when they were sent and received. These chains involved Secretary Clinton both sending e-mails about those matters and receiving e-mails from others about the same matters. There is evidence to support a conclusion that any reasonable person in Secretary Clinton's position, or in the position of those government employees with whom she was corresponding about these matters, should have known that an unclassified system was no place for that conversation. In addition to this highly sensitive information, we also found information that was properly classified as Secret by the U.S. Intelligence Community at the time it was discussed on e-mail (that is, excluding the later 'up-classified' e-mails).

"None of these e-mails should have been on any kind of unclassified system, but their presence is especially concerning because all of these e-mails were housed on unclassified personal servers not even supported by full-time security staff, like those found at Departments and Agencies of the U.S. Government—or even with a commercial service like Gmail.

"Separately, it is important to say something about the marking of classified information. Only a very small number of the e-mails containing classified information bore markings indicating the presence of classified information. But even if information is not marked 'classified' in an e-mail, participants who know or should know that the subject matter is classified are still obligated to protect it."

It sounded as though Comey were about to recommend that Clinton be charged. But then he delivered the bottom line: "In our system, the prosecutors make the decisions about whether charges are appropriate based on evidence the FBI has helped collect. Although we don't normally make public our recommendations to the prosecutors, we frequently make recommendations and engage in productive conversations with prosecutors about what resolution may be appropriate, given the evidence.

In this case, given the importance of the matter, I think unusual transparency is in order.

"Although there is evidence of potential violations of the statutes regarding the handling of classified information, our judgment is that no reasonable prosecutor would bring such a case."

Comey's July 5 presentation lasted fifteen minutes. Lynch, Yates, and Axelrod were stunned. They'd been totally blindsided. Comey and his top aides had been discussing the statement and how it would be conveyed since May. They'd had time to become comfortable with it. At Justice, it was a shock.

As Yates later put it, "I was stunned A, at the level of detail that he went into," and "B, that he then made judgments and said things like extremely careless." She felt Comey stressed the incriminating aspects, neglecting the elements that the case lacked. This was especially troubling because by long tradition, "We don't trash people we're not charging. And we don't get to just make value or moral judgments about their conduct." In her view, "that was way out of order."

Toscas described Comey's press conference as "beyond strange" and "incredibly dangerous" given the departure from department precedent, especially in the context of an ongoing presidential campaign. Lynch, too, thought Comey's statement was "a huge mistake."

Within minutes of Comey's appearance, Trump unleashed a barrage of tweets:

11:37 a.m.: The system is rigged. General Petraeus got in trouble for far less. Very very unfair! As usual, bad judgment.

11:39 a.m.: FBI director said Crooked Hillary compromised our national security. No charges. Wow! #RiggedSystem

---

That evening, Trump lit into Comey's decision at a raucous rally in Raleigh, North Carolina. "Today is the best evidence we have ever seen that our system is totally rigged. Hillary Clinton put the entire country in danger," he began. "It was confirmed today that she routinely sent classified emails on an insecure, private server that could be easily hacked by hostile foreign agents. And we learned that people she emailed were hacked and probably, I think maybe definitely were hacked by these hostile actors and these are bad, but very, very smart people. Our enemies may have a blackmail file on Crooked Hillary, and this alone means that she should not be allowed to serve as President of the United States."

Trump was interrupted by cheers. He continued, "We now know that she lied to the country when she said she did not send classified information on her server. She lied! She sent vast amounts of classified information including information classified as top secret. Top secret. OK? And this is where they said that she was extremely careless and, frankly, I say grossly incompetent. She would be such a lousy president. So sad. OK. The lives of American people were put at risk by Hillary Clinton so that she could carry on her corrupt, financial dealings and that's probably why she didn't want people to see what the hell she was doing. She went through extraordinary lengths to carry out a purge of her emails, 33,000 emails are missing and they say she's fine." He went on, "Like a criminal with a guilty conscience, Clinton had her lawyers delete, destroy and wipe away forever except I still say there are geniuses that can find them, 30,000—think of this, 30,000 emails. This, again, disqualifies her from service."

There was more applause. "We have a rigged system, folks," Trump said.

Referring to Bill Clinton's tarmac meeting with Loretta Lynch, Trump predicted Clinton would extend Lynch's tenure as attorney general. "If she wins, she's going to consider extending the attorney general and you know what, I'm not saying, I'm not knocking the attorney general, what I'm saying is how can you say that? It's a bribe," Trump said. "The attorney general sitting there saying, if I get Hillary off the hook I'm going to have four more years or eight more years, but if she loses I'm out of a job, it's a bribe. It's a disgrace. It's a disgrace.

"She's crooked Hillary!" To continuing cheers, he wound up, "Hillary Clinton can't keep her emails safe and you know what, folks, she sure as hell can't keep our country safe."

It was everything Comey had feared, and only a taste of what was to come.

FOUR

"THIS FEELS MOMENTOUS"

<hr />

Hillary Clinton, too, was in North Carolina that evening for a campaign rally with President Obama. Hoping to keep the focus on the president's long-awaited formal endorsement, she ignored Comey and his press conference. Her campaign had issued a brief statement that day saying it was pleased by the outcome, and "as the secretary has long said, it was a mistake to use her personal email and she would not do it again. We are glad that this matter is now resolved."

That it wasn't should already have been obvious.

The Obama endorsement was completely upstaged by the barrage of press coverage for Comey, which led the newscasts, made front-page headlines, and dominated the internet. Politicians predictably divided along party lines, but ominously for Clinton the mainstream press picked up on Comey's criticisms, much as Justice Department officials had feared.

CNN ran a feature: "Comey's 7 Most Damning Lines on Clinton," starting with "extremely careless."

As *The Washington Post* put it, "Though he recommended no criminal charges, Comey systematically dismantled the public explanations Clinton has offered to reassure the public about her email system for the past 15 months."

Patrick Healy, writing in *The New York Times*, noted that Clinton had spent months labeling Trump reckless, unprepared, and unfit to be president. "In just a few minutes of remarks, Mr. Comey called into question Mrs. Clinton's claims of superiority more memorably, mightily and effectively than Mr. Trump has over the entire past year. And with potentially lasting consequences."

At the FBI, the reaction to the media coverage was nonetheless one of considerable relief. No one had accused the bureau of being soft on Clinton or, as Strzok had worried, "mailing it in" on the investigation. *The Washington Post* found it "stunning" that Comey provided so much detail and "publicized his guidance before federal prosecutors had reached a final determination." But no one faulted Comey for taking matters into his own hands.

Not only had Comey emerged unscathed, but Democrats lavished praise on him. Nancy Pelosi called Comey a "great man," and the Senate minority leader, Harry Reid, praised his "integrity" and "competence."

AT 4:00 P.M. the next day, July 6, the entire Midyear team gathered in the attorney general's conference room to formally brief Lynch and Yates on the FBI's conclusions. Comey, McCabe, Baker, Rybicki, and Strzok attended from the FBI; Axelrod, Toscas, and other officials and prosecutors represented the Justice Department. David Margolis was there, even though he was struggling with advanced heart disease, which lent the gathering a certain gravitas.

Despite the simmering resentment they felt toward Comey, no one from the Justice Department said a word about the previous day's press conference.

Toscas opened with a review of the facts developed in the investigation and applicable law, which was so much more exculpatory toward Clinton than Comey had been that Yates wondered if they were even talking about the same case. The group spent some time discussing the gross negligence standard and the reasons why it had hardly ever been used. Still, the outcome of the meeting was never in doubt.

Lynch went around the room and asked each person if he or she agreed with the decision not to bring charges. As the senior career official, Margolis's view carried special weight. Citing the lack of precedent, he argued that to charge Clinton would be nothing more than "celebrity hunting," concluding, "We at the Department don't do that."

It was Margolis's last official act. He died six days later.

After the meeting, Lynch issued a brief statement: "Late this afternoon, I met with the FBI Director James Comey and career prosecutors and agents who conducted the investigation of Secretary Hillary Clinton's use of a personal email system during her time as Secretary of State. I received and accepted their unanimous recommendation that the thorough, year-long investigation be closed and that no charges be brought against any individuals within the scope of the investigation."

Midyear Exam was officially over. Or so it seemed.

There were still some loose ends to wrap up before the file was formally closed, mostly pro forma. One was the troubling Russian intelligence questioning Lynch's impartiality, which was still nagging at Comey.

A few weeks later McCabe met with Lynch for what's known as a "defensive briefing," intended to alert officials to intelligence that might personally affect them, even though, as in this case, the FBI didn't believe the information was credible or likely to become public. McCabe told her that the FBI believed the information had no investigative value and was taking no further action. Nor should she. But she should be aware the intelligence existed.

Lynch said she didn't know Wasserman Schultz, the Democratic National Committee chair, and had never spoken to her, but thanked him for bringing it to her attention.

When McCabe got back, Comey asked him how it went.

"Boss," McCabe replied, "it was the strangest thing. I don't want to read too much into this, but I'd feel a lot better if she'd said it wasn't true. All she said was, 'thank you for telling me.'"

———

REPUBLICANS GATHERED IN Cleveland on July 18 to nominate Donald Trump, and even before the opening speeches there was an undercurrent of seething anger and resentment toward Hillary Clinton and the elites she purportedly represented. "Crooked Hillary for Prison 2016" T-shirts sold briskly.

Speaking at a rally outside the arena, Trump's campaign adviser Roger Stone called Clinton "a short-tempered, foul-mouthed, greedy, bipolar, mentally-unbalanced criminal." Someone in the crowd yelled, "She's a reptile."

That night, just after Trump's formal nomination, the New Jersey governor, Chris Christie, took the stage to denounce Clinton. "Let's do something fun tonight," he told the crowd. "Tonight, as a former Federal Prosecutor, I welcome the opportunity to hold Hillary Rodham Clinton accountable for her performance and her character."

The crowd roared in gleeful anticipation.

Clinton "set up a private email server in her basement in violation of our national security," he continued. "Let's face the facts. Hillary Clinton cared more about protecting her own secrets than she cared about protecting America's secrets.

"And then, she lied about it, over, and over, and over again. She said, there was no marked classified information on her server. The FBI Director said, that's untrue. She said that she did not email any classified information. The FBI Director says, that's untrue. She said, all work-related emails were sent back to the State Department. The FBI Director said, that's not true. So, I say, Hillary Clinton, the charge of putting herself ahead of America, guilty or not guilty?"

"Guilty," the audience roared.

Thunderous applause made it hard for Christie to continue, but he pressed forward. "I got another question for you: I say, Hillary Clinton, lying to the American people about her selfish, awful judgment in making our secrets vulnerable. What's your verdict, guilty or not guilty?"

"Guilty," roared the crowd, even louder.

From the guilty cries emerged another refrain, barely discernible at first, but then growing in intensity until it filled the entire arena: "Lock her up!" Over and over the crowd chanted, "Lock her up!"*

Others at the convention picked up the refrain. "That's right, lock her up!" proclaimed Michael Flynn, the former three-star general and Trump's principal foreign policy adviser, after claiming Clinton considered herself "above the law."

The chant immediately became the defining image of the Trump campaign, a highlight of every Trump rally.

ON JULY 22, Democrats gathered in Philadelphia, and Clinton announced Virginia's Tim Kaine as her running mate. That same day, WikiLeaks took to Twitter:

> Today, Friday 22 July 2016 at 10:30am EDT, WikiLeaks releases 19,252 emails and 8,034 attachments from the top of the US Democratic National Committee—part one of our new Hillary Leaks series.

As Comey and others at the FBI had feared, it was the public release of the Guccifer haul, deliberately timed to wreak maximum havoc within the American political system. There were no bombshells (and, to Comey's relief, no sign of the troubling comments about Lynch), but some emails made clear the extent to which the supposedly neutral DNC had blatantly favored Clinton over Bernie Sanders. The revelations led to the resignation of Debbie Wasserman Schultz as party chair and disillusioned many of Sanders's idealistic young backers.

---

* The chant might have begun with Michael Stoker, a California delegate and ardent Trump supporter later named to an Environmental Protection Agency post. Stoker posted a video on Facebook showing him leading a group of delegates in the chant during Christie's remarks. "Trump Pick to Run Mediation Service Lands at EPA. What Happened?," *Bloomberg Law*, May 30, 2018.

The WikiLeaks founder, Julian Assange, wouldn't say whether Russia was his source, but news organizations widely reported the suspected link.

Half a world away, in Australia, the WikiLeaks disclosures set off alarm bells within the Australian intelligence service.

Months earlier, Erika Thompson, a political counselor at the Australian High Commission in London, had sent a classified cable describing a May 6 meeting she'd attended with Alexander Downer, a former Australian minister of foreign affairs, now high commissioner to the United Kingdom, the equivalent of ambassador, and George Papadopoulos, a foreign policy adviser to Trump.

Downer had initiated the meeting after being prompted by Thompson to learn more about Trump's worldview, now that it looked as if Trump might well win the nomination. The Australians thought the tanned, dark-haired, twenty-eight-year-old Papadopoulos seemed rather young and inexperienced to be a foreign policy adviser to a major presidential candidate, but Trump had publicly introduced him at a press event in March, describing him as "an energy and oil consultant, excellent guy." Since then, Papadopoulos had been trying to arrange a meeting between Putin and Trump.

Over drinks at the Kensington Wine Rooms, Papadopoulos ranged over a wide array of topics, but something stood out to Downer as particularly "interesting": that the Russians had "material that could be damaging" to Clinton, as Downer later described the conversation. Papadopoulos "said it would be damaging. He didn't say what it was," according to Downer.

Even more intriguing, Papadopoulos stressed that he had gotten "indications" that the Russian government could assist the Trump campaign by releasing the information anonymously so as to maximize the damage to Clinton.

Papadopoulos said much the same thing to another Australian he met in London at about the same time, who reported the conversation to the Australian mission. (His identity and what he disclosed remain classified.)

Downer had Thompson include all of this in the cable she sent a few days later, where it made little impression and might well have been forgotten to history. But after WikiLeaks, the reference suddenly made sense: the damaging "material" Papadopoulos referred to must have been the emails hacked from the Democratic National Committee. On July 26, the Australians turned the intelligence over to the CIA, which referred it to the FBI.*

That Russia might be behind the email release clearly got under Trump's skin. Three days after WikiLeaks released the emails, he tweeted that "the new joke in town" is that "Russia leaked the disastrous DNC emails." The next day, he tweeted that it was "crazy" to suggest Russia was "dealing with Trump." Later that day he added, "For the record, I have ZERO investments in Russia."

That evening Clinton was formally nominated in a well-orchestrated, history-making ceremony marred only by a group of Sanders delegates who walked out to protest the unfairness documented in the leaked emails. Clinton "just has to win now," Page texted Strzok during the televised proceedings. "I'm not going to lie, I got a flash of nervousness yesterday about Trump. The sandernistas have the potential to make a very big mistake here."

"I'm not worried about them," Strzok replied. "I'm worried about the anarchist Assange who will take fed information and disclose it to disrupt," referring to the WikiLeaks founder holed up in the Ecuadorian embassy in London.

The next day, at a press conference at his Doral golf resort in Florida, Trump seized on the hacked emails to stoke dissension among Democrats, opening his remarks by saying, "Debbie Wasserman Schultz, she totally rigged" the primary. "Bernie Sanders never had a chance."

Asked repeatedly about Russia, Trump said he had "nothing to do with Russia," had never met Putin, and had no business dealings there. He dismissed reports Russia was trying to interfere in the election. "It's

---

* The contents of the cable and exactly how it reached the FBI remain classified information. In a series of Twitter posts, and in a subsequent book, Papadopoulos maintained that Downer and Thompson were Australian spies working to discredit Trump. He also claimed Downer secretly recorded their conversation. Nothing has emerged to support those claims, and Downer denied recording him. The claims also seem inconsistent with the fact the Australians did nothing with the information until after WikiLeaks released the Clinton-related emails.

just a total deflection, this whole thing with Russia," he said. "If it is Russia, nobody even knows this, it's probably China, or it could be somebody sitting in his bed." After sidestepping a question about why he hadn't disclosed his tax returns, he returned to the subject: "It would be interesting to see—I will tell you this—Russia, if you're listening, I hope you're able to find the 30,000 emails that are missing. I think you will probably be rewarded mightily by our press."

AT HIS OFFICE in Trump Tower Manhattan, Michael Cohen found Trump's comments that he had "nothing to do with Russia" to be "interesting," as he later said, which was likely a considerable understatement. Cohen had been knee-deep in a project to build a Trump Tower in Moscow.

At forty-nine, Cohen, a lawyer who had dabbled in real estate and politics and owned a collection of taxi medallions, occupied a distinctive place in the Trump orbit. Although he had none of the Ivy League credentials so admired by Trump—he'd graduated from the Thomas M. Cooley Law School at Western Michigan University—he'd ingratiated himself with Trump by quoting passages from *The Art of the Deal* (he'd read it twice) and by demonstrating what Cohen later described as "blind loyalty," a trait prized by Trump. He bought an apartment in Trump World Tower across from the United Nations, as did his parents and in-laws. Cohen seemed unfazed that in return "Donald goes out of his way to treat him like garbage," Trump's campaign adviser Roger Stone told *The New York Times*. With his dark eyes and sagging lids, Cohen sometimes gave the appearance of a devoted basset hound.

Trump Tower Moscow was a possible $1 billion deal. Trump had signed a letter of intent to do the project in 2015. In May 2016, Cohen had been negotiating with Russian officials for Trump to attend the St. Petersburg International Economic Forum, Russia's answer to Davos, in mid-June. Cohen told Trump that Putin or the Russian prime minister, Dmitry Medvedev, might be there, and Trump agreed to go if Cohen could "lock and load" on a deal.

The trip was never firmed up, and progress had stalled with the Russian development partner, though Cohen hadn't yet told Trump that.

Nonetheless, after hearing during Trump's press conference that Trump had no business dealings with Russia, Cohen realized that was the "message" and the "party line," which, it went without saying, Cohen would follow.*

WITHIN TWENTY-FOUR HOURS of its delivery to the FBI, Strzok was poring over the Australian intelligence gleaned from Papadopoulos. His three weeks of relative calm following the Clinton announcement were over.

Strzok was stunned, not so much by the long-rumored revelation that Russians had hacked the Democratic National Committee as by the fact that they had communicated a willingness to help Trump at the expense of Clinton to a member of the Trump campaign. Did anyone within the Trump campaign take them up on the offer? If so, who?

Of course Strzok didn't simply accept the truth of the information at face value. During his years in counterintelligence, he'd learned to take anything involving the Russians with a big grain of salt. But this was coming from Australia, one of America's closest and most trusted allies, one of the so-called Five Eyes—the United Kingdom, Canada, New Zealand, Australia, and the United States—that share sensitive intelligence. Cursory research showed that Papadopoulos, though young and with scant experience, was indeed one of Trump's top foreign policy advisers.

Strzok had never encountered such a profoundly troubling allegation, and so far as he knew, no one else had either, even at the height of the cold war. Strzok's years working in counterintelligence had made him deeply distrustful of Russia. It wasn't just that Putin personally and Russia generally had felt disrespected and humiliated by the Western democracies after the end of the cold war. Strzok considered Russia an autocratic klep-

---

* After the press conference, Trump asked Cohen about Trump Tower Moscow, indicating he was well aware of the project at the time of the press conference. When Cohen told him it was "going nowhere," Trump responded, "Too bad." But after the election, the project appeared on a list of Trump Organization projects that needed to be "closed out."

tocracy that stood in opposition to everything America represented and the FBI tried to protect, starting with pluralism, tolerance, freedom of expression, and the rule of law. Russian interference in a presidential election was a direct and unprecedented attack on American democracy.

Strzok conveyed his reaction in a July 31 text to Page: "Damn this feels momentous. Because this matters. The other one did, too, but that was to ensure we didn't F something up. This matters because this MATTERS. So super glad to be on this voyage with you."

By "the other one," he meant the Clinton email case, which, however politically charged, paled by comparison to the profound implications of the Papadopoulos intelligence.

Strzok and others at the bureau spent the weekend doing additional research. Who besides Papadopoulos within the Trump campaign might be working with the Russians? It didn't take long for Strzok and other analysts working in counterintelligence to find additional troubling links: The foreign policy adviser Carter Page, who'd once worked at Merrill Lynch in Moscow and had since assiduously courted high-ranking Russian officials, had already been on the FBI's radar for three years. Trump adviser Michael Flynn sat next to Putin at a lavish Moscow dinner honoring a state-backed news channel in 2015 and received a $45,000 speaking fee. The campaign manager Paul Manafort had worked for Kremlin-backed officials in Ukraine. Any of them could have been a conduit between the Russians and the Trump campaign.

And then there were Trump's seemingly inexplicable affection and admiration for Putin.

The pattern was too conspicuous to ignore and lent credibility to the Australians' allegations. Strzok met with McCabe, Jim Baker, and Lisa Page to report on his findings, and the group briefed Comey later the same day. All agreed that a formal investigation needed to be opened, and on Sunday, July 31, the FBI launched "Crossfire Hurricane."*

---

* The code name was a reference to a Rolling Stones lyric from "Jumpin' Jack Flash," which begins, "I was born in a cross-fire hurricane." The line refers to Keith Richards's 1943 birth just outside London during the Nazi's World War II bombing campaign.

In the ensuing weeks, specific files were opened on Papadopoulos, Carter Page, Manafort, and Flynn.

Having just emerged from the Clinton investigation, which had already thrust the FBI into the perilous position of investigating the Democratic presidential candidate during the campaign, the FBI was now in the unprecedented position of also investigating advisers close to the Republican candidate, an investigation that might well ensnare Trump himself.

STRZOK AND ANOTHER agent flew to London the next day. With the election fast approaching, time pressure was intense. They showered, shaved, and changed into business suits at the U.S. embassy. That evening they met with the Australians Downer and Thompson. Both had clear recollections of their meeting with Papadopoulos and were very specific and precise about what he said, including the Russian offer to help the Trump campaign disseminate the damaging information on Clinton. Strzok and his colleague flew back the next morning.

Strzok briefed Comey, McCabe, Priestap, Baker, and Page. The reaction, without exception, was grave concern.

The group faced a dilemma with profound implications: whether to open a case file on Trump himself. What did Trump know about the Russian interference? What, if any, was his role?

There was no question that the Russians had hacked the DNC, had orchestrated the release through WikiLeaks, and did it to disrupt the election, hurt Clinton, and help Trump. Was that unilateral activity by the Russians, or was there cooperation by the Trump campaign? In the worst-case scenario, Trump might have sanctioned it and actively worked with the Russians. It was not out of the realm of possibility. The threshold for opening a case isn't that the subject has been proven guilty of anything but whether there's a basis for finding out. Trump clearly seemed to meet that threshold.

As a presidential candidate, however, he was not an ordinary subject. And the best-case scenario—equally plausible—was that Trump knew nothing about any of it.

The group also briefly considered whether the public interest called for some sort of disclosure. But that idea was discarded almost as soon as it was broached. Unlike the Clinton case, there had been no public referral to the FBI. The resulting furor would inevitably tarnish the reputations of those being investigated, as well as Trump, when no wrongdoing had been established. And the wisdom of the bureau's long-standing aversion to anything that might appear to be interfering in an election had been amply borne out in the Clinton case.

As Strzok told his colleagues, "God forbid we taint someone and impact a candidate and an election."

Given the recent problems with leaks, Comey imposed unusual strictures on Crossfire Hurricane. It went without saying that, like Midyear, it was a SIM, a sensitive investigative matter. The case files were divided among three field offices: Papadopoulos to Chicago, Page to New York, and Manafort and Flynn to D.C. But it would be managed from FBI headquarters. Knowledge of the probe was strictly confined to the top echelon of the FBI and agents working in counterintelligence. No one was allowed to mention the case at morning briefings, where agents would ordinarily give updates on progress in major investigations.

The FBI had to notify the Justice Department, where relations were still strained over the Midyear announcement. Strzok spoke to Toscas, his counterpart there, and urged him to keep the information within a small circle and, if possible, to withhold details from political appointees who had to be informed, even Yates and Lynch. Strzok feared that the subject of Crossfire Hurricane was "too juicy" not to leak.

The need for secrecy before the election also cramped the FBI's ability to get to the bottom of the matter. Operation Crossfire Hurricane had to rely on covert techniques, including the most covert of all—electronic surveillance and undercover agents.

BRUCE OHR, AGED fifty-four, and his wife, Nellie, fifty-three, were punctual for their breakfast meeting with a former British spy at Washington's venerable Mayflower Hotel on July 30. The pair—both bespectacled and slightly graying—hardly looked like characters out of a John Le Carré spy novel, but both had led surprisingly adventurous lives in and around the undercover world of Russian spies and drug traffickers.

Both Ohrs had illustrious résumés: after graduating from Harvard College, Bruce went on to Harvard Law, and Nellie received a Ph.D. in Russian history from Stanford. She later taught Russian studies at Vassar College and did research for the CIA. Nellie now focused on Russia as a researcher for Fusion GPS, an intelligence and consulting firm founded by Glenn R. Simpson along with some other former *Wall Street Journal* reporters.

Bruce Ohr had risen through the ranks of the Justice Department, focusing on drug trafficking and organized crime, especially Russian organized crime. As an associate deputy attorney general in the criminal division, he reported to Sally Yates.

Christopher Steele, in his early fifties with graying hair, was in town from London and joined them at their table. Bruce Ohr had known Steele for nearly a decade, since the American embassy in London arranged for the two to meet. Ohr was in London then to discuss Russian organized crime with British officials, and at the time Steele was head of the Russia desk for MI6, Britain's intelligence agency. Steele had been a British spy in Moscow in the 1990s and now ran his own consulting firm, Orbis Business Intelligence. Over the years, he and Ohr talked or had lunch about once a year and often discussed Oleg Deripaska, a Russian oligarch with ties to the Kremlin. Steele provided a regular stream of useful information about Deripaska to both the FBI and Ohr, and Ohr considered him a reliable source.

At their breakfast meeting. Steele reported that an attorney working for Deripaska had information that Trump's campaign adviser Paul Manafort had entered into some kind of business deal with Deripaska and Manafort had stolen money from him.

That wasn't the only link between a Trump campaign official and Russians of dubious character. Steele said that Carter Page, a name Ohr recognized from news reports as one of Trump's foreign policy advisers, had recently traveled to Russia, where he met with high-ranking Kremlin officials.

And most troubling to Ohr, Steele said he had information that a former head of the Russian Foreign Intelligence Service, the SVR, had said "they had Donald Trump over a barrel," according to notes Ohr made of the conversation—referring to compromising information that might expose Trump to blackmail.

As Ohr later said, "I was in a little bit of shock at that point."

Steele didn't reveal any of his sources, but Ohr didn't doubt his sincerity. Steele "was very alarmed by this information, which I think he believed to be true," Ohr later said. "And so I definitely got the impression he did not want Donald Trump to win the election." In his notes, Ohr went even further: Steele was "desperate" that Trump not be elected.

At the same time, Ohr was wary. "My impression is that Chris Steele believed his sources," he later said. "What I should say in addition, though, is that whenever you are dealing with information from Russia, you have to be careful, because it is a very complicated place. And so even information from a good source has to be looked at carefully."

Later that day Steele sent Ohr an email: "Great to see you and Nellie this morning, Bruce. Let's keep in touch on the substantive issues. Glenn is happy to speak to you on this if it would help."

"Glenn" was a reference to Glenn Simpson, the co-founder of Fusion, Nellie Ohr's employer. Fusion, in turn, had hired Steele and his firm to investigate Trump, first on behalf of Paul Singer, a billionaire Republican hedge fund manager, and then, after Trump won the nomination, on behalf of a law firm working for the Democratic National Committee and the Clinton campaign.

Steele had produced a series of relatively brief reports on the Trump campaign and its dealings with Russia. But as he indicated at his breakfast with Ohr, the magnitude of what he was hearing—the possibility that Trump campaign officials were working hand in glove with Russians and that Russia had compromising material on Trump—meant this was no ordinary assignment, but one he felt needed to be shared with American and British intelligence and national security concerns.

So in early July, Steele had met with an FBI agent based in Rome, someone he knew from prior cases, and shared with him the first few memos he'd produced for Fusion. The agent, Mike Gaeta, sent the material to the FBI's New York office, where no one took any immediate action. No one in New York knew anything about Crossfire Hurricane, and a counterintelligence operation involving a candidate for president wasn't within New York's purview.

After their breakfast, Ohr contacted McCabe, whom Ohr knew from McCabe's stint running the Russian organized crime task force in New York. As Ohr later put it, "Part of my job, as I saw it, as having been for a long time responsible for organized crime at the Department, was to try to gather as much information or introduce the FBI to possible sources of information."

Ohr met with McCabe and Page to pass on what he'd heard from Steele. "I tried to be clear that this is source information," Ohr later testified. He cautioned McCabe and Page, "I don't know how reliable it is. You're going to have to check it out and be aware. These guys were hired by somebody who's related to the Clinton campaign." He also mentioned that his wife worked for Fusion.

Ohr also followed up with Simpson, who had shared information about Russian organized crime with him for years, much of which he passed on to the FBI. Simpson mentioned his concerns that the Trump campaign was working with the Russians and mentioned several of the same names that Steele had: Paul Manafort and Carter Page, and another name—Michael Cohen.

Ohr would have preferred that Simpson speak directly to an FBI agent, but Simpson seemed more comfortable using Ohr as a go-between. McCabe and Page told Ohr to pass his information on to Strzok. Ohr, of course, had no way of knowing that the FBI had already launched Operation Crossfire Hurricane, and had opened case files on several of the names he'd just mentioned.

Alarmed by these latest developments—all of which came on top of and were consistent with the revelations from the Australian ambassador to London—Page texted Strzok on August 8: Trump is "not ever going to become president, right? Right?!"

Strzok replied, "No. No he's not. We'll stop it."

FIVE

"THE BAND IS BACK TOGETHER"

———

Just four days later, on August 12, 2016, Matthew Axelrod, who, like other Justice Department officials, was still seething over the FBI's handling of the Midyear announcement, called McCabe to express his concerns about another sensitive and secret matter—the FBI's investigation of the Clinton Foundation.

By then, four separate FBI field offices were looking into the Clinton Foundation's activities and donors—New York, Little Rock, Los Angeles, and Washington, D.C. The New York and Little Rock offices, in particular, were viewed by some within the Justice Department as hotbeds of anti-Clinton hostility, and agents there were agitating to ramp up their investigative activity, including issuing subpoenas, even as the presidential campaign was entering its final months. Axelrod warned McCabe that the FBI should ease off any overt investigative steps, like issuing subpoenas, until after the election, consistent with the department's long-standing aversion to activities that might influence an election.

With the tarmac incident still fresh in his mind, McCabe was shocked. "Are you telling me that I need to shut down a validly predicated investigation?" McCabe replied, in his recollection of the conversation. He couldn't remember ever getting such a call from a high-level official at Justice.*

———

* Axelrod has said he was simply stating long-standing Justice Department policy regarding elections.

That the FBI was investigating the Clinton Foundation was a closely guarded secret—like the Trump-Russia case, and nearly all investigations other than the anomalous Clinton email case. In congressional testimony in July defending his decisions in Midyear, Comey explicitly refused to say whether the FBI was examining the Clinton Foundation.

But there had been rampant speculation ever since the publication of the incendiary book *Clinton Cash: The Untold Story of How and Why Foreign Governments and Businesses Helped Make Bill and Hillary Rich*, by Peter Schweizer, an investigative journalist with ties to the Trump adviser Steve Bannon and the billionaire Trump financial backers Robert Mercer and his daughter Rebekah. Schweizer had worked on a film about Ronald Reagan with Bannon and was a senior editor at large for Bannon's *Breitbart News*. The Mercer Family Foundation helped fund the book with a $1.7 million contribution.

Clinton Cash suggested that Clinton donors had essentially traded cash for favors and influence at the State Department while Clinton was secretary of state. Clinton had entered into an agreement providing for State Department vetting of any contributions to the foundation from foreign governments, and the Clinton campaign provided a detailed rebuttal when the book was published in the spring of 2015. It said there was "zero evidence to back up its outlandish claims."

Still, the book was taken seriously by the mainstream press. Both *The New York Times* and *The Washington Post* got advance copies and, with the agreement of the publisher, pursued leads from the book. As Susan Milligan wrote in *U.S. News & World Report*, "When a source, no matter how agenda-driven, offers up actual, hard information, based on public records, the motivation becomes meaningless. And this is why Hillary Clinton and Bill Clinton (along with their loyal team of defenders) must expect news outlets to scour and report out every accusation" in *Clinton Cash*.

Like the email controversy, the foundation issues were self-inflicted by the Clintons. Their insistence they could run a foundation accepting major contributions while Hillary was secretary of state and then a candidate for president all but guaranteed controversy. There was no denying the allure to donors of the possibility that a well-timed donation, much like campaign contributions, might yield future benefits. The foundation was staffed with Clinton campaign officials and loyal allies, including Huma Abedin and Cheryl Mills, two Hillary aides at the center of the email affair.

As *The Boston Globe*'s editorial board observed on August 16, "The foundation should remove a political—and actual—distraction and stop accepting funding. If Clinton is elected, the foundation should be shut down." While it praised the foundation's "good causes," it added, "As long as either of the Clintons are in public office, or actively seeking it, they should not operate a charity, too."

Despite McCabe's reaction to Axelrod, neither he nor anyone else at FBI headquarters was all that impressed by the foundation case. Although a formal investigation had commenced, agents had uncovered little beyond the highly circumstantial evidence and innuendo in *Clinton Cash*. It was common knowledge that Clinton had used her tenure as secretary of state to burnish her résumé for a presidential run and knew that her every move would be scrutinized. She was advised by highly competent lawyers. How likely was it that she'd risk yet another scandal, let alone criminal prosecution, by trading favors for contributions to the foundation?

Given that the election was less than two months away, McCabe and Comey agreed that the FBI would ease off for now, and also that the case should be consolidated in the field office in Little Rock, where the foundation was nominally headquartered. Both moves infuriated agents in New York, where the foundation conducted most of its work; the agents there felt McCabe had told them to "stand down," as they later put it, and bowed to political pressure.

WITHIN THE FBI, there was also a spirited debate about how aggressively to pursue Crossfire Hurricane, because the more aggressive the investigation, the more likely it was to be discovered and publicized. Not only would that again plunge the FBI into the middle of an election, but it might also jeopardize a confidential source. As Strzok put it, "One of the debates on how to pursue this information was how much risk to put that sensitive source in because, in my experience, the more aggressive an investigation, the greater chance of burning or compromising that source."

On the other hand, there was urgency about getting to the bottom of it, because if Trump really was illegally colluding with the Russians, that was a fact of vital importance.

Page and Strzok tended to fall on opposite sides of the issue: Strzok wanted to be aggressive; Page felt the FBI could take its time, in large part because all the polls suggested it was highly unlikely Trump would win.

"We don't need to go at a total breakneck speed because so long as he doesn't become president, there isn't the same threat to national security," Page argued. "I mean if he is not elected, then, to the extent that the Russians were colluding with members of his team, we're still going to investigate that even without him being president, because any time the Russians do anything with a U.S. person, we care, and it's very serious to us."

"One school of thought, of which Lisa was a member," Strzok later testified, was "saying the polls, everybody in America is saying Secretary Clinton is the prohibitive favorite to be the next President, and therefore, based on that, these allegations about the Trump campaign, we don't need to risk that source. We can just take our time. We can run a traditional years-long counterintelligence operation, and we don't really need to worry because he's not going to be elected."

But Strzok argued that the FBI needed to move quickly, no matter what the polls said. "If candidate Trump is elected, we have months, and we may find ourselves in a position where we have these allegations potentially about people who are being nominated for senior national security roles, and then we're in a really bad spot because we don't know whether these allegations are true or false; we don't know the extent of these allegations and the truth and how extensive or not. So my advocacy was we need to pursue these cases in a way that will allow us to be responsible and protecting the national security of the United States."

Strzok texted Page after a discussion of the issue in McCabe's office.

"I want to believe the path you threw out for consideration in Andy's office—that there's no way he [Trump] gets elected," Strzok wrote, "but I'm afraid we can't take that risk. It's like an insurance policy in the unlikely event you die before you're 40."

As Strzok explained the text, "The analogy I am drawing is, you know, you're unlikely to die before you're 40, but nevertheless, many people buy life insurance. The similarity is that, regardless of what the polls are saying, that Secretary Clinton is the favorite to win, however likely or not it is who's going to win, just like life insurance, you have to take into account any potential possibility. You need to do your job regardless of whether it's highly likely or not."

COMEY USED THE occasion of the fifteenth anniversary of the September 11 attacks to remind all FBI employees that "Sunday marks 15 years since 3,000 innocent people were murdered in our country on a single, crystal-clear late summer morning. It somehow seems both yesterday, and a lifetime ago. Much has changed since then, but what matters most has not changed. We have shown the humility and agility to constantly improve, which is essential. But after 15 hard years, we have also stayed the same in the ways that matter most: our fidelity to doing things the right way; our bravery in the face of evil; and our integrity—the determination to always be honest and independent."

He said nothing about the extraordinary fact that the FBI was simultaneously scrutinizing both candidates for president of the United States.

ON SEPTEMBER 19, the file Steele had handed over to Agent Gaeta in Rome finally showed up in Strzok's email in-box. He read with mounting fascination what soon became known as the "Steele dossier," though at this early stage it consisted of only a few files.

Marked "Confidential/Sensitive Source" and dated June 30, the memo began,

Summary

—Russian regime has been cultivating, supporting and assisting TRUMP for at least 5 years. Aim, endorsed by PUTIN, has been to encourage splits and divisions in western alliance.

—So far TRUMP has declined various sweetener real estate business deals offered him in Russia in order to further the Kremlin's cultivation of him. However he and his inner circle have accepted a regular flow of intelligence from the Kremlin, including on his Democratic and other political rivals.

—Former top Russian intelligence officer claims FSB has compromised TRUMP through his activities in Moscow sufficiently to be able to blackmail him. According to several knowledgeable sources, his conduct in Moscow has included perverted sexual acts which have been arranged/monitored by the FSB.

—A dossier of compromising material on Hillary CLINTON has been collated by the Russian Intelligence Services over many years and mainly comprises bugged conversations she had on various visits to Russia and intercepted phone calls rather than any embarrassing conduct. The dossier is controlled by Kremlin spokesman, PESKOV, directly on orders. However it has not as yet been distributed abroad, including to TRUMP. Russian intentions for its deployment still unclear.

After this introduction, the dossier went into far more detail, especially regarding the "perverted" activities:

1. Source asserted that the TRUMP operation was both supported and directed by Russian President Vladimir PUTIN. Its aim was to sow discord and disunity both within the US itself, but more especially within the Transatlantic alliance which was seen as inimical to Russia's interests.

2. The Kremlin's cultivation operation on TRUMP also had comprised offering him various lucrative real estate development business deals in Russia, especially in relation to the ongoing 2018 World Cup

soccer tournament. However, so far, for reasons unknown, TRUMP had not taken up any of these.

3. However, there were other aspects to TRUMP's engagement with the Russian authorities. One which had borne fruit for them was to exploit personal obsessions and sexual perversion in order to obtain suitable "kompromat" (compromising material) on him. According to Source D, where s/he had been present, (perverted) conduct in Moscow included hiring the presidential suite of the Ritz-Carlton Hotel, where he knew President and Mrs. OBAMA (whom he hated) had stayed on one of their official trips to Russia, and defiling the bed where they had slept by employing a number of prostitutes to perform a "golden showers" (urination) show in front of him. The hotel was known to be under FSE control with microphones and concealed cameras in all the main rooms to record anything they wanted to.

The Moscow Ritz-Carlton incident involving TRUMP reported above was confirmed by Source E who said that s/he and several of the Staff were aware of it at the time and subsequently. S/he believed it had happened in 2013. Source E provided an introduction for a company ethnic Russian operative to Source F, a female staffer at the hotel when TRUMP had stayed there, who also confirmed the story. Speaking separately in June 2016, Source B (the former top level Russian intelligence officer) asserted that unorthodox behavior in Russia over the years had provided the authorities there with enough embarrassing material on the now Republican presidential candidate to be able to blackmail him if they so wished.

In many ways, Strzok was confounded by what he read, and not because of the salacious details about the visit to the Ritz-Carlton. While he was concerned at the possibility Trump might have exposed himself to blackmail, direct ties between Russia and the Trump campaign intended to influence the election were far more worrisome. Trump had been divorced twice, and he was known to be a womanizer, so it was hardly shocking that he might have engaged in lewd conduct in a foreign capital. It wasn't illegal or anything the FBI would ordinarily investigate. But it was so detailed and salacious that it seemed tailor-made to smear Trump and wreak havoc with his campaign. That was cause for concern.

So was the lack of what the FBI refers to as "actionable intelligence." Much of what was in the dossier could have been divined after the fact by any close observer. There was little the FBI could act upon. The dossier did not, for example, give any clues to what Russian intelligence operatives were doing now or planned to do—such as details of upcoming meetings with members of the Trump campaign the FBI could monitor.

Strzok knew something about the origins of the dossier and who was paying for it—not that it had ties to the Democratic National Committee and the Clinton campaign, but certainly that it was politically motivated to damage Trump. That didn't mean its contents weren't true, but when one assessed its veracity, motive needed to be considered.

More broadly, Strzok was well aware that Russia played a long-term intelligence game. Far more important than whether Trump won or lost was its goal of disrupting the American democratic process. The dossier seemed almost too well suited for that.

At the same time, much of it rang true. The FBI was already familiar with most of the names. The time frame appeared to be accurate. The FBI believed that the Russians were in fact trying to influence and disrupt the election.

And Strzok was convinced that Steele himself hadn't fabricated the documents. While Strzok didn't know Steele, others described him as cautious, with a long track record of valuable intelligence, a patriot who believed in the Western democracies.

Much like Ohr, Strzok didn't really trust anything that came out of Russia. But the FBI had to see what could be proven or disproven while still keeping the entire investigation a secret.

And true or not, if Strzok and Page wanted to "stop" Trump, they had just been handed the perfect weapon.

TWO DAYS AFTER the FBI received the Steele dossier, on September 21, the London tabloid the *Daily Mail* ran a front-page "exclusive":

Anthony Weiner carried on a months-long online sexual relationship with a 15-year-old girl during which she claims he asked her to dress up in "school-girl" outfits for him on a video messaging application and pressed her to engage in "rape fantasies," DailyMail.com can exclusively report.

The girl, whose name is being withheld by DailyMail.com because she is a minor, said the online relationship began last January while she was a high school sophomore and before Weiner's wife, Hillary Clinton's aide Huma Abedin, announced she was ending their marriage.

Weiner was aware that the girl was underage, according to DailyMail.com interviews with the girl and her father, as well as a cache of online messages.

In just three paragraphs, the British tabloid had laid out all the elements of a crime defined by New York Penal Law 235: disseminating indecent materials to minors.

Because it involved a minor, this incident was exponentially more threatening to Weiner than his prior much-publicized sexual escapades, which had ended his once-promising career in Congress, shattered his 2013 run for New York City mayor, and—after he sent lurid photos while in bed with his four-year-old son—finally caused Huma Abedin to leave him and file for divorce.

Through it all Clinton had loyally stood by her top aide. They were so close that Clinton referred to Abedin as a "second daughter." Bill Clinton officiated at her 2010 marriage to Weiner, then an up-and-coming Democratic congressman. Clinton had firmly rebuffed suggestions to distance herself from Abedin as the Weiner scandals mounted and Abedin loyally and painfully stood by her husband. Abedin was vice-chair of Clinton's campaign and by the candidate's side at a Hamptons fund-raiser when the *Daily Mail* story broke.

As *The New York Times* noted, Weiner's behavior "threatens to remind voters about the troubles in the Clintons' own marriage over the decades, including Mrs. Clinton's much-debated decision to remain with

then-President Bill Clinton after revelations of his relationship with
Monica Lewinsky. Ms. Abedin's choice to separate from her husband
evokes the debates that erupted over Mrs. Clinton's handling of the Lewinsky affair, a scandal her campaign wants left in the past."

In what would prove to be a spectacular miscalculation, the *Times* reported that Clinton's advisers "were confident Mr. Weiner's actions would
not hurt Mrs. Clinton."

FOLLOWING THE *Daily Mail* article, the New York field office and the
Manhattan U.S. attorney, Preet Bharara, took the lead in the Weiner investigation. On September 26, the government asked for and was granted
a search warrant and seized Weiner's iPhone, iPad, and laptop computer
the same day. One of the FBI's digital extraction technicians noticed
within hours that there were about 340,000 emails on the laptop. Among
the domain addresses were yahoo.com, state.gov, clintonfoundation.org,
clintonemail.com, and hillaryclinton.com. "Am I seeing what I think I'm
seeing?" the technician wondered.

At the technician's request, the computer was looked at by another
agent, who described it as an "oh shit" moment and agreed they needed to
report the discovery "up the chain" immediately. They also drafted an
email that began, "Just putting this on the record because of the optics of
the case."

Two days later, on September 28, the New York FBI office's assistant
director, Bill Sweeney, relayed news of the discovery during a weekly tele-
conference with FBI headquarters in Washington. Ordinarily, Comey
would have been presiding, but he was testifying that afternoon on Capitol Hill, so McCabe handled it. One participant said that Sweeney's revelation was like "dropping a bomb in the middle of the meeting" and stated
that "everybody realized the significance of this, like, potential trove of
information." He said Sweeney "very much emphasized the significance
of what he thought they had there."

But McCabe later had only a hazy memory of Sweeney's remarks.
Later that day, he told Comey, in passing, "Hey, Boss, I just want you to

know that the criminal squad in New York has got Anthony Weiner's laptop and I think it may have some connect to Midyear," or something to that effect, and he might have mentioned Abedin. But McCabe's comments didn't sink in. Comey didn't make the connection that Weiner was married to Abedin or that Clinton's emails had been found on his laptop.

Strzok texted Page that evening: "Got called up to Andy's earlier . . . hundreds of thousands of emails turned over by Weiner's atty to sdny, includes a ton of material from spouse. Sending team up tomorrow to review . . . this will never end." Strzok even considered going himself: "So I kinda want to go up to NY tomorrow, coordinate this."

A team was dispatched but didn't get very far. The search warrant used to seize Weiner's laptop covered only child pornography and disseminating indecent materials—not Hillary Clinton's emails. The U.S. attorney's office had told the agents they couldn't open and read the Clinton-Abedin emails without another search warrant, though it was okay to read the headers.

At this juncture, the New York agents thought the Midyear team in Washington was going to ask for guidance about getting a search warrant and get back to them. Strzok and others on the Midyear team were under the impression that agents in the New York office would continue processing the laptop and get back to them with more information about what was on it, a task that could easily take months—in "January, February 2017, whenever it gets done," according to Strzok. Others, too, thought the legal and technical issues involved in gaining access to the emails would take months to resolve, well after the upcoming election.

Any sense of urgency drained away. While sporadic discussions of the Weiner laptop continued within lower ranks at FBI headquarters, it wasn't even on Comey's radar. Strzok got back to the all-consuming task of the Russia investigation.

McCabe alerted the Justice Department about the Weiner laptop the first week in October and told a Justice Department lawyer he was sending an agent to review the emails. But both thought they would mostly be duplicates of what they'd already seen, given how thorough the investigation had been.

That was as far as it got. A few days later, on October 7, *The Washington Post* published a video showing Trump on his way to tape a 2005 episode of *Access Hollywood* in which Trump boasted to the host Billy Bush, "I don't even wait. And when you're a star, they let you do it. You can do anything. Grab them by the pussy. You can do anything." In the midst of the resulting furor, WikiLeaks released another batch of thousands of emails hacked from a Gmail account belonging to John Podesta, chair of the Clinton campaign. The Department of Homeland Security and the director of national intelligence issued a joint statement blaming the hack on Russia, noting that "only Russia's senior-most officials could have authorized these activities."

Two days later, FBI agents contacted Podesta, who told reporters on Clinton's campaign plane that he'd spoken to the FBI that weekend. "Russian interference in this election and apparently on behalf of Trump is, I think, of the utmost concern to all Americans, whether you're a Democrat or independent or Republican," Podesta said. And he suggested the Trump campaign might have been in on the leaks, noting that Trump's campaign adviser Roger Stone had boasted about his ties to the WikiLeaks founder, Julian Assange. "So I think it's a reasonable assumption to—or at least a reasonable conclusion—that Mr. Stone had advance warning and the Trump campaign had advance warning about what Assange was going to do," Podesta said. He also cited Trump's perplexing "bromance" with Vladimir Putin and added that Trump's foreign policy positions "are more consistent with Russian foreign policy than with U.S. foreign policy."

Podesta had just publicly revealed, perhaps inadvertently, the closely guarded secret that the FBI was indeed investigating Russian election interference and ties to the Trump campaign.

TOP OFFICIALS AT FBI headquarters were close to being overwhelmed by Russia—which is likely the main reason the Weiner laptop discovery fell through the cracks. For just as the new trove of Clinton emails was discovered, Strzok was helping put together a top secret application to the

Foreign Intelligence Surveillance Court for a court order authorizing electronic surveillance of Carter Page, the Trump campaign adviser with many suspicious ties to Russian officials. The application had to be reviewed and approved by Comey, and top FBI officials—McCabe, Priestap, and Baker among them—were all involved. Such FISA applications are also reviewed within the top ranks of the Justice Department.

The application for Page was submitted in October, sometime after October 7 (the most recent date mentioned in the application; the precise date the application was filed hasn't been disclosed).

"This application targets Carter Page," the application began. "The FBI believes Page has been the subject of targeted recruitment by the Russian Government."

The fifty-seven-page document reviewed in considerable detail the background of Operation Crossfire Hurricane and its origins. This included disclosures by Papadopoulos, as well as extensive material that remains classified. But Steele appears as a prominent source. "In July 2016, Page traveled to Russia and delivered the commencement address at the New Economic School," the application stated. "In addition to giving this address, the FBI has learned that Page met with at least two Russian officials during this trip. First, according to information provided by an FBI confidential human source (Source #1)"—a reference to Steele—"Page had a secret meeting with Igor Sechin, who is the President of Rosneft [a Russian energy company] and a close associate to Russian President Putin."

The application went into extensive detail about "Source #1" and his potential motivations. After describing the FBI's previous dealings with Steele and his reliability, the application stated that Steele was approached by an "identified U.S. person"—Glenn Simpson—"with whom Source #1 [had had] a long-standing business relationship." Simpson "never advised Source #1 as to the motivation behind the research into Candidate #1's ties to Russia." (Throughout the application, Trump is described only as "Candidate #1.") "The FBI speculates that the identified U.S. person was likely looking for information that could be used to discredit Candidate #1's campaign."

The application continued, "Notwithstanding Source #1's reason for conducting the research into Candidate #1's ties to Russia, based on Source #1's previous reporting history with the FBI, whereby Source #1 provided reliable information to the FBI, the FBI believes Source #1's reporting herein to be credible."

The application made no specific mention that the Clinton campaign or the Democratic National Committee was paying Fusion for the research, because neither Steele nor anyone at the FBI knew the identity of Simpson's clients, which was confidential information. But the FBI did "speculate" that the motive was to harm Trump—and made that clear to the court.

The application was granted by the five-judge FISA court.

As Crossfire Hurricane entered a new, more intense phase, the Clinton emails faded in importance. "We were consumed by these ever-increasing allegations" about Russian interference, Strzok later testified. By comparison, the discovery of a new trove of Clinton emails was "another thing to worry about. And it's important, and we need to do it," Strzok said. But at the same time, he faced a much more urgent question: "Is the government of Russia trying to get somebody elected here in the United States?"

As Strzok's boss, Bill Priestap, said, "My focus wasn't on Midyear anymore." He conceded, "Yes, we've got to review it. Yes, it may contain evidence we didn't know, but I'd be shocked if it's evidence that's going to change the outcome of the case because, again, aside from this, did we see enough information previously in which I felt confident that we had gotten to the bottom of the issue? I did." He continued, "As important as this was, in some ways it was water under the bridge. The issue of the day was what's going to be done to possibly interfere with the election."

For Comey himself, "it was Russia, Russia, Russia all the time."

CLINTON'S EMAILS MIGHT have been supplanted as the primary focus at FBI headquarters, but hardly anywhere else. Quick to sense a political opening after Christie's incendiary speech and the raucous chants of "lock her up" at the Republican convention, Trump rarely missed an opportunity to keep the issue alive. He brought it up repeatedly on the campaign trail and during the televised presidential debates.

"I didn't think I'd say this, but I'm going to say it, and I hate to say it," Trump told Hillary Clinton at the second televised debate, held in St. Louis on October 9. "But if I win, I am going to instruct my attorney general to get a special prosecutor to look into your situation, because there has never been so many lies, so much deception. There has never been anything like it, and we're going to have a special prosecutor."

Trump continued, "In my opinion, the people that are the long-term workers at the FBI are furious. There has never been anything like this, where emails, and you get a subpoena, you get a subpoena, and after getting the subpoena, you delete 33,000 emails." He continued, "You acid wash or bleach them, as you would say, a very expensive process."

Clinton tried to deflect the charge onstage, admitting again that she'd made a mistake by using a private server. She also pointed out that most of what Trump said was "absolutely false." (She was correct: she did not delete any emails after receiving a subpoena, nor did she or anyone else "acid wash" or "bleach" them.) "But I'm not surprised." She added, "It's just awfully good that someone with the temperament of Donald Trump is not in charge of the law in our country."

"Because you'd be in jail," Trump shot back.

One line in particular leaped out at FBI headquarters: "The people that are the long-term workers at the FBI are furious." Where had that come from? There had been no sign of widespread dissension within the FBI's rank and file. Still, there was mounting concern among some in Comey's inner circle that there was a germ of truth to Trump's claim. Some of the most vocal critics of the case's resolution and Comey's announcement appeared to be within the extended FBI community, perhaps not so surprising given the FBI's conservative leanings and some of the anti-Clinton remarks Page and Strzok had heard during the investigation. Retired agents, in particular—reflecting a generation that was even more white, male, and Republican than the current force—were stirring up dissent.

On October 7, the president of the Society of Former Special Agents of the FBI sent an email to headquarters, "Controversy over the Director/Clinton Email Situation," saying, "I continue to hear negative comments about the Bureau's handling of the Clinton email controversy from former agents. This is after a period where things seemed to quiet and comments mellowed."

As Lisa Page put it, the FBI had gotten "a ton of criticism from the formers about why we let her off the hook, and why she should have been prosecuted, and why if she had, if they had done this, they would have prosecuted, all those sorts of criticism."

Addressing the FBI's annual convention of special agents in charge in San Diego that month, Comey acknowledged, "I have gotten emails from some employees about this, who said if I did what Hillary Clinton did I'd be in huge trouble." At the same time, "What I'm getting from the left is savage attacks for violating policy and law by talking publicly about somebody who wasn't indicted, by revealing facts that you should've been prescribed from revealing by decades of tradition." As he pointed out, "It is a uniquely difficult time."

So Comey devoted a good part of his speech to explaining, yet again, his reasoning in the Midyear case. Back in Washington, at the behest of Michael Kortan, the FBI's head of public affairs, Page put together some talking points for answering questions about Midyear, especially from retired agents. Strzok, too, discussed the case in a conference call with former agents.

Despite these efforts to tamp down the controversy, on October 17 it broke into public view. *The Daily Caller*, a conservative, pro-Trump website co-founded by Tucker Carlson, the Fox News host and commentator, reported that "FBI agents say the bureau is alarmed over Director James Comey urging the Justice Department to not prosecute Hillary Clinton over her mishandling of classified information." The story named no sources but said, "According to an interview transcript given to The Daily Caller, provided by an intermediary who spoke to two federal agents with the bureau last Friday, agents are frustrated by Comey's leadership."

The only person quoted by name in the story was Joseph diGenova, a fierce Trump partisan, a Washington lawyer with close ties to Rudolph Giuliani, and a frequent guest on Carlson's TV show. "People inside the bureau are furious," diGenova maintained. "They are embarrassed." Then he turned his attack onto Comey personally. Comey was a "hack" and a "crook. They think he's fundamentally dishonest. They have no confidence in him. The bureau inside right now is a mess."

The whole story looked as if it were ginned up by diGenova and might easily have been dismissed as right-wing agitprop. But then Trump tweeted a link to the article, "EXCLUSIVE: FBI Agents Say Comey 'Stood in the Way' of Clinton Email Investigation," and "'Don't know how Comey can keep going.'"

THE WEINER LAPTOP investigation might have languished indefinitely but for the determined efforts of the New York case agent who examined the laptop's contents.* As the sole proprietor of what he now knew to be hundreds of thousands of emails with Clinton's name on them, and the election just a month away, he was, as he later put it, "a little scared." Even though "I'm not political" and "I don't care who wins this election," he feared the revelation that the bureau sat on such a trove "is going to make us look really, really horrible."

As he put it, "Something was going to come crashing down." Even though "I didn't work the Hillary Clinton matter. My understanding at the time was I am telling you people I have private Hillary Clinton emails, number one, and BlackBerry messages, number two. I'm telling you that we have potentially ten times the volume that Director Comey said we had on the record. Why isn't anybody here?" He also worried that Comey hadn't been informed. "As a big admirer of the guy, and I think he's a straight shooter, I felt like he needed to know that we got this. And I didn't know if he did."

Feeling he "had nowhere else to turn," on October 19 he went outside the normal chain of command and met with two prosecutors from the

---

* The FBI declined to identify the New York case agent who discovered the Clinton emails on Weiner's laptop and agitated to pursue the investigation.

Manhattan U.S. attorney's office. He figured if they "got the attention of Preet Bharara, maybe they'd kick some of these lazy FBI folks in the butt and get them moving."

The prosecutors got the sense that the agent was stressed and worried he'd be blamed if nothing more were done and the existence of the emails became public. He worried that "somebody was not acting appropriately, somebody was trying to bury this." Concerned that the agent might "act out," they briefed Bharara. Although the Clinton email investigation lay outside the Southern District's jurisdiction, Bharara had someone get in touch with Toscas at the Justice Department in case "something had fallen through the cracks."

The news that his message had gotten through came as a relief to the agent. "Not to sound sappy, but I appreciate you guys understanding how uneasy I felt about the situation," he said in an October 21 email to the Southern District prosecutors he'd met with. And he wrote to his boss and another agent in New York: The prosecutors "understood my concerns yesterday about the nature of the stuff I have on Weiner computer (ie, that I will be scapegoated if it comes out that the FBI had this stuff). They appreciated that I was in a tight spot and spoke to their chain of command who agreed." He now felt reassured "I did the right thing by speaking up."

TWO DAYS LATER, on October 23, the *Wall Street Journal* reporter Devlin Barrett broke the news that the Virginia governor McAuliffe's political action committee had given $467,500 to Jill McCabe's unsuccessful run for the state senate: "Clinton Ally Aided Campaign of FBI Official's Wife."

That came as news to McCabe, who, by design, had known nothing about contributions to his wife's campaign.

The FBI issued a statement, saying McCabe played no role in the campaign and at the time had no involvement in any Clinton investigations. The article also noted that McCabe had sought ethics guidance and had followed it.

Still, that McAuliffe had given such a large sum to Jill McCabe's campaign made Comey uneasy about the appearance of any influence or conflicts. He wished McCabe had told him (unaware that McCabe hadn't known). In that case, he would have assigned someone else to oversee the email investigation—not because he thought there was an actual conflict or that McCabe had done anything improper, but because it might be used "to undercut the credibility of the institution."

Those concerns were immediately borne out: Trump promptly tweeted a link to the article, and the Republican National Committee chair, Reince Priebus, issued a statement: "Given all we know about how the corrupt Clinton machine operates, it's hard not to see this as anything other than a down payment to influence the FBI's criminal investigation into Hillary Clinton's private email server."

Rudy Giuliani jumped on the news, calling the *Journal* story a "shot to the solar plexus" in an appearance on *Fox & Friends*. He added, "We've got a couple of surprises left."

THE DAY AFTER the *Wall Street Journal* story, Toscas asked McCabe about the status of the Weiner laptop, a subject that had largely slipped McCabe's mind. McCabe asked Strzok and Priestap and realized with some dismay that the investigation had languished. As Jim Baker put it, "We took our collective eyes off the ball, didn't pay attention to it, and when it came back and we were informed that it was not resolved, then it became a crisis."

Prompted by McCabe's questions, on October 26 Strzok and Toscas convened a conference call that included other Midyear team members, and they finally spoke directly to the New York case agent. He felt frustrated, as he put it, that they were "asking questions that I had already repeatedly answered in other calls." The laptop contained as many as 650,000 emails, and as the agent told them, "We could have every email that Huma and Hillary ever sent each other."

These appeared to include the emails from Clinton's earliest days as secretary of state—the time period when she was most likely to have explained or commented on her decision to use private email—which the FBI had been unable to retrieve through other means.

That revelation rekindled the sense of urgency that had briefly prevailed back in September. For Strzok this was the "tipping point" that this might not be just another case of duplicate emails. Strzok briefed Page, who described the development as "good news, in a bad news way"—good news, she explained, in the sense that "more evidence is always good news. It might either change our decision or outcome or further substantiate the outcome we reached." And bad news, because "I cannot believe we are, we are here. We are doing this again on October 26th. Like, oh, my goodness."

That same day, *The Wall Street Journal*'s Barrett again contacted Kortan, indicating he wasn't finished with the McCabe story. Now he was pursuing a lead that McCabe had tried to tamp down the FBI's Clinton Foundation investigation before the election, which, if true, suggested that McCabe had favored Clinton in the wake of his wife's McAuliffe-financed campaign.

In an email to Kortan, Barrett asked if it was "accurate" that, "in the summer, McCabe himself gave some instruction as to how to proceed with the Clinton Foundation probe, given that it was the height of election season and the FBI did not want to make a lot of overt moves that could be seen as going after her or drawing attention to the probe." He asked, "Anything else I should know?"

Kortan conferred with Page and McCabe, who suggested Page talk to Barrett and find out more about the story.

That same day, Giuliani again teased an upcoming "surprise" that would propel Trump to victory. Appearing again on Fox News, he said to expect "a surprise or two that you're going to hear about in the next two days.

"I'm talking about some pretty big surprise," he said.

Comey and McCabe wondered, what was Giuliani talking about? Was someone in the FBI, likely in New York, leaking?

Comey ordered the FBI's inspection division to launch an investigation. "I was concerned that there appeared to be in the media a number of stories that might have been based on communications reporters or non-reporters like Rudy Giuliani were having with people in the New York field office," Comey later explained. "In particular, in, I want to say mid-October, maybe a little bit later, Mr. Giuliani was making statements that appeared to be based on his knowledge of workings inside the FBI New York. And then my recollection is there were other stories that were in the same ballpark that gave me a general concern that we may have a leak problem—unauthorized disclosure problem out of New York." The same day as Giuliani's Fox appearance, McCabe hastily arranged a conference call with Lynch and the head of the FBI's New York office, who got "ripped by the AG on leaks," as he put it.

That same evening, Strzok and others briefed McCabe on the status of the Weiner laptop and their call with the New York case agent. Even though McCabe was going to be out of town the next day, they agreed it was urgent they brief Comey. Early the next morning—at 5:20—McCabe emailed: "Boss, The MYR team has come across some additional actions they believe they need to take. I think we should probably gather today to discuss implications if you have any space on your calendar. I am happy to join by phone. Will push to Lisa and Jim to coordinate if you are good."

Comey responded at 7:13 a.m., "Copy."

The Midyear team was waiting in Comey's conference room when the director walked in at 10:00 a.m. with a grin on his face. He had no idea what the meeting was about but was amused to see the familiar faces of the Midyear team gathered together once again. "The band is back to-gether," he observed. The grin quickly faded as he saw the sober looks around the conference table.

McCabe had called in, but Baker suggested he hang up. Comey, too, told him to "drop off" the call and added, "I don't need you on this call." McCabe was taken aback and upset; he was the one who had pushed for the meeting, and was intimately involved in the issues, but he nonetheless hung up. Lisa Page also left the room. While Comey said nothing explicit, everyone realized their departures had something to do with the firestorm that had erupted after the *Wall Street Journal* article.

Strzok led the briefing, and briefly reviewed the bizarre sequence of events in which Anthony Weiner's sexually explicit texts to a fifteen-year-old minor led to the discovery of hundreds of thousands of Hillary Clinton emails. It all seemed new to Comey. None of it jogged any memory of his having been told about it before.

Comey asked what they'd found in the emails. "We see evidence of many, many, many, thousands and thousands of emails from the period of Secretary Clinton's tenure as Secretary of State," Comey recalled being told. "Two, we see Verizon.Blackberry.net email metadata. We don't know what the content is, from the period of time when Secretary Clinton was using a BlackBerry, Verizon.BlackBerry.net account at the beginning of her tenure as Secretary of State. We think this may be the missing three months of emails."

If so, it was a potent discovery, because Clinton's motive—the elusive question of her intent—would have been most evident when she began using the private server. Comey asked if everyone felt they needed to review the contents of the emails to be sure they'd "turned over the necessary stones" and "be comfortable with the decision we made."

"Yes," Priestap replied. "We don't know with certainty what's in there. It could be information that we've not seen, you know, thus far, and so yes . . . in effect it's dereliction of duty to not, you know this thing is out here to pass it over. So yes, we've got to, we have to do it."

Strzok agreed, saying, "We have to pursue this material, because, you know, we would do it in any other case. And it is, you know, a pool of evidence that hypothetically, now understandably it's very speculative, but there is that possibility that it could change our outcome."

Priestap thought that unlikely. He felt that they'd already scoured so many emails that it was unlikely they'd discover any "smoking gun," as he put it, and if they did, it "would have shocked me." But "could it have been possible? Absolutely. That's why we had to review it."

Comey readily agreed that the FBI needed to get a search warrant and review the emails. As he later said, "We may be finding the golden missing emails that would change this case."

"How fast can you review and assess this?" Comey asked. The answer was weeks—maybe months—and not until long after the election. "Do it as quickly as you can, but do it well," Comey responded.

Going to court and applying for a warrant were overt investigative acts. Others would be aware or involved, including agents in New York and prosecutors in Preet Bharara's office. There was the ever-present danger, even likelihood, of leaks. According to Page, there was "a substantial and legitimate fear that when we went to seek the warrant in order to get access to the Weiner laptop, that the fact of that would leak."

More worrisome, with the decision to seek a warrant, Midyear "awoke from the dead," as Comey later put it. It was again an active investigation. The presidential election was exactly twelve days away. Comey wondered, now what?

SIX

"TO SPEAK OR TO CONCEAL"

With the discovery of the Weiner laptop and its contents, Comey now faced what he saw as a binary decision: "to speak or to conceal." Comey's own reputation for candor was on the line: he had represented to the American people that the Clinton email investigation was closed, something he deemed a "material fact." That was no longer true. To now remain silent would be "an affirmative act of concealment."

Once the information came out, because it was either announced or leaked, Comey's reputation for probity would be shredded, and his job as FBI director might well be in jeopardy. "I think he may have said, like, I could be impeached," Baker recalled.

Comey was well aware that Department of Justice policy discouraged (though didn't explicitly forbid) actions that might have an impact on elections, whether "that's a dogcatcher election or president of the United States."

As Comey told members of his staff, "Those are the doors. One says speak, the other says conceal. Let's see what's behind the speak door. It's really bad. We're eleven days from a presidential election."

"Okay, close that one, really bad," Comey said.

"Open the second one. Catastrophic." To conceal would be "catastrophic, not just to the Bureau, but beyond the Bureau." Comey elaborated: to conceal would subject the FBI and the Justice Department "to a corrosive doubt that you had engineered a cover up to protect a particular political candidate."

Given Comey's public commitment to unusual transparency in the email case, if he now concealed that the investigation had been reopened, he felt the consequence would be "generations-long damage to the credibility of the FBI and the Justice Department."

Comey was well aware Clinton was the overwhelming favorite to be the next president in every major poll. While he consciously tried to ignore that, he acknowledged, "I was operating in an environment where she was going to be the next president."

The likelihood of Clinton's election had obvious implications: if she was so far ahead, then announcing that the email investigation had been reopened was unlikely to affect the outcome. And if she were elected, and the FBI discovered incriminating evidence, "the moment she took office, the FBI is dead, the Department of Justice is dead and she's dead as president," Comey said.

There was also the ever-present danger of leaks. If Comey decided to remain silent, "we were quite confident that somebody is going to leak," Baker recalled. And then there would be "claims that we tried to play games with the election, and we tried to steer it in a certain way to help Hillary Clinton and hurt Donald Trump."

Posed in those terms, Comey's choice was between "really bad" and "catastrophic." Though discussions continued throughout the afternoon and evening, it was pretty clear where Comey was headed. As he'd said at the end of their meeting, "Welcome to the world of really bad."

Though excluded from the meetings, Page and McCabe both expressed strong reservations about Comey's plan. "Please, let's figure out what it is we HAVE first," Page texted Strzok that afternoon, noting the FBI might not even get the search warrant. "Then we have no further investigative step."

"Agreed," Strzok replied.

McCabe wrote to Page at 9:57 p.m. saying Baker had told him "about the notification and statement which the boss wants to send tomorrow. I do not agree with the timing but he is insistent."

"I also wildly disagree that we need to notify before we even know what the plan is," Page responded, adding, "I hope you can get some rest tonight."

THE NEXT MORNING, Trisha Anderson, the FBI's deputy general counsel, told Baker that after thinking about it overnight, "I have serious reservations about going down this road. I'm very concerned about this, Jim. Why? Well, because I'm concerned that we are going to interject ourselves into this process. We're going to interject ourselves into the election in a way that's, that potentially or almost certainly will change the outcome. And I am, I, Trisha, am quite concerned about that. And I'm concerned about us being responsible for getting Donald Trump elected."

Anderson, who like nearly everyone else at FBI headquarters was somewhat in awe of Comey, was reluctant to broach the subject with the director present. So Baker brought it up at that morning's discussion, and Anderson said, "I'm not so certain that this is the right thing to do."

While she didn't explicitly name Trump, and felt the mention of any candidate's name would be inappropriate, she expressed her concerns about affecting the outcome of an election. Everyone knew what she was talking about.

Anderson was also concerned that no one yet knew what was in the emails and whether they would have any impact on the conclusion. As she later explained, "It was unclear—and perhaps even unlikely—that the emails would be material to the investigation." And "no matter how carefully we wrote such a letter, the importance of the emails would be over-inflated and misunderstood. So, in my mind, and what I believe I argued in the meeting, was that we were about to do something that could have a very significant impact on the outside world even though what we had might not be material, yet people would very likely view it as such."

Comey firmly rejected her concerns. "I cannot consider that at all," he said. "Down that path lies the death of the FBI because if I ever start thinking about whose political ox will be gored by this or that, who will be hurt or helped, then we are done as an independent force in American life." He said he appreciated her raising the issue, which was likely on everyone's mind. But "I cannot consider it."

Anderson said she came around to Comey's view that disclosure was the better of two bad alternatives. Strzok, too, overcame any reservations he'd expressed to Page. McCabe, though excluded from the meeting, was firmly opposed—at least until the FBI knew what was in the emails—but when he spoke to Comey by phone after the meeting, Comey said, "I don't need you to weigh in on this decision."

By now Comey's mind was largely made up, and he asked Strzok to draft a letter notifying Congress. Comey felt so strongly that if he failed to inform Congress, "I ought to be fired, I ought to be hung out, I would be run out of town."

AFTER THE MEETING, Kortan and Page called *The Wall Street Journal*'s Devlin Barrett, who insisted that he had sources who had told him that McCabe told them to "stand down" on the Clinton Foundation investigation until after the election, implying that McCabe was trying to protect Clinton from any adverse publicity.

The agents had been barred from overt steps until after the election, but by the Justice Department, not by McCabe. On the contrary. McCabe had stood up to Axelrod when the subject came up in August. McCabe reminded Page about the Axelrod call and authorized her to tell Barrett about it. Surely, he reasoned, Barrett would drop that part of his story once he heard the anecdote, because it completely undercut the premise that McCabe was going easy on Clinton because of his wife's campaign donations.

Along with Comey, McCabe had the authority to approve press disclosures when it was in the public interest, though he'd never exercised it before. But Comey was mired in the Weiner laptop issues. So Kortan and Page spoke again to Barrett late that afternoon and told him about McCabe's response to Axelrod's call. Neither Page nor McCabe focused on the fact that they had just implicitly confirmed that there was a Clinton Foundation investigation.

COMEY HANDED THE unenviable task of conveying his decision to notify Congress about the Weiner laptop discovery to Rybicki, his chief of staff, who called Axelrod that same afternoon, October 27. Although Comey didn't call Lynch or Yates himself (in order, he said, to let them distance themselves), at least he was giving his nominal superiors advance notice and a chance to weigh in, in contrast to the July 5 announcement.

On the face of it, this was inconsistent. The risk that Justice Department involvement would be perceived as partisan was no less now than it had been in July. Comey himself was at something of a loss to explain it. He might have been subliminally troubled by the anger and distrust that his earlier decision had caused at the Justice Department. He might even have hoped that Lynch and Yates, his superiors in the government hierarchy, would give him a direct order not to send the letter. The burden of the Clinton investigation he'd donned in July now seemed incredibly heavy. On some level, it would be a relief to have someone lift it from his shoulders.

Rybicki told Axelrod that Comey planned to send a letter notifying Congress that the Clinton email investigation had been reopened. He stressed that Comey felt an ethical obligation. "The Director has testified. The Director believes that Congress has, now has a misimpression and so it's the Director's butt on the line," he told Axelrod. "He needs to do this. If he doesn't," he added, "it's not survivable for him."*

Axelrod was shocked and dismayed. This ran squarely counter to the department's long-standing policy of not interfering in an election, which was now only days away. He told Rybicki he'd have to discuss it with Yates and Lynch, but said it was "a bad idea."

Axelrod immediately briefed Lynch and Yates. As Lynch recalled it, "The Director's view was that he had to provide this information to Congress, that he was concerned about the information being leaked from the New York office." And "he also was concerned that if, if in fact he did not

---

* Rybicki said he didn't recall using the term "survivable" or suggesting Comey might be asked to resign or be fired.

provide this information to Congress, and either it was leaked or later on we discussed it in some Department-approved way, that it was not survivable." Lynch asked Axelrod what he meant by "survivable," and Axelrod said "that was just the phrase that Rybicki had used. It was not survivable," either for Comey or for the FBI as an institution.

Wittingly or not, Comey had put his superiors at Justice in what they considered an untenable situation.

All three thought notifying Congress at this juncture was a terrible idea, especially because no one yet knew what was in the emails. But as in July, they had no sense that Comey was seeking their advice. Rybicki had framed the issue as one of Comey's moral and ethical duty. A call from Lynch or Yates was unlikely to change his mind.

They recognized that Yates and Lynch had the authority to stop him, or at least order him not to make the disclosure. But then what?

In one scenario, Comey would defy them and send the notice to Congress. As Yates put it, we "weren't at all convinced that he would follow such an order not to do it." Lynch would then have to fire Comey or demand his resignation for insubordination. Nothing would have been gained, and the ensuing furor would only raise more questions about whether the Justice Department had tried to tip the scales in favor of Clinton.

Another scenario was that if Lynch ordered him not to notify Congress, he'd resign. Such was Comey's reputation stemming from the Ashcroft episode that this seemed highly likely. "That seemed like a very real possibility to us, particularly against the backdrop of the situation with John Ashcroft in the hospital room where he had the resignation letter drafted," Yates said. "That wasn't even an ethical obligation. That was something where he disagreed with them about the statutory authority there."

The reasons for Comey's resignation would surely become public, again placing Lynch and the Justice Department in the untenable position of trying to prevent an FBI director from discharging his perceived moral and ethical duty in what would appear to be an effort to protect the Democratic candidate for president.

A third scenario was that Comey obeyed the order. (Comey later said that he would have followed such a direct order.) Even this was highly problematic: as Axelrod put it, that "tees up an obstruction of Congress investigation" of Lynch, who might be accused of blocking Comey from correcting a statement—that the Midyear investigation was closed—that was no longer valid.

For Axelrod, none of those scenarios were "good for the policies and the procedures or the goals of keeping DOJ and FBI out of politics. None of those are good for the AG personally," or for the institutions.

There was another possible scenario, which was that Lynch could call Comey, feel out his intentions, and test his resolve to go through with the notice. But the two were never that close or had much rapport, certainly not after the discussion of the Clinton "matter" or the July 5 announcement.

As Yates put it, she'd witnessed Comey's reactions in many meetings with Justice Department officials, and his tendency "was very defensive of his agency and he would push back hard. I didn't think there was any way in the world he was going to go back to his people and say, I just got off the phone with the AG or I just got off the phone with the DAG and they convinced me that I really don't have this personal ethical obligation I've told all of you that I have." She felt the best strategy was to convince Rybicki, who might in turn be in a position to persuade Comey.

Axelrod conveyed in no uncertain terms "our building's view" that "the Director should not do this." It was "not only a really bad idea" that "violates our policies and procedures and traditions," but "it's contrary to how we do business. And actually, I used those exact words as well. It was contrary to how we do business."

The argument that notifying Congress violated department policy—the linchpin of Justice's opposition—didn't carry much weight with Comey, because the policy was always qualified by an "overriding public interest" in disclosure, which Comey deemed this to be.

A few rungs below Comey and Lynch, Strzok and Toscas also had a heated discussion, in which Toscas said, "This is BS. We don't talk about our stuff publicly. We don't announce things. We do things quietly."

He was also able to articulate more broadly the virtue in adhering to established principles—especially in extraordinary circumstances. He explained, "The institution has principles and there's always an urge when something important or different pops up to say, we might want to deviate because this is so different. But the comfort that we get as people, as lawyers, as representatives, as employees and as an institution, the comfort we get from those institutional policies, protocols, has, is an unbelievable thing through whatever storm, you know whatever storm hits us, when you are within the norm of the way the institution behaves, you can weather any of it because you stand on the principle."

But Toscas's reasoning didn't reach Comey, and even if it had, it's unlikely it would have tipped the scale between "really bad" and "catastrophic." What really struck Comey was that no one at Justice was telling him not to do it, or even reaching out to engage on the issue. Department officials could oppose his decision but bear no responsibility for the consequences, which Comey thought was a "cowardly way out." As in July, he realized, "it became my responsibility to take the hit."

Comey's letter reached Congress just before noon on October 28:

In previous congressional testimony, I referred to the fact that the Federal Bureau of Investigation (FBI) had completed its investigation of former Secretary Clinton's personal email server. Due to recent developments, I am writing to supplement my previous testimony. In connection with an unrelated case, the FBI has learned of the existence of emails that appear to be pertinent to the investigation. I am writing to inform you that the investigative team briefed me on this yesterday, and I agreed that the FBI should take appropriate investigative steps designed to allow investigators to review these emails to determine whether they contain classified information, as well as to assess their importance to our investigation. Although the FBI cannot yet assess whether or not this material may be significant, and I cannot predict how long it will take us to complete this additional work, I believe it is important to update your Committees about our efforts in light of my previous testimony.

Unlike in July, there would be no press conference and no further public statement, because the investigation was ongoing.

Seven minutes later, the news broke. The Utah Republican Jason Chaffetz tweeted, "FBI Dir just informed me, 'The FBI has learned of the existence of emails that appear to be pertinent to the investigation.' Case reopened." Within fifteen minutes, Fox reported "breaking news." The story immediately dominated the airwaves and internet.

So confident was Hillary Clinton of victory that at 12:37 p.m., even as the news was breaking, her campaign announced that during the final days of the campaign she'd be traveling to a traditional Republican stronghold, Arizona, and would be pouring money into another, Texas. National polls showed her rising on the trustworthiness scale and pulling even further ahead of Trump.

Clinton herself, and Democrats generally, seemed somewhat bewildered by the laptop discovery, not knowing what if anything was in the emails. Clinton didn't respond at all until that night. "We are 11 days out from perhaps the most important national election of our lifetimes," she said in Des Moines. "The American people deserve to get the full and complete facts immediately."

In a perceptive assessment, the former Democratic congressman Barney Frank told the *Times*, "It sounds like Comey is being supercareful and superthorough. He wanted to alert Congress quickly because he is being careful that nothing about these new emails would otherwise leak out. He usually wouldn't talk about things so early, but he wants to be careful."

Frank's main point—that no actual facts had emerged to change the outcome of the investigation—was lost in the furor that the case had been reopened, which many people assumed meant something damaging to Clinton had been discovered.

Trump, of course, pounced on the revelation, making no effort to conceal his glee. When he opened a rally that day in New Hampshire with an announcement that he had "breaking news," raucous cheers and chants of "Lock her up!" all but drowned him out. Once the crowd had quieted slightly, he continued, "Hillary Clinton's corruption is on a scale we have never seen before. We must not let her take her criminal scheme into the Oval Office." More cheers erupted. Then Trump softened his tone on the FBI and an investigation he had repeatedly insisted was "rigged."

"I have great respect for the fact that the FBI and the Department of Justice are now willing to have the courage to right the horrible mistake that they made," Trump said. "This was a grave miscarriage of justice that the American people fully understood."

Comey's letter and the resurrected email scandal were the lead news story for six out of the crucial seven days between October 29 (when the *Times*'s lead headline was "New Emails Jolt Clinton Campaign in Race's Last Days") and November 4, the Friday before the election, according to the media analysis website Memeorandum.

OVER THE WEEKEND, anonymous Justice Department sources vented their frustrations with Comey to *The Washington Post* in unusually blunt terms, with one saying, "Comey made an independent decision to alert the Hill. He is operating independently of the Justice Department. And he knows it."

In the article, Matt Miller, a former Justice Department spokesman, said, "Jim Comey forgets that he works for the attorney general. I think he has a lot of regard for his own integrity. And he lets that regard cross lines into self-righteousness. He has come to believe that his own ethics are so superior to anyone else's that his judgment can replace existing rules and regulations. That is a dangerous belief for an FBI director to have."

This line of criticism really got under Comey's skin, because it transformed what he considered two important virtues—being truthful and transparent—into moral failings, being "in love with my own righteousness." While he did worry about his ego, he was also proud he tried to do the right thing.

A colleague sent a copy of the article to Page, with the notation, "This is all Axelrod."

"Yeah. I saw it," Page replied. "Makes me feel WAY less bad about throwing him under the bus in the forthcoming CF article," referring to

Barrett's forthcoming *Wall Street Journal* article on McCabe and the Clinton Foundation.

"FBI in Internal Feud over Hillary Clinton Probe" was the headline on the *Wall Street Journal* website on October 30. It was hardly what Page was hoping for, especially after she'd spent so much time with Barrett. Her efforts hadn't persuaded the reporter to leave out the allegations about McCabe, although he included what she told him about Axelrod, who wasn't named in the story: "The Justice Department official [Axelrod] was 'very pissed off,' according to one person close to Mr. McCabe, and pressed him to explain why the FBI was still chasing a matter the department considered dormant. Others said the Justice Department was simply trying to make sure FBI agents were following longstanding policy not to make overt investigative moves that could be seen as trying to influence an election." But, the article continued, agents had been told to "stand down" on the Clinton Foundation investigation and "were told the order had come from the deputy director—Mr. McCabe."

The article hit a raw nerve with Comey. Reporting on the conversation with Axelrod, which cast Axelrod in an especially unflattering light, would only exacerbate tensions with the Justice Department. Moreover, no one had publicly confirmed the existence of a Clinton Foundation investigation; Comey himself had refused to do so in Congress. And who was the "source close to" McCabe? Obviously, there was another leak, already one of Comey's major worries. He suspected—but didn't know—it was Page.

Comey brought up the article at Monday morning's staff meeting. Page was taking notes. "Need to figure out how to get our folks to understand why leaks hurt our organization," she wrote. Afterward, he discussed the *Journal* article with McCabe. "Can you believe this crap? How does this stuff get out?" he said, or words to that effect, in Comey's recollection.

At that moment, McCabe could have clarified that Page was indeed the source "close" to McCabe, and he'd authorized her to speak to rebut the flagrantly false claim that McCabe had tried to suppress the foundation case. Doing so, of course, might have risked Comey's ire and, even worse, disappointment. McCabe hesitated, and then the moment passed.

A few days later, Comey asked McCabe to recuse himself from the email case and anything else having to do with Clinton, "in light of the controversy" over McAuliffe's donations to his wife's campaign. Although McCabe strenuously disagreed, he agreed to step aside.

NOT ALL THE media coverage of Comey's letter to Congress was critical. William Barr, a former attorney general under George H. W. Bush and a Trump supporter, wrote a spirited defense of Comey in *The Washington Post*, "James Comey Did the Right Thing." "Comey had no choice but to issue the statement he did," Barr wrote. "Indeed, it would have violated policy had he not done so."

Trump himself softened his tone on Comey. "I have to tell you, I respect the fact that Director Comey was able to come back after what he did," he said at a rally in Phoenix. "I respect that very much."

But all that week, Comey felt like a pariah, at least in Democratic precincts. In the House, Nancy Pelosi compared his letter to a "Molotov cocktail" and said Comey had become "the leading Republican political operative in the country—wittingly or unwittingly." At Comey's next meeting in the White House Situation Room, everyone avoided eye contact with him (except his friends John Brennan, CIA director, and James Clapper, director of national security).

So when Loretta Lynch asked Comey to stay behind for a private meeting after their weekly intelligence briefing, he wondered, how angry was she? Was she going to yell at him? Threaten him?

Lynch had indeed been angry. But she'd softened that morning when she saw him. Lynch thought Comey looked terrible, like he'd been run over by a truck.

Once they were alone, she asked, "How are you?"

"Well . . ." he began, his voice trailing off.

Lynch went to him and put her arms around him. "I thought you needed a hug."

"You knew I didn't want you to send that letter," Lynch said when they resumed their conversation.

Comey murmured his assent.

"Well, it's done now," she said. "The question is, how do we go forward?"

"I don't know," Comey said.

"Just tell me what was going on with you," Lynch said. "What were you thinking?"

Comey said it had been a "nightmare" and reviewed the unpalatable choice he faced between "really bad" and "catastrophic."

"Would they feel better if it leaked on November 4?" she asked.

"Exactly," Comey said. "I feel a little bit better. You're one of the few people who get it."

"I get it but I don't agree with it," Lynch replied.

"It's clear to me that there is a cadre of senior people in New York who have a deep and visceral hatred of Secretary Clinton," Comey said. And, "It is deep."

"I'm aware of that," Lynch said. "I wasn't aware it was to this level and this depth that you're talking about, but I'm sad to say that that does not surprise me. I am just troubled that this issue has put us where we are today with respect to this laptop."

"I hear you," Comey answered.

Lynch was sad Comey felt he had to shoulder the burden of the decision alone. She would gladly have taken some of the heat. They'd been friends for over twenty years.

As they left, Lynch smiled and said, "Try to look beat up."

It was the last time they spoke.

AS THE PRESIDENTIAL election neared, Christopher Steele, apparently frustrated by the FBI's inaction on his dossier, spoke to a reporter from *Mother Jones*, the progressive San Francisco–based magazine. On October 31, the Washington bureau chief and investigative reporter David Corn reported that "a former senior intelligence officer for a Western country who specialized in Russian counterintelligence tells *Mother Jones* that in recent months he provided the bureau with memos, based on his recent interactions with Russian sources, contending the Russian government has for years tried to co-opt and assist Trump—and that the FBI requested more information from him."

The former intelligence officer was obviously Steele, and speaking to the press about a confidential FBI investigation was a blatant violation of FBI rules for confidential intelligence sources. The next day, the FBI terminated its formal relationship with Steele and filed a memo to that effect, saying the cause was "confidentiality revealed."

But Steele was still a potential loose cannon. He had the dossier, and he knew the FBI was investigating the Trump campaign's ties to Russia. In terms of disrupting the election, Steele was a ticking time bomb.

Even as the FBI was distancing itself from Steele, on October 30 a Russian businessman involved in the Trump Tower Moscow sent Michael Cohen a text message alluding to potentially damaging tapes—presumably the ones described in the Steele dossier. "Stopped flow of some tapes from Russia but not sure if there's anything else. Just so you know," wrote Giorgi Rtskhiladze, who had been discussing the proposed Trump project with high-ranking officials, including the mayor of Moscow.

"Tapes of what?" Cohen asked.

"Not sure of the content but person in Moscow was bragging had tapes from Russia trip," Rtskhiladze responded. "Will try to dial you tomorrow but wanted to be aware. I'm sure it's not a big deal but there are lots of stupid people."

"You have no idea," Cohen replied.

Cohen relayed the conversation to Trump—meaning the Republican nominee knew about possibly embarrassing tapes a full week before the election.*

THE FBI OBTAINED a search warrant for Weiner's laptop on October 30, and the computer was physically transferred from New York to the bureau's operational technology division in Quantico, Virginia. The laptop contained 1,355,980 items and approximately 650,000 emails. While that

---

* Rtskhiladze later said he was told the tapes were "fake," but didn't mention that to Cohen. Nor did he explain how he had "stopped" them.

seemed a daunting and time-consuming task, technicians were able to narrow the Clinton-related emails to under 50,000. The FBI reviewed 6,827 emails that were either to or from Clinton and deemed 3,077 of those emails "potentially work-related." Strzok led the team that pored over each of these, working near twenty-four-hour days. They found thirteen email chains containing confidential information, though none were marked as classified. All were duplicates of emails that had already been examined.

On Friday, they told Comey they might finish before the election and made a final push to finish their review the next day. There was little disagreement that Comey should send another letter to Congress addressing the findings, although some worried that it was too close to the election to say anything. Strzok, for one, worried that anytime the FBI made an announcement, it only "reinvigorated" the news cycle, thrusting the FBI into the partisan wrangling. But there was no opposition at the Justice Department, which wanted Comey to correct any misimpressions that Clinton might still be charged, and lawyers there reviewed and signed off on a draft of the proposed letter.

The letter reached Congress on Sunday afternoon, November 6:

> I write to supplement my October 28, 2016 letter that notified you the FBI would be taking additional investigative steps with respect to former Secretary of State Clinton's use of a personal email server. Since my letter, the FBI investigative team has been working around the clock to process and review a large volume of emails from a device obtained in connection with an unrelated criminal investigation. During that process, we reviewed all of the communications that were to or from Hillary Clinton while she was Secretary of State. Based on our review, we have not changed our conclusions that we expressed in July with respect to Secretary Clinton. I am very grateful to the professionals at the FBI for doing an extraordinary amount of high-quality work in a short period of time.

As the *Times* put it, Comey's letter—his third public statement on the Midyear investigation—"swept away her largest and most immediate problem" but came "at the end of a rocky week for Mrs. Clinton that included wild, false speculation about looming indictments and shocking discoveries in the emails."

Trump immediately reverted to form—that Clinton "is being protected by a rigged system. It's a totally rigged system," as he said in Michigan on November 6 and at every subsequent rally.

Comey wanted nothing more to do with the election. He was, in his words, "too tired to care." He'd dedicated his career to the Department of Justice and the FBI in large part because they were institutions that stood apart from and above partisan politics. He had no plans to vote.

Comey had nonetheless achieved the dubious status of celebrity, or perhaps notoriety. That night he, his wife, and one of their daughters went out for dinner, where "Comey was spotted with a giant margarita at El Tio Tex Mex Grill," *The Washington Post* duly noted.

Perhaps because it drained the suspense from the Clinton email story rather than added to it, and had none of the "wild speculation" that had provided such good tabloid fare, Comey's November 6 letter got far less media attention. It wasn't even the lead news story that day; it was overshadowed by reports that a swarm of secret service agents had rushed Trump at a Nevada rally after someone in the crowd yelled, "Gun." (The man turned out to be unarmed.) The next day's news was dominated by the latest polls (which showed Clinton in a slight uptick, with a lead of 3.5 percentage points over Trump).

Strzok and Page never discussed any of their own work in terms of how it might affect the election. Strzok and Page had often advocated a tougher investigative approach toward Clinton and had even questioned issuing the November 6 letter exonerating her. None of their colleagues detected any hint of the political sentiments they expressed in what they assumed were confidential text messages.

Despite her lead in the polls, Page and Strzok weren't at all sure Clinton would win.

"The nyt probability numbers are dropping every day," a worried Page texted Strzok on November 3, referring to the *Times*'s online forecast. "I'm scared for our organization."

"Stein and moron are F'ing everything up, too," Strzok replied, referring to the Green candidate, Jill Stein, and the Libertarian Gary Johnson.

Four days later, the *Times* gave Clinton an 85 percent chance of winning, but added, "A victory by Mr. Trump remains possible."

"OMG this is F*CKING TERRIFYING," Strzok texted.

For the first time since he was old enough, McCabe decided not to cast a vote.

AT 2:35 ON the morning of November 9, 2016, Hillary Clinton called Trump to concede the election. *The New York Times* put aside the front-page headline it had mocked up, "Madam President."

"Trump Triumphs" was the headline that morning in both the *Times* and *The Washington Post*. Both *USA Today* and the *Los Angeles Times* referred to Trump's victory as a "stunning" upset.

Remarkably, nothing about the Russia investigation—including its very existence—had leaked. For those at the FBI privy to Operation Crossfire Hurricane, the result meant that in the worst-case scenario they were investigating, the Russian plot to undermine American democracy had succeeded beyond Putin's wildest dreams.

Comey was stunned by the election result. He felt numb. His wife was in tears. Comey desperately hoped he'd had nothing to do with the outcome. He consoled himself with the hope that the gravitas of the office would make Trump more presidential, and he'd shift toward governing from the center rather than cater to his base.

McCabe, too, was shocked. But he thought Clinton might have been more hostile toward the FBI, given the email investigation and Comey's letter reopening the case. Comey would surely have been replaced, and a new director would replace McCabe. But he also thought Trump and his campaign staff knew little about the role of the FBI and its tradition of independence. It would be a steep learning curve, especially with Crossfire Hurricane in progress.

Page and Strzok thought less about the consequences for the FBI.

"OMG I am so depressed," Page texted Strzok. "And honestly, I don't know if I can eat. I am very nauseous. I'm extremely depressed. Though today it's mostly not about work."

Two days later she wasn't feeling any better: "God, I'm really f-ing depressed. Bill [Priestap] just called to talk about the sentiment of everyone he was talking to."

"Sentiment about what?" Strzok asked.

"Thinks we had something to do with the outcome. I bought All the President's Men. Figure I needed to brush up on Watergate."*

COMEY WAS FEELING at a low point in late November, when he was in the Oval Office again with Obama, now a lame-duck president, and other national security leaders. After the meeting, Obama asked Comey to stay behind.

Once they were alone, Obama told him he didn't want to discuss any particular investigation but wanted to tell him something. "I picked you to be FBI director because of your integrity and your ability. I want you to know that nothing—nothing—has happened in the last year to change my view."

Comey felt tears welling up.

"That means a lot to me, Mr. President," Comey said. "I have hated the last year. The last thing we want is to be involved in an election. I'm just trying to do the right thing."

"I know," Obama reassured him.

---

* *All the President's Men* is the book by Bob Woodward and Carl Bernstein chronicling the Watergate scandal and the fall of President Richard Nixon.

SEVEN

"THERE WERE NO PROSTITUTES"

In the wake of victory, a more magnanimous Trump seemed to emerge, at least toward the vanquished foe he had so often branded a criminal. Trump's adviser Kellyanne Conway declared on MSNBC's *Morning Joe* that Trump didn't want to see Clinton prosecuted, despite the campaign chants to "lock her up." "If Donald Trump can help her heal then, perhaps, that's a good thing," Conway said.

Later that day, Trump elaborated during a visit to *The New York Times*. Asked about prosecuting Clinton, he said, "Look, I want to move forward, I don't want to move back. And I don't want to hurt the Clintons. I really don't. She went through a lot. And suffered greatly in many different ways. And I am not looking to hurt them at all. The campaign was vicious. They say it was the most vicious primary and the most vicious campaign. I guess, added together, it was definitely the most vicious." He reiterated, "I'm not looking to hurt them. I think they've been through a lot. They've gone through a lot. I think we have to get the focus of the country into looking forward."

In the following days, Trump began to put his stamp on the incoming administration as he announced top cabinet and national security appointments. For the pivotal post of attorney general, he chose Alabama senator Jeff Sessions. That Sessions would get a high-level appointment came as no surprise; he'd been the first (and for some time the only) senator to endorse Trump, turning his back on his fellow Republican senator

and frequent ally Ted Cruz. Sessions was a hard-line immigration opponent, fiercely opposed to any kind of amnesty for illegal immigrants, and
a supporter of Trump's proposed border wall.

He was also a controversial choice for a post like that of attorney general. His nomination to the federal bench had foundered thirty years earlier after a slew of racially tinged comments came to light, many made
while he was the U.S. attorney in Mobile, Alabama. And the post of attorney general wasn't Sessions's first choice; he'd asked for secretary of
defense or state, both rebuffed by Trump. Trump had never developed
much personal chemistry with Sessions and had to be prodded to give
him any cabinet-level job.

Comey didn't know what to make of the appointment. The only interaction he'd had with Sessions came after a speech in which Comey had
said it was hard for the FBI to hire cyber experts. "We may find people of
great technical talent who want to smoke weed on the way to the interview," Comey had said. At a subsequent Judiciary Committee hearing,
Sessions chastised Comey, saying smoking marijuana was no laughing
matter.

The following week, Trump made his first major foreign policy appointment, naming as his national security adviser Michael Flynn, the
former army general who had led "lock her up" chants during the campaign. Flynn is "one of the country's foremost experts on military and
intelligence matters and he will be an invaluable asset to me and my administration," Trump said, and the choice was warmly praised by Republicans. But Flynn's hard-line anti-Muslim views and an affinity for Russia
that mirrored the president's worried some. "Some of the policy positions
he's advocated, a kind of a newfound affinity for the Russians and Kremlin, concern me a great deal," said the California Democratic congressman Adam Schiff.

And Trump himself had ignored a warning from Obama that Flynn,
whom Obama had fired as head of the Defense Intelligence Agency, was
temperamentally unsuited for the job.

Press reports about Russian interference had only intensified since the
election. In an interview on Fox News, Trump dismissed them as another

attempt by Democrats to undermine his legitimacy. "I think it's ridiculous," he said. "I think it's just another excuse." As for the hacked DNC emails, no one knew "if it's Russia or China or somebody. It could be somebody sitting in a bed someplace."

The incoming White House chief of staff, Reince Priebus, said on Fox News, "This whole thing is a spin job," and asked why Democrats "are doing everything they can to delegitimize the outcome of the election."

In this, Priebus was only echoing Trump, who saw the entire issue of Russian interference through a single lens, which was not what it meant for American democracy but what it meant to him personally. Whether true or not, people would think Russia had tipped the scale for him, thereby rendering his historic victory illegitimate. As the press coverage continued, this theme became something of an obsession with Trump, who talked about it incessantly not only to Priebus but to almost anyone who would listen. To the White House communications director, Hope Hicks, he said Russia was going to be his "Achilles heel."

IN EARLY DECEMBER, Comey got a call from John McCain asking if they could meet in person. McCain, the venerable Republican senator from Arizona and former presidential nominee, was in open conflict with Trump, who'd denigrated McCain's status as a war hero on the campaign trail. "He's not a war hero," Trump had asserted. "He was a war hero because he was captured. I like people that weren't captured." McCain, in turn, withdrew his support for Trump's campaign after the *Access Hollywood* tape surfaced, saying Trump's "demeaning comments about women and his boasts about sexual assaults make it impossible to continue to offer even conditional support for his candidacy."

McCain had gotten a version of the Steele dossier in Halifax, Nova Scotia, in November. Partly because of his ongoing feud with Trump, he would have preferred to stay uninvolved and hand over the material as part of a congressional investigation. But his fellow Republicans had blocked that idea. So when McCain arrived at Comey's office on December 9, he handed over the folder. "You should have this," he said. Comey already had it, but didn't say so.

Later in December, yet another copy arrived via Bruce Ohr, who'd been given a memory stick by Glenn Simpson. Ohr didn't look at the contents of the flash drive, but assumed it contained the dossier. He didn't know, either, that the FBI already had multiple copies.

Comey felt tremendous pressure to resolve the issue of whether Trump or anyone in the Trump campaign had colluded with Russia before Trump was inaugurated, in part because Comey had already been accused of tipping the election. Despite their strenuous efforts, the FBI hadn't found much evidence of collusion, and nothing to connect Russia's election efforts to Trump himself. At this juncture, Comey felt it possible, even likely, that the FBI could close the Russia-Trump campaign investigation by the end of the year, and Trump could begin his presidency unencumbered by an ongoing investigation that might leak or otherwise become public at any time.

That all changed on December 29, when President Obama announced sanctions on Russia as "a necessary and appropriate response to efforts to harm U.S. interests."

The Steele dossier aside, the Obama administration had overwhelming evidence that Russia had tried to influence the election, but the president had been reluctant to publicize it before the election out of the same fears that the FBI had wrestled with: that he'd be accused of using classified government intelligence to favor Clinton. But now, with elections safely in the past, Obama felt comfortable taking action.

Trump shrugged off the need for any punitive measures. "I think we ought to get on with our lives," he told reporters at his Mar-a-Lago retreat, and later added, "It's time for our country to move on to bigger and better things."

Russia promised to retaliate in kind; expulsions of Russian diplomats were invariably met with a tit-for-tat expulsion of American diplomats from Russia.

So it struck Comey as exceedingly curious that the next day Putin said he wouldn't retaliate and would adopt a wait-and-see approach instead—a clear olive branch to the incoming Trump administration. "Great move on delay (by V. Putin)—I always knew he was very smart!" Trump tweeted. Suspicions within the FBI that Putin and Trump might be in league with each other immediately ratcheted up.

The next day, the White House asked the intelligence services for anything they had that might explain Putin's curious reaction. Comey had FBI agents review the secret intercept transcripts from the Russian embassy in Washington, D.C., from the week of the sanction announcement. (The Russian embassy was the subject of an ongoing FISA court order that authorized wiretaps on the embassy phones.)

Poring over the transcripts, agents discovered two startling phone calls between the Russian ambassador, Sergey Kislyak, and Michael Flynn, who knew each other and had met with Trump's son-in-law, Jared Kushner, at Trump Tower early in December. The first call, from Flynn to Kislyak, was on December 29, the day the sanctions were announced. Flynn asked Kislyak not to "escalate" the situation in response to the sanctions. Then, on New Year's Eve, Kislyak called Flynn to report that his request had been heard at "the highest levels" of the Russian government, obviously referring to Putin, and assured Flynn that it was his call that had precipitated the decision not to retaliate.

After Comey was briefed, he conveyed the information to the White House and top national security officials. Strzok and McCabe briefed their counterparts at the Department of Justice. The immediate mystery of Russia's benign reaction to the sanctions was solved: someone in the incoming Trump administration—Flynn—had intervened and helped bring about the result.

But it only deepened the question of ties between the Trump campaign and Russia. So far the Flynn investigation had yielded nothing of consequence, but here was a direct link between Flynn and the Russian government. The intercepted conversations might themselves be crimes; the Logan Act bars private citizens from negotiating with foreign governments, and Flynn was still a private citizen, albeit one who was advising an incoming president. The moribund Flynn investigation was suddenly alive again.

COMEY, OF COURSE, could say nothing about any of this when the time came for his annual New Year's letter to FBI personnel. But he did finally address lingering concerns about the Clinton investigation and its impact on him personally:

> *2016 was, to put it mildly, a challenging year, in which the FBI was the focus of a great deal of public attention for our work. As it always is, our work was subject to a fair amount of second-guessing. We try to stare hard at our own work, take feedback that is thoughtful, and always seek to be better.*

As for the Clinton email controversy,

> *I am uncomfortable spending time talking about me, but I am very grateful for the support so many of you have expressed in recent months. I would be lying if I said the external criticism doesn't bother me at all, but the truth is it doesn't bother me much because of the way we made decisions. At every turn last year, we were faced with choosing among bad options and making decisions we knew would bring a torrent of criticism. But at each turn, we asked ourselves only: Which option is most consistent with our values? Which option would honest, competent, and independent people choose? When you know you have made decisions thoughtfully and consistent with your values, it is freeing, in a way.*

Comey and other national security officials met with President Obama and Vice President Joe Biden on January 5, when they gathered in the Oval Office for an intelligence briefing on Russian interference. They'd already decided that they had little choice but to brief Trump about the contents of the dossier and that Comey was the man to do it. The FBI handled counterintelligence investigations, and Brennan and Clapper

were both Obama appointees who would soon be leaving. Comey agreed
he should handle it, though he wished it were otherwise.

There was little chance the dossier would remain a secret for long.
Senator McCain had a version, as did the Democratic senator Harry Reid,
and it was known to be circulating in Washington, D.C., intelligence and
media circles. CNN had already called the FBI press office to say it had
the dossier and was preparing to release it.

The point of such a "defensive" briefing was to prepare Trump for
potentially adverse publicity. But Comey's primary motive was somewhat more complex. He didn't really care whether Trump had consorted
with prostitutes. Even if it were true, Trump was a private citizen traveling
in Moscow, and what he did at the Ritz-Carlton was neither illegal nor any
of the FBI's business. But by briefing Trump, the FBI would achieve its
primary objective: the Russians couldn't blackmail the incoming
president—because Trump now knew that the FBI was already aware of it.

However compelling the logic, that didn't mean Comey was comfortable at the prospect of discussing salacious allegations about Trump with
the man himself, someone he'd never met. Given what he considered
Trump's worldview, in which all relationships were measured in terms of
who had the upper hand and could use it to extract the best deal, he
worried that Trump would see the disclosure simply as a matter of
leverage—that the FBI had something on him.

The legendary reputation of J. Edgar Hoover, the seemingly untouch-
able founding FBI director, had been tarnished by disclosures he kept secret files on presidents, information he deftly wielded to remain in power
for nearly five decades until he died of a heart attack. That was anathema
to Comey.

Comey thought he could defuse the idea that the FBI might use the
information against him by telling Trump that he personally wasn't under investigation. Jim Baker had argued against that, noting that while it
was technically true, it was "Jesuitical"; Trump's activities certainly fell
within the scope of the investigation, and he might well become the subject. Some at the FBI thought Trump already should be. But at this juncture, Comey was determined to work with Trump. He feared that if

Trump thought he was a target, he'd be at war with the FBI the moment he was inaugurated.

Toward the end of the meeting with Obama, Director of National Intelligence Clapper brought up the salacious material in the Steele dossier. Obama betrayed no reaction. "What's the plan for that briefing?" Obama asked, referring to the forthcoming session with Trump.

Clapper said Comey would be briefing Trump alone the next day, after the incoming president's regular national security briefing.

Obama said nothing but looked at Comey and raised both his eyebrows.

ON JANUARY 6, a motorcade of black SUVs carried Comey and other national security leaders from the airport to Trump Tower in Manhattan for Trump's final intelligence briefing before his inauguration, now just two weeks away. The focus would be Russian interference in the election, because President Obama was preparing to release a heavily edited version of the intelligence to the public before Trump's inauguration.

They entered from Fifty-sixth Street, shielded from the press corps waiting on Fifth Avenue. After they were seated in a conference room upstairs, Trump arrived with Vice President–elect Mike Pence, Sean Spicer, and the incoming national security team: Flynn; Mike Pompeo, his choice for CIA director; Tom Bossert, the homeland security adviser; and K. T. McFarland, the deputy national security adviser.

Clapper led the briefing, interrupted only once by Trump, who asked, "But you found there was no impact on the result, right?" Clapper explained that it wasn't their task to determine whether the Russian efforts had influenced the outcome. All he could say was there was no evidence any votes had been altered or compromised.

To Comey's surprise, Trump and his advisers asked no questions about what Russia was still doing and might do in future elections, or what the United States was doing to combat it. Instead, Priebus launched into a discussion about how they could "position" the intelligence with the media, stressing the finding that Russia had no impact on Trump's victory.

To Comey, this was spin, not fact. Trump and his advisers went on in this vein almost as though Comey and the others weren't there. Clapper had to interrupt to remind them, as he'd just said, that the intelligence agencies had not evaluated whether Russia had any influence on the outcome, only that it had tried.

As an experienced former prosecutor of organized crime, Comey couldn't help but think about how the Mafia drew its participants into its "family" by sharing confidences and strategy and getting everyone to agree. Trump and his team seemed instinctively to be doing much the same thing. It made Comey deeply uncomfortable, but he said nothing.

Trump finally wound up the discussion, and Priebus asked if there was anything else they needed to know.

The moment was at hand. Clapper said, "Well, yes," adding that he and the others would leave, and Comey would stay behind to discuss it with a smaller group.

"How small?" Trump asked.

"I was thinking the two of us," Comey said.

Priebus suggested that he and Pence remain as well, but Trump said, "Just the two of us."

Everyone else filed out.

"You've had one heck of a year," Trump said when they were alone. He praised Comey's handling of the email investigation, noting that Comey had repeatedly been put in an "impossible" situation. "You saved her and then they hated you for what you did later, but what choice did you have?" Trump said. Trump praised Comey's reputation and said he hoped he'd be staying on as FBI director.

"I intend to, sir," Comey said. It seemed an odd comment from Trump, given that Comey still had more than six years remaining in his ten-year term.

"Good," Trump replied.

Trying to maintain a matter-of-fact tone, Comey followed the script he'd worked out with McCabe, Baker, and the others at FBI headquarters. He said he needed to discuss some sensitive information that was circulating within the intelligence community because he didn't want Trump to be "caught cold" by some of the details. Then Comey turned to the most sensitive allegation: that the Russians had videotapes of Trump consorting with prostitutes in the Presidential Suite at the Ritz-Carlton in 2013. He spared Trump the lurid detail that the women had urinated on the same bed where the Obamas had slept.

"There were no prostitutes, there were never prostitutes!" Trump angrily interjected.

He didn't need to "go there," Trump said. Comey took that to mean that Trump didn't need to pay for sex. Almost to himself, Trump repeated the year "2013" and seemed to be searching his memory. He said that he always assumed that hotel rooms where he stayed were bugged, and Comey said that when he traveled abroad, he did, too.

Comey assured Trump that it wasn't that the FBI believed the allegations but that Trump needed to know the dossier existed and was being widely circulated. CNN had it and was looking for a "news hook." Comey said it was important the FBI not give it one by revealing it had the dossier or was looking into its substance, and he assured Trump the bureau was keeping it within a tightly controlled circle to prevent leaks.

Trump said he couldn't believe CNN had the dossier and hadn't run with it.

Comey explained that the information was "inflammatory" and the media would get "killed" if it ran with it without substantiating the allegations.

That an FBI director would be briefing a future president of the United States in private about such compromising personal information was so unprecedented, so bizarre, that Comey felt as if he were watching himself in a play or movie. It was something akin to an "out-of-body experience."

Trump suddenly started discussing women who'd falsely accused him of groping or grabbing them, again implying that his inherent sex appeal made any such moves unnecessary. Although he mentioned several of his accusers, Trump focused on a stripper who'd accused him of grabbing her (presumably a reference to Stephanie Clifford, the actress and stripper known as Stormy Daniels).

As Trump grew more agitated, Comey sensed the conversation was teetering on disaster. Now was the time to defuse the situation.

"We are not investigating you, sir," Comey said.

He said again that the information might be "totally made up" but that to protect Trump from any effort to coerce him, the FBI needed to understand what the Russians were doing and might do. And he wanted Trump to be aware that the allegations might surface at any time in the media.

The assurance seemed to calm Trump. He said he was grateful for the information and again praised Comey and said he looked forward to working with him. The two shook hands. Comey's private conversation with Trump had lasted only five minutes but felt much longer.

Comey left the conference room, passing Jared Kushner in the corridor as he left.

MCCABE, PAGE, BAKER, and Strzok were to varying degrees appalled by Trump's reaction when Comey briefed them on the meeting, as much by what Trump didn't say as by what he did. Trump could have denied the allegations; expressed outrage at the Russian attempt to interfere; urged Comey to get to the bottom of it as soon as possible; and pledged his full cooperation and that of his incoming administration. That was how they hoped an incoming president, faced with a blatant act of hostility from a foreign power, would have responded. Instead, Trump had denied there were prostitutes. That was hardly reassuring.

Still, they thought Comey had handled an exceptionally awkward encounter well. He'd stressed that the FBI was trying to protect the president. Trump had thanked him for sharing the information.

Their reactions showed how little they knew or understood Trump.

WITHIN FOUR DAYS of the Trump Tower meeting, word of the briefing had leaked. CNN didn't publish the Steele dossier, but it came close. On January 10, the network reported, "Classified documents presented last week to President Obama and President-elect Trump included allegations that Russian operatives claim to have compromising personal and financial information about Mr. Trump, multiple US officials with direct knowledge of the briefings tell CNN."

Trump immediately tweeted: "FAKE NEWS—A TOTAL POLITICAL WITCH HUNT"—his first use of the phrase "witch hunt" to describe the Russia probe.*

Just one hour later, *BuzzFeed News* published thirty-five pages of the dossier.

BuzzFeed News went to some lengths to justify what it knew would be a controversial decision to publish. In its introduction to the materials, it noted the dossier "has been circulating among elected officials, intelligence agents, and journalists for weeks" and had "acquired a kind of legendary status among journalists, lawmakers, and intelligence officials who have seen" it. *BuzzFeed News* also cautioned readers that much of the dossier's contents couldn't be verified, that it contained demonstrable errors, and that it had been compiled by a political opponent of Trump's.

Conway, on national television, maintained Trump was "not aware" of any such intelligence briefing (which was patently false). Michael Cohen, Trump's lawyer named in the dossier, called it "ridiculous" and a "fake story" (even though Cohen had told Trump about the possibility of embarrassing tapes).

Despite the disclaimers, the story was a bombshell. Even though CNN, the *Times*, the *Post*, *The New Yorker*, and other media outlets knew about the dossier and its contents and had declined to publish them, all now weighed in on the impact and significance of the revelations, driving massive traffic to *BuzzFeed*'s website. As the *Times* wrote the next day, the consequences of the story "have been incalculable and will play out long past Inauguration Day." Multiple congressional committees launched investigations.

Trump was beside himself, tweeting obsessively that the dossier was fake. He called Steele, its author, "sick." He also made direct calls to the

---

* Trump had occasionally used the phrase "witch hunt" before, notably to describe the investigation of Trump University in 2013 and charges of sexual harassment against his friend the former Republican presidential candidate Herman Cain in 2011. The phrase had been widely used to describe Senator Joseph McCarthy's pursuit of suspected communists, which might have resonated with Trump, given his close relationship with McCarthy's chief counsel, Roy Cohn.

intelligence officials who had just briefed him. Clapper emailed Comey, saying Trump had called him on January 11 to ask "if I could put out a statement. He would prefer of course that I say the documents are bogus, which, of course, I can't do."

Trump called Comey about 5:00 p.m. the same day. He seemed most concerned about how the dossier had "leaked." Comey explained that it wasn't really a leak, given that the dossier had been compiled by private parties who shared it widely and thus wasn't a government document. (On the other hand, someone had leaked the fact of the intelligence briefing, which gave CNN its "news hook" for reporting about the dossier.)

Trump told Comey he'd been thinking more about his 2013 trip to Moscow for the Miss Universe pageant and recalled that he hadn't even spent the night there. He'd gone to the Ritz-Carlton only to change his clothes and had flown back to New York the same night. Then he launched into the graphic incident Comey hadn't mentioned, but by now was dominating the news cycle: urinating on the bed, what Trump referred to as "golden showers."

"I'm a germophobe," Trump protested. "There's no way I would let people pee on each other around me. No way."

Comey laughed nervously. He found that unpersuasive: even a germophobe could have witnessed the incident from a safe distance. Nor did being there require an overnight stay. And Trump confirmed that he had been at the Ritz-Carlton. But Comey didn't say anything.

As Trump ended the call, Comey gazed out his large office windows at the lit monuments of the capital. Much as during the conversation at Trump Tower, he had trouble believing he had just had such a conversation with a man who, in a little more than a week, would be president of the United States.

"SOMETHING IS ROTTEN in the state of Denmark," began the column by the influential *Washington Post* columnist David Ignatius the next day, referring to "this past week of salacious leaks about foreign espionage plots and indignant denials."

What upset Comey and others in the intelligence community wasn't so much pointed references to the Steele dossier as what did appear to be a new leak:

> According to a senior U.S. government official, Flynn phoned Russian Ambassador Sergey Kislyak several times on Dec. 29, the day the Obama administration announced the expulsion of 35 Russian officials as well as other measures in retaliation for the hacking. What did Flynn say, and did it undercut the U.S. sanctions? The Logan Act bars U.S. citizens from correspondence intending to influence a foreign government about "disputes" with the United States. Was its spirit violated?

Comey was so concerned that he launched an investigation to determine the source of the leak.

Comey wasn't the only person alarmed by the disclosure. An angry Trump called Priebus: "What the hell is this all about?"

Priebus called Flynn, saying he'd spoken to the "boss" and Flynn needed to "kill the story."

Flynn had his deputy, K. T. McFarland, call the *Post* to deny the account (even though she was well aware that the column was accurate), and the *Post* updated the story to say that two Trump "team members" had called to deny the account, insisting that sanctions weren't discussed.

The next day, Trump's spokesman Sean Spicer told reporters Flynn had "reached out" to Kislyak only to convey holiday greetings and also denied that sanctions had been discussed. On Sunday, Pence appeared on *Face the Nation* and Priebus on *Meet the Press* to deny the *Post*'s reporting. Pence said he'd spoken to Flynn, and "those conversations that happened to occur around the time that the United States took action to expel diplomats had nothing whatsoever to do with those sanctions."

Comey, of course, knew none of this was true. And he wasn't the only one. Kislyak and the Russians knew that sanctions had been discussed. As the falsehoods mounted, concerns grew within the Obama administration, especially at the Justice Department. There, Sally Yates, the deputy attorney general, Axelrod, and Toscas were all convinced that Flynn was misleading other members of the incoming administration, lying to them about the substance of the December 29 conversation, which they in turn repeated to a national audience. Because the Russians knew Flynn was lying, they had leverage they could use with him. Yates felt the White House needed to be warned.

Yates called Comey to express the department's concern, but Comey was more concerned about the ongoing investigation than any immediate risk that the Russians might blackmail Flynn. He agreed that Flynn appeared to be lying, but why? What was it about his relationship with Kislyak he needed to conceal from others in the incoming administration? The fact of the lie added more fuel to the Flynn investigation. He persuaded Yates to hold off at least until the inauguration.

THAT SAME MONTH, Bill Priestap, the head of counterintelligence overseeing Crossfire Hurricane, approached McCabe about another sensitive matter. Priestap said an analyst—Jonathan Moffa—had brought to his attention that Page and Strzok were spending a lot of time together, and he worried Page was "monopolizing" Strzok's time. The analyst suspected the two were having an affair. Partly out of those concerns, Priestap had reduced Strzok's responsibilities, leaving him in charge only of domestic U.S. witnesses. He'd assigned another agent, Jennifer Boone, to oversee foreign ones.

Priestap also took his concerns directly to Strzok. He didn't ask him point-blank if he and Page were having an affair. As Priestap later said, "We all have our personal lives," and "I'm not the morality police." Still, he wanted Strzok to be aware that people were talking and that the impression they were having an affair was "out there."

While "there's no FBI policy that says you can't have an affair, and if you do, you're going to be punished," Priestap worried that in the extraordinarily sensitive circumstances of the Russia investigation, an affair, or even a perception of one, could make Strzok "vulnerable" to a foreign intelligence service. "This better not interfere with things, if you know what I mean," Priestap warned Strzok. "To me, the mission is everything," Priestap later explained.*

McCabe told Page that Priestap had brought up the issue. "I know you and Pete are friends, but you have to be more careful," he said. "People are talking, and this isn't good for you."

Page was acutely embarrassed, mortified that the issue had even come up, especially because the affair was now over. They were still friends, and still texting, at least until June, when Page finally cut off the exchange. She denied the two were romantically involved or had had an affair.

Priestap hadn't discussed the issue with Page; she reported to McCabe, not him. But Page sought him out and said she thought splitting responsibilities between Strzok and Boone was a mistake. She told him she hoped it wasn't because of the rumors of an affair, which weren't true.

Priestap felt uncomfortable discussing anything so personal with Page. But he was firm about the division of responsibilities and kept the witnesses divided between Strzok and Boone. At least Page thought the rumors had been laid to rest. And she and Strzok were more careful—or so they thought.

INAUGURATION DAY, January 20, was a bleak, rainy day in the nation's capital, and the tone of Trump's address matched the leaden skies. Wearing a wide bright red tie, the new president looked grim as he lambasted the ruling elite and made none of the usual pleas for national unity. The speech lasted just sixteen minutes.

Wearing the campaign's signature MAGA caps, Trump supporters thronged the National Mall, though just how many became the first controversy of the new administration. Independent estimates ranged from 300,000 to 600,000 people, far fewer than Obama had attracted four years earlier. Trump claimed the media deliberately minimized the crowd

---

* Strzok later denied that the affair posed any security risk. He testified that had any foreign agent ever approached him about it, he would have promptly reported the approach and the affair to his superiors.

size. From his vantage point, the crowd "looked like a million-and-a-half people," he said, and "went all the way back to the Washington Monument."

ON SUNDAY AFTERNOON, January 22, President Trump hosted a reception at the White House Blue Room for law enforcement officers who worked on the inauguration, and at the insistence of his staff Comey went, albeit reluctantly. He didn't want to give any impression that he and Trump were personally close, which meant avoiding one-on-one encounters or photos of him with the president. He positioned himself at the far end of the room from the entrance, near a window overlooking the South Lawn. He hoped his blue suit would blend in with the draperies.

Trump and his entourage entered with a blaze of lights, surrounded by TV cameras and photographers. The event was clearly being mounted as a publicity gambit.

"We're going to have a great eight years together, as we say," Trump began. "And again, the inauguration was such a success, and such a safety success. And we want to thank you all because it was really a very very special experience."

He singled out John Kelly, just sworn in as director of homeland security, "and your very beautiful wife." He asked Joe Clancy, director of the Secret Service, to step forward. "Stay up here with us," he said. "So let's, uh . . ." His eyes lit on Comey. "Oh and there's James. He's become more famous than me! Let's take some pictures and say hello to each other, okay? Where's a good spot? Right here?"

The cameras rolled as Comey walked the length of the blue carpet, thinking, "This is a complete disaster," and contemplating ways to avoid hugging the president or making any other gesture that might suggest fealty.

Once he was within range, Trump gripped Comey's hand and leaned in close to his ear. "I'm really looking forward to working with you," he said in a stage whisper.

When Comey described the encounter to his friend Benjamin Wittes, he said he was "disgusted." The way Trump had leaned in made it look like a kiss. Comey "regarded the episode as a physical attempt to show closeness and warmth in a fashion calculated to compromise him, especially before Democrats who already mistrusted him," Wittes recalled.

In the Mafia, a kiss signifies something more ominous: the imminent murder of the recipient.

THE NEXT DAY, in Sean Spicer's first press briefing as White House press secretary, he again claimed that Flynn hadn't discussed sanctions with the Russian ambassador. Now that Trump was president and Flynn his national security adviser, the threat that Russia might exert leverage over Flynn was no longer an abstraction. Comey and McCabe decided that it was time to act.

The next day, January 24, at 12:30 p.m., McCabe called Flynn at the White House on a secure phone line to say he had a "sensitive matter" to discuss. He said the media coverage of Flynn's contacts with Russian representatives had spawned some questions.

"You know what I said, because you guys were probably listening," Flynn said.

McCabe let that pass without comment, but as a national security expert Flynn probably did know that the Russian embassy was likely to be tapped.

Flynn professed amazement that so much confidential information had found its way into the media and asked McCabe if he thought it had been leaked. McCabe said the FBI was indeed concerned about recent "significant" leaks. But in the meantime, he was hoping Flynn would sit down with two FBI agents as "quickly, quietly and discreetly as possible." Flynn readily agreed, saying he was available that day. They settled on 2:30 p.m., less than two hours later, at Flynn's new White House office.

McCabe also said he felt the "quickest way" to get the interview done was to have Flynn meet alone with the agents. It was okay if he wanted someone from the White House counsel's office to be there, but then McCabe would have to get the Justice Department involved.

"It's fine, just send your guys down here," Flynn responded.

McCabe tapped Strzok and a more junior agent, Joe Pientka, for the mission, and they mapped out their strategy: to maintain a relaxed, congenial atmosphere, they wouldn't explicitly warn Flynn that any false statement to an FBI agent is a crime. (Flynn surely knew that.) If Flynn did deny something they knew had been said, they wouldn't argue or contradict him, but would ask the question using the exact words from the phone transcript in an effort to jog his memory.

The two agents arrived early, and Flynn gave them a brief tour of the West Wing. Strzok had never been in the White House by daylight and was struck by all the activity. Movers were carting boxes and moving art into the Oval Office, where Trump himself was supervising its placement. Flynn didn't introduce them, but praised the president's "knack" for interior design.

Once they settled into Flynn's office, Flynn seemed "relaxed and jocular," as Strzok later described him. He seemed "unguarded" and "clearly saw the FBI agents as allies," like fellow members of the administration who were going to help clear up the annoying press accounts. He seemed oblivious that they might be investigating him, despite McCabe's call.

In this atmosphere, Flynn seemed in no hurry, ranging from a discussion of hotels where he'd stayed, to his long work hours, to Islamic terrorism, which seemed to be a singular preoccupation. Strzok's occasional reminder "I'm sure you're busy and have other things to do" had no apparent effect, and Strzok was surprised that Flynn seemed to have so much time on his hands. Flynn struck Strzok as out of his depth and unsophisticated, such a contrast to the worldly, poised people surrounding Clinton and the White House officials he'd met during the Obama administration.

When the discussion finally turned to Russia, Flynn described his friendly relationship with Ambassador Kislyak and volunteered that his phone calls were to commiserate over the recent assassination of the Russian ambassador to Turkey ("and that was all") and the crash of a Russian military plane. Strzok knew, of course, that both statements were false.

Strzok got more specific: Had Flynn discussed the expulsion of the

Russian diplomats? Flynn said he hadn't, and reiterated what he'd said before about condolences. Did Flynn ask Kislyak not to "escalate" the situation or engage in a "tit for tat"—the exact words from the intercepted call. "Not really; I don't recall; it wasn't, 'don't do anything,'" Flynn replied.

Both Strzok and Pientka knew what was in the intercept, and it wasn't what Flynn said. But after they left, Pientka said, "For the life of me, it sure didn't look like he was lying."

Strzok agreed that Flynn's demeanor had betrayed none of the usual signs of deception. Flynn had hedged only one of his answers ("I don't recall"). He hadn't fidgeted, hesitated, or avoided eye contact. If he was consciously lying, he'd done a remarkable job.

Back at FBI headquarters, Strzok and Pientka briefed Comey and Mc-Cabe, calling attention to Flynn's confident demeanor. It was all the more baffling to McCabe, who pointed out that Flynn had indicated that he knew the conversation had been intercepted. But it didn't change the fact that, as McCabe put it, Flynn's statement "was in absolute, direct conflict" with the truth.

Comey had alerted Yates to the interview just before the agents went to the White House and briefed her on the outcome. She was "not happy" that once again the FBI had gone off on its own in a highly sensitive manner. But now Flynn was not only vulnerable to Russian influence; he had just committed multiple crimes by repeatedly lying to FBI agents. His position in the upper ranks of the Trump administration was clearly untenable. Before the investigation proceeded any further, the White House needed to be told.

Yates and a colleague met with the White House counsel, Don Mc-Gahn, at the White House two days later. The mild-mannered, anodyne McGahn, a longtime Republican operative who'd been the Trump campaign's general counsel, was a welcome contrast to some of the outsize personalities now in the White House. His specialty was the minutiae of campaign finance law—he'd served for five years as a George W. Bush appointee on the Federal Election Commission—but he knew less about foreign policy or criminal law.

At the meeting, Yates summarized the Flynn situation and expressed her concern that he might be compromised because the Russians would know Flynn had lied to, among others, the vice president. She said Flynn had been interviewed by the FBI two days before—surprisingly, something McGahn seemed to know nothing about. While Yates wouldn't say that Flynn lied to the FBI, too, she implied as much by saying he'd told the FBI the same things he had apparently told Pence and Priebus.

Yates got the impression McGahn realized it was serious, asking if the administration needed to fire Flynn. That seemed obvious, but Yates didn't feel it was her place to make that call.

For his part, McGahn got the impression the FBI hadn't really "pinned Flynn down" in a lie.

McGahn told Trump about Yates's visit that evening and had to explain Title 18, Section 1001 of the U.S. Code, which makes false statements to a government official a crime, as well as the Logan Act. Trump didn't want to fire Flynn; he thought doing so just weeks into his term would be terrible publicity. Still, Trump seemed angry and annoyed with Flynn. "Not again, this guy, this stuff," he said.

But the person he was really annoyed with might well have been Comey, whose seeming obsession with Russia had led to the salacious dossier and had now ensnared one of Trump's top advisers. When he dined later that evening with Dan Coats, his director of national intelligence, and other advisers, Trump was clearly preoccupied and troubled by Comey. He asked everyone at the dinner what they thought of the FBI director. While no one went so far as to suggest Trump fire him, their views were generally unfavorable: he was self-righteous, a grandstander. But Coats maintained Comey was a good director and suggested Trump spend more time with him before making any decision about his future.

Trump didn't waste any time. The next day, Comey was lunching at his desk when Trump himself called and asked, "Can you come over for dinner tonight?"

Comey said he could, not mentioning that he and his wife had dinner plans.

"Will 6:00 work?" Trump asked. "I was going to invite your whole family but we'll do it next time. Is that a good time?"

"Sir, whatever works for you."

"How about 6:30?"

Comey agreed, but the request made him "deeply uncomfortable," as he put it, given his mounting concern about Trump's respect for the independence of the bureau. But surely others would be there as well, serving as a buffer. Comey felt he had little choice but to accept a personal invitation from the new president. He canceled the date with his wife.

Trump was determined that it would be dinner for just the two of them. Priebus and Bannon had both tried to insinuate themselves, without success. Trump seemed oblivious that it might be inappropriate, or that he might want a witness to the conversation. "Don't talk about Russia, whatever you do," Priebus warned.

As Trump entered the Green Room that evening, he complimented Comey on being early. "I like people who are on time," he said. "I think a leader should always be on time." To Comey's dismay, he saw the table was set for just two. His name was written in calligraphy on a place card.

As plates of shrimp scampi were served, Trump asked, "So what do you want to do?"

Comey wasn't sure what he meant.

As Trump continued, it became clear he was asking if Comey wanted to continue as FBI director, although Comey had already assured him that he did. At various points, Trump said he'd heard good things about Comey and knew that people at the FBI thought highly of him; that he'd nonetheless understand if Comey wanted to "walk away" from the job given all he'd been through; and that Trump could make a change in FBI leadership if he wished but wanted to hear what Comey had to say.

It was obvious that Trump had invited him to dinner "and decided my job security was on the menu."

Comey had the distinct impression Trump wanted something in return for keeping him as FBI director—that Trump saw the director's position as a form of patronage.

Comey said he loved his job, thought he performed it well, and wanted to serve out his term.

That didn't seem to be enough. So Comey told Trump he could count on him to be "reliable." By that he meant he'd always tell him the truth, wouldn't leak, and wouldn't do any "sneaky things" or "weasel moves." But Comey said he wasn't political by nature; he wasn't on "anybody's side." That neutrality was in the president's—and the nation's—best interest, because it gave the FBI credibility. The public could trust it to resolve even the most politically charged investigations based on the facts and law, not ideology or power. It was the essence of the rule of law rather than survival of the strongest.

That seemed to make no impression on Trump.

Looking grave, Trump said, "I need loyalty. I expect loyalty."

Comey said nothing, his gaze locked with the president's. The silence continued.

An inner voice spoke to Comey: "Don't do anything. Don't you dare move."

Trump finally broke the deadlock, looking down at his plate and launching into a rambling monologue. He boasted about the size of the crowds at his inauguration; the massive amount of free media he'd generated; how vicious the campaign was. He praised his interior design talent, gesturing about the room and comparing the White House favorably to Mar-a-Lago. "This is luxury," he said. "And I know luxury." He again denied that he'd grabbed a porn star or groped a woman on an airplane.

And he offered a succinct analysis of the Clinton email investigation: "Comey 1," in which Comey had "saved her"; "Comey 2," in which he'd done what he had to do by notifying Congress; and "Comey 3," when he'd "saved Hillary again" but she "totally misplayed" that.

Two different times Trump brought up McCabe, asking if "your guy" has "a problem with me," because "I was pretty rough on him and his wife during the campaign."

Comey explained that, on the contrary, McCabe was "a true professional" and that "FBI people, whatever their personal views, they strip them away when they step into their bureau roles."

All in all, Trump seemed to be enjoying himself. But Comey noticed he never laughed, which made an impression.

Eventually, Trump again turned to the incident involving the Moscow prostitutes—the "golden showers thing," in Trump's words—and said he was thinking of asking the FBI to investigate the allegation and prove it was a lie. It upset him, he said, that his wife, Melania, might think there was "even a one percent chance" it was true.

Comey said it was up to the president, but that proving a falsehood was often difficult, and it would also suggest Trump himself was being investigated.

"Maybe you're right," Trump said, but asked Comey to think about it.

Trump said he was happy Comey wanted to stay on as director and repeated what good things he'd heard about him. Comey began to think he might escape relatively unscathed.

But Trump was nothing if not tenacious. "I need loyalty," he said again.

This time Comey couldn't just ignore him. "You will always get honesty from me," he said.

There was a pause. That wasn't what he'd asked for.

"That's what I want, honest loyalty," Trump finally said.

It was some kind of compromise. "You will get that from me," Comey promised.

As waiters arrived with vanilla ice cream, Trump broached the topic of Flynn, expressing irritation that he hadn't told him about a call from Britain's prime minister, Theresa May, for six days. Trump pointed to his head. "The guy has serious judgment issues."

But Trump said nothing about Flynn's recent interview with FBI agents. Perhaps no one had told him. Comey scrupulously avoided the subject, saying nothing about the FBI's ongoing probe.

The dinner had lasted about eighty minutes. As they rose from the table, Trump suggested Comey and his family come back for dinner sometime.

Comey froze.

"Or a tour," Trump said awkwardly. "Whatever you think."

EIGHT

"WHERE'S MY ROY COHN?"

Comey called McCabe from his SUV on the way home from the White House. McCabe was as shocked as Comey, especially about the request for "loyalty." It was blatantly inappropriate in any circumstances, but especially so when the director of an independent law enforcement agency was, at that very moment, investigating matters of grave national importance that touched on the president himself and many of his close associates.

As soon as he got home, Comey started typing a memo summarizing the conversation. He initialed and dated the four-page, single-spaced document when he finished typing it the next day. He'd never done such a thing after meeting with Obama or Bush, but he never felt the need to. Comey simply didn't trust Trump to tell the truth. And he had the sense he might need such a record someday, to protect both himself and the FBI as an institution. He made two copies. He kept one at home and took the other to the office, where he distributed it to his senior leadership team. He made it a practice to document every conversation he had alone with Trump.

THE SAME DAY as Comey's dinner with Trump, McGahn asked Sally Yates to return to the White House to continue the Flynn discussion. He said his staff had been examining the situation, concluding that Flynn had not violated the Logan Act, which had never been prosecuted in any event. But the administration didn't want to do anything that might interfere with any ongoing investigation of Flynn, such as firing him. As McGahn put it in a subsequent memo, "Yates was unwilling to confirm or deny that there was an ongoing investigation but did indicate that the Department of Justice would not object to the White House taking action against Flynn."

For her part, she couldn't understand what was taking so long. She agreed to provide the White House by the following Monday morning with the evidence that Flynn had lied. Afterward, she headed to the airport for a flight to Atlanta. She was still in the car when Axelrod called to tell her that Trump had just issued an executive order banning travelers from seven predominantly Muslim countries from entering the United States. Yates could hardly believe it; she had just been with McGahn, and he hadn't given her any warning.

Yates spent a hectic weekend overseeing legal research and staff meetings about the travel ban. She concluded the order was unconstitutional, motivated by discrimination against Muslims, a fundamental violation of the First Amendment guarantee of freedom of religion. After flying back to Washington, on Monday afternoon Yates issued a statement to all Justice Department personnel:

> For as long as I am the Acting Attorney General, the Department of Justice will not present arguments in defense of the Executive Order, unless and until I become convinced that it is appropriate to do so.

About five hours later, at a little past 9:00 p.m., Yates received a hand-delivered letter from the White House. It contained just one sentence:

> *I am informing you that the President has removed you from the office of Deputy Attorney General of the United States.*

THE NEXT DAY, Trump nominated Rod Rosenstein, the U.S. attorney in Baltimore, to replace her. Appointed to the post by President Bush in

2005, he was the country's longest-serving U.S. attorney and survived the controversial 2006 purge of U.S. attorneys implemented by Bush's attorney general, Gonzales. Rosenstein had an illustrious résumé: Wharton and Harvard Law School, where he was editor of the *Law Review*. Given his long tenure in Baltimore, he was well known within the FBI and generally regarded as a nonpartisan, competent prosecutor. His wire-rim glasses and slight build gave him something of a professorial appearance.

Comey had known Rosenstein for over fifteen years, and as deputy attorney general Comey had helped choose Rosenstein in 2005 to be the U.S. attorney in Baltimore. For his part, Rosenstein considered Comey "a role model," Rosenstein has said. "His speeches about leadership and public service inspired me." On October 27—the day before Comey sent his letter to Congress—Rosenstein had invited Comey to speak to lawyers in his office about ethics and leadership, and Comey also talked about his decision to announce the results of the Clinton investigation at a press conference without giving the Justice Department advance notice. Rosenstein didn't express any misgivings about Comey's approach. On the contrary, he praised Comey's leadership and thanked him for setting an inspiring example.

Later, at a lunch with his friend Benjamin Wittes, Comey described Rosenstein as a "solid," if not brilliant, "career guy," which, coming from Comey, was faint praise. "Rod is a survivor," Comey explained, and survivors have to make compromises. "So I have concerns," he said—especially given the kinds of compromises Rosenstein might be asked to make in a Trump administration.

ON SUNDAY, FEBRUARY 5, the conservative Fox News host and bestselling author Bill O'Reilly interviewed the president as part of the network's pregame Super Bowl show, a slot all but guaranteed to be a ratings blockbuster. It was a largely friendly interview, as Trump had expected when he agreed to do it. But then O'Reilly, a fervent anticommunist, turned to the subject of Russia.

"Do you respect Putin?" O'Reilly asked.

"I do respect Putin," Trump answered.

"Why?"

"Well, I respect a lot of people," Trump said. "But that doesn't mean I'm going to get along with them. He's a leader of his country. I say it is better to get along with Russia than not, and if they help us in the fight against ISIS, which is a major fight, and Islamic terrorism all over the world, major fight, that's a good thing. Will I get along with him? I have no idea."

"He's a killer though. Putin is a killer," O'Reilly asserted.

"There's a lot of killers," Trump said. "What, you think our country is so innocent?"

Comey didn't watch the program, but he saw the coverage and much of the outrage it inspired. It struck him as consistent with Trump's puzzling indifference to Russian interference in the election. Trump seemed to be "doubling down" on his reluctance to criticize the Russian government.

Three days later, on February 8, Priebus invited Comey to the White House for a "meet and greet," as Priebus put it, a "chance to get acquainted." As Comey was waiting outside the West Wing, Flynn, of all people, passed by, looking lean and still tan from his Christmas trip to the Dominican Republic. He offered Comey a few tips on staying fit.

Once alone, Priebus and Comey ranged over a variety of topics, starting with the travel ban. Because it wasn't an FBI focus, Comey didn't purport to be an expert, but he took issue with Yates, agreeing with Priebus that presidents have wide latitude when dealing with border security and the ban didn't, on its face, discriminate against Muslims.

Priebus turned to the Steele dossier and wanted to know how something so salacious had ended up in Comey's briefing to the president. Comey said portions of the intelligence had been corroborated by other sources; he "thought it very important that it be included" and "the incoming president needed to know the rest was out there." Comey added that at their recent dinner the president had expressed interest in having him investigate the "golden showers thing" but that Comey didn't want to create a narrative that they were investigating him.

Like Trump, Priebus was troubled by so many leaks. Comey explained that all presidents were "plagued" by them, and Priebus wanted to know if the FBI had ever caught a leaker. The bureau had, but "it was a rare thing because it almost always turned on our willingness to go after reporter records."

Then Priebus asked, "Is this a private conversation?"

Comey said it was.

"I want to ask you a question and you can decide if it's appropriate to answer," Priebus said. "Do you have a FISA order on Mike Flynn?"

Comey was silent as he pondered the question. The question was, of course, inappropriate. On the other hand, it was an opportunity to drive home the point he had repeatedly tried to make, which was that the White House and the FBI needed to keep a distance.

So he told Priebus that he would answer: there was no FISA order on Flynn. In the future, however, all such requests should go through the Justice Department. The FBI director would typically inform the attorney general and deputy, who, if appropriate, would notify the president. Direct communication with the FBI risked looking like improper interference with an investigation.

Priebus said he understood that and it was helpful.

"I understand your dinner with the President went well," he said, shifting topics again, adding that Trump wanted Comey to stay on as director. Comey explained that while the president could fire him at any time, he had a ten-year term, so there was no need to announce that the president had decided to keep him.

Priebus also expressed sympathy that people were holding Comey responsible for Trump's victory over Clinton. Her team had totally "misplayed" his final decision and "should have pushed it harder as good news." In any event, he added, "it wasn't the Russians' fault that she failed to campaign in Michigan," and it wasn't Comey's fault "that she set up her email the way she did."

"And it wasn't my fault that Huma Abedin forwarded emails to Anthony Weiner," Comey added.

Why wasn't it "gross negligence"? Priebus wanted to know. So Comey reviewed, yet again, the basis for the decision and the lack of proof on the question of intent.

After about twenty minutes, Priebus asked if Comey wanted to drop in on the president. Comey wondered if Priebus had absorbed anything he'd just said.

"No, no thanks," Comey said. Surely the president was too busy.

"Sit," Priebus insisted. "I'm sure he'd love to see you. Let me see if he's in the Oval."

To Comey's dismay, Trump was. Priebus brought Comey in; Spicer was just leaving, and they shook hands. Trump remained seated behind his large desk.

Trump, too, touched on the email investigation, musing that if Comey had charged Clinton, Trump might have run against Bernie Sanders. He wondered what that would have been like. And he again asked if Comey's deputy (he didn't seem to remember McCabe's name) had a "problem" with him, given how tough he'd been on him during the campaign. "The number two guy at the FBI took a million dollars from the Clintons," Trump asserted. Comey let that pass (which was false on three counts: it was his wife, not McCabe, who got the money; it wasn't a million dollars; and it didn't come from the Clintons). But Comey came to McCabe's defense, saying he was a "pro."

Had McCabe ever brought up Trump's attacks? Trump asked.

"Never," Comey said. He repeated that "Andy McCabe is a true pro" and "you'll come to value him." He said if McCabe had it to do over, he'd probably urge his wife not to run, but nonetheless the "guy put everything aside and did his job well."

Priebus brought up the dossier, and Trump repeated that it "really bothered him" if Melania had any doubts about it. He seemed eager to expand on his earlier denial: he hadn't stayed overnight in Russia and the "hookers thing is nonsense," although Putin had told him "we have some of the most beautiful hookers in the world."

Priebus kept trying to say something, but Trump ignored him.

The mention of Putin seemed to remind Trump of his recent interview with O'Reilly, whose question about Putin had been a "hard one," Trump said.

"What am I going to do?" he asked. "Say I don't respect the leader of a major country I'm trying to get along with?"

Priebus and Comey said nothing.

"I gave a good answer," Trump said. "Really, it was a great answer. I gave a really great answer." He looked at Comey.

"You think it was a great answer, right?"

There it was again, Comey thought—the loyalty test. Trump didn't seem to need an answer; silence would be acquiescence enough.

Comey wasn't going to give it to him.

"The first part of your answer was fine, Mr. President," he said. "But not the second part. We aren't the kind of killers that Putin is."

Comey saw Trump's jaw clench and a shadow pass over his face. Trump thanked Comey for stopping in, and Priebus wordlessly showed him out of the Oval Office.

ON FEBRUARY 8, Sessions was confirmed by his fellow senators as attorney general after a hard-fought process that focused on Sessions's civil rights record and his willingness to stand up to Trump. (Sessions said repeatedly that he wouldn't be a "rubber stamp.") He'd also faced some grilling about any ties to Russia. "I'm not aware of any of those activities," he said. "I have been called a surrogate at a time or two in that campaign and I did not have communications with the Russians." And in response to a written question—"Have you been in contact with anyone connected to any part of the Russian government about the 2016 election, either before or after election day?"—he answered no.

Sessions was immediately thrust into the middle of the festering Flynn situation. Despite Yates's visits to the White House, and the sense of urgency she thought she'd conveyed, nothing had been done about Flynn. But the day after Sessions's confirmation, *The Washington Post* published a detailed account of what had been mentioned in the Ignatius column, which was that Flynn "privately discussed U.S. sanctions against Russia with that country's ambassador to the United States during the month before President Trump took office, contrary to public assertions by Trump officials."

"Flynn on Wednesday denied that he had discussed sanctions with Kislyak. Asked in an interview whether he had ever done so, he twice said, 'No,'" the report continued.

But now Flynn backtracked. A day later, on Thursday, his spokesman told the *Post* "that while he had no recollection of discussing sanctions, he couldn't be certain that the topic never came up."

Continuing press coverage of Flynn and Kislyak was only keeping the Russia story alive, and Trump was upset. In a private meeting in the Oval Office, Trump grilled Flynn on the conversations; he even corrected Flynn on one of the exact dates, indicating he'd had a detailed briefing on the encounters. When Trump pressed him about what was discussed, Flynn conceded he "might" have discussed sanctions.

The day after the *Post* story, McCabe was at a White House briefing when McGahn asked him to stop by. McGahn's secretary led McCabe to the vice president's office, where Pence, Priebus, McGahn, and some staff members were waiting. Priebus said they wanted to see what evidence the FBI had gathered about Flynn, and, he said, "We want to see it right now."

McCabe obviously wasn't carrying it with him. He called Jim Baker to discuss the request, and someone at the FBI brought the material over. They regrouped in the White House Situation Room, and Pence started reading the file. "Oh, this is fine. No problem with this," he muttered as he read. "Fine, fine, fine." Then he got to the actual transcript of the call. His tone changed abruptly. He shook his head in disbelief. "This is totally opposite, and it's not what he said to me." Pence handed the materials back to McCabe and thanked him.

Afterward, Pence and Priebus concluded Flynn had lied to the vice president and others. It was inconceivable Flynn could simply have forgotten what was obviously the entire point of his initial and follow-up calls with Kislyak.

Priebus and McGahn told Trump he had to fire Flynn, a recommendation McGahn memorialized in a memo.

The next day, Flynn joined Trump for the weekend at Mar-a-Lago, where Trump hosted Japan's prime minister, Shinzo Abe. (After North Korea fired a ballistic missile that same weekend, Trump and Flynn worked out an official response to the test from the dining terrace of the club, prompting national security concerns.)

Sunday night, Flynn flew back with Trump on Air Force One. But for some reason, Trump still didn't fire him. Instead, he asked him directly if he'd lied to the vice president. Flynn prevaricated: he might have forgotten some of the details, but he didn't think he'd lied. That seemed to satisfy Trump. "Okay. That's fine. I got it," he said.

The next day, dismayed that Trump had failed to deliver the message, Priebus told Flynn point-blank that he had to resign. Flynn asked to see the president so he could say goodbye. Priebus ushered him into the Oval Office.

Trump got up, hugged Flynn, and shook his hand. "We'll give you a good recommendation," he said. "You're a good guy. We'll take care of you."

FLYNN ANNOUNCED HIS resignation the next day, still avoiding any concession that he'd lied. "Unfortunately, because of the fast pace of events, I inadvertently briefed the Vice President Elect and others with incomplete information regarding my phone calls with the Russian Ambassador," his resignation letter said. "I have sincerely apologized to the President and the Vice President, and they have accepted my apology."

And he effusively thanked Trump for his "personal loyalty."

Trump tweeted the next morning that the "real story" was leaks coming out of Washington.

At that day's press briefing at the White House, Sean Spicer offered a somewhat less sanitized version. "The President was very concerned that General Flynn had misled the Vice President and others," he said, adding that given sensitive national security concerns, "the President must have complete and unwavering trust for the person in that position. The evolving and eroding level of trust as a result of this situation and a series of other questionable instances is what led the President to ask for General Flynn's resignation."

Flynn was furious over Spicer's comments, which he thought went far beyond the approved talking points by mentioning "other questionable instances."

At the Justice Department, career officials remained mystified that it had apparently taken a *Washington Post* article to prompt action, when Yates had told McGahn everything he needed to know weeks earlier, including that Flynn was a security risk. They suspected Trump would have done nothing but for the publicity.

As the *Washington Post* article noted, "The White House appears to have let its repeated false statements about Flynn stand for weeks after that notification from Yates, and has yet to account for what it did with the warning she conveyed. The disclosures about Flynn have added to the swirling suspicion about the Trump administration's relationship with Moscow—suspicion based in part on Trump's repeated expressions of admiration for Russian president Vladimir Putin."

As Spicer was delivering his press briefing, Trump had lunch at the White House with Chris Christie and his wife, Mary Pat. After giving up his run for the Republican nomination, the New Jersey governor had endorsed Trump and had seemed in line for a top cabinet post or chief of staff. Then Trump had replaced Christie as head of his transition team, reportedly at the behest of his son-in-law, Jared Kushner. So it must have been awkward when Kushner joined them at the table.

At some point in the conversation, Trump brought up Flynn. "Now that we fired Flynn, the Russia thing is over," Trump said.

Christie laughed. "No way," he said. "This Russia thing is far from over." We'll "be here on Valentine's Day 2018 talking about this."

Kushner said that was "crazy."

"What do you mean?" Trump asked. "Flynn met with the Russians. That was the problem. I fired Flynn. It's over."

Kushner chimed in: "That's right, firing Flynn ends the whole Russia thing."

On the contrary, Flynn will be "like gum on the bottom of your shoe," Christie said.

As if to prove the point, that very moment Flynn called Kushner to vent his anger over Spicer's remarks. Seemingly oblivious to conventional courtesies, Kushner took the call at the table and carried on a conversation. "You know the President respects you," Kushner assured Flynn as the others listened. "The President cares about you. I'll get the President to send out a positive tweet about you later." As he spoke, Kushner turned toward Trump, who nodded in agreement (though he didn't tweet about Flynn that day).

When conversation resumed, Christie reminded Trump that he was both a former prosecutor and himself the subject of a major investigation.*

Based on that experience, firing Flynn would not end the investigation. Christie told the president that there was no way to shorten an investigation, but many ways to prolong it, including talking about it.

Despite that advice, Trump brought up Comey twice, making clear that the FBI director remained a preoccupation. Christie had a friendly relationship with Comey, and Trump asked him to call Comey and say the president "really likes him. Tell him he's part of the team." Trump again asked him to make the call toward the end of the lunch.

The suggestion made Christie uncomfortable. Trump was obviously ignoring his advice to avoid doing anything that might prolong an investigation. Christie decided to ignore the request.

JUST A FEW hours after Trump's lunch with Christie, at 4:00 p.m., Comey was back in the Oval Office with Trump, this time for a homeland security briefing. It was Comey's first White House meeting with Sessions present. Sizing up the new attorney general, Comey found him both "overwhelmed and overmatched" for his new job. Sessions reminded him of the hapless Gonzales, without Gonzales's kindness.

Trump seemed distracted, showed little interest in the discussion, and

---

* The so-called Bridgegate scandal, over the closing of lanes leading to the George Washington Bridge. Christie was never charged with any wrongdoing.

after about fifteen minutes brought it to an abrupt end with a dismissive "thanks, everybody." He pointed toward Comey. "I just want to talk to Jim."

Sessions and Kushner lingered as the other participants filed out, and Kushner chatted with Comey, mentioning how hard the email investigation must have been.

"Thanks, Jeff," Trump said to Sessions, indicating he should leave. Trump turned to his son-in-law. "Okay, Jared, thank you." Kushner followed Priebus out, leaving Comey, once again, alone with Trump.

The president wasted no time with pleasantries: "I want to talk about Mike Flynn."

Trump repeatedly stressed that Flynn "hadn't done anything wrong" in talking to Kislyak, apparently latching onto McGahn's conclusion that the conversation didn't violate the Logan Act. But Trump said he couldn't have Flynn going around misleading the vice president (a "good guy"); he had other issues with Flynn (which he didn't specify); and, in any event, he had a "great guy" to replace him. Spicer, he said, had done a "great job" that morning explaining things.

"Did you see my tweet this morning?" Trump asked, adding, "It's really about the leaks." He patted the gray phone set on his desk. He thought calls on "this beautiful phone" were strictly confidential, but recent conversations with the leaders of Mexico and Australia had leaked. It "makes us look terrible," he said. Moreover, he didn't remember saying the things that got leaked, and "they say I have one of the world's greatest memories."

What Flynn did wasn't wrong "in any way," but the leaks were terrible.

As usual, Comey had trouble getting a word in. Finally Trump stopped talking, and Comey said he, too, was eager to find leakers and would like to "nail one to the door as a message."

"We need to go after the reporters," Trump said. He mentioned the former *New York Times* reporter Judith Miller, who spent eighty-five days in jail for refusing to identify a source in the Scooter Libby affair before she named Libby as her source. "Ten or fifteen years ago we put them in jail and it worked," he said.

Comey said he believed in pursuing leaks aggressively, but going after reporters was "tricky," both for legal reasons and because the Department of Justice was cautious with members of the media.

Trump told him to talk to Sessions and see what they could do about that. Priebus opened the door, and Comey glimpsed Pence waiting outside. But Trump waved Pence off, saying he knew people were waiting but he needed a few more minutes.

Trump got back to the subject with which he'd opened the conversation. Flynn was a "good guy" who'd "been through a lot," Trump said. Flynn might have misled the vice president, but he didn't do anything wrong during the call.

"I hope you can see your way clear to letting this go, to letting Flynn go," Trump said. "He is a good guy. I hope you can let this go."

What could Comey say? The request was blatantly inappropriate. "I agree he is a good guy," Comey said awkwardly, and stopped. Even that wasn't really true. But caught off guard, alone with the president, Comey felt he had to say something.

Trump got up from his desk. As he walked Comey out, he mentioned again that reporters should be jailed. "They spend a couple days in jail, make a new friend, and they are ready to talk," he said.

FROM HIS CAR, Comey emailed McCabe, Baker, and his senior leadership team, "Now I have to write another memo."

Given the circumstances of their one-on-one meeting—alone, with Priebus and Kushner deliberately excluded so there would be no witnesses—Comey interpreted Trump's comment to "let this go" as a "directive." He had no intention of following it.

Comey also called McCabe to discuss Trump's request, which McCabe considered an "unqualified contradiction to what the Bureau stood for." McCabe had found each of Comey's conversations with Trump stranger and more inappropriate than the last. But he was willing to chalk them up to inexperience and not yet understanding the norms of government. But this was more sinister: an attempt to "manipulate the functions of government mainly for their own interests."

The next day, when Comey and McCabe and others at the bureau discussed the options, they decided to say nothing about it to Strzok or other investigators. Nor did there seem any point in briefing Sessions.

Comey did arrange to stay behind with the attorney general after their weekly threat briefing at the Justice Department. Seated in Sessions's secure conference room, he conveyed the message that the president wanted to go after leaks more aggressively, as promised. Then he said he never again wanted to be left alone with Trump. "That can't happen," Comey said. "You are my boss. You can't be kicked out of the room so he can talk to me alone."

Sessions didn't speak, but looked down at the table, his eyes darting from side to side.

THE FLYNN RESIGNATION—and why it took Trump so long to ask for it—continued to attract news coverage. "Michael Flynn, General Flynn is a wonderful man," Trump said on February 15, 2017, during an appearance with the Israeli prime minister, Benjamin Netanyahu. "I think he's been treated very, very unfairly by the media—as I call it, the fake media, in many cases. And I think it's really a sad thing that he was treated so badly."

Trump continued to send messages of support to Flynn, in what Priebus thought an effort to maintain Flynn's loyalty. He told Priebus to reach out to say the president still cared about him and felt bad about what happened to him. He told Flynn's deputy, McFarland, to tell him he should stay strong; he told Hicks to say the president wanted to make sure he was okay.

On February 14, another damaging Russia story ran in the *Times*: "Phone records and intercepted calls show that members of Donald J. Trump's 2016 presidential campaign and other Trump associates had repeated contacts with senior Russian intelligence officials in the year before the election, according to four current and former American officials."

Priebus thought the administration was getting "killed" in the press over Russia, so it was welcome news when McCabe stayed behind after an intelligence briefing at the White House that day and said the *Times* story was "overstated and inaccurate"; it was "total bullshit."

"What can we do about it?" Priebus asked. If he could refute the story, he knew he'd be seen as a hero in the West Wing. What if he got McCabe to deny it? The media couldn't ignore a statement from the deputy director of the FBI, and it would take the *Times* down a peg or two. But McCabe said he wasn't sure he could do that. A few hours later, he called to say he couldn't, because he'd have to discuss classified information.

"You just told me it's inaccurate and now you say you can't do anything? That's ridiculous," Priebus responded. McCabe said he'd ask again, but then he called to say the answer was still no.

"You're not being good partners," Priebus said, which McCabe took to mean both him personally and the FBI as an institution. Comey, too, weighed in, calling Priebus to remind him that he shouldn't be making such requests to the FBI.

Trump complained to McGahn that Comey was "acting like his own branch of government."

The next day, at a White House press conference, Trump was pummeled with more questions about Flynn and Russia. The president extolled Flynn as a "fine man" and said, "What he did wasn't wrong, what he did in terms of the information he saw. What was wrong was the way that other people, including yourselves in this room, were given that information, because that was classified information that was given illegally. That's the real problem. And you can talk all you want about Russia, which was all fake news, a fabricated deal to try and make up for the loss of the Democrats, and the press plays right into it."

Trump acknowledged Flynn "didn't tell the Vice President of the United States the facts, and then he didn't remember. And that just wasn't acceptable to me." (Curiously, Trump didn't say that Flynn had also dissembled with him.) As for the call to Kislyak to discuss sanctions, "It certainly would have been okay with me if he did," Trump said. "I would have directed him to do it if I thought he wasn't doing it. I didn't direct him, but I would have directed him because that's his job."

Asked more broadly about Russia, Trump again lambasted the media: "Well, the failing *New York Times* wrote a big, long front-page story yesterday. And it was very much discredited, as you know. It was—it's a joke." He continued, "Speaking for myself, I own nothing in Russia. I have no loans in Russia. I don't have any deals in Russia. President Putin called me up very nicely to congratulate me on the win of the election. He then called me up extremely nicely to congratulate me on the inauguration, which was terrific. But so did many other leaders—almost all other leaders from almost all other countries. So that's the extent. Russia is fake news. Russia—this is fake news put out by the media."

But over the next week, calls mounted for the appointment of a special counsel to investigate the Trump campaign's ties to Russia. "The gravity of the issues raised by the events that led to national security adviser Michael Flynn's resignation cannot be overstated or ignored," the minority leader, Senator Chuck Schumer, wrote in *The Washington Post*. "The American people, and indeed American democracy, require a thorough and independent investigation into what transpired and whether any criminal laws or constitutional precepts were violated." While that would normally fall within the purview of the attorney general, "in this case, given his deep and long-standing ties to President Trump and many of Trump's top advisers, Attorney General Jeff Sessions cannot lead such an investigation."

A few days later, Priebus was astonished when CNN reported (accurately) that he'd tried to get the FBI to refute the *Times* story and suggested that making such a request was a "violation of procedures." Priebus had only tried to refute the story because McCabe brought it up and said it was inaccurate. He and Trump both saw it as yet another leak, and who could it have been but someone at the FBI? Perhaps even Comey or McCabe himself. Trump lashed out at the FBI on Twitter: "The FBI is totally unable to stop the national security 'leakers' that have permeated our government for a long time. They can't even find the leakers within the FBI itself. Classified information is being given to media that could have a devastating effect on U.S. FIND NOW."

—————

ON FEBRUARY 28, Trump gave his first presidential address to a joint session of Congress. A seemingly new, conciliatory Trump was on view. He called for putting aside "trivial fights" and joining across party lines to improve health care and achieve tax and immigration reform. The media praised this much more traditionally "presidential" approach, and Trump basked in the glow of the favorable publicity.

For less than a day. The next morning, the vexing subject of Russia was again the lead story, and Trump saw the momentum from his speech vanish. *The Washington Post* reported that morning that Sessions himself had spoken with Kislyak, the Russian ambassador, twice while serving as a top adviser to the Trump campaign, once in a private meeting in Sessions's office.

Sessions struggled to reconcile this with his sworn testimony, arguing he met with the Russian ambassador in his capacity as a member of the Senate Armed Services Committee, not as a campaign adviser, and thus hadn't lied during his confirmation hearings. In a statement, he said he'd "never met with any Russian officials to discuss issues of the campaign" and promised to clarify his prior testimony.

Senator Al Franken, the Minnesota Democrat who had asked Sessions the question about contacts with Russians, called for Sessions's recusal: "It is now clearer than ever that the attorney general cannot, in good faith, oversee an investigation at the Department of Justice and the FBI of the Trump-Russia connection, and he must recuse himself immediately."

As the public furor over Sessions mounted, Trump called Comey at about noon, saying he just wanted to "check in" and see how Comey was doing. Comey was about to board a helicopter for a flight to Richmond but delayed his departure to take the call.

"I'm doing great," Comey said, but "I have a lot going on."

Comey praised Sessions, saying the attorney general seemed "to have hit the ground running" with a recent speech on violent crime.

"That's his thing," Trump responded.

But Trump didn't say anything more about Sessions, though it must have been the subject uppermost in his mind. He said only that Comey should "take good care" of himself and stop by to see him the next time he was at the White House.

The next morning, Trump summoned McGahn and told him to stop Sessions from recusing himself. Doing so would make Sessions look guilty of lying about his contacts with the Russian ambassador and, even worse, leave Trump without an ally overseeing the investigation.

McGahn dutifully delivered the message—repeatedly—but Sessions said he intended to follow the department's rules. McGahn tried calling anyone who might be able to influence Sessions, even the Senate majority leader, Mitch McConnell, to no avail. Sessions fielded a barrage of similar calls from other administration officials, suggesting Trump had enlisted a battery of supporters to lobby him.

But Sessions and the Justice Department lawyers advising him didn't believe he had any choice, even before the devastating *Post* article. Justice Department regulations state, "No DOJ employee may participate in a criminal investigation or prosecution if he has a personal or political relationship with any person or organization substantially involved in the conduct that is the subject of the investigation or prosecution, or who would be directly affected by the outcome." Sessions had a political relationship with Trump; Trump was involved in the conduct being investigated; and Trump had a huge stake in the outcome.

Sessions issued a statement that afternoon announcing, "I have decided to recuse myself from any existing or future investigations of any matters related in any way to the campaigns for President of the United States." At a press conference he added, "My staff recommended recusal," and "I have studied the rules and considered their comments and evaluation. I believe those recommendations are right and just."

Trump was livid. He convened a meeting with McGahn and Priebus. As the conversation became heated, Hicks called Bannon and told him to come to the Oval Office. When Bannon arrived, Trump was as angry as Bannon had ever seen him.

"I don't have a lawyer," Trump said, glowering at McGahn. "Where's my Roy Cohn?"

Cohn had won hopeless cases for him and did "incredible things" for him, Trump said.

That Trump would cite Roy Cohn as a positive role model left his audience speechless. As Joseph McCarthy's chief counsel, Cohn had aggressively assisted the senator's purge of suspected communists during the mid-1950s; Cohn had tried to identify and purge homosexuals in the military and government (despite his own homosexuality); and he'd been disbarred for unethical conduct. Cohn was a memorable character in Tony Kushner's acclaimed play *Angels in America*, portrayed as a lying, bitter, self-hating hypocrite dying of AIDS.

But for Trump, Cohn was a "winner and a fixer," someone who "got things done," in contrast to McGahn and Sessions, who now merited Trump's ultimate opprobrium—"weak."

By now, Trump was practically screaming. Referring to the previous attorneys general Bobby Kennedy and Eric Holder, Trump went on, "You're telling me that Bobby and Jack didn't talk about investigations? Or Obama didn't tell Eric Holder who to investigate?" They had protected the president. Holder had always stood up for President Obama and even took a contempt charge for him. Bobby Kennedy always had "his brother's back." Trump said he'd been told his entire life that he needed a great lawyer, a "bulldog."

Trump went so far as to say he wanted an attorney general he could tell "who to investigate."

Trump was so angry he told Priebus he didn't want him on Air Force One for a planned weekend at Mar-a-Lago, and he agreed to stay behind. Bannon said he'd fly down the next day on the Justice Department plane with Sessions and McGahn. Trump did have dinner with them and a few others on Saturday night and pulled Sessions aside to ask him to "unrecuse" himself. He again mentioned Kennedy and Holder as the kind of attorney general he needed to protect him.

Early the next morning, in what might have been an effort to change the subject, he tweeted the sensational claim that Obama had tapped his phone: "Terrible! Just found out that Obama had my 'wires tapped' in Trump Tower just before the victory. Nothing found. This is McCarthyism!"

And immediately after: "How low has President Obama gone to tapp my phones during the very sacred election process. This is Nixon/Watergate. Bad (or sick) guy!"

WITH SESSIONS'S RECUSAL from anything involving the Trump campaign, Rod Rosenstein's confirmation hearing on March 7 took on sudden significance, because, if confirmed as deputy attorney general, Rosenstein would be in charge of the Russia investigation. Democrats seized the occasion to renew their call for the appointment of a special counsel, but Rosenstein said he needed to know the facts before making that decision. He noted, however, that Lynch hadn't recused herself in the Clinton email case.

The Republican senator and Judiciary Committee chair, Charles Grassley, said he wouldn't schedule a vote on Rosenstein until Comey briefed Congress on the Russia investigation. So two days later, after extended discussions with Justice Department officials about what he could say, Comey briefed the so-called Gang of Eight—the congressional leaders who, in strict confidence, receive classified intelligence briefings—and confirmed, for the first time, that the Russia investigation existed. He identified the four subjects—Flynn, Page, Manafort, and Papadopoulos—and said that at that juncture Trump himself was not a subject.

Within days, Trump was in a "panic/chaos" about the Russia investigation, according to notes from McGahn's office dated March 12. Four days later, a Gang of Eight member, Richard Burr, chair of the Senate Select Committee on Intelligence, who had advised Trump during the campaign on national security matters, provided Comey's testimony to the White House. According to notes from McGahn's office dated March 16, Burr identified "4–5 targets": "Flynn (FBI was in—wrapping up)→DOJ looking for phone records"; "Comey→Manafort (Ukr + Russia, not campaign)"; "Carter Page ($ game)"; and "Greek Guy."

On March 20, Comey gave a similar briefing to the House Permanent Select Committee on Intelligence, chaired by a fierce Trump partisan, Representative Devin Nunes of California. In contrast to his Senate testimony, the hearing was public. Nonetheless, in consultation with the Justice Department, Comey had decided to confirm the existence of the investigation as being in the public interest—but not to say whether Trump (or anyone else) was being investigated. This was in part to protect Trump, because once Comey said publicly that the president was not personally under investigation, he'd have to correct the record if he ever was, much as Comey had to notify Congress once Clinton was again under investigation.

"As you know, our practice is not to confirm the existence of ongoing investigations, especially those investigations that involve classified matters, but in unusual circumstances where it is in the public interest, it may be appropriate to do so as Justice Department policies recognize. This is one of those circumstances," Comey began, and proceeded to confirm "that the FBI, as part of our counterintelligence mission, is investigating the Russian government's efforts to interfere in the 2016 presidential election and that includes investigating the nature of any links between individuals associated with the Trump campaign and the Russian government and whether there was any coordination between the campaign and Russia's efforts. As with any counterintelligence investigation, this will also include an assessment of whether any crimes were committed. Because it is an open ongoing investigation and is classified, I cannot say more about what we are doing and whose conduct we are examining."

Comey spent much of the ensuing five and a half hours fending off questions about who was being investigated, including Trump himself.

Adam Schiff, the ranking Democrat on the House Select Intelligence Committee, asked whether it was true that Trump's phones at Trump Tower had been tapped.

"With respect to the President's tweets about alleged wiretapping directed at him by the prior administration, I have no information that supports those tweets and we have looked carefully inside the FBI," Comey responded. "The Department of Justice has asked me to share with you that the answer is the same for the Department of Justice and all its components. The department has no information that supports those tweets."

Comey's testimony infuriated Trump. The next day, he was "beside himself," according to notes from McGahn's office. Not only had Comey failed to state that Trump himself wasn't being investigated, but he'd left the distinct impression that he was. (It was lost on Trump that saying he wasn't under investigation generated an obligation to say if he was.)

Perhaps even worse, Comey had undercut Trump's claim that his phones had been tapped. Comey had made him "look like a fool," Trump said.

And thanks to his "bombshell" confirming the conversation, Comey was all over the TV news broadcasts and the front pages. This was exactly the kind of grandstanding that so irked Trump, that had prompted his earlier comment that Comey "was more famous than me."

Trump called McGahn repeatedly that day to vent about Comey and threatened to fire him. The president got "hotter and hotter, get rid?" according to notes taken by McGahn's chief of staff. McGahn had a lawyer in his office research whether a president needed cause to fire an FBI director. (He concluded that he didn't but neglected to tell the president that.) McGahn spent much of the day running interference with the Justice Department and discouraging Trump from acting on his impulse to call the department himself and demand a statement that he wasn't under investigation.

The president was consumed with the issue throughout the week, complaining to Director of National Intelligence Dan Coats, "I can't do anything with Russia, there's things I'd like to do with Russia, with trade, with ISIS, they're all over me with this," and to the NSA director, Michael Rogers, that "the thing with the Russians" was "messing up" his ability to get things done. He also asked Rogers if he could do anything to refute the stories. The issue even overshadowed Trump's effort to overturn Obamacare, one of the signature promises of his campaign. That Friday, House Republicans abandoned efforts to repeal the Affordable Care Act after failing to come up with enough votes, even though they had a majority.

At about 8:15 a.m. on March 30, Trump finally called Comey, notwithstanding the repeated warnings about direct contact with the FBI director. The president began with a comment that Comey was getting more publicity than he was (which Comey considered a joke, showing how much he underestimated Trump's resentment at being upstaged). "I hate that," Comey said.

Then Trump said he was trying to run the country but the "cloud" of "this Russia business" was making that difficult. He said it had cost him the health care vote.

He again denounced the Steele dossier. He had nothing to do with Russia and had a letter saying he derived no income from Russia "from the largest law firm in D.C." As for consorting with "hookers," "Can you imagine me, hookers?" He had a "beautiful wife," and all this had been "painful" for her. He was going to sue Christopher Steele.

Comey listened; he'd heard variations of all this before.

Finally Trump asked what he could do to "lift the cloud." Comey said the FBI was moving as quickly as it could, and if it found nothing, Trump would have "our Good Housekeeping seal of approval." But the bureau needed to do its work unimpeded.

Trump claimed to agree, but returned to how hard this was making his job. He was being tough on Russia, ramping up production of oil (thereby driving down prices and Russia's oil revenues) and renewing America's nuclear weapons ("ours are 40 years old").

Trump wanted to know why Congress had held a hearing the previous week and why Comey had testified. Comey said he hadn't volunteered for the task but that legislators from both parties demanded it; Grassley had even threatened to block Rosenstein's confirmation. Comey assured Trump that he'd briefed the congressional leadership in greater detail, making clear—as Comey had told Trump before—that the president wasn't under investigation.

That was clearly what Trump wanted to hear. "We need to get that fact out," he said. And although he, Trump, hadn't done anything with the Russians, if one of his "satellites" had, it would be good to find out.

But, he said again, it would be good to get out that the FBI wasn't investigating him.

Trump abruptly turned to the subject of McCabe, someone he hadn't brought up again, because Comey had assured him he was an honorable guy.

"He is an honorable guy," Comey responded.

But "McAuliffe is close to the Clintons and gave him money," Trump said.

Comey had no idea why Trump was bringing up McCabe now (although McCabe's recent refusal to correct the *Times* story might well have been on his mind). Comey said McCabe was a professional, not motivated by politics, and was, indeed, an "honorable guy."

Trump returned to his main theme: he was trying to make deals for the country, and this "cloud" was making it difficult. He hated going to the upcoming G7 meeting with it hanging over him. Again, he said Comey should find a way to get out the fact that he wasn't being investigated.

Comey said he'd see what he could do, then called the acting deputy attorney general, Dana Boente, for guidance about how to respond. He also told Boente, as he had so many times, that he was uncomfortable taking calls from the president about an ongoing investigation.

ON APRIL 7, Trump's nominee Neil M. Gorsuch was confirmed as a justice of the Supreme Court, fulfilling a Trump campaign pledge to replace Antonin Scalia, who had died in February 2016, with a similarly reliable conservative justice. *The New York Times* called Gorsuch's confirmation a "triumph" for Trump and said the president "now has a lasting legacy: Judge Gorsuch, 49, could serve on the court for 30 years or more."

In a statement, Trump hailed Gorsuch as "a deep believer in the rule of law."

But Trump didn't take much time to savor his victory or reward his allies and staff, like McGahn, who had helped make it happen. Instead, he fretted about Comey.

Just four days later, on April 11, shortly before 8:30 a.m., Trump called Comey again. Trump's patience was wearing thin. There were no pleasantries this time, or even pointed comments about Comey's celebrity. Trump wanted to ask what Comey had done about his request to publicize the fact he wasn't under investigation. Comey said he'd sought guidance from Dana Boente at the Justice Department but hadn't heard back.

"Who's that?" Trump asked.

Trump reminded Comey that he was "trying to do work for the country, visit with foreign leaders, and any cloud, even a little cloud, gets in the way of that. They keep bringing up the Russia thing as an excuse for losing the election."

Comey suggested Trump have people in the White House contact the Justice Department about a statement, which was the proper channel, rather than coming to him.

Trump seemed to agree but then added, "Because I have been very loyal to you, very loyal, we had that thing, you know."

Comey didn't immediately respond. He didn't ask Trump what "thing" he meant. He again urged Trump to have someone contact the Justice Department.

The two turned to a few other matters, and then Trump told Comey, unconvincingly, that he was doing a "great job."

It was the last time they spoke.

NINE

"I KNOW YOU TOLD ME NOT TO"

A few hours after speaking to Comey, Trump taped an interview with another friendly network host, Maria Bartiromo of Fox Business, in which he both hinted ominously about Comey's future and signaled that his preoccupation with the Clinton email case was far from over, however magnanimous he'd seemed right after the election.

"People are still wondering, though, they're scratching their heads, right, so many Obama-era staffers are still here," Bartiromo said, before singling out Comey. "Was it a mistake not to ask Jim Comey to step down from the FBI at the outset of your presidency? Is it too late now to ask him to step down?"

"No, it's not too late, but, you know, I have confidence in him," Trump answered. "We'll see what happens. You know, it's going to be interesting."

Trump seemed to suggest that Comey's and Clinton's self-interests had aligned in the email investigation, both exonerating Clinton and turning Comey into a celebrity. "Don't forget, when Jim Comey came out, he saved Hillary Clinton," Trump said. "People don't realize that. He saved her life, because—I call it Comey 1. And I joke about it a little bit. When he was reading those charges, she was guilty on every charge. And then he said, she was essentially OK. But he—she wasn't OK, because she was guilty on every charge. But Hillary Clinton won—or Comey won. She was guilty on every charge."

"Yes," Bartiromo agreed.

Trump continued, "Director Comey was very, very good to Hillary Clinton, that I can tell you. If he weren't, she would be, right now, going to trial."

"Are you going to push that?"

"I don't want to talk about that," Trump said.

Afterward, the White House communications director, Hope Hicks, suggested references to Comey be cut from the interview, but Trump disagreed, saying he wanted them left in. They were included when the interview broadcast the next day, prompting widespread speculation about Comey's future. Aaron Blake in *The Washington Post* described the remarks as "a half vote-of-confidence and a half you-better-watch-your-back to Comey. 'We'll see what happens' isn't exactly promising that Comey will be around forever."

Only later that afternoon did Trump disclose to Priebus, McGahn, and others that he had defied instructions not to talk to Comey about the Russia investigation and had done so twice. "I know you told me not to, but I called Comey anyway," the president said.

Trump said Comey agreed he could make a statement that Trump wasn't under investigation as long as the Justice Department approved, and, as Comey had suggested, he told McGahn to make some calls. Comey would be testifying in Congress on May 3; that might be the ideal time. His failure to do so, Trump warned McGahn, would be "the last straw."

McGahn called Dana Boente, who relayed his conversation with Comey, saying the calls from Trump had made Comey uncomfortable. Nor was Boente eager to have Comey make a statement defending Trump. He thought it could backfire politically and would only lead to more calls for a special counsel. That, of course, was not what Trump wanted to hear.

In any event, it was soon no longer Boente's problem: Rosenstein was confirmed as deputy attorney general on April 25 and assumed oversight of the Russia investigation.

EVEN AS TRUMP was blaming Comey for "saving" Clinton, Clinton supporters increasingly blamed him for her narrow loss, with a growing body of data to support their argument.

On May 3, Nate Silver, the widely respected statistician, analyst, and founder of the FiveThirtyEight website, published a lengthy analysis of the 2016 presidential election, stating flatly that "Hillary Clinton would probably be president if FBI Director James Comey had not sent a letter to Congress on Oct. 28."

While Silver didn't dismiss other factors, "the impact of Comey's letter is comparatively easy to quantify. At a maximum, it might have shifted the race by 3 or 4 percentage points toward Donald Trump, swinging Michigan, Pennsylvania, Wisconsin and Florida to him, perhaps along with North Carolina and Arizona. At a minimum, its impact might have been only a percentage point or so. Still, because Clinton lost Michigan, Pennsylvania and Wisconsin by less than 1 point, the letter was probably enough to change the outcome of the Electoral College."

Clinton reached a similar conclusion in an interview with Christiane Amanpour, CNN's international anchor, at a women's conference in New York, her first extended public remarks since her loss. "If the election had been on October 27th, I'd be your president. It wasn't," Clinton said. "It wasn't a perfect campaign," Clinton said. "There is no such thing. But I was on the way to winning until a combination of Jim Comey's letter on October 28th and Russian WikiLeaks raised doubts in the minds of people who were inclined to vote for me but got scared off. And the evidence for that intervening event is I think compelling, persuasive."

Clinton's comments, which drew widespread media attention, were on Comey's mind the next day, when he made yet another appearance in Congress, this time before the Senate Judiciary Committee. The committee chair, Charles Grassley, introduced Comey with a comment sure to get under Trump's skin: "As the old saying goes, for somebody as famous as you, you don't need any introduction."

In her opening comments, Dianne Feinstein, Democrat of California, echoed Clinton's comments: "I join those who believe that the actions taken by the FBI did, in fact, have an impact on the election." Comey responded, "Look, this is terrible. It makes me mildly nauseous to think that we might have had some impact on the election. But honestly, it wouldn't change the decision. Everybody who disagrees with me has to come back to October 28 with me and stare at this and tell me what you would do. Would you speak or would you conceal? And I could be wrong, but we honestly made a decision between those two choices that even in hindsight—and this has been one of the world's most painful experiences—I would make the same decision."

Richard Blumenthal, Democrat of Connecticut, asked a series of questions about the Russia investigation. "Have you ruled out anyone in the campaign that you can disclose?"

Comey said he wasn't "comfortable" answering that.

"Have you—have you ruled out the President of the United States?"

Had he been so inclined, this would have been the perfect moment to deliver what Trump so desperately wanted, which was a statement he wasn't under investigation. But all Comey said was, "I don't want people to over-interpret this answer, I'm not going to comment on anyone in particular, because that puts me down a slope of—because if I say no to that then I have to answer succeeding questions. So what we've done is brief the chair and ranking on who the U.S. persons are that we've opened investigations on. And that's—that's as far as we're going to go, at this point."

"But as a former prosecutor, you know that when there's an investigation into several potentially culpable individuals, the evidence from those individuals and the investigation can lead to others, correct?" Blumenthal pressed.

"Correct," Comey answered. "We're always open-minded about—and we follow the evidence wherever it takes us."

"So potentially, the President of the United States could be a target of your ongoing investigation into the Trump campaign's involvement with Russian interference in our election, correct?"

Comey was a little tongue-tied. "I just worry—I don't want to answer that—that—that seems to be unfair speculation. We will follow the evidence, we'll try and find as much as we can and we'll follow the evidence wherever it leads."

Blumenthal, too, asked about the email case: "Do you have any regrets or are there any things you would do differently in connection with either the comments you made at the time you closed the investigation or when you then indicated to Congress that you were in effect reopening it?"

"The honest answer is no," Comey replied. "I've asked myself that a million times because, Lordy, has this been painful. The only thing I regret is maybe answering the phone when they called to recruit me to be FBI director when I was living happily in Connecticut." He continued, "I've gotten all kinds of rocks thrown at me and this has been really hard but I think I've done the right thing at each turn. I'm not on anybody's side. So hard for people to see that. But I—look, I've asked that a million times. Should you have done this, should you have done that, and I—the honest answer—I don't mean to sound arrogant—I wouldn't have done it any differently. Somehow I'd have prayed it away, wished it away, wished that I was on the shores of the Connecticut sounds, but failing that I don't have any regrets."

COMEY TESTIFIED FOR nearly four hours, wrapping up about 2:00 p.m. At the White House, where Sessions, McGahn, and Sessions's chief of staff, Jody Hunt, were meeting with the president, Trump asked how Comey had done. McGahn told him Comey had declined to say whether the president himself was under investigation. Trump was visibly enraged and turned his ire toward Sessions.

"This is terrible, Jeff," Trump exclaimed. "It's all because you recused. AG is supposed to be the most important appointment. Kennedy appointed his brother. Obama appointed Holder. I appointed you and you recused yourself. You left me on an island. I can't do anything."

He added, "I have foreign leaders saying they are sorry I am being investigated."

Sessions defended himself as best he could. He didn't have any choice; the law required that he step aside. Sessions tried to shift the focus to Comey, suggesting Trump needed a "new start" at the FBI and he should consider replacing Comey.

TRUMP WAS STILL fuming the next day. He complained repeatedly to Steve Bannon that Comey had "told me three times I'm not under investigation. He's a showboater. He's a grandstander. I don't know any Russians. There was no collusion."

Bannon warned Trump that it was too late to fire Comey. "That ship had sailed," Bannon said. And in any event, it wouldn't do any good. The president could fire the FBI director, but he couldn't fire the FBI.

That afternoon, Comey met with Rosenstein at the Justice Department, at Rosenstein's request, and gave him some advice about his new job, because Comey had served in the same capacity. Among other topics, Comey urged him to make sure he got enough sleep and exercise. Rosenstein didn't say anything about Trump, but Comey, alluding to Trump's penchant for one-on-one contacts, said that "one of your folks is going to have to straighten out the relationship between the White House and Department of Justice."

Rosenstein thanked him profusely for the advice. He didn't give any hint that trouble might be brewing at the White House.

IT WAS POURING rain that Friday evening when Trump arrived by helicopter at his Bedminster, New Jersey, Trump National Golf Club. Stephen Miller, who was one of Trump's closest advisers, the architect of much of his populist agenda, and Jared Kushner joined him for dinner in the neo-Georgian clubhouse with its large white pillars.

Since leaving the White House that afternoon, Trump had made up his mind.

Miller took notes as Trump dictated a draft of a letter to Comey. "While I greatly appreciate you informing me that I am not under investigation concerning what I have often stated is a fabricated story on a Trump-Russia relationship pertaining to the 2016 presidential election," Trump began, "please be informed that I, and I believe the American public—including Ds and Rs—have lost faith in you as Director of the FBI."

Fearful of leaks from within the White House, Trump swore everyone to secrecy.

Miller used his notes to come up with a draft letter, which Trump edited throughout the weekend (he had time on his hands after a round with the golfing great Greg Norman was rained out). Trump also watched Comey's May 3 testimony on television (or at least parts of it), which only angered him even more.

As Trump had directed, the letter began by stating, "While I greatly appreciate your informing me, on three separate occasions, that I am not under investigation concerning the fabricated and politically-motivated allegations of a Trump-Russia relationship with respect to the 2016 Presidential Election, please be informed that I, along with members of both political parties and, most importantly, the American Public, have lost faith in you as the Director of the FBI and you are hereby terminated."

With its convoluted syntax it was hardly a model of efficient prose, nor was the rest of the letter, which ran to four pages. It faulted Comey's May 3 testimony, his handling of the Clinton email investigation, and his failure to identify and hold leakers accountable. The letter said Comey had asked Trump to keep him on as FBI director and that Trump had said he would "consider" it. But the president had concluded he had "no alternative" but to find a new leader for the FBI "that restores confidence and trust."

The letter accomplished several Trump objectives: It finally got on the public record that Trump wasn't being investigated. It enabled Trump to reiterate his anger over leaks. It tapped into Democratic anger at Comey over the email investigation, affording Trump some bipartisan cover.

No one that weekend took issue with Trump's decision to fire Comey or seemed to anticipate that it might prompt a political firestorm. On the contrary, Trump seemed to think that Comey was genuinely unpopular, both inside the FBI and with the public at large, and that his decision would be met with applause.

Despite Trump's admonition, Miller didn't want Priebus to be blind-sided, so he called Priebus to say that Trump had been thinking about the "Comey situation" and there would be an important discussion about it at the White House the next day.

As it turned out, it wasn't much of a discussion. Trump summoned Priebus, McGahn, Miller, and members of their staffs. "I'm going to read you a letter," he began. "Don't talk me out of this. I've made my decision." He then read the opening paragraphs of the letter firing Comey that he and Miller had drafted. Trump added that Miller had researched the issue, and he was free to terminate Comey without cause.

No one pushed back on the idea. But in an effort to at least slow things down, McGahn suggested that he and other White House lawyers confer with Sessions and the newly confirmed Rosenstein.

When the delegation from the Justice Department arrived at noon, McGahn broke the news that Trump was going to fire Comey. Neither Sessions nor Rosenstein objected or seemed all that surprised, and they piled on with their own criticisms of Comey. Their reactions reassured McGahn; no one, for example, suggested that firing Comey might be considered obstruction of justice.

At 5:00 p.m., the group met with the president, who said he'd watched Comey's testimony over the weekend. Something's "not right" with Comey, Trump maintained. He asked for Sessions's and Rosenstein's recommendation, and both concurred that Comey should be removed. Sessions said he'd already made that suggestion, and Rosenstein criticized Comey's handling of the Clinton case.

The only issue was how to handle it. Trump handed out copies of his letter drafted over the weekend. McGahn suggested that Comey be allowed the more graceful option of resignation, but Trump firmly overruled him: he wanted him fired. Trump seemed to like the idea that Sessions and Rosenstein draft a letter and memorandum urging Trump to fire Comey, making it look as if the president were simply responding to a Justice Department suggestion. He told Rosenstein to draft the memo, which he wanted to see first thing in the morning. "Put the Russia stuff in the memo," Trump directed.

Rosenstein disagreed, because his argument for removing Comey had nothing to do with Russia. Trump said he'd "appreciate it" if Rosenstein put it in anyway.

After the meeting, Rosenstein told colleagues that his reasons for firing Comey were not the same as the president's.

AS HIS FATE was being decided at the White House, Comey himself was a continent away, preparing for his visit to the Los Angeles field office. McCabe was in charge at headquarters.

On the afternoon of May 9, two agents from the FBI's internal inspection division stopped by to interview him about the multiple leaks that had plagued the bureau. The mystery of Giuliani's sources had never been solved. Other instances, too, were under investigation, including a story about a McCabe staff meeting that had appeared in *Circa News*, a website owned by the conservative Sinclair Broadcast Group—an investigation that McCabe himself had ordered. But when the two agents had settled at the conference table in his office, their questions shifted to the now-all-but-forgotten October 30 *Wall Street Journal* story, which contained Axelrod's claim that McCabe had ordered FBI agents to "stand down" on the Clinton Foundation investigation until after the election. Expecting questions about *Circa News*, McCabe was surprised. The agents produced a copy of the article to refresh his memory, which McCabe quickly reviewed and initialed.

Since that story appeared, leaks had become a near obsession at the White House, in Congress, and even within the FBI itself. McCabe himself had repeatedly admonished the New York office over leaks. Comey had expressed his dismay over what appeared to be a leak in the *Journal* article.

McCabe said the article was accurate but that he "had no idea where it came from" and he hadn't authorized anyone to disclose it, according to notes of the interview. McCabe had described the August 12 call from

Axelrod to numerous people, suggesting the agents "would not get anywhere" by asking who else might have known about the call.

The agents concluded that McCabe "had not personally shared that
information with the media, and he considered it a leak." They left about
five minutes later, and McCabe was soon engulfed in far more consuming
matters.

ROSENSTEIN'S MEMO HAD duly landed on Trump's desk that morning. It
was addressed to the attorney general with the heading "Subject: Restoring Public Confidence in the FBI."

Despite some obligatory nods to Comey as an "articulate and persuasive speaker about leadership and the immutable principles of the Department of Justice," it was a searing indictment of the FBI director, all the
more surprising given Rosenstein's long-professed admiration for him.

"I cannot defend the Director's handling of the conclusion of the investigation of Secretary Clinton's emails, and I do not understand his refusal to accept the nearly universal judgment that he was mistaken,"
Rosenstein wrote. Ignoring the bipartisan praise Comey had reaped after
his July 5 announcement (not to mention the warm reception Rosenstein
himself gave Comey, or Trump's praise for Comey's October 28 letter),
Rosenstein continued, "Almost everyone agrees that the Director made
serious mistakes; it is one of the few issues that unites people of diverse
perspectives."

> The Director was wrong to usurp the Attorney General's author-
> ity on July 5, 2016, and announce his conclusion that the case should
> be closed without prosecution. It is not the function of the Director to
> make such an announcement. At most, the Director should have said
> the FBI had completed its investigation and presented its findings to
> federal prosecutors. . . .
> [Despite] a well-established process for other officials to step in
> when a conflict requires the recusal of the Attorney General, . . . the

Director announced his own conclusions about the nation's most sensitive criminal investigation, without the authorization of duly appointed Justice Department leaders.

Compounding the error, the Director ignored another longstanding principle: we do not hold press conferences to release derogatory information about the subject of a declined criminal investigation. Derogatory information sometimes is disclosed in the course of criminal investigations and prosecutions, but we never release it gratuitously. The Director laid out his version of the facts for the news media as if it were a closing argument, but without a trial. It is a textbook example of what federal prosecutors and agents are taught not to do.

Rosenstein cited a list of legal experts who, with benefit of hindsight, now faulted Comey's judgment:

> I agree with the nearly unanimous opinions of former Department officials. The way the Director handled the conclusion of the email investigation was wrong. As a result, the FBI is unlikely to regain public and congressional trust until it has a Director who understands the gravity of the mistakes and pledges never to repeat them. Having refused to admit his errors, the Director cannot be expected to implement the necessary corrective actions.

The memo made no mention of Russia. Nor had Trump ever expressed any concern about Comey's departures from Justice Department norms in the email case—only that he'd reached the wrong conclusion in recommending Clinton not be charged. So it's surprising that Trump told McGahn he liked the memo, as well as Sessions's brief letter that accompanied it.

That came as a relief to lawyers in McGahn's office, who were appalled by the letter Trump and Miller had drafted. At least Rosenstein's memo avoided the subject of the Russia investigation, and in that regard was a vast improvement. Trump's and Miller's original letter was "not to see the light of day," and it was better to offer "no other rationales" beyond those cited in Rosenstein's memo, according to notes from McGahn's chief of staff. One note even asked, "Is this the beginning of the end" of Trump's presidency?

None of that deterred Trump from publicizing the fact that he wasn't under investigation. He ordered Miller to include in a new cover letter that Comey had informed the president three times that he was not under investigation. McGahn and Priebus both objected, but Trump overruled them. James Burnham, a lawyer in McGahn's office, noted that that was "the only line the President cared about." He was determined to make the point that Comey had repeatedly denied him.

At about 5:00 p.m., Spicer was summoned to the Oval Office and handed a statement that Trump himself had dictated:

> Today, President Donald J. Trump informed FBI Director James Comey that he has been terminated and removed from office.

FOX NEWS CHEERED the news and embraced Trump's stated rationale. On his show that evening, the Fox host Sean Hannity blasted Comey as "a national embarrassment" who "has failed you, the American people, on a spectacular level" by not subjecting Hillary Clinton to "the criminal prosecution she deserves." The Fox commentator Jesse Watters called Comey "corrupt" for not going after Clinton and the Clinton Foundation.

The *Wall Street Journal* editorial page, indulging its long-standing disdain for Comey, praised the decision and headlined an editorial "Comey's Deserved Dismissal":

> The reality is that Mr. Comey has always been most concerned with the politics of his own reputation. He styles himself as the last honest man in Washington as he has dangled insinuations across his career about the George W. Bush White House and surveillance, then Mrs. Clinton and emails,

and now Mr. Trump and Russia. He is political in
precisely the way we don't want a leader of America's premier law-enforcement agency to behave.

But they were exceptions. The major networks and digital and print
media nearly all raised questions about why Comey was fired, and many
featured congressional critics like the Senate Judiciary Committee member Patrick Leahy, the Vermont Democrat. "No one should accept President Trump's absurd justification that he is now concerned that FBI
Director Comey treated Secretary Clinton unfairly," Leahy said in a statement. "This is nothing less than Nixonian."

Representative John Conyers of Michigan, ranking Democrat on the
Judiciary Committee, sent a letter to both Rosenstein and McCabe demanding that the Justice Department and the FBI preserve all documents
relating to both Comey's dismissal and the Russia investigation. "The
Trump administration cannot be allowed to interfere any further in this
investigation," the letter said. "Nothing less than the integrity of our leading independent law enforcement agency and the credibility of our democracy are at stake."

Evidently channel surfing beyond the echo chamber of Fox News,
Trump called Chris Christie that evening, upset that he was getting
"killed" in the media, as he put it. What could he do?

"Did you fire him because of what Rod wrote in the memo?" Christie
asked.

"Yes," Trump replied.

Then he should "get Rod out there" to defend the decision, Christie
recommended.

Trump said he'd call Rosenstein right away, but it was the White
House press office that first reached out to say the White House wanted
to release a statement saying it was Rosenstein's idea to fire Comey.

Rosenstein balked, telling other Justice Department officials he wasn't
going to be part of a "false story."

Trump himself called Rosenstein soon after. He said he'd been watching Fox News, and the coverage had been "great."

But Trump wanted Rosenstein to do a press conference to say firing Comey was all his idea.

Rosenstein again refused and told the president that if he gave a press conference, he'd tell the truth: it wasn't his idea.

This apparently prompted a call from Priebus to the Justice Department public affairs office, in which he was "screaming" that Rosenstein had to do a press conference.

Sessions, too, called the White House to warn that Rosenstein was getting upset.

Spicer, who had earlier said he wouldn't be saying anything more about Comey's firing that day, was hurriedly summoned for an interview with Fox Business News. Afterward, he was spotted in bushes near the White House trying to avoid other reporters. Finally he emerged, agreeing to take ten minutes of questions, though only in darkness. "Just turn the lights off. Turn the lights off," he ordered as cameras rolled. "We'll take care of this. Can you just turn that light off?"

Spicer told reporters Trump knew nothing about firing Comey until he received the memo from Rosenstein, along with the letter from Sessions recommending that he be fired.

"It was all him," Spicer said, meaning Rosenstein.

"It was all him?" a reporter asked.

"That's correct," Spicer said. "I mean, I can't, I guess I shouldn't say that, thank you for the help on that one. No one from the White House. That was a DOJ decision."

WHEN MCCABE REACHED the White House that evening for his 6:30 appointment, Trump's bodyguard, Keith Schiller, showed him to the Oval Office. McCabe had been to the West Wing many times for meetings, but he'd never before been in the Oval Office. McGahn, Pence, and Priebus were there, sitting in a row of wooden chairs across from Trump, who was behind his large desk. Trump rose and shook hands with McCabe, who took the remaining seat in the row of chairs.

There was as yet no sign from Trump himself that he was getting "killed" in the media; the president seemed in unusually high spirits and gleeful as he reenacted firing Comey for McCabe's benefit. He had to do it, he said, because of the bad decisions Comey had made in the email investigation and, he added, for many other unspecified reasons.

Was McCabe aware that Comey had told him on three separate occasions that he was not under investigation? Trump asked.

McCabe said yes, he knew Comey had told Trump that.

People at the FBI were "thrilled" he'd fired Comey, Trump asserted. People there "really disliked Jim Comey," they were "really happy" he was gone, and it was a "great thing."

McCabe said that in his experience, most people in the FBI felt positively about Comey.

"I heard you were part of the resistance," Trump continued.

McCabe asked what he meant by that.

"I heard that you were one of the people that did not support Jim Comey. You didn't agree with him and the decisions that he'd made in the Clinton case. And is that true?"

"No, sir," McCabe replied. "That's not true. I worked very closely with Jim Comey. I was a part of that team and a part of those decisions."

McCabe knew he'd just given all the wrong answers.

TEN

SEVEN DAYS IN MAY

I f Trump thought he was getting "killed" on Tuesday night, it was worse by Wednesday morning. Firing Comey had set off a firestorm in the media and in Congress, with renewed calls for the appointment of a special counsel. There was widespread skepticism that the idea to fire Comey had come from Rosenstein and had nothing to do with Russia.

"Why now?" asked the Senate Democratic leader, Chuck Schumer. "If the administration had objections to the way Director Comey handled the Clinton investigation, they had those objections the minute the President got into office. But they didn't fire him then. Why did it happen today?"

"If Deputy Attorney General Rosenstein does not appoint an independent special prosecutor, every American will rightly suspect that the decision to fire Director Comey was part of a cover-up," Schumer said.

Members of both committees investigating ties between Russia and the Trump campaign expressed concerns. "The decision by a President whose campaign associates are under investigation by the FBI for collusion with Russia to fire the man overseeing that investigation, upon the recommendation of an Attorney General who has recused himself from that investigation, raises profound questions about whether the White House is brazenly interfering in a criminal matter," said Representative Adam Schiff, the ranking Democrat on the House Intelligence Committee. Even a Republican, Richard Burr, head of the Senate Intelligence

Committee, said he was "troubled by the timing and reasoning of Director Comey's termination."

AFTER BEING INTERRUPTED the night before by his summons to the White House, McCabe and his top leadership reconvened that morning in McCabe's conference room. While they were discussing the previous day's turn of events, McCabe's secretary interrupted to tell him the president himself was on the line. Surprised, McCabe took the call. Everyone stayed in the room and listened to McCabe's end of the conversation.

Trump proposed a presidential visit to FBI headquarters and invited McCabe to the White House to discuss it. He expected an enthusiastic reception; he told McCabe he'd received "hundreds" of messages of support from FBI personnel since firing Comey.

But simply arranging a visit didn't require a call from the president. Trump quickly shifted the topic to what seemed the real reason: He'd seen Comey on television boarding a government plane for his return to Washington, after he'd been fired. How had that happened?

McCabe said he'd authorized it. He'd discussed the matter with Baker and other FBI lawyers, and no one saw any reason to stop Comey from flying back, given that the plane and its crew had to return anyway.

"That's not right!" Trump exploded. "I never approved that!"

McCabe said he was sorry Trump disagreed with the decision.

"I want you to look into that," Trump persisted. McCabe wondered, what was he supposed to look into? He'd authorized it; there wasn't anything left to investigate.

McCabe's answers only seemed to further enrage the president. He said he wanted Comey banned from FBI headquarters and all FBI property. He didn't want Comey coming in to collect any personal effects.

People listening in the room were stunned that the president would be so petty and vindictive.

Trump's anger at Comey seemingly spent, he asked McCabe about his wife, Jill, the object of so much of Trump's scorn on the campaign trail.

"She's fine," McCabe replied. His wife had taken her loss in stride and had resumed her career as a medical doctor and the task of raising their three children.

"That must have been really rough," Trump said. "To lose. To be a loser."

Everyone in the room saw McCabe's face stiffen.

Trump hung up. Strzok texted Page again: "We need to lock in" the investigation. "In a formal chargeable way. Soon."

McCabe was already of the same mind. After the comments about his wife and the tone of the call, which everyone had heard, it seemed possible—even likely—that McCabe would be fired any moment. He asked Priestap, Strzok, and the Russia team to figure out what needed to be done to "put the Russia case on absolutely solid ground in an indelible fashion that were I removed quickly or reassigned or fired that the case could not be closed or vanish in the night without a trace."

THAT MORNING THE president hosted Sergey Lavrov, the Russian foreign minister, and the ubiquitous Kislyak, the Russian ambassador, in the Oval Office. Trump and Putin had agreed to the meeting during a phone call the week before, and details had been completed that weekend in Bedminster while Trump and Miller were planning Comey's ouster.

That a meeting with Russians the day after he fired the FBI director might be considered ill-timed never seems to have occurred to Trump. He boasted to his Russian guests, "I just fired the head of the FBI. He was crazy, a real nut job," according to a written summary of the meeting that was read to a *New York Times* reporter. He also explicitly linked the decision to the Russia investigation. "I faced great pressure because of Russia. That's taken off."

Trump assured them, "I'm not under investigation."

THUS FAR, the FBI had uncovered no overt acts by Trump linking him to the Russians, the "articulable factual basis," which is grounds for opening a case file. But in firing Comey, Trump had just handed the FBI one.

Until now, Strzok had agreed that opening a case on the president himself was premature. But firing the director, as he told his colleagues, "was a very real tangible event adversely impacting our ability to conduct an investigation."

As Baker later put it, "Not only would it be an issue about obstructing an investigation, but the obstruction itself would hurt our ability to figure out what the Russians had done, and that is what would be the threat to the national security. Our inability or our—the inability or the delays, the difficulties that we might have with respect to trying to figure out what the Russians were doing, because our main objective was to thwart them."

Taken in context—Trump's admiration for Putin, his attempts to protect Flynn, his efforts to co-opt Comey, his disparagement of the investigation as a "witch hunt"—his firing of Comey forced the FBI to contemplate what Baker referred to as an "extreme" and unnerving possibility: that the president of the United States might be "acting at the behest of [Russia] and somehow following directions, somehow executing their will. That was one extreme. The other extreme is that the President is completely innocent, and we discussed that too."

AFTER HIS LATE night before the cameras, Sean Spicer reported for U.S. Navy Reserve duty, so the deputy White House press secretary, Sarah Huckabee Sanders, conducted the packed press briefing that began that day just before 2:00 p.m.

"The President, over the last several months, lost confidence in Director Comey," Sanders said in her opening remarks. "The DOJ lost confidence in Director Comey. Bipartisan members of Congress made it clear that they had lost confidence in Director Comey. And most importantly, the rank and file of the FBI had lost confidence in their director. Accordingly, the President accepted the recommendation of his Deputy Attorney General to remove James Comey from his position."

The NBC White House correspondent Hallie Jackson had the first question: "Yes or no, did the President direct Rod Rosenstein to write this memo on James Comey?"

"No," Sanders answered. The president had "lost confidence in Director Comey, and, frankly, he'd been considering letting Director Comey go since the day he was elected. But he did have a conversation with the Deputy Attorney General on Monday, where they had come to him to express their concerns. The President asked they put those concerns and their recommendation in writing, which is the letter that you guys have received."

"So it's the White House's assertion that Rod Rosenstein decided on his own, after being confirmed, to review Comey's performance?" Jackson continued.

"Absolutely."

ABC's Jonathan Karl pressed Sanders on the point: "Sarah, isn't it true that the President had already decided to fire James Comey, and he asked the Justice Department to put together the rationale for that firing?"

"No."

"When did he make the decision?"

"He made the decision for—the final decision to move forward with it was yesterday. But I know that he's been contemplating it for a while." She added, "I did speak directly to the President and heard directly from him that he, again, had been considering letting Director Comey go pretty much since the day he took office, but that there was no request by him to have a review at the Department of Justice."

"But was the reason for the firing what was written by the Deputy Attorney General? Is that why he did it?" Karl asked again.

"That was, I think, the final piece that moved the President to make that quick and decisive action yesterday," Sanders said.

"What did he mean in the letter that he wrote informing Comey that he was being fired—he said, on three separate occasions Comey had told him that 'I am not under investigation.' What were those three occasions that the FBI Director told the President that he wasn't under investigation?"

"I'm not going to get into the specifics of their conversations, but I can tell you that Director Comey relayed that information to the President."

Charlie Spiering of *Breitbart News* asked if Trump wanted to "shut down what he's called a 'taxpayer-funded charade' investigation."

"He wants them to continue with whatever they see appropriate and sees fit, just the same as he's encouraged the House and Senate committees to continue any ongoing investigations," Sanders replied, trying to head off any intimation of obstruction. "Look, the bottom line is any investigation that was happening on Monday is still happening today," she said. "That hasn't changed. And, in fact, we encourage them to complete this investigation so we can put it behind us and we can continue to see exactly what we've been saying for nearly a year, there's no evidence of collusion between the Trump campaign and Russia. And we'd love for that to be completed so that we can all move on and focus on the things that, frankly, I think most of Americans are concerned with."

"What gives you such confidence that the rank and file within the Bureau lost faith in the FBI Director?" another reporter asked, and then quoted from a letter by an FBI agent: "The vast majority of the Bureau is in favor of Director Comey. This is a total shock. This is not supposed to happen. The real losers here are 20,000 front-line people in the organization because they lost the only guy working here in the past 15 years who actually cared about them."

"We've heard from countless members of the FBI that say very different things," Sanders replied, echoing what the president had been repeating. "In fact, the President will be meeting with Acting Director McCabe later today to discuss that very thing—the morale at the FBI—as well as make an offer to go directly to the FBI if he feels that that's necessary and appropriate."

Sanders spoke to Trump after the press conference, and he told her what a good job she'd done—notwithstanding that what she'd said bore almost no resemblance to reality.

MCCABE WAS, at that very moment, at the White House for his meeting to discuss Trump's visit. Schiller again showed him to the Oval Office.

Trump was behind his desk, and the wooden chairs were in the same place as the night before. McCabe took a seat next to Priebus and McGahn.

Trump couldn't stop talking about what a great decision it was to fire Comey and how happy it had made people at the FBI. So many people "hated" the man, Trump asserted. Trump said he was pleased to see so many people applauding his decision on TV, evidently referring to Comey's critics on Fox News. Had McCabe seen that?

No, he hadn't, McCabe said. What he didn't say was that what he'd seen was the opposite: people at the FBI were dejected.

"We've had so many FBI people calling us, sending us messages to say they're so glad the director is gone," Trump said.

McCabe wondered who at the FBI would be calling the White House. Everyone there knew such direct contact was inappropriate, especially given recent events.

"Well, sir, I don't know. I guess it's possible," McCabe equivocated. "But most people seem shocked and surprised by what happened. They will rebound. We will move on. Right now people are just trying to figure things out."

That wasn't what the president wanted to hear. He asked again, were people glad he was gone?

"Some people were frustrated with last summer's outcome on the Clinton case," McCabe acknowledged. "It's possible that some of these people are glad. Other than that, I've seen no evidence that people are happy about the director being fired."

"You know, your only problem is your wife," Trump said, again bringing up Jill's unsuccessful campaign.

"She's a bright and independent woman and I've always supported her," McCabe replied.

Evidently frustrated by McCabe's responses, Trump turned to the stated purpose of the meeting, which was his proposed triumphal visit to FBI headquarters. McCabe thought it a terrible idea, even a potential disaster. It was astonishing that Trump would suggest such a thing when so many questions were being raised about the independence of the bureau and Trump's attempts to exert undue influence over it. And then there was the reality of how people felt about Comey's firing, as opposed to the delusion that Trump seems to have embraced. Trump might even be booed.

But what could McCabe say? "It's always a good idea to visit your people at the FBI," McCabe said.

"Do you think it would be a good idea for me to come down now?" Trump asked.

"Come whenever you want," McCabe said halfheartedly.

Trump turned to McGahn. "Don, what do you think? Do you think I should go down to the FBI and speak to the people?"

"If the acting director of the FBI is telling you he thinks it's a good idea for you to come visit the FBI, then you should do it," McGahn said, deftly putting the onus back on McCabe.

Trump turned back to McCabe. "Is that what you're telling me?"

The question hung in the air. Trump and McGahn stared at him. McCabe realized that he was being maneuvered into "inviting" Trump to speak at the FBI, which was no doubt how it would be portrayed. But to say no probably meant he, too, would be fired. That put too much at risk. Losing his job over a visit from Trump wasn't worth it.

A visit would be fine, McCabe said.

"FBI people love me," the president continued. "At least 80 percent voted for me. Who did you vote for?"

No one in a position of authority had ever asked McCabe that question. He was completely unprepared. As the silence lengthened, he stammered something along the lines of "I played it down the middle," which even he knew was a nonanswer.

Trump gave him an odd, sideways look. McCabe had told him all he needed to know.

The discussion turned to the logistics of the visit: Trump would come that Friday, May 12; McCabe told him the Hoover Building's spacious open courtyard would accommodate the largest crowd. "Make sure that courtyard is full," Trump said.

THE NEXT MORNING, McCabe, Baker, and Lisa Page arrived on Capitol Hill for a previously scheduled worldwide threats briefing—McCabe's first appearance in Congress as acting director, and his first ever in a public hearing. Comey was supposed to have done that, and McCabe had considered backing out. But he wanted to send a message that the FBI was functioning smoothly despite the upheaval.

He knew he'd be asked about Comey's firing, which would thrust him into the awkward position of either dissembling to support the White House narrative or being direct, which would contradict it. He'd practiced answering the question the night before and that morning with Page. "You've got to defend us," she pleaded. "You have to defend him."

McCabe wasn't prepared for the media circus that awaited him as he, Baker, and Page got out of the car. McCabe was suddenly the object of intense curiosity. Reporters shouted questions at him as he tried to maneuver through the crowd to the hearing room. Senator Dianne Feinstein could barely get through the crowd. "Finally, a gentleman," she said when Baker stepped aside so she could pass.

When they got into the room, McCabe took his seat at the table with Coats and Pompeo. They faced what seemed a wall of photographers stationed just feet away as camera flashes popped. McCabe was dazed. No one had prepared him for this.

Martin Heinrich, Democrat of New Mexico, was the first to bring up Comey's firing. "We've heard in the news claims that Director Comey had lost the confidence of rank and file FBI employees. You've been there for 21 years. In your opinion, is it accurate that the rank and file no longer supported Director Comey?"

It was exactly the question McCabe had been rehearsing with Page. He decided to be direct, even at the risk of further offending the president.

"No, sir, that is not accurate," he said. "I can tell you, sir, that I worked very, very closely with Director Comey from the moment he started at the FBI. I was his Executive Assistant Director of National Security at that time; then worked for him running the Washington Field Office; and of course I've served as Deputy for the last year. I can tell you that I hold Director Comey in the absolute highest regard. I have the highest respect for his considerable abilities and his integrity, and it has been the greatest privilege and honor of my professional life to work with him."

He continued, "I can tell you also that Director Comey enjoyed broad support within the FBI and still does to this day. We are a large organization. We are 36,500 people across this country, across this globe. We have a diversity of opinions about many things. But I can confidently tell you that the majority, the vast majority, of FBI employees enjoyed a deep and positive connection to Director Comey."

Later in the hearing, Senator Marco Rubio, the Florida Republican, asked if "the dismissal of Mr. Comey in any way impeded, interrupted, stopped, or negatively impacted any of the work, any investigation, or any ongoing projects at the Federal Bureau of Investigation."

"As you know, Senator, the work of the men and women of the FBI continues despite any changes in circumstance, any decisions," McCabe assured him. "So there has been no effort to impede our investigation to date. Quite simply put, sir, you cannot stop the men and women of the FBI from doing the right thing, protecting the American people and upholding the Constitution."

AFTERWARD, Sanders doubled down on her earlier claim, now suggesting that she herself had spoken to FBI employees: "I have heard from countless members of the FBI that are grateful on the president's decision, and we may have to agree to disagree."*

Sanders later told lawyers for Mueller that her reference to "countless members of the FBI" was a "slip of the tongue" and her assertion that rank-and-file FBI agents had lost confidence in Comey was a comment she made "in the heat of the moment" that was "not founded on anything."

---

* An enduring mystery is the identity of any of the "countless" FBI employees whom the White House "heard from," in Sanders's account, or who contacted Trump to communicate how happy they were that Comey had been fired, as Trump repeatedly claimed, or even whether such employees exist.

But it's implausible that Sanders would have experienced multiple such slips of the tongue. It seems more likely that she heard the claims from Trump, given how closely her remarks mirrored his. Some at the FBI have speculated that Trump was repeating hearsay from Giuliani, who was in regular contact with disgruntled former agents, but the claim had no factual basis.

But McCabe had come through his first public trial by fire. Baker was impressed by how McCabe rose to the occasion, and Page was proud of him for defending the bureau and telling the truth about morale.

McCabe had always been the consummate anonymous Washington insider. He'd spent over twenty years in the capital cultivating anonymity. No one recognized him. That night he and his wife had dinner at Fiola, an Italian restaurant close to FBI headquarters. When he got up after paying the check, everyone in the restaurant gave him a standing ovation.

SANDERS'S ONGOING STATEMENTS pinning the Comey firing on Rosenstein had prompted another wave of press calls to the Justice Department, where Sessions and Rosenstein remained conspicuously silent. But her repeated insistence that it was Rosenstein, not Trump, who initiated Comey's firing was deeply troubling to both. Both knew it was untrue. More worrisome, it put Rosenstein in legal jeopardy: if this was all his idea, then he might be accused of obstructing the Russia investigation.

Both Sessions and Rosenstein complained repeatedly to McGahn and others on his staff that the White House was disseminating a false narrative. There's no indication that Sessions or Rosenstein threatened to go public with what had really happened, but they wouldn't have needed to; their objections would have been enough to suggest the possibility.

McGahn and his staff also knew that Trump's version wasn't true; they'd seen the letter Miller had drafted laying out the real reasons. Finally McGahn agreed that the story the White House was pushing—that the Justice Department had initiated Comey's firing—was "factually wrong" and asked his staff to work with the communications staff to correct the record.

But Trump took matters into his own hands. He told McGahn's staff that his communications team "could not get the story right," so he was "going on Lester Holt" to say what really happened, referring to the *NBC Nightly News* anchor. "Never forget, no one speaks for me but me," Trump said just before the interview. The communications people "don't know what they're talking about. But I do, believe me," Trump said.

At the White House, Holt and Trump sat in chairs facing each other in front of French doors flanked by flags. Trump immediately blasted Comey as "a showboat, he's a grandstander, the FBI has been in turmoil. You know that, I know that. Everybody knows that. You take a look at the FBI a year ago, it was in virtual turmoil, less than a year ago, it hasn't recovered from that."

Trump did, in an important sense, correct the record that he had largely created, saying Rosenstein's recommendation was irrelevant, and the reason he fired Comey was Russia—not his handling of the Clinton investigation. "Oh I was gonna fire [Comey] regardless of recommendation," Trump said. Rosenstein "made a recommendation but regardless of recommendation I was going to fire Comey knowing, there was no good time to do it. And in fact when I decided to just do it, I said to myself, I said, you know, this Russia thing with Trump and Russia is a made-up story, it's an excuse by the Democrats for having lost an election that they should have won." He repeated, "This was an excuse for having lost an election."

"Okay, are you angry with, angry with Mr. Comey because of his Russia investigation?" Holt asked.

"I just want somebody that's competent. I am a big fan of the FBI, I love the FBI."

Trump said he knew firing Comey wouldn't end the Russia investigation. "Look, let me tell you. As far as I'm concerned, I want that thing to be absolutely done properly. When I did this now I said, I probably, maybe will confuse people, maybe I'll expand that, you know, lengthen the time because it should be over with, in my opinion, should have been over with a long time ago. Because all it is, is an excuse, but I said to myself, I might even lengthen out the investigation but I have to do the right thing for the American people. He's the wrong man for that position."

Holt asked why Trump mentioned in his letter that Comey told him three times he wasn't under investigation.

"Because he told me that," Trump said. "I had a dinner with him. He wanted to have dinner because he wanted to stay on. We had a very nice dinner at the White House."

"He asked for the dinner?"

"A dinner was arranged, I think he asked for the dinner. And he wanted to stay on as the FBI head. And I said I'll, you know, consider and we'll see what happens. But we had a very nice dinner. And at that time he told me you are not under investigation. Which I knew anyway.

"Then during a phone call he said it. And then during another phone call he said it. So he said it once at dinner and then he said it twice during phone calls."

And did you ask, "Am I under investigation?"

"I actually asked him, yes. I said, 'If it's possible would you let me know am I under investigation?' He said, 'You are not under investigation.'"

"Did you ask him to drop the investigation?"

"No. Never."

Trump had now confirmed what many had suspected: that Rosenstein's memo was a pretext and Trump had fired Comey because of Russia. Any lingering doubts about whether to open a case against Trump vanished. For why would the president have gone to such lengths to conceal his real motive, unless he knew what he had done was wrong?

TRUMP MIGHT HAVE thought he'd dispatched Comey and thereby rid himself of the Russia investigation, but Comey himself had other ideas. Once he was fired, it was obvious that the Justice Department needed to appoint a special counsel to oversee the Russia investigation. A special counsel would remove it from direct political influence and keep it one step further from the White House. But after the events of that week, starting with his betrayal by Sessions and Rosenstein, Comey no longer trusted the Justice Department's leadership to do the right thing. As Comey later put it, "Something was needed that might force them to do the right thing"—like a news article suggesting Trump's real intent in firing Comey.

Two of Comey's closest confidants—Columbia law professor Daniel Richman and his friend Ben Wittes—furious at how Trump was spinning Comey's firing, asked if Comey "would try to stop us" if they talked to the press.

Still exhausted by recent events, Comey said he didn't care. "Do what you think is right," he said.

The result was an explosive article in *The New York Times* on May 11. Relying on two "associates" of Comey's as sources, the *Times* reporter Michael Schmidt described in considerable detail and accuracy Comey's dinner with Trump on January 27:

> The conversation that night in January, Mr. Comey now believes, was a harbinger of his downfall this week as head of the FBI, according to two people who have heard his account of the dinner.
>
> As they ate, the president and Mr. Comey made small talk about the election and the crowd sizes at Mr. Trump's rallies. The president then turned the conversation to whether Mr. Comey would pledge his loyalty to him.
>
> Mr. Comey declined to make that pledge. Instead, Mr. Comey has recounted to others, he told Mr. Trump that he would always be honest with him, but that he was not "reliable" in the conventional political sense.

As Comey had hoped, the article triggered a new wave of calls for a special counsel. The attorneys general of nineteen states and the District of Columbia sent a much-publicized letter to Rosenstein: "As the chief law enforcement officers of our respective states, we view the President's firing of FBI Director James Comey in the middle of his investigation of

Russian interference in the presidential election as a violation of the public trust. As prosecutors committed to the rule of law, we urge you to consider the damage to our democratic system of any attempts by the administration to derail and delegitimize the investigation."

The *Times* account drew vehement denials from the White House. "We don't believe this to be an accurate account," Sanders told the *Times*. "The integrity of our law enforcement agencies and their leadership is of the utmost importance to President Trump. He would never even suggest the expectation of personal loyalty, only loyalty to our country and its great people."

In a Fox News interview with Jeanine Pirro, Trump himself flatly denied asking Comey for loyalty: "No. No, I didn't. But I don't think it would be a bad question to ask." He denied it to Spicer, too, but added, "Who cares?"

TRUMP ALSO RESPONDED with a barrage of tweets. "Russia must be laughing up their sleeves watching as the U.S. tears itself apart over a Democrat EXCUSE for losing the election," he tweeted late on May 11. Early the next morning, he followed up with "Again, the story that there was collusion between the Russians & Trump campaign was fabricated by Dems as an excuse for losing the election"; and then "When James Clapper himself, and virtually everyone else with knowledge of the witch hunt, says there is no collusion, when does it end?"*

But he saved his most provocative tweet for James Comey: "James Comey better hope that there are no 'tapes' of our conversations before he starts leaking to the press!"—an apparent reference to the *Times* story and the conflicting accounts of what was said at the dinner.

The tweet set off a frenzy of speculation: Had Trump secretly taped his former FBI director? Trump and the White House coyly refused to say.

---

* James Clapper, the former director of national intelligence, had testified on May 8 that he wasn't aware of any evidence of collusion during his tenure, not that it didn't exist.

IN THIS HIGHLY charged environment, the former attorney general William Barr weighed in to defend Trump's ouster of Comey and lend his support to Rosenstein's reasoning. Writing in *The Washington Post*, Barr ignored his earlier praise for Comey's decision in the same newspaper. He now argued that Comey's "basic misjudgment" about how to handle the Clinton investigation "boxed him in, compelling him to take increasingly controversial actions giving the impression that the FBI was enmeshed in politics."

"Once Comey staked out a position in July," Barr continued, "he had no choice on the near-eve of the election but to reopen the investigation when new evidence materialized. Regrettably, however, this performance made Comey himself the issue, placing him on center stage in public political discourse and causing him to lose credibility on both sides of the aisle. It was widely recognized that Comey's job was in jeopardy regardless of who won the election."

And "no matter how far along the president was in his own thinking, Rosenstein's assessment is cogent and vindicates the president's decision."

ON FRIDAY MORNING McCabe had his first meeting with Rosenstein in his new capacity as acting director. It was a routine discussion with staff members present, but afterward McCabe asked to speak to Rosenstein alone.

When the others left, they stayed in their seats on opposite sides of the conference table. McCabe told Rosenstein he needed to help him coordinate requests to interview witnesses in the Russia investigation now that multiple congressional committees were pursuing the issue. Typically, the FBI needed to have the first—and in some cases the only—access to key witnesses to protect the investigation. "I need your help on this," McCabe said.

Rosenstein said fine, no problem, but he didn't seem to be really concentrating.

His gaze shifted toward the closed door to the room, somewhere off in the distance. His eyes looked glassy. His voice wavering, his eyes teared up. He said he couldn't believe what was happening. The White House was trying to make it look as if it were his idea to fire Comey. That wasn't true. The president had asked him to write the memo only after announcing that he was firing Comey. Rosenstein was obviously struggling to keep his emotions in check.

McCabe was shocked Rosenstein was confiding in him, essentially calling the president a liar; they barely knew each other. But he wanted to be compassionate.

"Are you okay?" McCabe asked.

"No."

"Are you getting any sleep?"

"No."

"Is your family okay?"

Rosenstein said there were news trucks parked outside his house. His wife and family were upset.

There was a pause; then Rosenstein said, "There's no one here I can talk to about this. There's no one I can trust." Rosenstein seemed again to be struggling to hold his emotions in check.

After a pause, he asked if McCabe thought he should appoint a special counsel, and McCabe said yes, it would be a good idea. Rosenstein said he'd always considered Jim Comey a friend and mentor, someone he looked up to. "The one person I wish I could talk to is Jim Comey."

"Good luck with that," McCabe thought, but said nothing. He was startled by the idea that Rosenstein wanted to seek guidance from Comey, whom he had just helped fire.

McCabe left the meeting in a state of shock.

AS SOON AS he reached his office, McCabe confided in Page that Rosenstein seemed in a fragile emotional state and had said he wanted to talk to Comey. Page was equally astonished. In her view, Rosenstein had just betrayed Comey and helped fire him, and now wanted to confide in him?

Surely Rosenstein wasn't so naive that when asked to write his memo, he had no idea to what use it would be put. McCabe and Page had fervently hoped that Rosenstein would stand up to Sessions and the White House and defend the FBI. But now "we really are alone," she said.

McCabe agreed. Still, he felt he owed Rosenstein more thoughtful comments on the question of a special counsel. Everyone in the Obama administration had been dead set against naming one in the Clinton email case. The ill-fated consequences of that decision were now clear. Had Clinton been cleared by a special counsel, there would have been no need for Comey to make any announcement, and the FBI could have stayed out of politics, its integrity and reputation intact.

McCabe made an appointment to see Rosenstein again that afternoon at 4:00.

IN THE MIDST of this fraught and hectic environment, that afternoon the FBI's inspection division sent McCabe an email following up on his May 9 interview about media leaks, which had now shifted almost entirely to the *Wall Street Journal* article. The email included a sworn statement summarizing McCabe's earlier statements—"My assessment of the referenced portion of the article is that it is basically an accurate depiction of an actual telephonic interaction I had with a Department of Justice (DOJ) executive. I do not know the identity of the source of the information contained in the article," and "I gave no one authority to share any information relative to my interaction with the DOJ executive with any member of the media"—and asked him to review and sign it.

McCabe didn't respond, and the email disappeared into a queue of unanswered messages from that day.

As scheduled, McCabe and Rosenstein met in the deputy attorney general's elegant private office at 4:00 p.m. McCabe sat on the sofa, Rosenstein in an armchair facing him.

McCabe pushed strenuously for a special counsel: "You have to do this." He added, "The Attorney General has recused himself. It's a mess. We need someone independent to oversee this." Without a special counsel, the FBI and the Justice Department would face intense criticism going forward that could destroy their credibility.

Rosenstein didn't disagree, but he knew how strongly the White House opposed the idea. He worried it would cost him his job, and he wanted to stay on to help choose a new FBI director. Clearly still preoccupied by his memo, Rosenstein said again that it wasn't his idea; the president had already decided to fire Comey. In fact, based on conversations he'd had with Sessions, Rosenstein said he'd known since January that Trump would fire Comey. (January, of course, was when Comey told Trump about the Steele dossier and the "golden showers thing.")

The meeting ended with no resolution of the special counsel issue. Rosenstein didn't seem to feel any sense of urgency.

THE NEXT DAY, which was a Saturday, Sessions and Rosenstein interviewed McCabe at the Justice Department to be the permanent FBI director. Trump would be making the decision, of course, but they'd be screening candidates and passing their observations on to the White House. Rosenstein acted as though nothing had happened the day before.

McCabe assumed the interview was little more than a pretense, given Trump's hostile comments about him and his wife, not to mention his already tenuous relationship with the president. Sessions and Rosenstein seemed cordial, but McCabe's apprehensions were soon confirmed: Sessions showed McCabe an iPhone screenshot of McCabe and his family wearing the "Dr. Jill McCabe for State Senate" T-shirts.

McCabe found himself explaining that they were at a swim meet; the T-shirts had just arrived; they'd put them on so a family friend could take a photo; the shot had gotten on Facebook. In any event, it was taken before McCabe had anything to do with the Clinton case. As McCabe spoke, he knew he was wasting his breath. Sessions looked unconvinced. "Of all the important issues facing the FBI, here we are talking about T-shirts," McCabe thought.

"Honestly, if I could be so bold," McCabe finally said, "I think you should look hard and well to find the best candidate from outside the

FBI," effectively withdrawing from consideration. He pledged to do everything he could to get a new director up to speed as quickly as possible. He thought they should know that he would be eligible for retirement with a pension in March 2018, less than a year away. He planned to retire then and move into the private sector.

ON SUNDAY MORNING Rosenstein called McCabe using his cell phone, and indicated that he was grappling with the issue of a special counsel. "Have you had a chance to talk to that guy I mentioned?"—a clear reference to Comey. He'd be interested to hear his thoughts on whether he should appoint one. McCabe said he'd get back to him.

McCabe held a conference call that afternoon with Baker, Page, and others to discuss the possibility of bringing in Comey but quickly decided against the idea. Comey was now a private citizen; he shouldn't be privy to sensitive internal deliberations. More fundamentally, he was right in the middle of the issue: his termination was the prime reason for appointing a special counsel. McCabe conveyed the decision to Rosenstein, who never brought it up again.

On Monday morning, May 15, McCabe convened a small group involved in the Russia investigation—Baker, Priestap, Page, and Strzok—to address the momentous issue of opening a formal investigation of the president.

Strzok had earlier resisted such efforts, but lying about Trump's reasons for firing Comey had put him over the edge. As he'd texted Page, "We need to open this."

After all, no one at the FBI knew what was coming next. They'd already experienced an unprecedented barrage of attacks from the White House. In his brief tenure, Rosenstein had inspired no confidence that he'd protect them or the integrity of the Russia probe. Either he'd told Trump to fire Comey, in Trump's first version, or he'd been complicit in it by writing the memo. If Trump wanted him to, he might well shut down the investigation.

And Comey's firing was the culmination of a series of events that had created a "corrosive and threatening environment," as Strzok told his colleagues. "We can't leave this alone," he argued.

As McCabe later said, "There were a number of things that caused us to believe that we had adequate predication or adequate reason and facts, to open the investigation. The president had been speaking in a derogatory way about our investigative efforts for weeks, describing it as a witch hunt, publicly undermining the effort of the investigation. The president had gone to Jim Comey and specifically asked him to discontinue the investigation of Mike Flynn which was a part of our Russia case. The president, then, fired the director. In the firing of the director, the president specifically asked Rod Rosenstein to write the memo justifying the firing and told Rod to include Russia in the memo. Rod, of course, did not do that. That was on the president's mind. Then, the president made those public comments that you've referenced both on NBC and to the Russians which was captured in the Oval Office. Put together, these circumstances were articulable facts that indicated that a crime may have been committed. The president may have been engaged in obstruction of justice in the firing of Jim Comey."

And they discussed another sensitive potential case: Sessions. McCabe had received multiple letters from Senators Franken and Leahy that Sessions had lied in his testimony that he'd had no contact with Russians. Comey and McCabe had brought the issue to Dana Boente and then to Rosenstein; both Justice Department officials had urged them to hold off. But the Comey firing had lent new urgency to the task before Trump could do anything more to impede it.

The decision was unanimous to open formal investigations of both the president and Sessions.

ON TUESDAY, MAY 16, McCabe met with Rosenstein at 12:30 p.m. to brief him on the FBI's decision and the need for McCabe to brief the Gang of Eight in Congress. Given the gravity of the allegations, McCabe wanted both the legislative and the executive branches of government to be fully informed, so no one could credibly call the investigations a rogue operation or "witch hunt."

Legislators would no doubt press Rosenstein about naming a special counsel, and McCabe thought he needed to be ready to answer— preferably by saying he would. Rosenstein's chief of staff, James Crowell IV, was also at the meeting, and he agreed.

If anything, Rosenstein looked even worse than he had the previous Friday. He obviously hadn't slept much. He launched into another account of his trip to the White House and Trump's request for his memo, this time in greater detail. McCabe heard for the first time about the long, rambling letter Trump had dictated to Miller terminating Comey. Rosenstein's memo was just a pretense. Worst of all, Rosenstein maintained, was being pressured to hold a press conference the night Comey was fired.

As he talked, Rosenstein grew more animated, flailing his hands and arms. At times he got up and walked around the table. At one point he was so upset he went into an adjoining bathroom to compose himself. Everyone in the room listened—and watched—in anxious silence.

At some point in his increasingly disjointed monologue, Rosenstein brought up the Twenty-fifth Amendment (providing for the removal of the president if he "is unable to discharge the powers and duties of his office") and said he thought at least two cabinet-level officers were willing to support such a move—Sessions and Director of Homeland Security John Kelly.

McCabe was startled and wondered if any such effort was really under way or existed only in Rosenstein's feverish speculation. But the FBI played no role in invoking the Twenty-fifth Amendment, so McCabe let it go.

"I wonder what Trump really intended when he fired the Director," Rosenstein mused.

McCabe said he wondered the same thing.

"How would we know or collect evidence?" Rosenstein pondered his question. Then he said, "I never get searched, no one ever searches me" at the White House, he said.

McCabe thought that was odd. He didn't get searched either. No one with a security clearance did.

"I could record the President," Rosenstein said. "I could wear a recording device. They wouldn't know it was there."

What? McCabe was startled. His mind raced. Was Rosenstein serious? It seemed so. "Oh my God; time out; let's think about this," McCabe thought to himself.

"Uh, let me go back and talk to the team," McCabe said. "I'll come back to you."

"YOU'RE NOT GOING to believe this," McCabe told Page and Baker as soon as he got back. When he told Baker about Rosenstein's offer to wear a wire and record the president, Baker threw his hands up and looked at the ceiling. McCabe thought Baker was going to "have a heart attack," he said later.

After he collected himself, Baker said, "That's a bridge too far. We're not there yet."*

Rosenstein called McCabe later that afternoon and asked him to return at 7:00 p.m. to continue their discussion. This time McCabe brought Page, who took detailed notes and, if needed, could also serve as a witness to some of Rosenstein's far-fetched proposals. Rosenstein was surrounded by a larger entourage this time.

Rosenstein immediately launched into another recounting of his visit to the White House. Even though the president had already decided to fire Comey, "they acted like they cared about my opinion," he said with a hint of bitterness. And Trump had told him to "put Russia in the memo."

Then Rosenstein mentioned McCabe's "political problem," meaning his wife, and said that Comey's defense of McCabe was one of the reasons Trump had fired him. Rosenstein brought up the T-shirts, yet again, and accused McCabe of engaging in prohibited political activity.

---

* In later testimony, Baker described McCabe as "sort of stunned, surprised, didn't know how to really react" to the suggestion that Rosenstein wear a wire. There was no doubt in McCabe's mind that Rosenstein was serious.

Rosenstein seemed even more disjointed than the day before; McCabe thought he was at the end of his rope. He hopped from topic to topic. One moment he proposed candidates for special counsel. The next, FBI director. He mentioned Bob Mueller and John Kelly; for which job was unclear.

At one point he said the president wanted Kelly to run both Homeland Security and the FBI. "You've got to be kidding," McCabe said.

It's the president's "strategy for disruption," Rosenstein said.

At one point Rosenstein took a call from McGahn, inviting McCabe to the White House for an interview with Trump to be FBI director. Evidently, McCabe was a finalist, notwithstanding the White House hostility Rosenstein had just mentioned.

And—"as I've already told Andy"—Rosenstein volunteered to wear a wire to secretly record the president.

Rosenstein brandished a copy of the Trump-Miller letter he'd mentioned the day before. He handed it to McCabe. McCabe read it with mounting incredulity: here was documentary proof that Trump had lied about his reasons for firing Comey.

McCabe took the copy back to his office, put it in a sealed envelope, and placed it in his office safe.

ELEVEN

"THIS IS THE END OF MY PRESIDENCY"

On May 16, 2017, Comey woke abruptly at 2:00 a.m. with a sudden realization: if Trump really had tapes of their conversations, then independent proof existed that the president had not only asked for his loyalty but asked him to drop the Flynn investigation, too, both of which Trump had denied. Comey had assumed it would be his word against Trump's, which is one reason he'd written the memos and put them in secure locations.

For the past week, Comey had been trying to get Trump out of his head. But Trump kept taunting him by tweeting. If those tapes really existed, someone had to get them. Comey couldn't count on Rosenstein to make the demand. But a special counsel would, Comey reasoned. And if people knew about his memos, there would be more pressure to appoint a special counsel. Comey lay awake the rest of the night mapping out a strategy.

Later that morning, Comey contacted his friend and media go-between Daniel Richman, the Columbia law professor. He said he was emailing him a memo that he urgently "needed to get out." Richman said he'd do it. He already knew the drill: he'd again contact Michael Schmidt at the *Times*.

Comey could, of course, simply have gone himself to Schmidt, or countless other reporters. It wasn't because he was "leaking" and needed the protection of anonymity; there was no classified information in his memos. As a private citizen, he was free to describe a conversation with the president. But if Comey were the named source, he'd have the media camped at his driveway. As he later put it, it would be "like feeding seagulls at the beach."

Soon after, Richman sent Comey a one-word text: "Done."

That same day Schmidt had a sensational scoop: "President Trump asked the FBI director, James B. Comey, to shut down the federal investigation into Mr. Trump's former national security adviser, Michael T. Flynn, in an Oval Office meeting in February, according to a memo Mr. Comey wrote shortly after the meeting."

While the story said the *Times* didn't have a copy of the memo, "one of Mr. Comey's associates read parts of it to a Times reporter."

"I hope you can see your way clear to letting this go, to letting Flynn go," Trump told Comey, according to the memo. "He is a good guy. I hope you can let this go."

AS THE FUROR from the *Times* story raged, McCabe showed up that afternoon for his job interview at the White House. As he sat outside the Oval Office, he could hear Trump, Priebus, Spicer, and other staff members yelling over the sound of the television, where commentators were talking about nothing except the Comey memo. "Who leaked this? How did this get out?" McCabe overheard someone say.

The communications director, Hope Hicks, was sitting at a desk nearby. Should McCabe be hearing this? He offered to move. "No, no, you're fine right there," she said.

Hicks interrupted Trump to say the Iowa senator Charles Grassley was calling. An ardent Trump supporter, Grassley was one of McCabe's fiercest critics in Congress. He'd seized on the campaign contributions issue to send a barrage of letters to the Justice Department complaining about McCabe.

Finally the group filed out, and McCabe went in. Trump was behind his desk as usual, and Priebus, Sessions, and McGahn had stayed behind. There was no sign of Rosenstein.

"I was just talking to Senator Grassley," Trump said. "Boy, he's no fan of yours."

"I'm aware of that," McCabe said, and mentioned, in what he thought was a lighthearted tone, the fourteen letters Grassley had sent to the Justice Department complaining about him.

McCabe's irony was lost on the president. Trump launched into a long and detailed account of his electoral triumph in North Carolina. (Why, McCabe had no idea.) He returned to the theme that people in the FBI loved him: "Ninety percent love me." (It had been 80 percent the last time.)

That gave McCabe an opening for something he'd wanted to say. He reminded Trump that he'd asked him whom he voted for, and "I didn't give you a straight answer." Trump indicated he should go on, and McCabe said, "I did not vote in the 2016 election. I have considered myself a Republican my whole life, and I have always voted for the Republican candidate for president, except in 2016." Because of the ongoing investigations during the campaign, "I thought it would be inappropriate for me to cast a vote," he explained.

Priebus and McGahn said nothing. The president narrowed his eyes, squinting, gazing at McCabe.

"So, we're looking for a new director now, and here you are," Trump finally said. "Isn't that great? This is terrific for you. How do you feel about that?"

McCabe said he was honored and happy to be considered. He loved the FBI, and being director would be the ultimate way to serve. He mentioned Louis Freeh, the only former FBI agent to have served as director.

"Well, it's great," Trump went on. "I don't know if you're going to get it, but if you don't, you'll just go back to being a happy FBI guy, right?"

Trump rattled off the names of other people he was interviewing for the job. Then he ended the interview without having asked a question about how McCabe would run the bureau or what he perceived to be its biggest challenges. "This has been great," Trump said dismissively. "And who knows? You might get it."

One name Trump didn't mention was Robert Mueller, although Mueller, too, was at the White House that day to meet with the president and McGahn. Mueller was there to "offer a perspective on the institution of the FBI," Bannon recalled, and the White House had even thought of "beseeching" Mueller to return to head the FBI. But Mueller hadn't shown any interest in his old job, and "he did not come in looking for the job," Bannon said.

MCCABE WENT STRAIGHT from his White House interview to Capitol Hill, stopping en route to pick up Page and Baker. Rosenstein and his entourage came in their own SUV. Rosenstein called McGahn from the vehicle to break the news he was appointing a special counsel. He knew it was the last thing Trump wanted, but he told McGahn the White House should welcome the news.

While McCabe and Rosenstein were waiting in a room in the basement of the Capitol, the House Intelligence Committee chair, Devin Nunes, came in, even though he'd recused himself from the Russia investigation in April amid allegations he'd leaked classified information to the White House. "He's not supposed to be here," McCabe said, and Rosenstein went over to talk to him. When he returned, Rosenstein said Nunes had insisted he was staying. "I can't force him to leave," Rosenstein said. So much for the confidentiality of what was supposed to be a top secret proceeding, McCabe thought.

The remaining members of the Gang of Eight filed in with their staff members. McCabe and Rosenstein sat at the head of a long table. Chuck Schumer and the Democrats sat on one side of the table to their left (Nancy Pelosi didn't attend but sent a staff member); Mitch McConnell, Paul Ryan, and the Republicans faced them across the table. McCabe had an outline in front of him. He'd already gone over what he'd say with Rosenstein.

McCabe summarized Operation Crossfire Hurricane, reminding them of what Comey had already briefed them on, including the original four subjects, Carter Page, Papadopoulos, Flynn, and Manafort. No one had any questions or comments.

Then McCabe said the FBI had added two case files to Crossfire Hurricane, both counterintelligence investigations. One was President Trump. The other was Attorney General Sessions.

No one said anything. Some Democrats shook their heads; the Republicans cast their gaze downward at the table.

McCabe went on, explaining the predicate acts in both cases—the firing of Comey and its implications, for Trump; and the false statement about Russian contacts, for Sessions.

No one raised any objections. No one suggested the FBI was overstepping any bounds. There was some nodding of heads, as if the reasoning made perfect sense. The Republicans looked resigned to the inevitable.

Paul Ryan was the only one who asked a question, about whether a counterintelligence investigation was also a criminal investigation. Yes, McCabe answered. The FBI was investigating both collusion with the Russians and obstruction; either or both could result in criminal charges.

Then Rosenstein stepped in and announced he'd appointed a special counsel. Everyone at the table seemed surprised. Rosenstein fielded mostly procedural questions, including how a special counsel could be removed.

It was all over in little more than half an hour.

ROSENSTEIN ISSUED A formal order that same day:

> By virtue of the authority vested in me as Acting Attorney General, including 28 U.S.C. §§ 509, 510, and 515, in order to discharge my responsibility to provide supervision and management of the Department of Justice, and to ensure a full and thorough investigation of the Russian government's efforts to interfere in the 2016 presidential election, I hereby order as follows: (a) Robert S. Mueller III is ap-

pointed to serve as Special Counsel for the United States Department of Justice. (b) The Special Counsel is authorized to conduct the investigation confirmed by then–FBI Director James B. Comey in testimony before the House Permanent Select Committee on Intelligence on March 20, 2017, including: (i) any links and/or coordination between the Russian government and individuals associated with the campaign of President Donald Trump; and (ii) any matters that arose or may arise directly from the investigation; and (iii) any other matters within the scope of 28 C.F.R. § 600.4(a). (c) If the Special Counsel believes it is necessary and appropriate, the Special Counsel is authorized to prosecute federal crimes arising from the investigation of these matters.

Sessions was still in the Oval Office after interviewing candidates for FBI director when Rosenstein called. Trump, McGahn, and Sessions's chief of staff, Jody Hunt, who was taking notes, waited while Sessions stepped out to take the call.

He came back in and broke the news.

The president looked stricken. He slumped back in his chair. "Oh my God. This is terrible. This is the end of my presidency. I'm fucked."

In Trump's view, this was all Sessions's fault. "How could you let this happen, Jeff?" he angrily asked. The post of attorney general was his most important appointment, and Sessions had "let him down." He again compared Sessions unfavorably to Bobby Kennedy and Eric Holder. "You were supposed to protect me."

Instead, "Everyone tells me if you get one of these independent counsels it ruins your presidency. It takes years and years and I won't be able to do anything. This is the worst thing that ever happened to me."

Sessions should resign, Trump said. Sessions said he would, and left, as did Hunt and McGahn.

Hope Hicks, still sitting at her desk outside the office, described Trump as "extremely upset." She'd seen him in such a state only once before, which was after the *Access Hollywood* tape was released.

AS HE LEFT the Capitol that evening, McCabe felt a great sense of relief and satisfaction. Now that Rosenstein had appointed a special counsel, he felt he'd fulfilled his most important and urgent mission as acting director. Now that the case was officially open, FBI agents delivered a notice requiring the White House to preserve all documents related to Comey's dismissal, and McGahn told the staff not to send out any burn bags while he sorted things out.

McCabe went home, opened a can of beer, and drank it standing by the kitchen island, reflecting on the dizzying events of the past week.

Comey had been fired, and McCabe thrust into a leadership role. The FBI had opened a formal investigation of the president, with the knowledge and approval of both the Justice Department and Congress. No one had raised any objections. The Russia investigation was on solid ground. It didn't matter now if Trump fired him, or Rosenstein or Sessions, for that matter. There was no way Trump could stop the investigation or shut it down without the world knowing.

McCabe felt he'd been sprinting toward some kind of finish line all week. Now it felt as if he'd crossed it. He could stop running.

WITTINGLY OR NOT, Rosenstein could not have found a special counsel more closely aligned with the values espoused by Comey, whom Rosenstein had just helped fire.

Any hopes of Rosenstein that Trump might "welcome" the appointment of a special counsel, especially one of Mueller's unblemished reputation and stature, were quickly dashed. Early the next morning Trump tweeted, "This is the single greatest witch hunt of a politician in American history!"

And Trump was already suspicious of Mueller, whom he accused of conflicts of interest, especially what he called a "nasty" dispute the two had had over Mueller's onetime membership in the Trump National Golf Club in Potomac Falls, Virginia.

But Trump's was a solitary voice among elected officials. Democrats were predictably elated, but even Republican allies of the president praised Rosenstein's decision to name a special counsel and his choice of Mueller.

Senator Grassley, the head of the Judiciary Committee who'd been so critical of Comey and McCabe, issued a statement saying he had "a great deal of confidence" in Rosenstein "and I respect his decision." "Mueller has a strong reputation for independence, and comes with the right credentials for this job," Grassley said.

The Republican Susan Collins of Maine, a member of the Senate Intelligence Committee, said Mueller "has sterling credentials and is above reproach. He is well respected on both sides of the aisle and will inspire public confidence in the investigation."

The mainstream media lavished praise on Rosenstein's decision. "If President Trump thought that by sacking the FBI director, James Comey, he could kill off the investigation into his associates' ties to the Russian government and its attempt to deliver him the White House, he was wrong," *The New York Times* editorialized. "The investigation will go on, now under the leadership of a former FBI director—and this one the president can't fire on his own." Rosenstein "has done the nation a service in choosing Mr. Mueller, one of the few people with the experience, stature and reputation to see the job through."

In a dissenting view, the *Wall Street Journal* columnist Kimberley Strassel warned that Mueller was "part of the brotherhood of prosecutors" who "see themselves as a legal elite, charged with a noble purpose." Worse, he was "a longtime colleague of none other than James Comey." Still, what Strassel saw as defects could as easily be seen as virtues.

None of the praise for Mueller made any impact on Trump, who continued to fume about Mueller's appointment and Sessions's treachery. If anything, it only heightened his anger and resentment: the more praise for Mueller, the harder it would be to demonize him.

Later that day, Sessions returned to the White House to submit his resignation, as the president had demanded during his humiliating dressing-down the evening before. He handed it to Trump. "Pursuant to our conversation of yesterday, and at your request, I hereby offer my resignation," the letter began.

Trump took the letter and put it in his inside jacket pocket. Then he asked Sessions if he wanted to stay on as attorney general. Sessions equivocated. Trump asked him again, and then again, almost as if Trump wanted to see Sessions beg for the job. Finally Sessions said he wanted to stay, but added the decision was up to the president.

With Sessions's humiliation complete, Trump shook his hand and didn't accept his resignation. But he kept the letter.

ROBERT MUELLER DIDN'T waste any time. On May 18, the day after he was named special counsel, he and two close associates he'd already named to his team, Aaron Zebley, his former chief of staff at the FBI, and James Quarles, one of his law partners, arrived at FBI headquarters for a briefing on progress in the Russia case. McCabe, Page, Strzok, and Moffa all attended, and Moffa led the briefing. As usual, Page freely offered her observations and opinions.

Afterward, Mueller asked McCabe, "Who was that woman in there? At the end of the table. I want her for my team."

When McCabe told her the news, Page resisted. She was trying to spend more time with her young children and husband. She knew Mueller's reputation and that working for him would be a full-time, seven-day-a-week commitment. She didn't want to abandon McCabe just as he was stepping into his role as acting director.

"You don't say 'no' to Bob Mueller," McCabe cautioned. "For better or worse, I never said 'no' to Bob Mueller."

Page got the message: If the acting director of the FBI never turned down a request from Mueller, then what right did she have?

The next day, she sat down alone with Mueller. "I'm unbelievably honored and grateful" to be asked, she said, but wanted him to know she had two young children.

"Well, family comes first," Mueller said, though she doubted he (or any other men of his generation) really knew what that meant. If something blew up at 5:00 p.m. on a Friday, no one was going to leave the office.

But Page agreed to sign on for forty-five days, long enough for his team to get up and running.

Not long after, Mueller asked Strzok to join as well (unaware, of course, of his relationship with Page). "You'd be very good," Mueller said.

Strzok, too, had doubts, though not because of family commitments. Leaving his job at FBI headquarters for a special counsel investigation, no matter how important or prestigious, was not a standard path for advancement at the FBI. He was in line to be a special agent in charge for a major city, and then a top headquarters job. Going with Mueller might be no more than a path to early retirement.

Page urged Strzok not to take up Mueller on his offer, both for those reasons and because, under the circumstances of their prior affair, she didn't think the two of them should be working so closely together.

On the other hand, Strzok, too, was reluctant to say no to Mueller. And it was a chance to work on what could be the case of a lifetime.

The two debated the issue that week in an exchange of text messages.

"A case which will be in the history books," Strzok said. "A million people sit in AD [assistant director] and staff jobs. This is a chance to DO. In maybe the most important case of our lives."

"No way, dude. I really don't think you should do it," Page answered. She also expressed doubts about her own abilities in such a high-powered group, but a friend encouraged her because "I lean in and have a stronger work ethic than anyone she knows."

Strzok was quick to bolster her confidence: "You have passion and curiosity, which is more than half of the battle anyway."

As for himself, "I personally have a sense of unfinished business," and "Now I need to fix it and finish it."

"You shouldn't take this on," Page persisted. "I promise you, I would tell you if you should." She continued, "We can't work closely on another case again," but "I want you to do what is right for you."

"Sigh. Yeah, I suppose that's right. But god we're a good team. Is that playing into your decision/your advice to me?"

"No, not at all," Page replied. "I just think we're both ready for a change. Truly." And Page said they needed to consider the "realistic outcomes" of the investigation, which included a finding that Trump hadn't colluded with the Russians.

"You and I both know the odds are nothing," Strzok responded. "If I thought it was likely, I'd be there no question. I hesitate in part because of my gut sense and concern there's no there there."*

Given the evidence he'd seen so far, Strzok was dubious that there was some kind of massive conspiracy with Trump at the center in the role of Mafia don. He thought it more likely that "it was a bunch of corrupt incompetents with individual agendas engaged in unethical and illegal activity," as he put it.

Still, the possibility remained that Trump was working in a clandestine manner with a foreign power to win the presidency of the United States. As Strzok later said, "People were desperate to work on this. It was like parents volunteering their firstborn children for the war, because everyone understood the gravity and how important an endeavor it was."

In the end, Strzok, too, said yes.

Mueller was able to assemble a highly accomplished and experienced team of prosecutors. Some, like Zebley (whose nickname was the "energizer bunny"), he brought with him from his law firm, WilmerHale. Others filled niches of expertise. Most Mueller had known for years, and they were devoted to him.

Federal law barred Mueller from asking anyone's political affiliation. (In the heavily Democratic District of Columbia, where the primary usually decides the outcome in local elections, many voters register as Democrats, even if they vote for Republican presidential candidates.) Nonetheless, every applicant's record was scoured for partisan political activism—conservative or liberal—which was disqualifying.

---

* Gertrude Stein coined the phrase "There is no there there" to describe her hometown of Oakland, California.

Within the team the issue of political affiliation never surfaced; no one knew or cared, so long as it had no impact on their work. That didn't stop the topic from being one of obsessive interest to Trump and his supporters, especially after *The Wall Street Journal* reported that Andrew Weissmann had attended Hillary Clinton's election night party in New York. That did prompt some discussion within the Mueller team, but no one thought it disqualified him. Weissmann primarily worked on the Manafort case, not on the Trump case.

Zebley had represented Justin Cooper, the Clinton aide who installed the server at the Clintons' residence and was a witness in the email case. But that didn't make him a Clinton partisan or pose a conflict.

And Mueller himself, of course, was a Republican.

Trump had less to fear from any political bias than from the team's deeply held belief in the rule of law.

THE SATURDAY AFTER Mueller was appointed, May 20, Rosenstein called McCabe to ask him to meet with Mueller that weekend to discuss logistics. They gathered in Rosenstein's office the next day. Zebley was there from Mueller's team, along with one of Rosenstein's staff. McCabe brought Carl Ghattas from the FBI's national security team.

An entirely different Rosenstein was on display from the previous week: Mueller's appointment had relieved some of the pressure on him, but gone was any sense of warmth or willingness to confide in McCabe. And instead of logistics, he confronted McCabe with the photo of him in his wife's campaign T-shirt. "You should think about recusing," Rosenstein told him.

McCabe was startled and upset. It wasn't fair. As he'd already told Sessions and McGahn during his job interview, McCabe told Rosenstein that the bureau had already thoroughly examined the issue of his wife's campaign and McAuliffe's contributions and concluded there was no conflict. McCabe had done nothing wrong. He offered to produce internal FBI memos that had reached that conclusion.

But Rosenstein persisted. Finally McCabe said, "If anyone should be recusing himself, it's you." After all, Rosenstein was a major witness to Comey's firing. "You're involved in this."

The comment infuriated Rosenstein. He told McCabe and Ghattas to leave the room so he could talk to Mueller.

When they returned, Rosenstein looked sullen. "I'm not getting involved in this," Mueller said. "It's not in my scope. You guys have to figure this out."

TRUMP WAS SUPPOSED to name his choice for a new FBI director that week, but didn't. He wasn't that happy with any of the candidates he'd met. Trump left the next day for his first foreign visit as president, to Saudi Arabia followed by Israel. Accompanying him on Air Force One was an entourage that included Melania, Jared Kushner and Ivanka, Bannon, and Priebus. That the president was leaving a capital consumed by scandal, intrigue, the firing of the FBI director, and the appointment of a special counsel drew numerous comparisons to Richard Nixon's trip to Egypt at the height of the Watergate crisis.

During the flight Priebus asked Trump about Sessions's resignation letter. Both he and Bannon worried Trump might use it as leverage with Sessions, as a kind of "shock collar," as Priebus put it. As long as Trump had the letter, he had "DOJ by the throat," Priebus said. He and Bannon had told Sessions they'd get the letter back from the president with a notation that he was not accepting it. But Trump told Priebus on the plane that the letter was back at the White House, somewhere in the residence.

In fact it was in Trump's pocket. On the flight to Tel Aviv he pulled it out and brandished it before some of his other senior advisers and asked what he should do with it.

Back in Washington, Priebus again asked for Sessions's letter. Trump "slapped the desk" and said he'd left it at their hotel. But Trump subsequently opened his desk drawer, pulled out the letter, and showed it to the White House staff secretary, Rob Porter.

Back from the trip, Trump kept up a steady drumbeat of criticisms of

Mueller and what Trump considered the special counsel's conflicts. As the president later tweeted, "Is Robert Mueller ever going to release his conflicts of interest with respect to President Trump, including the fact that we had a very nasty & contentious business relationship, I turned him down to head the FBI (one day before appointment as S.C.) & Comey is his close friend."

He also complained that the law firm where Mueller had been a partner, WilmerHale, had taken on clients who challenged Trump policies, such as his tough stand on immigration. The firm also represented the Trump family members Ivanka and Jared Kushner.

But even his closest advisers had trouble taking any of these complaints seriously. Mueller had resigned from Trump National in 2011 and asked in a letter to the club if a pro rata portion of his initiation fee could be refunded. The club's controller had replied that he would be placed on a waiting list, which was the club's usual refund policy. That had been the end of the correspondence. There was nothing "nasty" about it, or even a dispute. Why Trump thought otherwise—or was even aware of such a minor administrative detail—was a mystery.

Trump hadn't "turned down" Mueller to be FBI director; he'd sought Mueller's advice, but Mueller neither applied for nor asked for the position.

That a large law firm like WilmerHale had clients opposed to some of Trump's policies wasn't a conflict for Mueller. Trump wasn't hiring WilmerHale to represent him. And Mueller hadn't had any involvement with Ivanka or Kushner, who were prospective witnesses in the investigation.

Mueller and Comey weren't even close friends, though the fact that Mueller and Comey seemed cut from the same cloth (as *The Wall Street Journal* had noted) is probably what most unnerved Trump.

Bannon told Trump that his complaints about Mueller were "ridiculous," and the issue about the golf club fees was both "ridiculous and petty."

McGahn, too, told Trump the purported conflicts were "silly."

Trump ignored them.

Trump took his complaints about Mueller to McGahn and asked him to reach out to Rosenstein. Now that a special counsel was investigating Trump for possible obstruction of justice, McGahn was a key potential witness, which made contacting Rosenstein even more inappropriate. McGahn said he wouldn't do it and told Trump he should enlist one of his personal lawyers.

Even then, it was a bad idea. It would "look like still trying to meddle in [the] investigation" and "knocking out Mueller" would be "[a]nother fact used to claim obst[ruction] of just[ice]," according to notes of the conversation. The notes also indicate that McGahn warned Trump that his "biggest exposure" was not the act of firing Comey but his "other contacts" and "calls" and his "ask re: Flynn."

On May 23, the Justice Department said its ethics lawyers had reviewed potential conflicts involving Robert Mueller and "determined that Mr. Mueller's participation in the matters assigned to him is appropriate."

A WEEK LATER, Trump finally sent Sessions's resignation letter back to him, and only then because McGahn and Bannon had kept insisting on it. On it he'd scrawled "not accepted."

That same day, Trump interviewed yet another candidate to be FBI director: Christopher A. Wray, apparently at the behest of Chris Christie. (Wray had represented Christie in the Bridgegate scandal, and the two had been friends since they worked together as young lawyers in the Justice Department.) But Wray had also worked closely with Comey, as an assistant attorney general when Comey was the deputy, and Mueller, when Mueller was FBI director. The Yale-educated Wray was also cut from the same mold of elite former prosecutors that had troubled the *Wall Street Journal* editorial writers.

Nonetheless, a week later Trump tweeted the news: "I will be nominating Christopher A. Wray, a man of impeccable credentials, to be the new Director of the FBI. Details to follow."

ALMOST EXACTLY ONE month after he was fired, Comey appeared on Capitol Hill to testify before the Senate Intelligence Committee investigating Russian influence on the presidential election. In the wake of the explosive reporting on his memos and Trump's request for loyalty and interference in the Flynn investigation, Comey had maintained his silence. The public's curiosity had reached fever pitch. For better or worse, Comey was the man of the hour, eclipsing anything he'd experienced before, even at the height of the Ashcroft controversy.

Spectators started lining up at 4:15 a.m. to get one of the coveted seats in the hearing room. All the major television networks aired live coverage, and more than eighteen million viewers initially tuned in, rising to nearly twenty million as Comey's testimony continued. Millions more watched on live streaming services.

"When I was appointed FBI Director in 2013, I understood that I served at the pleasure of the president," Comey began. "Even though I was appointed to a 10-year term, which Congress created in order to underscore the importance of the FBI being outside of politics and independent, I understood that I could be fired by a president for any reason or for no reason at all. And on May the ninth, when I learned that I had been fired, for that reason I immediately came home as a private citizen. But then the explanations, the shifting explanations, confused me and increasingly concerned me. They confused me because the president and I had had multiple conversations about my job, both before and after he took office, and he had repeatedly told me I was doing a great job, and he hoped I would stay. And I had repeatedly assured him that I did intend to stay and serve out the years of my term. He told me repeatedly that he had talked to lots of people about me, including our current Attorney General, and had learned that I was doing a great job, and that I was extremely well-liked by the FBI workforce.

"So it confused me when I saw on television the president saying that he actually fired me because of the Russia investigation, and learned again from the media that he was telling privately other parties that my firing had relieved great pressure on the Russian investigation. I was also confused by the initial explanation that was offered publicly that I was fired because of the decisions I had made during the election year. That didn't make sense to me for a whole bunch of reasons, including the time and all the water that had gone under the bridge since those hard decisions that had to be made. That didn't make any sense to me. And although the law required no reason at all to fire an FBI director, the administration then chose to defame me and more importantly the FBI by saying that the organization was in disarray, that it was poorly led, that the workforce had lost confidence in its leader. Those were lies, plain and simple. And I am so sorry that the FBI workforce had to hear them, and I'm so sorry that the American people were told them."

Comey also saw his opening statement as a way to make the farewell speech he hadn't been able to deliver:

> I worked every day at the FBI to help make that great organization better, and I say help, because I did nothing alone at the FBI. There are no indispensable people at the FBI. The organization's great strength is that its values and abilities run deep and wide. The FBI will be fine without me. The FBI's mission will be relentlessly pursued by its people, and that mission is to protect the American people and uphold the constitution of the United States. I will deeply miss being part of that mission, but this organization and its mission will go on long beyond me and long beyond any particular administration.
>
> I have a message before I close for my former colleagues of the FBI but first I want the American people to know this truth: The FBI is honest. The FBI is strong. And the FBI is and always will be independent. And now to my former colleagues, if I may.

At this point Comey struggled to hold back tears: "I am so sorry that I didn't get the chance to say goodbye to you properly. It was the honor of my life to serve beside you, to be part of the FBI family, and I will miss it

for the rest of my life. Thank you for standing watch. Thank you for doing so much good for this country. Do that good as long as ever you can."

In written comments distributed to the committee, Comey gave a
detailed account of his interactions with the president: the January 6
briefing at Trump Tower; the January 27 dinner; the February 14 meeting in the Oval Office; the March 30 and April 11 phone calls.

As senators began their questioning, he elaborated on why he wrote
the memos. "I was honestly concerned he might lie about the nature of
our meeting so I thought it important to document," he said, the "he"
being Trump. "I knew there might come a day when I would need a record of what had happened, not just to defend myself, but to defend the
FBI and our integrity as an institution and the independence of our investigative function."

Comey confirmed that one of his top advisers (whom he didn't name,
but was Jim Baker) had warned him not to tell Trump he wasn't being
investigated because "inevitably his behavior, his conduct will fall within
the scope of that work." But Comey had disagreed. "I thought it was fair
to say what was literally true. There was not a counterintelligence investigation of Mr. Trump, and I decided in the moment to say it, given the
nature of our conversation."

And the reason he felt so uncomfortable about the president's request
for loyalty was "the reason that Congress created a 10-year term is so that
the director is not feeling as if they're serving at, with political loyalty
owed to any particular person. The statue of justice has a blindfolds on.
You're not supposed to peek out to see whether your patron was pleased
with what you're doing."

Senator Dianne Feinstein asked why Comey hadn't been firmer with
Trump when he brought up the subject of Flynn.

"Maybe if I were stronger, I would have," Comey answered. "I was so
stunned by the conversation that I just took in. The only thing I could
think to say, because I was playing in my mind—because I could remember every word he said—I was playing in my mind, what should my response be? That's why I carefully chose the words."

He mentioned the tapes: "Look, I've seen the tweet about tapes. Lordy, I hope there are tapes. I remember saying, 'I agree he is a good guy,' as a way of saying, I'm not agreeing with what you asked me to do. Again, maybe other people would be stronger in that circumstance."

Senator Jack Reed, a Rhode Island Democrat, asked why Comey thought he'd been fired.

"It's my judgment I was fired because of the Russia investigation," Comey said. "I was fired in some way to change the way the Russia investigation is being conducted. That is a very big deal. And not just because it involves me. The nature of the FBI and the nature of its work requires that it not be the subject of political consideration. And on top of that, you have the Russia investigation itself is vital, because of the threat. And I know I should have said this earlier, but it's obvious: if any Americans were part of helping the Russians do that to us, that is a very big deal. And I'm confident if that is the case, Director Mueller will find that evidence."

Angus King, the Maine independent, asked Comey what he thought Trump meant when he said "something like, I hope or I suggest or would you, do you take that as a directive?"

"Yes," Comey said. "It rings in my ear as: Will no one rid me of this meddlesome priest?"

"I was just going to quote that," King said. "In 1170, December 29, Henry II said, who will rid me of this meddlesome priest, and the next day, he was killed."*

COMEY CAME ACROSS as both humble and credible. Trump was furious over Comey's testimony and the massive media attention it generated, especially Comey's admission that he'd "leaked" memos detailing what were supposed to be private conversations with Trump. Minutes after Comey finished testifying, Trump dispatched his personal lawyer, Marc

---

* The reference is to Thomas à Becket, the archbishop of Canterbury who refused to bow to the king's will and was murdered by four of the king's knights in Canterbury Cathedral after Henry II expressed a wish to be rid of him. The line "Will no one rid me of this meddlesome priest?" is used in the 1964 film *Becket*. While Henry's exact words aren't known, the phrase conveys the sense that a ruler's wish is a command, and thus was an apt analogy for Comey.

Kasowitz, to put a positive spin on Comey's testimony and brand Comey a liar and a leaker. "The President also never told Mr. Comey, 'I need loyalty, I expect loyalty' in form or substance," Kasowitz said at a press conference. "Of course, the Office of the President is entitled to expect loyalty from those who are serving in an administration, and, from before this President took office to this day, it is overwhelmingly clear that there have been and continue to be those in government who are actively attempting to undermine this administration with selective and illegal leaks of classified information and privileged communications. Mr. Comey has now admitted that he is one of these leakers.

"In sum, it is now established that the President was not being investigated for colluding with the Russians or attempting to obstruct that investigation," Kasowitz concluded. "As the Committee pointed out today, these important facts for the country to know are virtually the only facts that have not leaked during the long course of these events."

The next day, at a press conference with the president of Romania, ABC News chief White House correspondent Jonathan Karl said Comey "did say, under oath, that you told him to let the Flynn—you said you hoped the Flynn investigation he could let—"

"I didn't say that," Trump interrupted.

"So he lied about that?"

"Well, I didn't say that," Trump repeated. "I mean, I will tell you I didn't say that."

"And did he ask you to pledge . . ."

"And there would be nothing wrong if I did say it, according to everybody that I've read today," Trump went on. "But I did not say that."

"And did he ask for a pledge of loyalty from you?* That's another thing he said."

"No, he did not."

"So he said those things under oath. Would you be willing to speak under oath to give your version of those events?" Karl asked.

"One hundred percent," Trump said. As for Comey, "I hardly know

---

* Karl obviously meant to ask: "Did you ask for a loyalty pledge from him?"

the man. I'm not going to say, I want you to pledge allegiance. Who would do that? Who would ask a man to pledge allegiance under oath? I mean, think of it. I hardly know the man. It doesn't make sense. No, I didn't say that, and I didn't say the other."

"So if Robert Mueller wanted to speak with you about that you would be willing to talk to him?"

"I would be glad to tell him exactly what I just told you, Jon," Trump replied.

TRUMP SPENT THE weekend fuming over the press coverage and venting about Mueller's conflicts. Priebus and Bannon were so worried that Trump might precipitously order Rosenstein to fire Mueller that they summoned Christopher Ruddy to the White House. Ruddy, the chief executive of the conservative Newsmax Media, a longtime conspiracy theorist, and a Trump confidant dubbed the "Trump whisperer" by *The Washington Post*, was a reliable media conduit. Priebus told Ruddy he hoped they wouldn't have another blowup like the one that followed Comey's firing. So Ruddy agreed to send up a trial balloon.

Ruddy appeared that evening on PBS's *NewsHour* with Judy Woodruff. "Is President Trump prepared to let the special counsel pursue his investigation?" Woodruff asked.

"Well, I think he's considering perhaps terminating the special counsel. I think he's weighing that option." Ruddy went on, "I mean, Robert Mueller, there are some real conflicts. He comes from a law firm that represents members of the Trump family. He interviewed the day before, a few days before he was appointed special counsel with the president, who was looking at him potentially to become the next FBI director."

Afterward, Sean Spicer issued a statement that "Mr. Ruddy never spoke to the president regarding this issue," which prompted Ruddy to send a text message to ABC News: "Spicer issued a bizarre late night press release that a) doesn't deny my claim the president is considering firing Mueller and b) says I didn't speak to the president about the matter—

when I never claimed to have done so." He reiterated that "Trump is definitely considering it . . . it's not something that's being dismissed."

Ruddy might not have spoken to Trump directly, but his comments hadn't come out of thin air. In that sense, the gambit worked: there was an immediate media outcry, and Sanders had to deny that the president intended to fire Mueller. "While the president has the right to, he has no intention to do so," she told reporters on Air Force One the next day, adding that that's what the president told her to say.

And Ruddy's comments prompted Senator Susan Collins to ask Rosenstein, when he testified before the Senate Appropriations Committee, what would happen if Trump ordered him to fire Mueller.

"Senator, I'm not going to follow any order unless I believe those are lawful and appropriate orders," Rosenstein replied. "Special counsel Mueller may be fired only for good cause, and I am required to put that cause in writing. That's what I would do. If there were good cause, I would consider it. If there were not good cause, it wouldn't matter to me what anybody says."

The Republican Speaker of the House, Paul Ryan, warned Trump not to fire Mueller. "The best thing to do is to let Robert Mueller do his job," Ryan said. "I think the best case for the president is to be vindicated by allowing this investigation to go on thoroughly and independently."

But Trump again ignored the advice. The president called Sessions at home and asked if he'd "unrecuse" himself and referred to "all of it," which Sessions took to mean the Russia investigation and oversight of Mueller. Trump's magnanimity toward Hillary Clinton having apparently run its course, he asked Sessions to direct the Department of Justice to investigate and prosecute Hillary Clinton. Sessions did neither.

On June 14, *The Washington Post* disclosed that Trump's most cherished concession from Comey—that Trump himself was not under investigation—was no longer true. "Special Counsel Is Investigating Trump for Possible Obstruction of Justice, Officials Say," the headline read, which was quickly trumpeted by cable networks. "Trump had received private assurances from then–FBI Director James B. Comey starting in January that he was not personally under investigation," the story reported. "Officials say that changed shortly after Comey's firing."

The revelation set off a rapid-fire series of tweets by Trump that were angry and frustrated even by Trump standards:

"They made up a phony collusion with the Russians story, found zero proof, so now they go for obstruction of justice on the phony story. Nice."

"You are witnessing the single greatest WITCH HUNT in American political history-led by some very bad and conflicted people!"

"Crooked H destroyed phones w/ hammer, 'bleached' emails, & had husband meet w/AG days before she was cleared- & they talk about obstruction?"

"After 7 months of investigations & committee hearings about my 'collusion with the Russians,' nobody has been able to show any proof. Sad!"

And, in a pointed criticism of Rosenstein:

"I am being investigated for firing the FBI Director by the man who told me to fire the FBI Director! Witch Hunt."

Wittingly or not, the tweets confirmed that the president was, indeed, under investigation.

Trump also called Chris Christie to ask what he thought about getting rid of Mueller. Like just about everyone else outside the right-wing fringe, Christie was against it. He said there weren't any legitimate grounds for removing him and Trump would lose even Republican support in Congress if he did.

Despite the overwhelming advice not to do it, Trump set out to get rid of Mueller.

TRUMP CALLED MCGAHN at 10:31 on the night of the *Post* story and told him he wanted Mueller removed. He told McGahn to call Rosenstein and tell him to fire Mueller because of the special counsel's multiple conflicts.

"You gotta do this. You gotta call Rod," Trump said.

McGahn had no intention of doing so, but all he said was that he'd see what he could do. If he did nothing, maybe Trump would forget, or think better of it.

McGahn was at home on Saturday, June 17, when the president called him from Camp David just before 2:30 p.m. This time Trump was more insistent: "Call Rod. Tell Rod that Mueller has conflicts and can't be the Special Counsel." Trump added that "Mueller has to go" and "Call me back when you do it."*

Worn down by the president's demands and eager to get him off the phone, McGahn agreed, even though he wasn't going to do it.

McGahn felt trapped. He thought of Robert Bork, who fired the Watergate special prosecutor, Archibald Cox, in what became known as the Saturday Night Massacre. The resulting public outcry had helped doom Bork's nomination to the Supreme Court, and Bork complained he was "tired of it being portrayed as the only thing I ever did."

McGahn had no intention of becoming another Bork. But what would he say the next time the president called? McGahn saw only one way out, which was to resign.

---

* McGahn later testified that both calls from the president occurred on June 17. However, phone records show only one call that day and another on June 14. McGahn said it was possible Trump's demands to get rid of Mueller took place in those two calls.

TWELVE

"THE WORST DAY OF MY LIFE"

McGahn told his personal lawyer, chief of staff, Bannon, and Priebus that he was resigning. He was deliberately vague about the reasons; he told Priebus only that Trump had asked him to "do crazy shit." Bannon and Priebus pleaded with him to stay, and Bannon stressed that his legacy would be the makeup of the Supreme Court. But McGahn drove to the White House to pack his belongings and draft a resignation letter.

On Monday, June 19, McGahn nonetheless showed up for work. When he saw the president, Trump said nothing about Mueller or his weekend calls.

TRUMP CONTINUED TO remind people that he could have Mueller fired anytime he wanted. But after the aborted attempt with McGahn and repeated warnings from just about everybody around him—including Priebus and Bannon—not to interfere with the special counsel, Trump shifted his focus, aiming his fire at the beleaguered Sessions, whom he saw as the root of the problem.

Unlike Mueller, Sessions reported directly to him. Trump could bend the attorney general to his will, and, if not, he could try to get him to resign. If that failed, he could fire him, even though his advisers had repeatedly warned that doing so risked arousing the ire of Sessions's former colleagues in the Senate. But now that Sessions, too, was being investigated by the FBI—something that Trump surely knew—he had added leverage. Once rid of Sessions, Trump could name a new attorney general in the mold of Holder or Bobby Kennedy, someone who could protect him.

And replacing Sessions with an unconflicted attorney general had the added advantage of sidelining Rosenstein, who had defied him when Trump asked him to do a press conference after Comey was fired and, after all, was the one who decided to name a special counsel and chose Mueller. The president's disdain for both men was evident from their nicknames: "Mr. Magoo" for Sessions, and "Mr. Peepers" for Rosenstein.*

In the Oval Office on June 19, Trump met alone with his former campaign manager Corey Lewandowski and began a campaign to get rid of Sessions. "Write this down," Trump directed, and then dictated a public statement Sessions should make.

Lewandowski hastily took notes: "I know that I recused myself from certain things having to do with specific areas. But our POTUS . . . is being treated very unfairly. He shouldn't have a Special Prosecutor/Counsel b/c he hasn't done anything wrong. I was on the campaign w/ him for nine months, there were no Russians involved with him. I know it for a fact b/c I was there. He didn't do anything wrong except he ran the greatest campaign in American history."

Seemingly oblivious to the fact that Sessions had recused himself from anything related to Russia, Trump wanted Sessions to restrict Mueller to investigating future Russian interference: "I am going to meet with the Special Prosecutor to explain this is very unfair and let the Special Prosecutor move forward with investigating election meddling for future elections so that nothing can happen in future elections."

If Sessions delivered that statement, he'd be the "most popular guy in the country," Trump said.

---

* According to *The Washington Post*. Mr. Magoo starred in a 1950s cartoon series. Mr. Peepers was the mild-mannered, bespectacled schoolteacher in an eponymous 1950s sitcom. Both characters did, in fact, physically resemble Sessions and Rosenstein. But Trump denied ever using the nicknames or even knowing who the characters were. "Why Trump Denies Calling Sessions and Rosenstein 'Mr. Magoo' and 'Mr. Peepers,'" *Vox,* April 23, 2018.

Lewandowski kept the notes but didn't deliver the message to Sessions. A month later, Trump asked him if he'd talked to Sessions. Lewandowski hadn't, but said he would soon. If Sessions didn't meet with him, Trump said, Lewandowski should tell Sessions he was fired.

Needless to say, Lewandowski was in no position to fire the attorney general. As he later told Priebus, "What can I do? I'm not an employee of the administration. I'm a nobody." Lewandowski didn't deliver the message.*

Later that day, Trump and Hope Hicks met in the Oval Office with three *New York Times* reporters, Peter Baker, Maggie Haberman, and Michael Schmidt, who'd broken the Comey memos story. Instead of following Hicks's advice to steer clear of anything having to do with the special counsel investigation, Trump managed to tar Sessions, Rosenstein, Mueller, and Comey while again accusing Comey of perjury.

After a brief discussion of Russian interference in the election, Trump segued into the dossier: "Now, that was totally made-up stuff, and in fact, that guy's being sued by somebody. . . . And he's dying with the lawsuit. I know a lot about those guys, they're phony guys. They make up whatever they want. Just not my thing—plus, I have witnesses, because I went there with a group of people." Trump continued, "I had a group of bodyguards, including Keith [Schiller]. . . . He said, 'What kind of crap is this?' I went there for one day for the Miss Universe contest, I turned around, I went back. It was so disgraceful. It was so disgraceful."

Referring to Comey, "When he brought it to me, I said this is really made-up junk. I didn't think about anything. I just thought about, man, this is such a phony deal."

From there he moved to Mueller. Hicks later said she tried to throw herself between Trump and the reporters and stop him, to no avail. "A special counsel should never have been appointed in this case."

"Was that Sessions's mistake or Rosenstein's mistake?" Schmidt asked.

"Look, Sessions gets the job. Right after he gets the job, he recuses himself."

---

* Lewandowski gave the notes to a White House staff member and asked him to take them to Sessions, but no one ever did.

"Was that a mistake?" Baker asked.

"Well, Sessions should have never recused himself, and if he was going to recuse himself, he should have told me before he took the job, and I would have picked somebody else."

"He gave you no heads up at all, in any sense?" Haberman asked.

"Zero," Trump replied. "So Jeff Sessions takes the job, gets into the job, recuses himself. I then have—which, frankly, I think is very unfair to the president. How do you take a job and then recuse yourself? If he would have recused himself before the job, I would have said, 'Thanks, Jeff, but I can't, you know, I'm not going to take you.' It's extremely unfair, and that's a mild word, to the president. So he recuses himself. I then end up with a second man, who's a deputy."

"Rosenstein," Haberman clarified.

"Who is he? And Jeff hardly knew. He's from Baltimore."

Trump continued, "Yeah, what Jeff Sessions did was he recused himself right after, right after he became attorney general. And I said, 'Why didn't you tell me this before?' I would have—then I said, 'Who's your deputy?' So his deputy he hardly knew, and that's Rosenstein, Rod Rosenstein, who is from Baltimore. There are very few Republicans in Baltimore, if any. So, he's from Baltimore. Now, he, we went through a lot of things. We were interviewing replacements at the FBI. Did you know Mueller was one of the people that was being interviewed?

"He was sitting in that chair. We had a wonderful meeting. The day before! Of course, he was up here, and he wanted the job."

The next day, Mueller "is appointed special counsel," Trump went on. "I said, what the hell is this all about? Talk about conflicts? But he was interviewing for the job. There were many other conflicts that I haven't said, but I will at some point. So Jeff Sessions, Jeff Sessions gave some bad answers."

Baker asked, "What would cause you—what would be the line beyond which if Mueller went, you would say, 'That's too far, we would need to dismiss him'?"

"Look, there are so many conflicts that everybody has," Trump answered, none more glaring than Rosenstein's: "Then Rosenstein becomes extremely angry because of Comey's Wednesday press conference, where he said that he would do the same thing he did a year ago with Hillary Clinton, and Rosenstein became extremely angry at that because, as a prosecutor, he knows that Comey did the wrong thing. Totally wrong thing. And he gives me a letter, O.K., he gives me a letter about Comey. And by the way, that was a tough letter, O.K. Now, perhaps I would have fired Comey anyway, and it certainly didn't hurt to have the letter, O.K. But he gives me a very strong letter, and now he's involved in the case. Well, that's a conflict of interest."

Trump had just made the same point as had McCabe at his Sunday meeting with Rosenstein and Mueller.

"Do you know how many conflicts of interests there are? But then, then Comey also says that he did something in order to get the special counsel. He leaked. The reason he leaked. So, he illegally leaked.

"So think of this, Mike," Trump went on. "He illegally leaks, and everyone thinks it is illegal, and by the way, it looks like it's classified and all that stuff. So he got—not a smart guy—he got tricked into that, because they didn't even ask him that question."

Trump reminded the reporters that he could have "ended the whole thing." Then he questioned the very premise that the FBI should operate independently of the White House, blaming Richard Nixon and Watergate for the idea. "Nothing was changed other than Richard Nixon came along," he said, which was "pretty brutal, and out of courtesy, the FBI started reporting to the Department of Justice. But there was nothing official, there was nothing from Congress. There was nothing—anything. But the FBI person really reports directly to the president of the United States, which is interesting. You know, which is interesting. And I think we're going to have a great new FBI director."

As for Comey, "His testimony is loaded up with lies, O.K.?"

At that point Ivanka showed up with Trump's granddaughter Arabella Kushner, who'd turned six years old two days earlier.

"My granddaughter Arabella," Trump said. "Say hello to them in Chinese."

"Ni hao."

"She's great. She speaks fluent Chinese. She's amazing. She spoke with President Xi. Honey? Can you say a few words in Chinese? Say, like, 'I love you, Grandpa.'"

"Wo ai ni, Grandpa."

"She's unbelievable, huh? Good, smart genes."

TO HICKS'S DISMAY, the *Times* led with Trump's criticisms of Sessions and that Trump had accused Comey "of trying to leverage a dossier of compromising material to keep his job." But Trump told Hicks he "loved" the interview and how the media covered it.

Despite all the hints, Jody Hunt, Sessions's chief of staff, told Priebus the attorney general had no intention of resigning and questioned what getting rid of Sessions would accomplish anyway: there was an investigation before, and there would be an investigation after.

Three days after the *Times* interview, Trump stepped up the pressure. He tweeted, "So many people are asking why isn't the A.G. or Special Council looking at the many Hillary Clinton or Comey crimes. 33,000 emails deleted?" Three minutes later, he added, "What about all of the Clinton ties to Russia, including Podesta Company, Uranium deal, Russian Reset, big dollar speeches etc."

The same morning, en route to Norfolk, Virginia, with Priebus, Trump said the country had lost confidence in Sessions. Priebus took notes: "Need a letter of resignation on desk immediately." Sessions had "no choice" but "must immediately resign."

Priebus warned again that the Department of Justice and Congress would "turn their backs" on the president, but Trump brushed aside his concerns. When Priebus told McGahn about Trump's directive to demand Sessions's resignation, McGahn told him not to do it and told Priebus to consult his personal lawyer. They considered the possibility they'd both have to resign rather than carry out the president's order.

"Did you get it? Are you working on it?" Trump asked Priebus that afternoon. Priebus, buying time, said he'd get Sessions's resignation but warned him Rosenstein and others at the Justice Department would likely quit, too, triggering a crisis and massive bad publicity. Trump agreed to hold off until after the Sunday news shows. To Priebus's relief, he didn't press the matter after that.

But Trump didn't give up his public attacks on Sessions. Starting Monday, he issued a series of tweets assaulting Sessions for not pursuing Clinton. He also took another swipe at McCabe:

"So why aren't the Committees and investigators, and of course our beleaguered A.G., looking into Crooked Hillary's crimes & Russia relations?"

"Attorney General Jeff Sessions has taken a VERY weak position on Hillary Clinton crimes (where are Emails & DNC server) & Intel leakers!"

"Why didn't A.G. Sessions replace Acting FBI Director Andrew McCabe, a Comey friend who was in charge of Clinton investigation but got . . . big dollars ($700,000) for his wife's political run from Hillary Clinton and her representatives. Drain the swamp!"

Trump later unleashed another series of tweets and comments attacking Sessions, one of which—"I put in an Attorney General that never took control of the Justice Department"—prompted a rare response from Sessions.

"I took control of the Department of Justice the day I was sworn in," Sessions said in a prepared statement, and added, "While I am Attorney General, the actions of the Department of Justice will not be improperly influenced by political considerations."

The next day, the president tweeted, "'Department of Justice will not be improperly influenced by political considerations.' Jeff, this is GREAT, what everyone wants, so look into all of the corruption on the 'other side' including deleted Emails, Comey lies & leaks, Mueller conflicts, McCabe, Strzok, Page, Ohr, FISA abuse, Christopher Steele & his phony and corrupt Dossier, the Clinton Foundation, illegal surveillance of Trump campaign, Russian collusion by Dems—and so much more. Open up the papers & documents without redaction? Come on Jeff, you can do it, the country is waiting!"

But for the moment, Sessions had survived.

EMBEDDED IN TRUMP'S barrage of tweets that July were two aimed at the "Amazon" *Washington Post*, one of his favorite targets now that Amazon's founder, Jeff Bezos—someone far richer than Trump—had bought it. On July 23, he complained that "The Amazon Washington Post has gone crazy against me." In the second, the same day, he seemed to threaten antitrust action:

"In my opinion the Washington Post is nothing more than an expensive (the paper loses a fortune) lobbyist for Amazon. Is it used as protection against antitrust claims which many feel should be brought?"

The *Post* responded that "Trump has made the false claim about The Post serving as a lobbyist for Amazon multiple times," and said the newspaper operates with complete independence from Bezos.

Ominously for McCabe, after two months of relative calm since Mueller's appointment, he was again on the president's radar: "Problem is that the acting head of the FBI & the person in charge of the Hillary investigation, Andrew McCabe, got $700,000 from H for wife!" Trump tweeted on July 25.

McCabe heard about the tweet on the news; he didn't follow Twitter or have an account. Putting aside the flagrant falsehood that McCabe himself had taken money from Hillary Clinton, the mere fact the president of the United States was attacking him personally and implying he'd done something corrupt came as a shock.

McCabe's wife, too, was upset. She blamed herself for running for office, taking money from McAuliffe, and somehow besmirching her husband's career. McCabe tried to reassure her that those were just pretexts to undermine him. The real issue was the Russia investigation.

Jim Baker called to ask if McCabe was okay.

McCabe decided he'd try to make light of it. He began a meeting that morning by saying he hadn't seen the news. "Anything new?" he asked. But his quip generated only some awkward laughter.

HAVING FAILED TO deliver Sessions's resignation, Priebus was soon ousted himself. On Friday, July 28, while sitting on the tarmac on Air Force One in Washington, Trump tweeted, "I would like to thank Reince Priebus for his service and dedication to his country. We accomplished a lot together and I am proud of him!"

Priebus emerged from the plane in a driving rain, dashed to a waiting car, and left without further comment. "Reince is a good man," Trump told reporters after he disembarked.

Trump named John F. Kelly his new chief of staff. Just weeks later, Trump dispatched Bannon, too. For all his brash populism, Bannon had often been a voice of reason in curbing Trump's impulses.

The same rainy afternoon that Priebus was ousted, Lisa Page answered her phone at FBI headquarters, where she'd returned as special counsel to McCabe after completing her forty-five-day stint with Mueller. On the phone was Julie McConnell, a lawyer with the inspector general's office. McConnell asked if Page could come in for an interview that day. Her tone sounded serious.

"What are you looking at?" Page asked.

"Potential political bias," McConnell said.

That was news to Page. She thought the inspector general was looking at leaks. "Can you tell me anything more?"

"We're looking at certain text messages that reveal potential political bias in the Hillary Clinton email investigation," she said. "You're not just a witness. You're a subject," McConnell added ominously.

Page froze. "I'm sorry, I think I need to get a lawyer."

Her first impulse was to call McCabe. "Hey, I just got a call from the IG. I'm a subject, but about what?" she asked.

"Stop, Lees," McCabe said, using her nickname. "Stop talking." He didn't want to hear anything. He was a potential witness. "I just got a call, too. I'm going over this evening."

Page's mind raced. She knew the inspector general had obtained text messages from her FBI-issued phone. She and Strzok had often discussed news and political developments, but she didn't remember saying anything that might suggest bias.

But that wasn't what really terrified her. If they had the texts, then they knew about the affair.

MCCONNELL AND TWO other lawyers were waiting when McCabe got to the inspector general's office. Daniel Beckhard seemed in charge and did most of the questioning. McCabe went alone. When they'd called earlier asking him to come over, McCabe had said he didn't feel comfortable testifying without a lawyer present, given that he was a subject of the leak investigation. But he'd been assured "it's not about you. There's something else we need to show you." When he arrived, he reiterated that he wouldn't discuss anything about himself. Beckhard told him that was fine.

Stacked on a conference table were copies of thousands of Page's and Strzok's texts. After McCabe read a few, it was obvious that Page and Strzok had been romantically involved. They'd also made some intemperate political comments. McCabe knew it would be bad—bad for the FBI, bad for the special counsel, bad for him—and most of all catastrophic for Page and Strzok, two people he valued, respected, and considered friends.

And he knew to a near certainty the texts would leak or be made public. They perfectly fit the Trump narrative that the FBI was biased and out to get him.

The lawyers for the inspector general didn't seem to be thinking about the implications. They were obsessively focused on decoding the often cryptic texts. They peppered McCabe with questions about what Page and Strzok meant. How was he supposed to know? McCabe said he didn't want to speculate.

Then the lawyers showed him text messages from Page dated October

27, 28, and 30, 2016—text messages sent to him. These were messages in which Page discussed the *Wall Street Journal* article and included the text to McCabe where Page said she felt "WAY less bad" about throwing Axelrod "under the bus in the forthcoming CF article."

Beckhard said they weren't sure what CF related to, but perhaps it was the Clinton Foundation. "Do you happen to know?"

"I don't know what she's referring to," McCabe said.

"Or perhaps a code name?"

"Not one that I recall, but this thing is like right in the middle of the allegations about me, and so I don't really want to get into discussing this article with you," McCabe said.

"Was she ever authorized to speak to reporters in this time period?" one of the lawyers asked; another was talking at the same time, which McCabe found confusing.

As McCabe had already pointed out, the lawyers were now violating the assurance that he wouldn't be questioned about his own role. But, reeling from the shock of the Page-Strzok texts, McCabe went ahead and answered, "Not that I'm aware of." He hoped that would end it.

Beckhard asked again about Page's texts suggesting she was talking to Barrett, the *Wall Street Journal* reporter. "I was not even in town during those days," McCabe answered. "So I can't tell you where she was or what she was doing."

McCabe later said he felt "disconnected" from the questioning, worrying about the personnel crisis he'd just been handed and how he'd deal with it. As the questions mounted, he had the sense things were coming "unglued."

McCabe finally said he wouldn't answer any more questions about himself. Before he left, the lawyers told him not to discuss the texts with Page and Strzok.

WHILE SHE WAITED anxiously outside McCabe's office, Page called Jim Baker and asked for suggestions for a lawyer, even though she didn't know how she'd pay for one.

As darkness fell, the top leadership gradually left their offices adjoining the same corridor. No one made eye contact with her. After about an hour, McCabe returned, looking grave. Page followed him into his office and sat on the sofa. McCabe took a seat in an adjacent chair.

"Should I be stressed?" Page asked. "Or not stressed?"

"You should be stressed," McCabe answered.

"Lisa, they have thousands of your text messages." He held his hand above his knee to show high the stacks were. "It's clear there was a personal relationship there."

Page nodded her head yes, looking down, fighting tears. "I'm sorry, Andy," she said softly.

"I know you are," he said.

There was nothing McCabe could say that would make her feel any worse than she felt at that moment.

McCabe said he'd discuss her situation with Baker and other top officials, but she couldn't stay as his special counsel. As she left the office, Page felt it was the worst day of her life.

McCabe had already decided that Strzok could no longer remain on the Mueller team. It wasn't because he felt Strzok had ever shown any political bias in his work—on the contrary. Nor was having an affair against any rules. But the fact that the inspector general was investigating bias—even if he eventually concluded there was none—would be used to undermine the credibility of the special counsel, especially in the intensely charged political environment of the moment. McCabe couldn't take that risk.

He called Strzok at home. As he placed the call, he realized he was about to upend Strzok's career and marriage. McCabe didn't realize that the same could be said of himself.

MCCABE THOUGHT STRZOK took the bad news surprisingly well. When Page called Strzok the next day—breaking her silence with him—he was reassuring, telling her they'd both survive. Their affair wasn't any of the government's business. They were entitled to their political views and to express them in a private setting. Page thought that was naive. "You're going to need a lawyer," she said.

Strzok met with Mueller the next day. Strzok understood that for appearances' sake, he had to leave. Mueller seemed grave, deeply saddened at the loss of his top FBI agent.

When he returned to the FBI, Dave Bowdich, the acting deputy, assigned Strzok to human resources, the equivalent of Siberia for someone who'd been one of the bureau's brightest stars. Strzok had never been in anything but operations. Everyone knew something bad must have happened, but Bowdich told Strzok not to say anything. "This isn't forever," Bowdich told him. "Be a good soldier, work hard, and keep quiet. We don't want to risk Trump getting this and blowing it up."

CHRISTOPHER WRAY WAS overwhelmingly confirmed to be the next FBI director by the Senate on August 1. That same day, McCabe phoned Beckhard at the inspector general's office.

Over the weekend, McCabe had been replaying the shocking events of the previous Friday. He said he wanted to correct any errors or misimpressions he might have made. McCabe explained that Page had dealt with the *Wall Street Journal* reporter, Barrett, on a previous article in an effort to correct inaccuracies. McCabe was out of town and "may have authorized" Page to talk to Barrett again "because she had previously worked with McCabe on the issues raised by his wife's political campaign and was very familiar with those issues." He added that Michael Kortan, the head of public affairs, "also knew about the situation."

Sessions swore in Wray as director at the FBI the next day as Wray's wife and McCabe stood nearby. (Trump didn't attend.) In a meeting with top leadership, Wray tried to put people at ease. He described himself as "somewhere between Jim Comey and Bob Mueller," meaning he wasn't as outgoing and gregarious as Comey but would be more open and communicative than Bob "Say Nothing" Mueller. He assured people he had no immediate plans for any personnel moves, which meant McCabe would stay on as deputy. But McCabe told him, as he had Sessions and Rosenstein, that he planned to retire when he became eligible in March.

SINCE THE TERRIBLE day McCabe learned about the texts, Lisa Page had trouble sleeping. Already thin, she lost over fifteen pounds. Still, she showed up for work. McCabe had agreed that she could work under Jim Baker. It was meaningful work and she felt safe there, at least for the time being. She knew there was rampant speculation about her sudden move, but she kept her head down and tried to ignore it.

Even though she was now a subject of the inspector general's investigation, Page wasn't unduly concerned when FBI inspectors met with her on August 7. Page thought they were still looking in to the *Circa News* leak, so she didn't bring her lawyer. She was surprised when they suddenly asked about the *Wall Street Journal* article instead. "But that's an entirely new topic," she protested.

"Are you familiar with it?"

"Yes. I talked to the reporter," Page readily acknowledged. She didn't think it was a secret.

The lawyers looked stunned. "You did?"

Page told them the whole saga. She'd been authorized to do so by McCabe, and Kortan had been on both calls to the reporter with her, so he also knew about it.

Page signed a sworn statement to that effect a week later and turned over her notes of the conversation with Barrett.

This, of course, flatly contradicted McCabe's prior statements. McCabe had already clarified his answers to the inspector general, and he reached out to do the same with the FBI lawyers. On August 18, he met with them, and they showed him the article again. According to their interview memo, McCabe "looked at it, and he read it. And as nice as could be, he said yep. Yep, I did, although he said he did not recall specifically doing it." McCabe "took responsibility, or he took ownership of it," and said he was "okay with it."

One of the lawyers, Mark Morgan, responded, "We put a lot of work into this based on what you've told us. I mean, even long nights and weekends working on this, trying to find out who amongst your ranks of trusted people would, would do something like that."

McCabe just looked down, nodded, and said, "Yeah, I'm sorry." He added, "There was a lot going on at the time."

The FBI lawyers turned over the information to the inspector general, who opened a formal investigation of McCabe two weeks later.

ON A LATE summer Friday, Michael Cohen had breakfast near his weekend home in the Hamptons with Emily Jane Fox, a *Vanity Fair* reporter. After being subpoenaed by the House and Senate Intelligence Committees investigating Russia, he'd just submitted documents on the Trump Tower Moscow deal and written testimony, which he'd also released to the press. On display that morning was his legendary loyalty to Trump, which he seemed eager to talk about. Cohen lamented that his lawyer had banned him from speaking to Trump. "At times I wish I were there in D.C. more, sitting with him in the Oval Office, like we used to at Trump Tower, to protect him," Cohen told Fox. "I feel guilty that he's in there right now almost alone." And later in the interview, he said, "I'm the guy who protects the president and the family. I'm the guy who would take a bullet for the president."

So it should have come as no surprise that Cohen was on "message" and toed the "party line" that Trump had laid down at his press conference the previous summer. "I assume we will discuss the rejected proposal to build a Trump property in Moscow that was terminated in January of 2016; which occurred before the Iowa caucus and months before the very first primary," Cohen stated in his written testimony and later repeated under oath during the committee hearings—even though the project had not been "terminated" and was still under way months later. He added, "I'm very proud to have served Donald J. Trump for all these years, and I'll continue to support him."

Cohen later said he released his opening remarks to "shape the narrative" and make sure other witnesses knew what he was saying so they, too, could stay on message. Afterward, Trump's lawyer called to tell Cohen the president was pleased with his statement.

HAVING ABANDONED, AT least for the time being, his efforts to get rid of Mueller or Sessions, Trump renewed his efforts to punish Comey, whose treachery still infuriated the president. He had his lawyer in the Russia investigation, John Dowd, write a long letter to Rosenstein airing Trump's festering grievances and complaining that Mueller was "inexplicably not investigating the official misconduct of former FBI Director James Comey involving his unlawful conduct and testimony." Dowd continued, "It is particularly troubling that it was Mr. Comey's plainly deliberate, unlawful conduct and false Congressional testimony which precipitated your appointment of Special Counsel Mueller. Indeed, Mr. Comey publicly bragged about it.

"I further understand that the Department of Justice has failed to open and commence a full Federal Grand Jury investigation into the obviously corrupt closing of the e-mail investigation of Secretary Clinton including the highly irregular and bizarre conduct of Mr. Comey and then Attorney General Lynch. Nor has it addressed the corruption investigation of the Clinton Foundation."

Trump kept up the same refrain with Sessions, complaining that the Justice Department should be pursuing Clinton rather than him. "Wow, FBI confirms report that James Comey drafted letter exonerating Crooked Hillary Clinton long before investigation was complete. Many people not interviewed, including Clinton herself. Comey stated under oath that he didn't do this—obviously a fix? Where is Justice Dept?" Trump tweeted in October. He followed up with another tweet: "ANGER & UNITY" over a "lack of investigation" of Clinton and "the Comey fix," and concluded, "DO SOMETHING!"

Republicans in Congress were also keeping up the pressure on the FBI. In late October, House Speaker Paul Ryan announced that the FBI had agreed to turn over documents related to the controversial Steele dossier.

The announcement alarmed Christopher Steele, who, despite sporadic efforts to reestablish his relationship with the FBI, hadn't made any progress. But he was still in regular contact with Bruce Ohr at the Justice Department.

"Can we have a word tomorrow, please?" Steele wrote in an email to Ohr. "Just seen a story in the media about the Bureau handing over docs to Congress about my work and relationship with them. Very concerned about this. People's lives may be endangered." Ohr conveyed his worries to the FBI. "I can give you an FBI contact if and when it becomes necessary" to protect the source, Ohr wrote to Steele afterward.

Later, Steele did speak to another FBI agent and eventually cooperated with Mueller.

THAT MONTH THE Mueller investigation produced its first conviction: George Papadopoulos, whose comment to an Australian diplomat had set the entire probe in motion. When questioned by FBI agents, Papadopoulos made numerous false statements, all designed to minimize his contact with Russians trying to elect Trump. In that regard, he, too, toed the Trump party line.

When questioned by the FBI, Papadopoulos had readily identified his source for the Clinton "dirt" remark—Joseph Mifsud, a mysterious Maltese professor based in London with ties to the Kremlin. The FBI had interviewed Mifsud when he was passing through Washington, but he had lied, too. Mifsud left the country and stayed beyond the reach of U.S. authorities.

In July, Papadopoulos was arrested after landing at Dulles International Airport. In October he pleaded guilty to making false statements to the FBI.

"I made a terrible mistake, for which I have paid a terrible price, and am deeply ashamed," he told the judge at his sentencing. He said he'd lied to "create distance between the issue, myself, and the president." His lawyer was more explicit: "The President of the United States hindered this investigation more than George Papadopoulos ever could."

Impressed by his contrition, the judge sentenced him to just fourteen days in jail.

ON NOVEMBER 29, the inspector general's lawyers again questioned McCabe under oath. It was clear by now they were closing in on him.

McCabe said he'd clarified his answers in his phone call on August 1 after spending "a lot of time thinking about it" over the weekend and that "on further recollection, yeah, I remember authorizing Page and Kortan to talk to *The Wall Street Journal*." He said, "It was important to me that Beckhard and you all did not have the misimpression about the authorization that I had given to, to Kortan and Page to interact with Devlin Barrett on that article."

McCabe said he didn't want the inspector general's office to "start heading off in a direction on" Kortan and Page "that would not have been accurate."

But then, Beckhard pointed out, McCabe did know where Page had been despite his earlier answer he didn't know because he was out of town.

"Yeah, and as I've said before, and she made clear, I was very concerned, as I think I said at that time, uncomfortable about discussing things that I thought were outside the scope," McCabe responded. "And I felt like that's the direction that the questions were coming from. I didn't feel comfortable saying, you know, vouching for what was in Strzok's and Page's texts and saying what they meant. I had not thought about the *Wall Street Journal* article and the conversations we had around it in quite a long time. And so, I misspoke."

ON DECEMBER 1, Michael Flynn pleaded guilty to lying to the FBI about conversations with the Russian ambassador and agreed to cooperate with Mueller's investigation. This came as no surprise to Trump or his attorneys: Flynn had withdrawn from a joint defense agreement he had with the president nine days earlier, signaling he was about to make a deal. Trump's lawyer John Dowd had left a voice mail for Flynn's lawyer that appeared to be a veiled threat as well as encouragement to remain in the president's fold.

"I'm sympathetic," Dowd began. "I understand your situation, but let me see if I can't state it in starker terms. It wouldn't surprise me if you've gone on to make a deal with, and work, with the government." He continued, "If, on the other hand, we have, there's information that implicates the President, then we've got a national security issue, or maybe a national security issue, I don't know, some issue, we got to deal with, not only for the President, but for the country." He added, "We need some kind of heads-up, just for the sake of protecting all our interests."

Without specifically mentioning a pardon, Dowd reminded him, "Remember what we've always said about the President and his feelings toward Flynn and, that still remains."*

THE NEXT DAY, the president tried to focus attention on his sweeping tax bill, which had just won approval in the Senate. Following the debacle of failing to repeal Obamacare, it was the biggest legislative success of his tenure. "It was a fantastic evening last night," he told White House reporters before boarding his helicopter. "We passed the largest tax cut in the history of our country," a typical exaggeration (it was not even close to being the largest).

But reporters quickly asked about Flynn. Trump said he wasn't worried about his cooperation. Asked if the president still stood behind him despite the guilty plea, Trump said, "We'll see what happens." To McCabe and others at the FBI, this was appalling: as if Trump's support for an admitted criminal were conditioned on what Flynn did—or didn't—say.

Trump followed up with a series of supportive comments about Flynn while taking swipes at his usual targets: "So General Flynn lies to the FBI and his life is destroyed, while Crooked Hillary Clinton, on that now fa-

---

* Dowd was furious the recording was made public, and accused Mueller of trying to "smear and damage the reputation of counsel and innocent people."

mous FBI holiday 'interrogation' with no swearing in and no recording, lies many times . . . and nothing happens to her? Rigged system, or just a double standard?" Trump tweeted. And "I feel badly for General Flynn. I feel very badly. He's led a very strong life," he said later.

TOWARD THE END of November, Lisa Page heard from a reporter that Strzok had been removed from Mueller's team because of anti-Trump texts. There were also rumors that the texts revealed an affair.

Page froze. "I can't talk about that," she said.

Page was stricken. One hope to which she'd clung on even the darkest days was that the affair wouldn't become public knowledge. The inspector general had agreed it wasn't relevant. It violated no FBI or Justice Department policies. It was purely salacious. Yet now someone was peddling the story.

Page didn't think the timing was an accident, coming just as Flynn's guilty plea was making headlines. Casting aspersions on her and the FBI was one way to divert attention from Flynn's potentially damaging cooperation. Page braced herself.

The next day, her lawyer, Amy Jeffress, called with more bad news. The *Post*'s Devlin Barrett—the same reporter with whom Page had tangled over the *Wall Street Journal* story when he was a reporter there—had called. He, too, knew about Strzok and the affair.

Barrett also called Kortan, the FBI's head of public affairs. *The New York Times* was calling, too. Kortan alerted Strzok, who felt betrayed that someone had leaked such personal information. But he felt there was nothing he could do or say to stop it.

Page, on the other hand, called Barrett. "Please don't destroy my life," she pleaded. "The IG is not looking at the affair. It's not against any policy. It's not part of any investigation."

"My source says it is," Barrett said.

"Call the IG and confirm it," Page begged. She said she'd give Michael Horowitz, the inspector general, permission to discuss it with him.

Barrett said he'd already cleared the story with Martin Baron, the *Post*'s top editor. But he said he'd call Horowitz. Page thought she'd at least bought some time.

But minutes later, the story appeared online with a joint byline, Barrett and Karoun Demirjian.

After stating that Strzok had been removed over text messages, the third paragraph read, "During the Clinton investigation, Strzok was involved in a romantic relationship with FBI lawyer Lisa Page, who worked for Deputy Director Andrew McCabe, according to the people familiar with the matter, who spoke on the condition of anonymity because of the sensitivity of the issue.

"The Post repeatedly sought comment from Strzok and Page but got no response."

Page was devastated, and furious with Barrett. She called the reporter again: "Don't lead me on when you have no intention of doing it." She hung up on him before he could respond.*

Page texted her mother in Los Angeles to warn her that the shocking news was coming: "It's true and I don't want to talk about it."

As Page had feared, news of the affair overshadowed everything else in her life. To the *New York Post*, she and Strzok were now "those cheatin' FBI lovebirds." On Fox News, they were the "FBI's anti-Trump lovebirds." The media camped out at her house. Her job search came to an abrupt halt.

Trump leaped on the revelation. "Tainted (no, very dishonest?) FBI 'agent's role in Clinton probe under review.' Led Clinton Email probe," he tweeted early the next morning, followed by "Report: 'ANTI-TRUMP FBI AGENT LED CLINTON EMAIL PROBE' Now it all starts to make sense!" And then: "After years of Comey, with the phony and dishonest Clinton investigation (and more), running the FBI, its reputation is in Tatters—worst in History! But fear not, we will bring it back to greatness."

---

* *The New York Times* actually broke the story of Strzok's removal over the texts but said nothing about an affair, even though *Times* reporters knew about it. See "A Top FBI Agent Taken Off Inquiry," *New York Times,* December 3, 2017.

The tirade prompted a rare response from Eric Holder, Obama's attorney general: "Nope. Not letting this go. The FBI's reputation is not in 'tatters.' It's composed of the same dedicated men and women who have always worked there and who do a great, apolitical job. You'll find integrity and honesty at FBI headquarters and not at 1600 Penn Ave right now."

A FEW DAYS after Flynn's guilty plea, Trump asked Sessions to stay behind after a cabinet meeting and again asked him to "unrecuse." "You'd be a hero," the president told him. Porter was on hand taking notes: "Not telling you to do anything. [Alan] Dershowitz says POTUS can get involved. Can order AG to investigate. I don't want to get involved. I'm not going to get involved. I'm not going to do anything or direct you to do anything. I just want to be treated fairly."

"We are taking steps; whole new leadership," Sessions responded, according to Porter's notes.

Among those steps, apparently, was a demotion for Bruce Ohr, Steele's Justice Department contact. Jim Crowell, Rosenstein's chief of staff, and Scott Schools, the department's most senior career attorney, summoned Ohr to say he was being removed from the office of the deputy attorney general, because "news articles" were about to reveal his dealings with Steele and his wife's position at Fusion and Ohr hadn't given the department "timely notice" of those relationships (even though Ohr had told several Justice Department officials). But Ohr could keep his job as head of the organized crime drug enforcement task force.

That didn't last long. On December 7, Fox News reported, "Evidence collected by the House Permanent Select Committee on Intelligence chaired by Rep. Devin Nunes, R-Calif., indicates that Ohr met during the 2016 campaign with Christopher Steele, the former British spy who authored the 'dossier.'" Four days later, Fox reported that Ohr's wife worked for Fusion.

The next day, Jay Sekulow, one of Trump's personal lawyers, told the *Axios* columnist Mike Allen, "The Department of Justice and FBI cannot ignore the multiple problems that have been created by these obvious conflicts of interests. These new revelations require the appointment of a Special Counsel to investigate."

Ohr and his wife soon became two of Trump's favorite Twitter targets, even though hardly anyone knew who Ohr was. Trump threatened to revoke Ohr's security clearance and later told reporters Ohr was a "disgrace." He tweeted, "How the hell is Bruce Ohr still employed at the Justice Department? Disgraceful! Witch Hunt!"

This time Ohr was told that Sessions and Rosenstein didn't want him to have further direct contact with anyone at the White House. Ohr was removed as head of the drug task force and assigned to a low-ranking staff position in the criminal division.

ON DECEMBER 12, the embattled Justice Department took another step that was sure to please Trump. It released to Congress—and in an even more unusual move, invited selected reporters to the Justice Department to review—375 of the raw Page-Strzok texts. There was no effort to explain their meaning or put them in a broader context. Given that they were obtained as part of the inspector general's review of the FBI's handling of the Clinton email case, they would ordinarily have been produced—if at all—only after that investigation and report were finished. But it was nowhere near being done.

In one concession to common decency, the Justice Department withheld texts that were purely personal and reflected the affair. Still, just about everyone at the FBI—most of all Strzok and Page themselves—were stunned at this departure from Justice Department policy. And they were furious that it had been Rosenstein himself who had made the decision.

Rosenstein defended his decision the next day at a hearing of the House Judiciary Committee. He said he'd approved the decision to give the texts to Congress after consulting with Horowitz but didn't say why he took the added step of briefing the media. "Our goal," he said, "is to make sure that it is clear to you and the American people that we are not concealing anything that's embarrassing to the FBI."

That was an understatement. A few of the raw texts, taken out of context, were incendiary:

> August 16, 2015, Strzok: "[Bernie
> Sanders is] an idiot like Trump. Figure
> they cancel each other out."

> February 13, 2016, Strzok: "Oh, [Trump's]
> abysmal. I keep hoping the charade will
> end and people will just dump him."

> March 4, 2016, Page: "God trump is a
> loathsome human."

> Strzok: "Omg [Trump's] an idiot."

> Page: "He's awful."

> Strzok: "God Hillary should win
> 100,000,000–0."

> Page: "Also did you hear [Trump] make a
> comment about the size of his d*ck
> earlier? This man cannot be president."

> July 19, 2016, Page: "Donald Trump
> is an enormous d*uche."

> July 21, 2016, Strzok: "Trump is a
> disaster. I have no idea how destabilizing
> his Presidency would be."

October 20, 2016, Strzok: "I am riled up.
Trump is a fucking idiot, is unable to
provide a coherent answer."

The texts dominated news coverage for days and suddenly put Mueller and the FBI on the defensive. Their release provided a field day for speculation by right-wing conspiracy theorists. Page and Strzok stood by helplessly as what they thought were private political opinions they were entitled to hold were distorted beyond recognition. To their dismay, no one stepped forward to defend them and the integrity of their work—not Comey, not McCabe, not Mueller, and certainly not their new boss, Christopher Wray. Wray said only that he would "hold people accountable after there has been an appropriate investigation, independent and objective, by the inspector general."

On Fox News, Trump allies like Sean Hannity avidly cast the revelation of the texts in apocalyptic terms. "This is very profound because on a level far deeper than Watergate ever was here, there is corruption at the highest levels," Hannity said on December 14. "This is no longer paranoia, it's provable fact that the fix was in here. You have James Comey. Then you have the pro-Hillary, anti-Trump Peter Strzok and then his girlfriend Lisa Page, yeah, they are the ones going to save America with what they are doing." He continued, "I don't even know what to say. I mean I don't even know what to say. Wouldn't you define this as obstruction?"

Newt Gingrich, the former Republican House Speaker and strong Trump ally, responded, "At every level, this is undermining our system of justice. It is violating the law. It's very likely all of these people will end up going to jail."

Congressman Andy Biggs, Republican of Arizona, also interviewed on Fox News, stated, "In any other country, we would call it a coup when you abuse the power of the police state to basically disenfranchise or just eliminate, if you will, the acting president. That's what was being done here."

That day, as he left for a visit to the FBI Academy, Trump commented, "It's a shame what's happened with the FBI. But we're going to rebuild the FBI. It will be bigger and better than ever. But it is very sad when you look at those documents. And how they've done that is really, really disgraceful, and you have a lot of very angry people that are seeing it. It's a very sad thing to watch, I will tell you that."

A WEEK AFTER their release, the "Lovebirds" texts still dominated cable news, which lent itself to rampant speculation about their meaning and ever darker conspiracy theories. In this highly charged atmosphere, McCabe testified before the House Judiciary Committee on December 21. The designated topic was the FBI's handling of the Clinton email case, but questions inevitably turned to the raging topic of the day. And questions from more sympathetic Democrats gave McCabe an opportunity to defend himself against some of the more extreme accusations, even if it was a closed-door session from which the press was excluded.

David Cicilline, a Democrat from Rhode Island, asked, "Mr. McCabe, was there any effort at the FBI to stop Donald Trump from being elected President of the United States?"

"No, sir."

"Is there any effort at the FBI currently to launch a coup against the President of the United States?"

"No, sir."

The congressman continued, "You've come under attack in a way that you've described as having devastating consequences for you and your family. Are you allowed publicly to respond?"

McCabe shook his head no.

"Could you speak, Mr. McCabe, a little bit more about that? We are seeing—we've seen it in this committee, we've seen it on television—what appears to be an intentional campaign to undermine the work of the FBI, the professionalism of the men and women who risk their lives to keep our country safe, and even the Department of Justice. Would you talk a little bit about what the impact of that is on the agency and the danger you think it poses—if you think it poses any danger—to the rule of law in this country?"

"You've asked quite a lot there," McCabe answered. "First, as I have said before, the men and women of the FBI remain committed to the most righteous mission on earth, and that is protecting Americans wherever they are, in whatever they do, and upholding the Constitution. I have no doubt that the men and women of the FBI will remain committed to and continue to execute that mission in an effective and professional and independent way. So that's what we do. That's our job. No matter what anyone says or how—what directions the winds blow around us, we will stay focused on that mission and continue doing that job."

McCabe elaborated on his role in removing Strzok from the Mueller investigation, even though Strzok's political views were his own business and there wasn't any evidence they'd affected his work.

McCabe said that after he learned about the texts, "I made the decision to remove him from the investigation that evening. I came back from my meeting with the inspector general. I met with a very small group of my fellow leaders. We discussed Peter's reassignment, and we discussed where we would place him."

Jamie Raskin, a Maryland Democrat, asked, "Now, just to take the devil's advocate's position, someone might have said, well, he expressed very vigorous criticism and opinions of Governor O'Malley, of Bernie Sanders, of Donald Trump, other people. Why was he not entitled to those private opinions expressed in the texts? Could he have made the argument that it didn't affect his public performance?"

"He certainly could and he certainly may," McCabe said. "What I knew at that point was that the inspector general was investigating Mr. Strzok and Ms. Page for potential political bias. And simply the existence of that investigation I felt was—could place in jeopardy the work of the special counsel's team, and I did not—I could not possibly take that risk."

Raskin asked of Strzok, "Did he in any way contaminate the entire investigation with bias because of those private texts that he sent?"

"Not in any way that I am aware of, sir," McCabe replied.

Elijah Cummings, also a Maryland Democrat, asked McCabe much the same question: "In your long and distinguished career at the FBI, have you ever let your personal political views, whatever they might be, influence you in any way with regard to your actions as an FBI agent?"

"No, sir."

"Did you ever let the fact that your wife ran for State Senate, or anything that occurred related to her campaign, influence or impact, in any way, your official actions as an FBI agent?"

"No, sir."

"What is your reaction to those personal attacks against you, and, more broadly, against the FBI as an institution?"

"Well, you have given me a lot to unpack there," McCabe responded.

"Let me tell you something," Cummings said. "I'm concerned about the tearing down of the reputation of the FBI, and it is painful."

"Yep."

"Because I think it's an attack on our very democracy. That's my feeling. But I'm just wondering what—I mean, how the men and women, these men and women who go out every day and give their blood, their sweat, their tears, wondering if they're going to come home, I mean, I'm just wondering how you and how they are affected."

"Yeah. So if I could speak just for a minute about my personal experience over the last year. And I'll tell you it has been enormously challenging. My wife is a wonderful, brilliant, caring physician who was drawn to take a run at public life because she was committed to trying to expand health insurance coverage for the people of the State of Virginia. That was the one and only thing that raised her interest in running for office when she was approached with the possibility of doing so. And having started with that noble intention, to have gone through what she and my children have experienced over the last year has been—it has been devastating."

Cummings asked for a "general idea" of what that was like.

"The constant reiteration of the lies and accusations about things that she allegedly did, or I allegedly did, in support of her campaign, despite the fact that we've consistently tried to tell folks the truth about what happened, has been very, very frustrating."

Two days later, Trump did exactly that, with an error-filled tweet: "How can FBI Deputy Director Andrew McCabe, the man in charge, along with James Comey, of the Phony Hillary Clinton investigation (including her 33,000 illegally deleted emails) be given $700,000 for wife's campaign by Clinton Puppets during investigation?"

And Trump followed up the same day with his first reference to McCabe's eligibility to retire: "FBI Deputy Director Andrew McCabe is racing the clock to retire with full benefits. 90 days to go?!!!"

THIRTEEN

DEEP STATE

T rump began the New Year of 2018 by tweeting another attack on
the Justice Department, referring to it this time as the "Deep State
Justice Department." There was nothing new in his calls for jail
time for Clinton and Comey. But it did mark his first public use of a phrase
that had become ubiquitous among his adoring media chorus.*

Newt Gingrich elaborated on the theme, calling Mueller "the tip of
the deep state spear aimed at destroying or at a minimum undermining
and crippling the Trump presidency" on Twitter. He added, "The brazen
redefinition of Mueller's task tells you how arrogant the deep state is and
how confident it is it can get away with anything."

"Deep State" soon joined "witch hunt" and "lock her up" in the pan-
theon of repetitive Trumpisms.

The term appears to have first been used in the 1990s to describe bu-
reaucratic resistance to the Turkish dictator Recep Tayyip Erdogan. But
its use in the United States picked up after a 2014 Bill Moyers television
interview with the author Mike Lofgren, a Republican former congressional staff member. It quickly made the leap from PBS to right-wing conspiracy theorists like Alex Jones, who accused the Deep State of plotting
to assassinate Trump.

In an essay to accompany the Moyers interview, Lofgren posited,

---

* Bannon said Trump picked up the phrase from watching Sean Hannity. Bannon himself mocked
the use of the phrase and said it was ridiculous.

There is the visible government situated around
the Mall in Washington, and then there is another,
more shadowy, more indefinable government that
is not explained in Civics 101 or observable to
tourists at the White House or the Capitol. The
former is traditional Washington partisan politics: the tip of the iceberg that a public watching
C-SPAN sees daily and which is theoretically
controllable via elections. The subsurface part of
the iceberg I shall call the Deep State, which operates according to its own compass heading regardless of who is formally in power.

IN MID-JANUARY, TRUMP was diverted from Mueller and the Russia investigation by yet another scandal, this one involving payoffs to a porn star.
On January 12, *The Wall Street Journal* reported that Michael Cohen
"arranged a $130,000 payment to a former adult-film star a month before
the 2016 election as part of an agreement that precluded her from publicly
discussing an alleged sexual encounter with Mr. Trump, according to
people familiar with the matter."

Michael Cohen, who spent nearly a decade as
a top attorney at the Trump Organization, arranged payment to the woman, Stephanie Clifford, in October 2016 after her lawyer negotiated
the nondisclosure agreement with Mr. Cohen.

In a statement to the *Journal*, Cohen said, "This is now the second
time that you are raising outlandish allegations against my client. You
have attempted to perpetuate this false narrative for over a year; a narrative that has been consistently denied by all parties since at least 2011,"
but he stopped short of explicitly denying payments had been made.

When Cohen sought guidance from Trump (again defying his lawyer's order not to talk to the president), Trump told him to say the president "was not knowledgeable" about the transaction. Cohen subsequently released a statement to that effect: "In a private transaction in 2016, I used my own personal funds to facilitate a payment of $130,000" to Clifford. "Neither the Trump Organization nor the Trump campaign was a party to the transaction," and "neither reimbursed me for the payment, either directly or indirectly."

Trump's lawyer sent Cohen a text: "Client says thanks for what you do."

WITH PRIEBUS GONE, McGahn was increasingly isolated at the White House. He and Trump were now communicating mostly through lawyers. On the other hand, his status as a key witness to the Comey firing gave him a certain amount of job security. Still, as should have been obvious, McGahn was fast falling from favor with the president.

Matters came to a head after *The New York Times*, on January 25, disclosed that Trump had ordered McGahn to get rid of Mueller but had backed down after McGahn refused and threatened to quit—all of which was true.

"Fake news, folks. Fake news. A typical New York Times fake story," Trump said en route to the World Economic Forum in Davos, Switzerland.

Through various lawyers and other intermediaries, Trump asked McGahn to refute the story. McGahn wasn't about to lie. He refused, saying the article was largely accurate.

A week later Trump was still fulminating. The story was "bullshit," he told Rob Porter, the White House staff secretary who was emerging as the president's preferred confidant. McGahn had leaked it to make himself look good. Trump said he wanted McGahn to write a letter refuting the story "for our records" because McGahn was a "lying bastard." He added that if McGahn didn't write such a letter, "then maybe I'll have to get rid of him."

When Porter dutifully conveyed the message, McGahn refused, saying the story was true. He waved off the president's threat to fire him, saying the "optics would be terrible."

The next day, in an Oval Office meeting with McGahn and the president's new chief of staff, John Kelly, Trump told McGahn he needed to correct the *Times* story. "I never said to fire Mueller. I never said 'fire,'" Trump insisted. "This story doesn't look good. You need to correct this. You're the White House counsel. Did I say the word 'fire'?"

"What you said is, 'Call Rod [Rosenstein], tell Rod that Mueller has conflicts and can't be the Special Counsel,'" McGahn responded.

"I never said that," Trump said. He only wanted McGahn to tell Rosenstein about Mueller's conflicts and then let Rosenstein decide how to proceed.

Trump had said no such thing. McGahn asserted again that Trump had said, "Call Rod. There are conflicts. Mueller has to go."

At this juncture the conversation was getting "a little tense," in Kelly's view.

So would McGahn do a correction? Trump asked.

"No," McGahn said.

Plainly annoyed, Trump noticed McGahn was writing on a legal pad. "What about these notes?" he asked. "Why do you take notes? Lawyers don't take notes. I never had a lawyer who took notes."

McGahn said a "real lawyer" takes notes because they create a record and aren't a bad thing.

"I've had a lot of great lawyers, like Roy Cohn," Trump said. "He did not take notes."

DESPITE TRUMP'S EARLIER public statements that he'd gladly submit to an interview by Mueller and his team, on January 29 Trump's lawyers John Dowd and Jay Sekulow submitted a twenty-page letter refusing Mueller's request to interview the president. It also constituted a detailed defense of the charges being investigated, focusing on the president's unique status as chief executive officer. The memo took the sweeping—and in the view of many legal experts radical—view that a president could not be charged for doing something that was within his constitutional prerogative, such as firing Comey, no matter what his motive. They also took the opportunity to attack the FBI and the Department of Justice—a thinly veiled attack on Mueller himself.

"It is abundantly clear to the undersigned that all of the answers to your inquiries are contained in the exhibits and testimony that have already been voluntarily provided to you by the White House and witnesses, all of which clearly show that there was no collusion with Russia, and that no FBI investigation was or even could have been obstructed," Trump's lawyers wrote.

"It remains our position that the President's actions here, by virtue of his position as the chief law enforcement officer, could neither constitutionally nor legally constitute obstruction because that would amount to him obstructing himself, and that he could, if he wished, terminate the inquiry, or even exercise his power to pardon if he so desired."

They continued, "We express again, as we have expressed before, that the Special Counsel's inquiry has been and remains a considerable burden for the President and his Office, has endangered the safety and security of our country, and has interfered with the President's ability to both govern domestically and conduct foreign affairs. This encumbrance has been only compounded by the astounding public revelations about the corruption within the FBI and Department of Justice which appears to have led to the alleged Russia collusion investigation and the establishment of the Office of Special Counsel in the first place. . . .

"We respectfully decline to allow our client to testify," the letter continued, and the lawyers took aim again at the FBI: "As is now apparent with the benefit of subsequent developments, the firing of Mr. Comey has led to the discovery of corruption within the FBI at the highest levels. . . .

"It is also worth responding to the popular suggestion that the President's public criticism of the FBI either constitutes obstruction or serves as evidence of obstruction. Such criticism ignores the sacred responsibility of the President to hold his subordinates accountable—a function not unlike public Congressional oversight hearings. After all, the FBI is not above the law and we are now learning of the disappointing results of a lack of accountability in both the DOJ and FBI."

And they reinforced McCabe's and Trump's point that Rosenstein had an obvious conflict, given that he was a critical witness for the defense:

> As you also know, far from merely signing off on a Presidential decision or taking a weak or indirect action indicating a tacit or pressured approval, Mr. Rosenstein actually helped to edit Mr. Comey's termination letter and actively advised the President accordingly. It is unthinkable that a President acting (1) under his Constitutional authority; (2) on the written recommendation and with the overt participation of his Deputy Attorney General; and (3) consistent with the advice of his Attorney General, to fire a subordinate who has been universally condemned by bipartisan leadership could then be accused of obstruction for doing so.

In sum,

> What all of the foregoing demonstrates is that, as to the questions that you desire to ask the President, absent any cognizable obstruction offense, and in light of the extraordinary cooperation by the President and all relevant parties, you have been provided with full responses to each of the topics you presented, obviating any need for an interview with the President. As all of the evidence demonstrates, every action that the President took was taken with full constitutional authority pursuant to Article II of the United States Constitution. As such, these actions cannot constitute obstruction, whether viewed separately or even as a totality.

ON SUNDAY EVENING, January 28, Christopher Wray summoned McCabe to his office at the Hoover Building. Since Wray's arrival, McCabe had tried to do everything he'd promised, which was to get Wray up to speed before McCabe reached his retirement date, now less than two months away. Wray had generally listened attentively, revealing little about himself. Their relationship was professional and polite, if not especially warm or close.

It was thus a shock to McCabe that as soon as he arrived, Wray said he was removing him as deputy director. Michael Horowitz, the inspector general, had briefed Wray the day before on progress in the leak investigation, which was nearing completion. Horowitz had told him that McCabe was going to be charged with multiple counts of "lack of candor" regarding his testimony about the *Wall Street Journal* article.

McCabe tried to defend himself; neither he nor his lawyer had as yet had a chance to respond to any proposed findings. McCabe stressed that he'd voluntarily corrected any misstatements. Wray wasn't interested in the details. He said McCabe had a choice: he could choose to leave his position, or Wray would remove him.

McCabe thought about it overnight. The next morning, he said he'd remain on the payroll, but effectively end his twenty-one-year career at the bureau. He didn't want another job; after being deputy and acting director, anything would be a demotion. And he wasn't going to pretend the move was voluntary. He had enough vacation time to get to his retirement date. Or so he thought.

Just about everyone at the FBI was stunned by McCabe's sudden departure and Wray's faint praise. Obviously something very bad had happened. No one knew what.

THE WEEK OF March 12, the inspector general finally delivered a draft "Report of Investigation of Certain Allegations Relating to Former FBI Deputy Director Andrew McCabe" to the FBI's Office of Professional Responsibility. Just twenty-four hours later, the office notified McCabe it was recommending he be fired.

McCabe finally got a copy. Its conclusions were more devastating than anything McCabe had imagined:

We found that, in a conversation with then-Director Comey shortly after the WSJ article was published, McCabe lacked candor when he told Comey, or made statements that led Comey to believe, that McCabe had not authorized the disclosure and did not know who did. This conduct violated FBI Offense Code 2.5 (Lack of Candor—No Oath).

We also found that on May 9, 2017, when questioned under oath by FBI agents, McCabe lacked candor when he told the agents that he had not authorized the disclosure to the WSJ and did not know who did. This conduct violated FBI Offense Code 2.6 (Lack of Candor—Under Oath).

We further found that on July 28, 2017, when questioned under oath by the OIG in a recorded interview, McCabe lacked candor when he stated: (a) that he was not aware of Special Counsel having been authorized to speak to reporters around October 30 and (b) that, because he was not in Washington, D.C., on October 27 and 28, 2016, he was unable to say where Special Counsel was or what she was doing at that time. This conduct violated FBI Offense Code 2.6 (Lack of Candor—Under Oath).

We additionally found that on November 29, 2017, when questioned under oath by the OIG in a recorded interview during which he contradicted his prior statements by acknowledging that he had authorized the disclosure to the WSJ, McCabe lacked candor when he: (a) stated that he told Comey on October 31, 2016, that he had authorized the disclosure to the WSJ; (b) denied telling INSD agents on May 9 that he had not authorized the disclosure to the WSJ about the PADAG call; and (c) asserted that INSD's questioning of him on May 9 about the October 30 WSJ article occurred at the end of an unrelated meeting when one of the INSD agents pulled him aside and asked him one or two questions about the article. This conduct violated FBI Offense Code 2.6 (Lack of Candor—Under Oath).

Lastly, we determined that as Deputy Director, McCabe was authorized to disclose the existence of the CF Investigation publicly if such a disclosure fell within the "public interest" exception in applicable FBI and DOJ policies generally prohibiting such a disclosure of an ongoing investigation.

However, we concluded that McCabe's decision to confirm the existence of the CF Investigation through an anonymously sourced quote, recounting the content of a phone call with a senior Department official in a manner designed to advance his personal interests at the expense of Department leadership, was clearly not within the public interest exception. We therefore concluded that McCabe's disclosure of the existence of an ongoing investigation in this manner violated the FBI's and the Department's media policy and constituted misconduct.

The OIG is issuing this report to the FBI for such action as it deems appropriate.

Under FBI guidelines, subjects are typically given thirty days to respond. McCabe was told he had less than a week. On Thursday, he spent four hours with Scott Schools, who'd replaced David Margolis at the Justice Department. McCabe stressed how confusing the questioning had been, veering abruptly from the *Circa News* article the questions were supposed to be about to a *Wall Street Journal* article he barely remembered and wasn't prepared for. He'd been blindsided, too, after he was summoned to the Justice Department and was shown the Page-Strzok texts. His mind was still reeling from that revelation when, over his protests, he was again aggressively questioned about the *Wall Street Journal* article. When McCabe had the time to consider what he'd said and realized he'd made some misstatements, he'd corrected his testimony—as have countless witnesses called by the FBI.

Schools betrayed little reaction, but McCabe thought he'd made a strong case. Part of him couldn't believe that after an illustrious career at the highest levels of the bureau, he was about to be fired.

Friday was McCabe's last day on the payroll; he'd be eligible to retire on Sunday. It didn't matter if he were terminated for cause on Monday;

he'd still receive full retirement benefits, which included a pension and health care. He and his family celebrated as best they could with a dinner Friday night.

McCabe was watching CNN at about 10:00 p.m. when the reporter Laura Jarrett broke in with the news that he'd been fired. She called it a "stunning blow tonight to the man who had climbed to the highest echelons of the FBI."

On some level McCabe knew it was coming. Still, the news felt like a punch in the gut. And the timing—late on a Friday night, just in time to cost him his retirement benefits—seemed obviously vindictive. He was not going to go quietly.

"This attack on my credibility is one part of a larger effort not just to slander me personally, but to taint the FBI, law enforcement, and intelligence professionals more generally," McCabe said in a statement released by his law firm. "It is part of this Administration's ongoing war on the FBI and the efforts of the Special Counsel investigation, which continue to this day. Their persistence in this campaign only highlights the importance of the Special Counsel's work."

Many at FBI headquarters were stunned that standard dismissal procedures had been accelerated and McCabe was fired hours before he was eligible to retire. Strzok, for one, thought it was morally wrong and malicious. Under the circumstances, it looked as if FBI and Justice Department leadership were trying to curry favor at the White House at McCabe's expense.

President Trump could barely contain his satisfaction, saying in a late-night tweet. "Andrew McCabe FIRED, a great day for the hard working men and women of the FBI—A great day for Democracy," he wrote. "Sanctimonious James Comey was his boss and made McCabe look like a choirboy. He knew all about the lies and corruption going on at the highest levels of the FBI!"

ON MARCH 22, John Dowd, considered a voice of moderation on Trump's legal team who had orchestrated the delicate balance between cooperat-

ing and keeping Trump from testifying, resigned, presumably over differences in strategy. As Dowd's voicemail had vividly demonstrated, a large
part of that strategy had been aimed at keeping others from turning
against the president, a classic lawyers' dilemma in any case involving possible conspiracies. So far, Trump had been remarkably adept at keeping
everyone in the fold while stopping short of outright witness tampering.
Of course Trump didn't need to say the obvious, which was that he had a
unique incentive to encourage cooperation: the power of the pardon.

Paul Manafort had clearly gotten the intended message: After
Manafort and his former business partner Rick Gates were indicted in
October, Manafort had reassured his fellow defendant that he had talked
to the president's personal counsel who said they should "sit tight" and
"we'll be taken care of," even though he said no one actually used the
word "pardon."

But then, on April 9, FBI agents searched Cohen's home, hotel room,
and office pursuant to a search warrant. Trump was outraged. That afternoon, at a meeting with military commanders to discuss Syria, he instead
vented his frustrations with Mueller and the Russia investigation.

"So I just heard that they broke into the office of one of my personal
attorneys—a good man," Trump began. "And it's a disgraceful situation.
It's a total witch hunt. I've been saying it for a long time. I've wanted to
keep it down. We've given, I believe, over a million pages worth of documents to the Special Counsel. They continue to just go forward. And here
we are talking about Syria and we're talking about a lot of serious things.
We're the greatest fighting force ever. And I have this witch hunt constantly going on for over 12 months now—and actually, much more than
that. You could say it was right after I won the nomination, it started.

"And it's a disgrace. It's, frankly, a real disgrace. It's an attack on our
country, in a true sense. It's an attack on what we all stand for.

"So when I saw this and when I heard it—heard it like you did—I said,
that is really now on a whole new level of unfairness."

After repeating "there was no collusion at all. No collusion," he continued with a familiar attack on Mueller and his team. "This is the most biased group of people. These people have the biggest conflicts of interest

I've ever seen. Democrats all—or just about all—either Democrats or a couple of Republicans that worked for President Obama, they're not looking at the other side; they're not looking at the Hillary Clinton—the horrible things that she did and all of the crimes that were committed. They're not looking at all of the things that happened that everybody is very angry about, I can tell you, from the Republican side, and I think even the independent side. They only keep looking at us.

"So they find no collusion, and then they go from there and they say, 'Well, let's keep going.' And they raid an office of a personal attorney early in the morning. And I think it's a disgrace.

"So we'll be talking about it more. But this is the most conflicted group of people I've ever seen. The Attorney General made a terrible mistake when he did this, and when he recused himself. Or he should have certainly let us know if he was going to recuse himself, and we would have used a—put a different Attorney General in. So he made what I consider to be a very terrible mistake for the country. But you'll figure that out.

"All I can say is, after looking for a long period of time—and even before the Special Counsel—because it really started just about from the time I won the nomination. And you look at what took place and what happened, and it's a disgrace. It's a disgrace."

Clinton was obviously still an obsession: "And the other side is where there are crimes, and those crimes are obvious. Lies, under oath, all over the place. Emails that are knocked out, that are acid-washed and deleted. Nobody has ever seen—33,000 emails. . . . So I just think it's a disgrace that a thing like this can happen."

Trump was especially furious when he learned that it was Rosenstein who approved the search warrant for Cohen.

One reason for Trump's vehement reaction might have been that Cohen was no Flynn, or even Manafort, but an intimate confidant who had full knowledge about the Moscow project as well as the Stephanie Clifford payoff—and who knew what else.

Even though they weren't supposed to be talking, a few days later Trump called Cohen to "check in." The president urged Cohen to "hang in there" and "stay strong." Then a friend of Trump's called Cohen to say that he was with "the Boss" at Mar-a-Lago and the president "loves you." Another mutual friend told him, "Everyone knows the boss has your back."

Given Cohen's public statements of loyalty, he seemed unlikely to turn against the president, especially because the Trump Organization was paying Cohen's legal fees, which he told *Vanity Fair* were now in the seven figures. Still, any white-collar defense lawyer knew how intense the pressure to cooperate with the government could become. And neither Trump nor his lawyers knew exactly what the FBI agents might have gotten as a result of the searches.

A time-honored way to keep a witness in line was to make sure his lawyer had a close relationship with the president's lawyers. Robert Costello fit the bill. He was close to Giuliani, and Costello told Cohen he had a "back channel of communication" to the president's lawyer, a channel that was "crucial" and "must be maintained." Costello wrote in an email to Cohen that he'd spoken to Giuliani, and the conversation was "Very Very Positive. You are 'loved' . . . they are in our corner. . . . Sleep well tonight, you have friends in high places."

Even so, Cohen worried that after the searches he was "an open book." He didn't want his payments to women on behalf of Trump to be revealed. His statements—lies, actually—to Congress about the Trump Tower Moscow project were an especially "big concern."

But he felt better after talking to Trump's lawyer. Cohen told him he'd been a "loyal servant" and asked what was in it for him. The lawyer responded that Cohen should stay on message; the investigation was a witch hunt; and everything would be fine. Cohen resolved to toe the party line and stay a part of the team.

On April 24, at a press conference with the French president, Emmanuel Macron, ABC's Jonathan Karl asked if Trump would consider a pardon for Cohen.

Trump glared at him. "Stupid question."

JOHN DOWD'S EXIT from Trump's legal team, and the arrival of Giuliani, marked a fundamental shift to a far more combative strategy toward the special counsel and his allies at the FBI and the Justice Department. Gone were the lawyers who'd counseled moderation and who had persuaded Trump not to fire Mueller, Rosenstein, or Sessions. Firing McCabe might have earned Sessions and Rosenstein goodwill and some time. But after the Cohen raid, the president's patience with them was clearly wearing thin.

"Much of the bad blood with Russia is caused by the Fake & Corrupt Russia Investigation, headed up by the all Democrat loyalists, or people that worked for Obama," Trump tweeted on April 11, just two days after the Cohen raid. "Mueller is most conflicted of all (except Rosenstein who signed FISA & Comey letter). No Collusion, so they go crazy!"

Trump summoned Rosenstein to the White House the next day, ostensibly to talk about turning Russia-related documents over to Congress. There was widespread speculation that Rosenstein would be fired, so much so that hundreds of former Justice Department employees signed a letter demanding that Congress "swiftly and forcefully respond to protect the founding principles of our Republic and the rule of law" if Trump fired Rosenstein, Mueller, or any other senior Justice Department officials. Even Sessions weighed in, warning McGahn that if Trump fired Rosenstein, Sessions would have to resign.

Rosenstein emerged from the meeting with his job intact, and Trump avoided another Saturday Night Massacre. Rosenstein, by then, knew all the details of the inspector general's report—an investigation that had begun within the FBI to find the source of leaks to Giuliani and had ended up instead focusing exclusively on McCabe. The report was released to the public the next day.

Many at the FBI were stunned by the report and its conclusion that McCabe, of all people, had lacked candor. Most people admired and respected McCabe, especially for the way he'd stepped up and steered the bureau through the treacherous period after Comey was fired. It made no sense that McCabe would lie, when both Lisa Page and Michael Kortan knew exactly what had happened, and readily volunteered the story when the investigators finally got around to asking. And the report made no mention of the incredible pressure McCabe was under when he was questioned about a distant *Wall Street Journal* story that, by then, seemed insignificant.

On the other hand, the report gave pause to many, even friends of McCabe's. Comey clearly had a different recollection. The sacred obligation to tell the truth was something that had been drummed into them from their first days in the FBI.

No one had been closer to McCabe than Page. As she later testified, "I have never seen Andy lie, ever, under any circumstances. I have never seen Andy do anything other than make the right decision and often the hard decision, even when it has been personally unpopular or professionally unpopular. I have consistently seen him make hard decisions because they were the right thing to do." She continued, "The findings of the inspector general are entirely inconsistent with the man I know and have worked very closely with for the last 4 years of my career. And I cannot—I simply don't agree with those conclusions."

But McCabe had no one willing or able to publicly defend him.

Trump, on the other hand, could barely contain his glee. "DOJ just issued the McCabe report—which is a total disaster," he tweeted. "He LIED! LIED! LIED! McCabe was totally controlled by Comey—McCabe is Comey!! No collusion, all made up by this den of thieves and lowlifes!"

BY THEN, Trump must have had a pretty good inkling of what was coming in Comey's new book, *A Higher Loyalty*, which was scheduled for publication on Tuesday, April 17. Copies and excerpts were circulating on the previous Thursday. And ABC was already touting its upcoming Sunday night *20/20* interview of Comey by George Stephanopoulos as a blockbuster, revealing that Comey had gone so far as to compare Trump to a mob boss.

Trump had already taken to Twitter, calling Comey "a proven LEAKER & LIAR. Virtually everyone in Washington thought he should be fired for the terrible job he did—until he was, in fact, fired. He leaked CLASSIFIED information, for which he should be prosecuted. He lied to Congress under OATH. He is a weak and . . . untruthful slime ball who was, as time has proven, a terrible Director of the FBI. His handling of the Crooked Hillary Clinton case, and the events surrounding it, will go down as one of the worst 'botch jobs' of history. It was my great honor to fire James Comey!"

And "Big show tonight on @seanhannity!" Trump tweeted, promoting Sean Hannity's segment that night on Fox News. Saying he was inspired by a video clip teasing Comey's upcoming interview with Stephanopoulos, Hannity used the occasion to attack the "obvious Deep State crime families trying to take down the president," consisting of the Clinton "family," the Comey "family," and the Mueller "family."

"Mr. Comey, you're really going to compare the sitting president of the United States to a mob boss so you can make money?" Hannity went on. "If he's going to use a sweeping analogy, I've decided tonight we're going to use the Comey standard . . . and make some comparisons of our own," including "the Clinton crime family," the "Mueller crime family," and Mueller's "best friend," Comey.

Initially stunned by the events of the previous May, Comey hadn't planned to write a book, and certainly not a Trump tell-all. When two fast-rising Washington literary agents, Keith Urbahn and Matt Latimer, called to propose a book, he turned them down. But he did suddenly have time on his hands. He wanted to do something he thought was useful. His wife encouraged him. He had a lot of pent-up thoughts about the president and what he was doing to the American system of justice. And the agents dangled the prospect of a multimillion-dollar advance.

So he called them back and said he'd write a book on leadership. The agents were blunt: a book on leadership wouldn't sell. A book about Trump would. So the previous summer, he'd reached a deal to write a hybrid memoir-leadership book, hence the subtitle: *Truth, Lies, and Leadership*. Comey stopped doing interviews and speeches and refused all comment on Trump.

There was fierce competition among networks for the first interview. Initially, Comey favored NBC's Lester Holt, but ABC offered a radio tour and more affiliates, so he went with Stephanopoulos. Stephanopoulos and his producers were thorough; they spent time with Comey's family; visited his New Jersey boyhood home; and conducted a five-hour interview with Comey himself, all of which got reduced to one hour of airtime that focused almost entirely on Trump and went far beyond anything Comey said in the book.

As advertised, Comey repeatedly compared Trump to a Mafia boss.

"How strange is it for you to sit here and compare the president to a mob boss?" Stephanopoulos asked.

"Very strange. And I don't do it lightly," Comey answered, "and I'm not trying to, by the way, suggest that President Trump is out breaking legs and—you know, shaking down shopkeepers. But instead, what I'm talking about is that leadership culture constantly comes back to me when I think about my experience with the Trump administration. The—the loyalty oaths, the boss as the dominant center of everything, it's all about how do you serve the boss, what's in the boss's interests. It's the family, the family, the family, the family."

He repeatedly criticized Trump's character.

"You write that President Trump is unethical, untethered to the truth. Is Donald Trump unfit to be president?" Stephanopoulos asked.

"I don't buy this stuff about him being mentally incompetent or early stages of dementia," Comey said, bestowing faint praise. "He strikes me as a person of above average intelligence who's tracking conversations and knows what's going on. I don't think he's medically unfit to be president. I think he's morally unfit to be president.

"A person who sees moral equivalence in Charlottesville, who talks about and treats women like they're pieces of meat, who lies constantly about matters big and small and insists the American people believe it— that person's not fit to be president of the United States, on moral grounds. And that's not a policy statement. Again, I don't care what your views are on guns or immigration or taxes.

"There's something more important than that that should unite all of us, and that is our president must embody respect and adhere to the values that are at the core of this country. The most important being truth. This president is not able to do that. He is morally unfit to be president."

Not only that, but "the challenge of this president is that he will stain everyone around him. And the question is, how much stain is too much stain and how much stain eventually makes you unable to accomplish your goal of protecting the country and serving the country?"

Later, Stephanopoulos asked, "Do you think the Russians have something on Donald Trump?"

In an answer sure to enrage the president, Comey said, "I think it's possible. I don't know. These are words I never thought I'd utter about a president of the United States, but it's possible."

"That's stunning," Stephanopoulos said. "You can't say for certain that the president of the United States is not compromised by the Russians?"

"It is stunning and I wish I wasn't saying it, but it's just—it's the truth. I cannot say that. It always struck me and still strikes me as unlikely, and I would have been able to say with high confidence about any other president I dealt with, but I can't. It's possible."

Even as the segment aired, Trump launched a new wave of Twitter attacks, calling Comey a "slimeball" and "slippery" and suggesting he be jailed. "The big questions in Comey's badly reviewed book aren't answered like, how come he gave up Classified Information (jail), why did he lie to Congress (jail), why did the DNC refuse to give Server to the FBI (why didn't they TAKE it), why the phony memos, McCabe's $700,000 & more?"

The interview dominated the news all week. "If there was any chance that President Trump and James B. Comey could have avoided all-out war, it ended Sunday night," the *Times* wrote. Comey called Trump "a serial liar who treated women like 'meat,' and described him as a 'stain' on everyone who worked for him. He said a salacious allegation that Mr. Trump had cavorted with prostitutes in Moscow had left him vulnerable to blackmail by the Russian government. And he asserted that the president was incinerating the country's crucial norms and traditions like a wildfire. He compared the president to a mafia boss."

Comey was taken aback that the distilled interview focused so much on Trump—he called it "vertigo inducing"—and that his observation Trump was "morally unfit," which wasn't in the book, became the centerpiece of massive media coverage. But his literary agents were right about what would sell. Thousands of people greeted him at stops on his book tour, so many he couldn't autograph all their copies. He vaulted to the top of the bestseller lists, selling 600,000 copies during the first week alone.

Reviews were mostly positive ("compelling" was a common adjective), but there were whiffs of criticism from reviewers who blamed Comey for Trump's being president in the first place. And, in entering the partisan fray, Comey threw any claim to objectivity to the winds, emerging as a fierce anti-Trump partisan.

As the columnist Frank Bruni wrote in the *Times*, "James Comey's book is titled 'A Higher Loyalty,' but it surrenders the higher ground, at least partly. To watch him promote it is to see him descend. Not to President Trump's level—that's a long way down. But Comey is playing Trump's game, on Trump's terms. And in that sense, he has let the president get the better of him."

And Comey faced criticism from within the ranks of retired FBI agents, echoing thoughts that many current employees were reluctant to say, at least on the record. Nancy Savage, executive director of the Society of Former Special Agents of the FBI, told *The Guardian* that Comey, "and a number of other FBI employees who worked directly for him, have damaged the agency." She called the book "tasteless at best. There is a total lack of dignity."

The former senior agent Bobby Chacon said of Comey, "I worked for him. He did a lot of good things at the FBI. He was popular and I didn't like the way the White House sacked him. But he made mistakes and now has been overtaken by his emotions. I'm surprised he has been dragged down into street-fighting with Trump."

In the wake of Comey's ABC interview and book tour, Trump's approval ratings actually rose, from a low of 37 percent on December 13 to 44 percent in early May, according to RealClearPolitics.

ON JUNE 8, 2018, William Barr, the former attorney general who'd kept up a drumbeat of public support for Trump, sent an unsolicited nineteen-page memo to Rosenstein at the Justice Department, arguing that Trump should not be required to testify in any obstruction inquiry and that Mueller was out of bounds by even asking. Barr later acknowledged that it was the only time he'd sent such an unsolicited memo to the department.

In essence, Barr argued that firing Comey and asking him to "let this go" of the Flynn matter were within a president's constitutionally pre-scribed duties, and thus could not be the basis for a criminal charge.

Barr indicated he didn't think obstruction, in Trump's case, was a "real crime." "I know you will agree that, if a DOJ investigation is going to take down a democratically-elected President, it is imperative to the health of our system and to our national cohesion that any claim of wrongdoing is solidly based on evidence of a real crime—not a debatable one," Barr wrote in the memo. "It is time to travel well-worn paths; not to veer into novel, unsettled or contested areas of the law; and"—in a clear barb aimed at Mueller and his team—"not to indulge the fancies by overzealous pros-ecutors."

Barr wrote that he was "deeply concerned" about the institution of the presidency, but given Trump's ongoing humiliation of Sessions, and the degree to which Barr's memo staked out the same position as Trump's defense lawyers, it inevitably led to speculation inside the Justice Depart-ment that Barr was auditioning for a triumphal return to Pennsylvania Avenue.

ON JUNE 14, Michael Horowitz, the inspector general, released his long-awaited report on the FBI's handling of the Clinton email investigation. The report harshly criticized Comey for the way he disclosed the results of the case at his July 5 press conference. "We concluded that Comey's unilateral announcement was inconsistent with Department policy and violated long-standing Department practice and protocol by, among other things, criticizing Clinton's uncharged conduct," the report stated. "We also found that Comey usurped the authority of the Attorney General."

And "although we acknowledge that Comey faced a difficult situation with unattractive choices, in proceeding as he did, we concluded that Comey made a serious error of judgment."

That's what drew the most press. "Inspector General Blasts Comey" was the headline in *The Washington Post*; "Comey's Actions 'Extraordinary and Insubordinate,'" reported CNN.

And the revelation of the "No, no, he won't. We'll stop it" text from Strzok—which hadn't been included in the earlier release—triggered a new wave of conspiracy theories and references to a "Deep State."

As the CNN editor at large Chris Cillizza accurately observed, "Those seven words are what Trump and his allies will seize on—casting them as definitive proof that the 'deep state' not only didn't want him to win but was actively working to keep him from the White House."

The White House said the report "reaffirmed the president's suspicions about Comey's conduct and the political bias among some of the members of the FBI."

But nearly lost in the sensational details were some sobering conclusions that threw cold water on the Deep State conspiracy theorists: The inspector general found no reason to question the decision not to charge Clinton. He found that any political bias or opinions had not affected the outcome. Far from coddling or protecting Clinton, the report noted, Page and Strzok "advocated for more aggressive investigative measures in the Midyear investigation, such as the use of grand jury subpoenas and search warrants to obtain evidence."

The report concluded, "We found no evidence that the conclusions by the prosecutors were affected by bias or other improper considerations; rather, we determined that they were based on the prosecutors' assessment of the facts, the law, and past Department practice. We therefore concluded that these were legal and policy judgments involving core prosecutorial discretion that were for the Department to make."

In short, after seventeen months and hundreds of interviews, the inspector general found no reason to reopen the Clinton case or doubt its conclusions.

Even though they felt exonerated, the report nonetheless cast a harsh spotlight, yet again, on Page and Strzok. A week later, Strzok was told his job status was under review. (Much to her relief, Page had already found a job with a private law firm.)

After thirty days, Strzok was told he would be terminated, but he could appeal. Strzok met with Candice M. Will, the head of the FBI's Office of Professional Responsibility. He argued strenuously that he'd never lied or engaged in any illegal activity. At the end of the day, all he'd done was express some personal opinions in what he thought was a strictly private setting. None of his personal views had impacted his work, as the inspector general had concluded.

To his pleasant surprise, in their next meeting, Will agreed with him. She told him he'd be suspended for sixty days but could return and "get back out there."

Strzok was elated. He signed a so-called last-chance agreement in which he agreed to the suspension and gave up his rights of appeal. He understood he'd be on probation: if he screwed up, he'd be fired.

Strzok was at home when two agents delivered a letter, which he assumed was the agreement countersigned by Will. But when he opened it, it was from Bowdich, whom Wray had named his deputy. Bowdich overruled Will. Strzok was fired.

"Deeply saddened by this decision," Strzok wrote on Twitter. "It has been an honor to serve my country and work with the fine men and women of the FBI."

Trump was far more outspoken. "Agent Peter Strzok was just fired from the FBI—finally," Trump tweeted. "The list of bad players in the FBI & DOJ gets longer & longer. Based on the fact that Strzok was in charge of the Witch Hunt, will it be dropped? It is a total Hoax. No Collusion, No Obstruction."

Seemingly oblivious to the findings of the inspector general, Trump added, "Just fired Agent Strzok, formerly of the FBI, was in charge of the

Crooked Hillary Clinton sham investigation. It was a total fraud on the American public and should be properly redone!"

THAT SPRING TRUMP formally added Rudy Giuliani, who'd been informally advising him for months, to his legal team. Giuliani combined the skills of a practiced TV commentator with decades of experience as a prosecutor. But his most important attribute might have been that Trump actually followed Giuliani's advice.

Soon after Giuliani's arrival, the president's risky dalliances with Michael Cohen stopped. The Trump Organization stopped paying Cohen's legal bills. An increasingly desperate Cohen was no longer feeling the love.

Cohen turned to television on July 2. In his first public comment since the raid on his office, Cohen told ABC's George Stephanopoulos, "My wife, my daughter and my son have my first loyalty and always will. I put family and country first."

Stephanopoulos reminded Cohen of his pledge to "take a bullet."

"To be crystal clear, my wife, my daughter and my son, and this country have my first loyalty," Cohen said.

And Cohen hired a lawyer who was openly hostile to Trump: Lanny Davis, a longtime Democrat best known for his prolonged and passionate defense of an embattled Bill Clinton.

Mueller handed over many aspects of the Cohen investigation (such as the payments to Stephanie Clifford) to federal prosecutors in New York. They were outside the scope of Mueller's mandate, and his doing so also served the purpose of placing probes of Trump into more than one set of prosecutorial hands. (An enduring lesson of Kenneth Starr's investigation of Clinton was that it was a mistake to combine the Whitewater and Monica Lewinsky cases, because Clinton allies needed to demonize only one prosecutor.)

Cohen pleaded guilty to eight felonies in New York on August 21. He immediately implicated Trump in the Clifford payments and said during his plea hearing that he had worked "at the direction of the candidate in making those payments."

In stark contrast, Paul Manafort refused to cooperate or testify in his own defense. That same day a jury declared Manafort guilty on eight felony counts.

Trump leaped on the disparity in an interview with the *Fox & Friends* host Ainsley Earhardt. As for Cohen, "he makes a better deal when he uses me. Like everybody else. And one of the reasons I respect Paul Manafort so much is he went through that trial—you know they make up stories. People make up stories. This whole thing about flipping, they call it, I know all about flipping. For 30, 40 years I've been watching flippers. Everything's wonderful and then they get 10 years in jail and they—they flip on whoever the next highest one is, or as high as you can go. It—it almost ought to be outlawed. It's not fair."

As for a pardon for Manafort, "I have great respect for what he's done, in terms of what he's gone through. . . . He worked for many, many people many, many years, and I would say what he did, some of the charges they threw against him, every consultant, every lobbyist in Washington probably does."

(In an apparent effort to curb Trump's worst instincts, Giuliani later walked back Trump's remark and said any discussion of a pardon would be inappropriate.)

IN EARLY SEPTEMBER, the Justice Department provided Congress with many of the missing Page-Strzok texts that had fueled a wave of conspiracy theories, which soon appeared in the media. No one had been trying to conceal them. It had merely been a technical glitch, and the inspector general's team had managed to recover them. In contrast to the first batch, they were relatively innocuous.

Page did finish *All the President's Men*. "Did you know the president resigns in the end?!" she'd texted in March.

"What?!?! God, that we should be so lucky," Strzok answered.

Trump and his allies leaped on a text saying, "I want to talk to you about media leak strategy with DOJ before you go," which Strzok sent Page on April 10.

"More text messages between former FBI employees Peter Strzok and Lisa Page are a disaster and embarrassment to the FBI & DOJ," Trump tweeted. "This should never have happened but we are learning more and more by the hour. 'Others were leaking like mad' in order to get the President!"

But Strzok's lawyer issued a statement that the text referred to a meeting at the Justice Department to discuss a strategy to stop leaks, not a plot to leak.

A little more than a week later, on Friday, September 21, *The New York Times* had another scoop. "The deputy attorney general, Rod J. Rosenstein, suggested last year that he secretly record President Trump in the White House to expose the chaos consuming the administration, and he discussed recruiting cabinet members to invoke the 25th Amendment to remove Mr. Trump from office for being unfit," the reporters Adam Goldman and Michael Schmidt revealed.

"*The New York Times*'s story is inaccurate and factually incorrect," Rosenstein said in a statement. "I will not further comment on a story based on anonymous sources who are obviously biased against the department and are advancing their own personal agenda. But let me be clear about this: Based on my personal dealings with the president, there is no basis to invoke the 25th Amendment."

The *Times* story added, "A Justice Department spokeswoman also provided a statement from a person who was present when Mr. Rosenstein proposed wearing a wire. The person, who would not be named, acknowledged the remark but said Mr. Rosenstein made it sarcastically."

No one, however, mentioned (nor did the *Times* report) that Rosenstein had made the offer to record the president twice in front of McCabe alone—none in a sarcastic tone—and that Page had taken notes on one of those occasions.

Still, a close reading of Rosenstein's response showed that he didn't really deny anything specific in the story. Rosenstein had just handed Trump all the ammunition he needed to fire him. Hardly anyone expected Rosenstein to survive the weekend.

On Friday evening, Rosenstein met with John Kelly, the chief of staff, at the White House and offered to resign. He also called McGahn with the same offer. But Kelly and McGahn thought only the president could accept his resignation. Neither was eager for a replay of a Comey-type disaster just weeks before the midterm elections.

On Monday, Rosenstein was still in his job, but the Justice Department was deluged with press calls about his imminent ouster. Sarah Flores, the chief spokesperson, started drafting a statement for Sessions. Rosenstein headed to the White House. News channels broke into coverage of the Kavanaugh Supreme Court hearings to report he was on his way to resign.

But Comey's perception that Rosenstein was a "survivor" proved apt. Just before 1:00 p.m., Sanders, the White House press secretary, tweeted that Rosenstein and the president had had an "extended conversation," presumably by phone, because Trump was in New York for the United Nations General Assembly meeting. She added that they'd meet in person on Thursday, which gave Rosenstein at least a three-day reprieve.

On Wednesday, during a press conference at the United Nations, Trump described his Monday talk with Rosenstein as "a good talk. He said he never said it, he said he doesn't believe it. He said he has a lot of respect for me, and he was very nice, and we'll see."

By Thursday, with everyone at the White House consumed by the Kavanaugh hearings, Trump postponed their get-together. It was only in October, after Kavanaugh was confirmed, that Rosenstein and Trump spoke in person on a flight to Florida. Trump didn't fire him or ask for his resignation. A White House spokesman said they discussed routine Justice Department matters, and Trump said only that the conversation was "great."

If, indeed, Rosenstein told Trump he "never said it"—either in the Monday conversation or on the plane or both—he had just given the president further leverage over him. It was one thing to vaguely describe a newspaper story as inaccurate. It was another to mislead the president, as Michael Flynn had discovered.

In many ways, it was even better for Trump than carrying around a resignation letter in his pocket. He now had ample grounds for firing Rosenstein, the man overseeing the Russia investigation, whenever he wanted.

AMERICAN VOTERS WENT to the polls on November 6 in what was overwhelmingly interpreted as a referendum on the tumultuous presidency of Donald Trump. The next day, Trump was in a surprisingly upbeat mood, given that Republicans lost a net thirty-nine seats and Democrats seized control of the House, giving them the capacity to launch investigations of the president that the Republican-controlled House had stalled.

"It was a big day yesterday," Trump exulted at a news conference. "An incredible day," adding, "This election marks the largest Senate gains for a President's party in a first midterm election since at least President Kennedy's in 1962."

Even then, he veered into the Russia investigation, nearly taunting the Democrats to pursue it. "I keep hearing about investigations fatigue. Like from the time—almost from the time I announced I was going to run, they've been giving us this investigation fatigue. It's been a long time. They got nothing. Zero. You know why? Because there is nothing. But they can play that game, but we can play it better."

Later, CNN's Jim Acosta returned to the subject: "On the Russia investigation. Are you concerned that you may have indictments . . ."

"I'm not concerned about anything with the Russia investigation because it's a hoax," Trump interrupted. "That's enough. Put down the mic," the president directed.

A White House aide tried to grab the microphone, but Acosta resisted.

"Mr. President, are you worried about indictments coming down in this investigation?" he finally asked.

"I'll tell you what: CNN should be ashamed of itself having you working for them. You are a rude, terrible person. You shouldn't be working for CNN."

Trump avoided a question about the fate of Sessions, but even before the press conference Kelly had called and demanded Sessions's resignation that day. Sessions delivered a letter to the White House, which Kelly accepted. Trump didn't give him the courtesy of a personal send-off.

"Dear Mr. President, at your request I am submitting my resignation," Sessions wrote. He added, in what many took to be a pointed jab at Trump's almost constant efforts to subvert the Mueller probe, "Most importantly, in my time as attorney general we have restored and upheld the rule of law."

In a slap at Rosenstein, who, as the deputy, would ordinarily have stepped in as acting attorney general, Trump instead named Matthew Whitaker, a little-known former Iowa football player and Iowa U.S. attorney whose principal qualifications seemed to be his close relationship with the Iowa senator Charles Grassley—a fierce critic of the Comey and McCabe FBI—and his hostility to Mueller's investigation.

Whitaker was widely distrusted by career lawyers at the department as a blatantly partisan advocate for Trump. Just before his appointment to the Justice Department, he'd gone so far in a CNN interview as to propose starving Mueller for funds. "I could see a scenario where Jeff Sessions is replaced with a recess appointment and that Attorney General doesn't fire Bob Mueller, but he just reduces his budget so low that his investigation grinds to almost a halt," Whitaker had said. In a radio interview he said, "There is no criminal obstruction of justice charge to be had here. The evidence is weak. No reasonable prosecutor would bring a case on what we know right now."

Whitaker's appointment drew immediate condemnation from Democrats in Congress and a lawsuit that tried (unsuccessfully) to block his appointment. Even Republican senators were wary. Referring to Mueller's work, Lamar Alexander of Tennessee said, "No new Attorney General can be confirmed who will stop that investigation." There was little chance that Whitaker would secure Senate confirmation.

That was of little concern to Trump and his legal advisers. A reliable and far more illustrious alternative to Whitaker was waiting in the wings. One month later, Trump announced that he'd chosen William Barr to be his new attorney general. "He was my first choice from day one," he told reporters.

With Republicans in control of the Senate, Barr was easily confirmed over Democratic objections to his pro-Trump op-ed pieces and unsolicited legal memo.

ON NOVEMBER 20, Trump's lawyers finally submitted written answers to a limited number of questions from the Mueller team. "What I can tell you is they're complete and detailed," Rudolph Giuliani said in an interview. "But there's nothing there I haven't read in a newspaper."

As agreed, the answers were limited to the time period before Trump became president and excluded any questions related to obstruction of justice. But that left one precarious area for the president: Trump Tower Moscow, which did relate to Russia, and any efforts by Trump to influence Cohen's testimony, which overlapped the obstruction probe. And neither Trump nor his lawyers, at this juncture, knew what Cohen was telling Mueller.

Mueller and his lawyers had asked Trump to describe the timing and substance of discussions he had with Cohen about the project, whether they discussed a potential trip to Russia, whether the president "at any time direct[ed] or suggest[ed] that discussions about the Trump Moscow project should cease," or whether the president was "informed at any time that the project had been abandoned"—all subjects Cohen had addressed.

"I had few conversations with Mr. Cohen on this subject," Trump responded. "As I recall, they were brief, and they were not memorable. I was not enthused about the proposal, and I do not recall any discussion of travel to Russia in connection with it." He continued, "I vaguely remember press inquiries and media reporting during the campaign about whether the Trump Organization had business dealings in Russia. I may have spoken with campaign staff or Trump Organization employees regarding responses to requests for information, but I have no current recollection of any particular conversation, with whom I may have spoken, when, or the substance of any conversation. As I recall, neither I nor the

Trump Organization had any projects or proposed projects in Russia during the campaign other than the Letter of Intent."

That answer was exceptionally vague and didn't answer any of Mueller's specific questions.

Nine days later, Cohen pleaded guilty to making false statements to Congress about Trump Tower Moscow and agreed to cooperate with Mueller. That same day Trump told reporters that he had decided to scrap the project, although "there would have been nothing wrong if I did do it. If I did do it, there would have been nothing wrong. That was my business. . . . It was an option that I decided not to do. . . . I decided not to do it. The primary reason . . . I was focused on running for President. . . . I was running my business while I was campaigning. There was a good chance that I wouldn't have won, in which case I would've gotten back into the business. And why should I lose lots of opportunities?"

That contradicted Cohen's version that the project was still on a list of Trump Organization projects at the time of the inauguration; that Trump had never terminated it; and, in Trump's written answer, that he had "no current recollection" of any specific conversation about it.

So Mueller's lawyers asked again whether Trump had participated in any discussions about the project being abandoned, including when he "decided not to do the project."

"The President has fully answered the questions at issue," Trump's lawyers curtly responded.

Cohen was sentenced to three years in prison on December 12.

"Time and time again, I felt it was my duty to cover up his dirty deeds rather than to listen to my own inner voice and my moral compass," Cohen told the judge. "My weakness can be characterized as a blind loyalty to Donald Trump, and I was weak for not having the strength to question and to refuse his demands."

WITH GIULIANI IN charge of his legal team, and the Mueller probe now in seemingly safe hands with Barr as attorney general, Trump eased off his attacks on Mueller and the Justice Department. His advisers said he was well aware by this point that even if he wanted to or needed to, it was too late to remove Mueller. Mueller had given up his efforts to interview Trump, or even insist on more written answers to his existing questions.

Speculation in the media turned from whether Trump would have Mueller fired to when Mueller would deliver his feverishly anticipated report. There was a flurry of rumors in February that delivery was imminent. CNN reported, "Attorney General Bill Barr is preparing to announce as early as next week the completion of special counsel Robert Mueller's Russia investigation, with plans for Barr to submit to Congress soon after a summary of Mueller's confidential report." *The Washington Post* reported, "The special counsel's investigation has consumed Washington since it began in May 2017, and it increasingly appears to be nearing its end, which would send fresh shock waves through the political system." *Vanity Fair* observed, "The great national psychodrama that has touched every corner of our politics and culture over the past two years is coming to an end."

By mid-March 2019, it had still not arrived, which only added to the suspense. Then, the week of March 18, the rumors heated up again. By Friday morning, they were at a fever pitch. Media crews staked out the special counsel's offices and the Justice Department.

A *New York Times* reporter spotted Giuliani at the Trump International Hotel down the street from the White House, waiting as anxiously as everyone else in the city. "They said it was going to be at noon or 12:30," Mr. Giuliani told the reporter.

At 4:00 p.m., thunder rumbled, followed by a hailstorm.

At almost precisely that moment, an inconspicuous security guard from Mueller's office slipped by news crews waiting outside the Justice Department and delivered a thick envelope to Rod Rosenstein.

The Mueller report had arrived.

CONCLUSION

The decision to make any or all of the Mueller report public, as well as how to react to its recommendations, fell to Barr, the new attorney general, and Rosenstein. Rosenstein was no longer overseeing the investigation, but had remained immersed in it.

The report's conclusions didn't come as much of a surprise to them: in a top secret meeting on March 5, 2019, Mueller had briefed them on his conclusions and explained his reasoning behind them. Forty-eight hours after receiving it, on Sunday, March 24, Barr summarized Mueller's findings in a letter to congressional leadership.

The "investigation did not establish that members of the Trump Campaign conspired or coordinated with the Russian government in its election interference activities," Barr stated.

As for obstruction of justice, Mueller hadn't reached any conclusion. Instead, "the report sets out evidence on both sides of the question and leaves unresolved what the Special Counsel views as 'difficult issues' of law and fact concerning whether the President's actions and intent could be viewed as obstruction," Barr stated. He added that Mueller stated, "While this report does not conclude that the President committed a crime, it also does not exonerate him."

"Deputy Attorney General Rod Rosenstein and I have concluded that the evidence developed during the Special Counsel's investigation is not sufficient to establish that the President committed an obstruction-of-justice offense," Barr continued. "In making this determination, we noted that the Special Counsel recognized that 'the evidence does not establish that the President was involved in an underlying crime related to Russian election interference,' and that, while not determinative, the absence of such evidence bears upon the President's intent with respect to obstruction."

Barr seemed to be suggesting that absent an underlying crime—in this case, collusion with Russia—Trump's intent couldn't be to obstruct.

For the first time in years—since the summer before the election—Trump was out from under the "cloud" of potential criminal prosecution. But the president seemed more angry than relieved and made clear that the Mueller report was likely to be just the opening salvo in a renewed attack on the people he blamed for the investigation.

As he was boarding Air Force One that Sunday for his return from a weekend at Mar-a-Lago, Trump made a brief statement to reporters:

> So, after a long look, after a long investigation, after so many people have been so badly hurt, after not looking at the other side where a lot of bad things happened, a lot of horrible things happened, a lot of very bad things happened for our country—it was just announced there was no collusion with Russia. The most ridiculous thing I've ever heard.
>
> There was no collusion with Russia. There was no obstruction, and—none whatsoever. And it was a complete and total exoneration. It's a shame that our country had to go through this. To be honest, it's a shame that your President has had to go through this for—before I even got elected, it began. And it began illegally. And hopefully, somebody is going to look at the other side. This was an illegal takedown that failed. And hopefully, somebody is going to be looking at the other side.
>
> So it's complete exoneration. No collusion. No obstruction.

Rudy Giuliani and Jay Sekulow, Trump's primary lawyers, called the CNN anchor Wolf Blitzer that afternoon. The Mueller report "completely exonerated the president, it is quite clear, no collusion of any kind, including the entire Trump campaign, which raises the question, why did this ever start in the first place?" Giuliani said.

As to the obstruction, "the key there is that the attorney general and the deputy attorney general made the conclusion that you don't have obstruction when there's no underlying crime," Sekulow continued. "I think that we've said from the outset that this was a situation where there was no collusion, there was no obstruction, and now we have the weight of the Department of Justice agreeing with us."

Citing the fact that Mueller stated explicitly that the report did not "exonerate" Trump, Blitzer asked, "What's your reaction to that?"

"If you go on to the next two paragraphs, Wolf, the attorney general does kind of a brilliant analysis of it," Giuliani answered. "He says that he and Deputy Attorney General Rod Rosenstein have concluded that the evidence is not sufficient to establish the president committed obstruction of justice. Then he goes even further and points out that basically under settled law, it's almost impossible to have obstruction of justice if there's no underlying crime. A brilliant lawyer-like analysis. Then he concludes with a very strong statement, 'in cataloging the president's actions, many of which took place in public view, the report identifies no actions that in our judgment,' that's Rosenstein and Barr, 'constitute obstructive conduct.'

"That is a complete exoneration by the attorney general and Rod Rosenstein."

The reality was far more complex, as became clear from a letter Mueller sent to Barr on March 27 and elaborated on in a phone call. For the tight-lipped Mueller to criticize Barr, someone he'd known for thirty years, and in writing, was an extraordinary step and came as a shock to lawyers at the Justice Department.

As we stated in our meeting of March 5 and reiterated to the Department early in the afternoon of March 24, the introductions and executive summaries of our two-volume report accurately summarize this Office's work and conclusions. The summary letter the

Department sent to Congress and released to the public late in the afternoon of March 24 did not fully capture the context, nature, and substance of this Office's work and conclusions. . . . There is now public confusion about critical aspects of the results of our investigation. This threatens to undermine a central purpose for which the Department appointed the Special Counsel: to assure full public confidence in the outcome of the investigations.*

On April 18, Barr addressed the nation from the Justice Department, with Rosenstein standing impassively just behind him. "I am committed to ensuring the greatest possible degree of transparency concerning the Special Counsel's investigation, consistent with the law," Barr stated, announcing the release of a redacted version of the report.

Despite the warning in Mueller's letter, Barr seemed even more intent on clearing the president. This time he didn't mention that Mueller had declined to exonerate Trump on the issue of obstruction. And, without the benefit of any testimony by the president (because Trump had refused to testify about obstruction), Barr leaped to what seemed extremely sympathetic conclusions about the president's cooperation and state of mind.

"President Trump faced an unprecedented situation," Barr said. "As he entered into office, and sought to perform his responsibilities as President, federal agents and prosecutors were scrutinizing his conduct before and after taking office, and the conduct of some of his associates. At the same time, there was relentless speculation in the news media about the President's personal culpability. Yet, as he said from the beginning, there was in fact no collusion. And as the Special Counsel's report acknowledges, there is substantial evidence to show that the President was frustrated and angered by a sincere belief that the investigation was undermining his presidency, propelled by his political opponents, and fueled by illegal leaks." Barr continued, "This evidence of non-corrupt motives weighs heavily against any allegation that the President had a corrupt intent to obstruct the investigation."

---

* None of this was known to the public, however, until April 30, when *The Washington Post* reported on and published the text of Mueller's letter.

Barr had now had two occasions on which to promote his view of Trump's innocence before the public had a chance to actually read the Mueller report. His views of Trump's innocence were magnified by the media echo chamber dedicated to the Trump cause. Just how far apart Barr's views were from Mueller's—as well as why Mueller would have felt compelled to write his letter complaining about Barr's characterizations— was abundantly clear once the Mueller report itself was available.

Mueller demolished the notion propounded by Barr and the president's lawyers that proving obstruction requires the existence of an underlying crime—the heart of the president's defense.

Quoting a series of controlling Supreme Court cases, Mueller laid out precisely the opposite: that "an improper motive can render an actor's conduct criminal even when the conduct would otherwise be lawful and within the actor's authority."

For good measure, Mueller added, "Obstruction-of-justice law 'reaches all corrupt conduct capable of producing an effect that prevents justice from being duly administered, regardless of the means employed.'"

"An 'effort to influence' a proceeding can qualify as an endeavor to obstruct justice even if the effort was 'subtle or circuitous' and 'however cleverly or with whatever cloaking of purpose' it was made." "The verbs '"obstruct or impede" are broad' and 'can refer to anything that blocks, makes difficult, or hinders.'"

Mueller's position makes perfect sense: the legal system can only function if it operates unimpeded by the myriad ways a defendant might seek to improperly influence the outcome. That's as true for the innocent as for the guilty. Subjects of investigations may have many motives to conceal behavior that, while it may not be criminal, is nonetheless embarrassing, dishonest, or greedy. Countless defendants have been prosecuted for and convicted of obstructing justice where there was no underlying criminal activity.

Trump would seem a textbook case, because the ways his campaign benefited from Russian interference undermined the legitimacy of his election victory, giving him a motive to conceal it.

Because Trump refused to testify except through limited written answers to questions, he had minimal risk of committing perjury. Not only is perjury a crime, but lying is often evidence of a guilty state of mind. Trump's sworn, written answer about Trump Tower Moscow was hardly candid, and hard to square with Cohen's testimony. At best, Trump's statement could be deemed misleading.

And apart from that sworn statement, Mueller's report documented scores of false public statements by Trump bearing on aspects of the investigation, from denying that he'd ever told Comey that he wanted "loyalty" or asked him to "let . . . go" of the Flynn case, to claiming that he fired Comey over his handling of the Clinton email case, to denying that he tried to have Mueller fired—to name just a few examples. While not perjury, they indicate Trump was determined to conceal embarrassing and potentially damaging truths.

Besides what is in Mueller's voluminous report, there remain questions about what Mueller did not include, especially any mention of the tumultuous days after Comey was fired, when Rosenstein proposed secretly recording the president. Mueller heard testimony about those events. Yet the report makes no mention of them. It is silent about what transpired between Rosenstein and Trump in their one-on-one meetings, including the flight to Florida. Each time, against seemingly long odds, Rosenstein emerged with his job intact. What did he offer Trump in return? What threats, explicit or implied, did Trump bring to bear? Rosenstein's interactions with the president might well have constituted yet another potential obstruction count.

"The only commitment I made to President Trump about the Russia investigation is the same commitment I made to the Congress: so long as I was in charge, it would be conducted appropriately and as expeditiously as possible," Rosenstein told *The Washington Post*. "Everyone who actually participated in the investigation knows that."

Many of Trump's reckless efforts to thwart the investigation were unsuccessful, thanks to the determination of Priebus, McGahn, and others. But in Rosenstein's case, the argument can be made that Trump got the result he wanted: exoneration on collusion with Russia and a swift verdict of not guilty on obstruction—a verdict delivered in tandem by Barr, a longtime apologist for and defender of Trump, and Rosenstein.

Failure to reach a decision on obstruction was no doubt the most controversial aspect of Mueller's report. Barr himself said he was taken aback when he learned of Mueller's position during their March 5 meeting.

Because the Justice Department has ruled that indicting a sitting president is unconstitutional, Mueller explained, "Fairness concerns counseled against potentially reaching that judgment when no charges can be brought. The ordinary means for an individual to respond to an accusation is through a speedy and public trial, with all the procedural protections that surround a criminal case. An individual who believes he was wrongly accused can use that process to seek to clear his name. In contrast, a prosecutor's judgment that crimes were committed, but that no charges will be brought, affords no such adversarial opportunity for public name-clearing before an impartial adjudicator."

Mueller might not have concluded that Trump committed a crime. But the conclusions he did reach, set forth in the introduction to his 448-page report, are devastating in their own right:

> Our investigation found multiple acts by the President that were capable of exerting undue influence over law enforcement investigations, including the Russian-interference and obstruction investigations. The incidents were often carried out through one-on-one meetings in which the President sought to use his official power outside of usual channels. These actions ranged from efforts to remove the Special Counsel and to reverse the effect of the Attorney General's recusal; to the attempted use of official power to limit the scope of the investigation; to direct and indirect contacts with witnesses with the potential to influence their testimony.

The report continues, "The President's efforts to influence the investigation were mostly unsuccessful, but that is largely because the persons who surrounded the President declined to carry out orders or accede to his requests."

In considering the full scope of the conduct we investigated, the President's actions can be divided into two distinct phases reflecting a possible shift in the President's motives. In the first phase, before the President fired Comey, the President had been assured that the FBI had not opened an investigation of him personally. The President deemed it critically important to make public that he was not under investigation, and he included that information in his termination letter to Comey after other efforts to have that information disclosed were unsuccessful. Soon after he fired Comey, however, the President became aware that investigators were conducting an obstruction-of-justice inquiry into his own conduct. That awareness marked a significant change in the President's conduct and the start of a second phase of action. The President launched public attacks on the investigation and individuals involved in it who could possess evidence adverse to the President, while in private, the President engaged in a series of targeted efforts to control the investigation. For instance, the President attempted to remove the Special Counsel; he sought to have Attorney General Sessions unrecuse himself and limit the investigation; . . . and he used public forums to attack potential witnesses who might offer adverse information and to praise witnesses who declined to cooperate with the government.

Quoting Supreme Court precedent, the report concluded that no person "in this country is so high that he is above the law."

Because we determined not to make a traditional prosecutorial judgment, we did not draw ultimate conclusions about the President's conduct. The evidence we obtained about the President's actions and intent presents difficult issues that would need to be resolved if we were making a traditional prosecutorial judgment. At the same time, if we had confidence after a thorough investigation of the facts that the President clearly did not commit obstruction of justice, we would so state. Based on the facts and the applicable legal standards, we are unable to reach that judgment. Accordingly, while this report does not conclude that the President committed a crime, it also does not exonerate him.

Mueller left it to Congress and ultimately the American people to resolve those "difficult issues."

MAY 29, 2019, was Robert Mueller's last day as special counsel. He marked the occasion with a televised statement that lasted less than ten minutes. He read from a prepared script and provided a succinct synopsis of his report. He reiterated that "if we had had confidence that the president clearly did not commit a crime, we would have said so." Despite burning public curiosity, he said he would have nothing further to say about the matter. "The report is my testimony," he said. "I would not provide information beyond that which is already public in any appearance before Congress." He declined to take any questions: "I do not believe it is appropriate for me to speak further about the investigation or to comment on the actions of the Justice Department or Congress."

By then, it had dawned on Trump that the Mueller report was not the complete exoneration he'd claimed but rather a devastating and detailed critique. "I think Mueller is a true Never Trumper," Trump said while on the South Lawn of the White House before leaving on the Marine One helicopter. As for Mueller's team of lawyers, they are "some of the worst human beings on Earth."

WHETHER TRUMP COMMITTED a crime or an impeachable offense or engaged in conduct unfitting for a president pledged to uphold the law and Constitution are serious questions. But others, too, remain subjects of intense public debate and interest. With the delivery of the Mueller report, the inspector general's various investigations into conduct by the FBI and the Justice Department, and multiple investigations by both branches of Congress, there's ample evidence to answer many of these:

- Did Hillary Clinton escape prosecution in the email investigation because the FBI favored her over Donald Trump?

The FBI did an exhaustive investigation, as did the inspector general. Classified information was transmitted over Clinton's personal email accounts and through her servers, although there's no evidence it was obtained by foreign powers. But there wasn't any evidence that that was Clinton's intent, or even that she knew about it.

Although a "gross negligence" standard might have enabled a prosecution with a lesser standard than criminal intent—and the FBI's Jim Baker argued that position initially—no case had ever been brought in such circumstances. Multiple FBI lawyers and agents and career Justice Department officials, including the much-revered and independent David Margolis, thought charging Clinton would amount to "celebrity hunting," in Margolis's words.

As the inspector general noted, the former attorney general Alberto Gonzales was not charged in similar circumstances. It might not have been necessary to go quite so far as to say "no reasonable prosecutor" would bring such a charge, as Comey did. But it's hard to imagine a jury would convict Clinton under such circumstances. And bringing a charge on such flimsy grounds would likely have ended her candidacy when she was the front-runner, sowing electoral chaos and possibly handing the nomination to her rival Bernie Sanders. The FBI could rightly have been criticized for a near-unthinkable intrusion into the democratic process.

Once the Weiner laptop surfaced, Comey had little choice but to reopen the investigation. The FBI had to obtain a search warrant, a step that might well have become public. Given how many people knew about the existence of the newly discovered emails—including many people in the leak-prone New York office—their existence was almost certain to become public. That not only would have damaged Clinton even more but would have seriously harmed the reputation of the FBI. Even Loretta Lynch recognized that, no doubt one of the reasons she gave Comey a hug.

Moreover, the fact that Comey reopened the Clinton investigation just days before the election and notified Congress, thereby making it public, is utterly inconsistent with any bias against Trump and in favor of Clinton. Many still blame Comey for Clinton's loss.

- Did Comey cost Clinton the election?

Comey's October 28 letter to Congress reopening the email investigation can only have damaged Clinton's campaign. But there's no way of knowing how many, if any, votes it actually cost her. However persuasive Nate Silver's analysis, it was Clinton herself who decided to use her private email account for State Department business. It was Bill Clinton who barged in on Loretta Lynch on the Phoenix tarmac. And it was decades of obfuscation—about her cattle futures trading, about her Whitewater investment, and about her husband's infidelities and sexual misconduct—that led some voters to doubt Clinton's integrity and truthfulness, including her claims about the emails.

After all, Comey cleared Clinton a few days later after a massive, round-the-clock effort by FBI agents. Perhaps, as Trump maintained, Clinton "misplayed" that good news. If so, Comey can hardly be blamed. And for anyone but Clinton, that final exoneration should have laid the matter to rest.

- Was Comey's decision to make the July 5 announcement about Clinton "insubordinate and extraordinary," as the inspector general concluded?

Comey was well aware that he was departing from FBI and Justice Department policy, as were his advisers and the FBI leadership. Comey did it for one reason: to protect public confidence in the FBI as an independent, nonpartisan, and trustworthy agency. After Obama's public statement, after Lynch's comment about "matters," and especially after Bill Clinton's ill-timed visit on the tarmac, Comey became convinced that any decision to exonerate Clinton would be tainted as partisan.

To criticize her actions as "extremely careless" while declining to recommend charges was also a departure from Justice Department policy. The description—especially in the initial draft, when it was "grossly negligent"—came perilously close to the language of the Espionage Act. But Comey felt some characterization was important to ward off criticism that the FBI was favoring her and ignoring what was an inappropriately risky handling of state secrets.

Appointing a special counsel—a step Comey weighed at several junctures—would have avoided the appearance of a conflict and thus any need for Comey to intervene. The last special counsel, Kenneth Starr (whose title was independent counsel), had led to Bill Clinton's impeachment and all but ended his presidency. With that precedent in mind, naming a special counsel for Clinton would surely have seriously damaged her candidacy, no matter the outcome. Once Comey knew she was unlikely to be charged, naming a special counsel would likely have done irreparable damage to the FBI. In any event, it was up to the Justice Department to name a special counsel.

As Comey said many times, there were no good choices and certainly no perfect ones. At the time—after July 5, but before he reopened the investigation in October—Comey drew bipartisan praise for his decision, even from Nancy Pelosi. Loretta Lynch, whose authority Comey arguably usurped, seemed content to have Comey bear the burden and the controversy of making the decision.

Had Huma Abedin kept Clinton's emails off her husband's laptop, no one would have second-guessed Comey's decision to make the announcement.

- Was the opening of the Russia investigation motivated by hostility to Trump, using a salacious and bogus dossier funded by the Clinton campaign?

The Russia investigation began after George Papadopoulos, a Trump campaign adviser, told Australia's ambassador to the United Kingdom, Alexander Downer, that Russia had damaging information about Hillary Clinton. Downer passed that information to Canberra, which initially did nothing. Only after WikiLeaks published the first of the hacked Clinton campaign emails did it forward the information to the Americans.

Australia is one of the United States' closest allies, and Downer was a respected and reliable source.

The subsequent arrival of the Steele dossier, in mid-September, reinforced the FBI's concerns but had only marginal value. The FBI—Strzok in particular—distrusted anything with a Russian provenance. He was immediately concerned that so little of it could be either verified or disproven. Most of it was not, in his words, "actionable intelligence." He knew as well that while Putin and Russia might well have preferred Trump over Clinton, Russia's true objective wasn't to elect any particular candidate but something much more profound and disturbing: to undermine America's democracy and sow chaos in its electoral system. The dossier was perfectly designed to do that.

At the same time, much of the dossier was accurate and corroborated other facts known to the FBI. The FBI had every reason to mention it in its FISA application on Carter Page, even though the application by no means rested on it. Even now, most of the dossier remains neither proven nor disproven, including its salacious account of Trump's visit to the Ritz-Carlton.

Most compelling, the FBI in fact opened a case file not on Trump but only on four of his campaign associates who had direct ties to Russia. The bureau had every reason to do so, and three of the four (Papadopoulos, Flynn, and Manafort) ended up being indicted or pleading guilty to crimes.

Had the FBI been motivated by animus to Trump, it could have opened a file in the summer or fall of 2016, and there were those inside the bureau who argued that it should have. Yet Comey held off.

Even after Trump asked for Comey's "loyalty" and to "let . . . go" of the

Flynn investigation, Comey delayed out of an abundance of caution. Only after Comey was fired, and McCabe's job seemed to be hanging by a thread, did the FBI open a file on Trump. McCabe went to the Justice Department, where he sought and obtained Rosenstein's approval. McCabe and Rosenstein then briefed the congressional leadership, including the Republican Speaker of the House and majority leader of the Senate. No one raised any objections.

For the fact that he fired Comey and thus became the subject of an FBI investigation into collusion with Russia and obstruction of justice, Trump has no one to blame but himself. As Bannon said, firing Comey was the biggest mistake "maybe in modern political history."

- Does a "Deep State" exist, and did it plot a coup to overthrow an American president?

Trump is hardly the first president to face resistance from, and to express hostility toward, elements of the federal bureaucracy. As the *New Yorker* editor David Remnick wrote in a 2017 essay (even before Trump had begun using the phrase), "Eisenhower warned of the 'military-industrial complex'; L.B.J. felt pressure from the Pentagon; Obama's Syria policy was rebuked by the State Department through its 'dissent channel.' But to use the term as it is used in Turkey, Pakistan, or Egypt is to assume that all these institutions constitute part of a subterranean web of common and nefarious purpose."

"The problem in Washington is not a Deep State; the problem is a shallow man—an untruthful, vain, vindictive, alarmingly erratic President," Remnick concluded.

Even Mike Lofgren, whose essay propelled the phrase into the current national conversation, has been alarmed by the way it's been weaponized by Trump and his chorus of supporters. "There is something about Trump that senior operatives, either within the Beltway or in their corporate bastions, don't like," Lofgren wrote in a 2017 essay for the Lobe Log website. "His disgusting vulgarity and unhinged ranting embarrasses people who like to think of themselves as professionals. And, of course, the caterwauling about the Deep State by White House trolls may deceive people into thinking that the Deep State, however one defines it, and Donald Trump are in mortal combat."

Yet "a glance at Trump's policy choices shows that this theory is nonsense. His cabinet, filled with moguls from Big Oil, mega-banking, investment, and retail, makes George W. Bush's cabinet look like a Bolshevik workers' council."

It's not that no "Deep State" exists, in Lofgren's view, but that Trump himself is a willing part of it. Legislation like Trump's tax code—one of his few major accomplishments—was largely designed and implemented by a Treasury secretary (Steven Mnuchin) and the top White House economic adviser (Gary Cohn) who are both alumni of Goldman Sachs—a linchpin of the "Deep State."

Steve Bannon told me that the "deep state conspiracy theory is for nut cases. America isn't Turkey or Egypt." There is an entrenched bureaucracy, but "there's nothing 'deep' about it," he said. "It's right in your face."

James Comey, the ostensible high mandarin of the Deep State, told me he'd never heard the phrase until after he was fired. Trump's idea of a Deep State "is both dead wrong and dead right," he said. "There's no Deep State looking to bring down elected officials and political leaders that represents some deep-seated center of power," Comey said. "But it's true in a way that should cause Americans to sleep better at night. There's a culture in the military, in the intelligence agencies, and in law enforcement that's rooted in the rule of law and reverence for the Constitution. It's very deeply rooted and, thank God, I think it would take generations to destroy."

AFTER RESIGNING AS attorney general, Jeff Sessions consulted with friends and advisers about whether to run for his old Senate seat from Alabama. Charles Cooper, Sessions's lawyer, said the FBI closed its investigation of Sessions without recommending any charges, and did so even before Sessions knew such an investigation existed. The FBI has made no public comment.

Donald McGahn, the White House counsel who defied Trump's directive to get rid of Mueller and refused his requests to publicly dispute accounts of the incident, left the White House on October 17, after cooperating extensively with the special counsel. More than anyone else in the White House, McGahn saved Trump from his most reckless impulses and what would have been an even more damning report and greater likelihood of impeachment.

For that he received no gratitude from the president. "I was NOT going to fire Bob Mueller, and did not fire Bob Mueller," Trump tweeted after the Mueller report was released. "In fact, he was allowed to finish his Report with unprecedented help from the Trump Administration. Actually, lawyer Don McGahn had a much better chance of being fired than Mueller. Never a big fan!"

Trump replaced McGahn with Pat Cipollone, a Washington lawyer who was an adviser and speechwriter for Barr when he was attorney general in the 1990s.

Rod Rosenstein announced his resignation on April 29, 2019, effective May 11. In a letter to Trump he praised the president while professing faith in the rule of law: "I am grateful to you for the opportunity to serve; for the courtesy and humor you often display in our personal conversations; and for the goals you set in your inaugural address: patriotism, unity, safety, education, and prosperity, because 'a nation exists to serve its citizens.' The Department of Justice pursues those goals while operating in accordance with the rule of law. The rule of law is the foundation of America. It secures our freedom, allows our citizens to flourish, and enables our nation to serve as a model of liberty and justice for all."

In a speech in New York on April 25, Rosenstein again pointedly stressed the rule of law and quoted the president (as he had on multiple occasions) saying, "We govern ourselves in accordance with the rule of law rather than the whims of an elite few or the dictates of collective will." But the statement was actually less than a full-throated endorsement of the proposition by Trump. The president made the comment in prepared remarks commemorating Law Day, and Rosenstein omitted the first words of the full quotation: "Law Day recognizes that we govern ourselves in accordance with the rule of law." Trump didn't explicitly say he embraces the proposition.

After leaving office, Rosenstein dropped any pretense of cordial relations with Comey, let alone admiration. "The former director is a partisan pundit, selling books and earning speaking fees while speculating about the strength of my character and the fate of my immortal soul," Rosenstein told a Baltimore audience on May 13. "That is disappointing."

Rosenstein's supporters have said the former deputy attorney general deserves credit for seeing the Mueller investigation through to its conclusion even if that meant denying accounts of his post–May 9 behavior, capitulating to Trump by writing the letter justifying Comey's firing, and delivering the scalps of McCabe and Strzok—in essence, that the end justified whatever means were necessary.

In his Baltimore speech, Rosenstein assessed his tenure: "I took a few hits and made some enemies during my time in the arena, but I held my ground and made a lot of friends. And thanks to them, I think I made the right calls on the things that mattered."

Since publishing his book, Comey has taught a course in ethical leadership at the College of William & Mary, his alma mater. He has lectured at law schools, including Chicago, Stanford, and Yale. Still, Comey's friends are dismayed that his career in public service was cut short and is unlikely to resume anytime soon, if ever.

Comey's emergence as a writer and his position as a firsthand witness to Trump's methods have earned him a prominent place on the nation's editorial pages. Writing in *The New York Times* on May 1, 2019, Comey said he was baffled by how Barr and Rosenstein handled the Mueller report.

How could Barr "start channeling the president in using words like 'no collusion' and FBI 'spying'"? Comey asked. "And downplaying acts of obstruction of justice as products of the president's being 'frustrated and angry,' something he would never say to justify the thousands of crimes prosecuted every day that are the product of frustration and anger?"

And how could Rosenstein "give a speech quoting the president on the importance of the rule of law? Or on resigning, thank a president who relentlessly attacked both him and the Department of Justice he led for 'the courtesy and humor you often display in our personal conversations'?"

Comey's answer: "Accomplished people lacking inner strength can't resist the compromises necessary to survive Mr. Trump and that adds up to something they will never recover from."

On May 28, in *The Washington Post*, Comey took on the "Deep State" conspiracy theorists. "The conspiracy theory makes no sense. The FBI wasn't out to get Donald Trump. It also wasn't out to get Hillary Clinton. It was out to do its best to investigate serious matters while walking through a vicious political minefield.

"But go ahead, investigate the investigators, if you must. When those investigations are over, you will find the work was done appropriately and focused only on discerning the truth of very serious allegations. There was no corruption. There was no treason. There was no attempted coup. Those are lies, and dumb lies at that. There were just good people trying to figure out what was true, under unprecedented circumstances."

FOLLOWING IN COMEY'S footsteps, in February 2019 McCabe published a memoir, *The Threat: How the FBI Protects America in the Age of Terror and Trump*. McCabe also had a star turn on national television, in his case *60 Minutes*, where he was courageous (or foolish) to so publicly criticize Trump and the Justice Department while he was under criminal investigation, and therefore still at their mercy.

The Threat shot to the top of national bestseller lists. McCabe will no doubt need whatever royalties the book earns, for his ordeal didn't stop with his being fired and denied his retirement benefits. The Justice Department referred the inspector general's report to the U.S. attorney for the District of Columbia. McCabe remains under criminal investigation for perjury (and perhaps other crimes), as a result of his statements about the source of the *Wall Street Journal* article.

McCabe has said he is constrained by the ongoing investigation about what he can say in his defense. In his book, he said, "I had done my best to answer the questions accurately—and when I realized I needed to clarify and correct what I had said, I did so voluntarily, without being prompted." He added that he was filing a lawsuit to challenge his firing and how it was handled, as well as the inspector general's conclusions.

With the ongoing attacks by Trump and the unresolved issue of criminal charges, McCabe hasn't found a job in the private sector.

ON APRIL 25, 2019, President Trump launched a renewed attack on Lisa Page and Peter Strzok. Appearing on his preferred news program, *Hannity* on Fox, Trump said, "These two were beauties. There is no doubt about it. They were going hog wild to find something about the administration which obviously wasn't there."

He continued, "These were the two that talked about the insurance policy just in case Hillary Clinton loses. If she loses, we've got an insurance policy. Well, that was the insurance policy.

"Now, she lost and now they are trying to infiltrate the administration to—really, it's a coup. It's spying. It's everything that you can imagine. It's hard to believe in this country that we would have had that."

Page and Strzok haven't had the national platform available to Comey and McCabe. While it hasn't been easy, given the harsh public spotlight cast on their affair, they've both managed to preserve their marriages. They've had little choice but to be more open and honest with their spouses. Page has been working at a Washington law firm. Strzok hasn't found a job in the private sector, but he, too, is working on a book. Both testified under oath in congressional hearings, which gave them an opportunity to address their critics.

"What would you say to those who allege that the special counsel's probe has become irredeemably tainted because you and Lisa Page were once a part of the Russia investigation," the Democrat Jerrold Nadler of New York asked Strzok.

"I'd say that is utterly nonsense," Strzok answered.

He went on, "I never, ever considered or let alone did any act which was based on my personal belief. My actions were always guided by the pursuit of the truth, and moreover, anything I did was done in the context of a much broader organization." He continued, "When you look at the totality of what occurred, the procedures that were followed, demonstrably followed and followed in accordance with law and our procedures, they were complete. They were thorough. They were absolutely done with no motive other than a pursuit of the truth."

The Illinois Democrat Raja Krishnamoorthi asked Strzok if he was aware of any FBI or Justice Department investigations motivated by political bias, and he answered no. "That's not who we are," he said. "What distresses me the most are people's suggestion that the FBI is the sort of place where that even could possibly occur is destructive to the rule of law and the mission of the FBI to protect the United States."

When it was Page's turn, Elijah Cummings asked, "Do you agree with the President's statement that the FBI's reputation is in tatters and is the worst in history?"

"Well, it is now," Page answered.

"And why do you say that?"

"Because we continue to be a political punching bag. Because some private texts about our personal opinions continue to be used as a broad brush to describe the entire activity of 36,500 individuals. Because we have been caught up in a place that we never could have possibly imagined, because all of us did the job that was asked of us."

"Is that painful?"

"It's horrendous, sir."

BY MID-2019, PRESIDENT Trump appeared to have the White House counsel, attorney general, and FBI director he wanted. Certainly none is a Roy Cohn, Trump's model for the ideal lawyer. But the Justice Department's release of the Strzok-Page texts, its publicizing of their affair, the handling of Strzok's termination, the demotion of Ohr, and the harsh treatment of McCabe raise disturbing questions about their willingness to stand up to a president and preserve the long tradition of independent law enforcement and the rule of law.

Rosenstein prided himself on seeing Mueller over the finish line. But at what cost? Who emerged the victor in this epic contest? Trump was exonerated of collusion with the Russians, and Barr and Rosenstein moved swiftly to free him from any threat of obstruction of justice charges. More broadly, Trump appears to have gained considerable sway over the institutions that dared to investigate him and thwarted his repeated demands that Hillary Clinton be prosecuted.

On May 13, Barr assigned John Durham, the U.S. attorney in Connecticut, to lead a probe into the origins of the Russia investigation and the roles of the FBI and the Justice Department. In an interview on *60 Minutes*, Barr said that "if foreign elements can come in and affect it," referring to the presidential election, "that's bad for the republic. But by the same token, it's just as dangerous to the continuation of self-government and our republican system, that we not allow government power, law enforcement or intelligence power, to play a role in politics, to intrude into politics, and affect elections."

Sounding every bit the "Deep State" convert, Barr continued, "Republics have fallen because of a Praetorian Guard* mentality where government officials get very arrogant, they identify the national interest with their own political preferences and they feel that anyone who has a different opinion is somehow an enemy of the state. And there is that tendency that they know better and that they're there to protect as guardians of the people. That can easily translate into essentially supervening the will of the majority and getting your own way as a government official."

"And you are concerned that that may have happened in 2016?" asked CBS's chief legal correspondent, Jan Crawford.

"Well, I just think it has to be carefully looked at because the use of foreign intelligence capabilities and counterintelligence capabilities against an American political campaign to me is unprecedented and it's a serious red line that's been crossed," Barr replied.

---

* The Praetorian Guard was the elite unit of the Imperial Roman Army that protected the emperor. It later engaged in political intrigues, in some cases overthrowing emperors and choosing their successors, starting with the assassination of Caligula in AD 41.

THE ULTIMATE TEST of their independence will be the willingness of the FBI and the Justice Department to satisfy Trump's seemingly insatiable thirst for vengeance. For the president hasn't simply declared victory.

At a White House press conference on May 23, the NBC White House correspondent Peter Alexander pointed out, "Sir, the Constitution says treason is punishable by death. You've accused your adversaries of treason," and asked, "Who specifically are you accusing of treason?"

"Well, I think a number of people."

"Who are you speaking of?"

"If you look at Comey; if you look at McCabe; if you look at probably people—people higher than that; if you look at Strzok; if you look at his lover, Lisa Page, his wonderful lover—the two lovers, they talked openly."

Trump elaborated on their alleged misdeeds and concluded, "That's treason."

ACKNOWLEDGMENTS

A t Penguin Press, my editor, Ann Godoff, immediately embraced the idea, saw its potential, shepherded my reporting, and stepped in with words of encouragement along the often twisted path to its finish. Her assistant, Casey Denis, kept me on schedule. Elisabeth Calamari, executive publicity and marketing associate, greeted my book with enthusiasm.

My long-time agent, Amanda Urban, has been involved in every step of the process from proposal to publication. Her sense of timing has been especially invaluable, and I'm grateful she pushed me to finish when I did.

Brian Gordon served as researcher and fact checker and worked with great speed, efficiency, and accuracy.

Steve Coll, dean of the Columbia Journalism School and a noted author himself, was incredibly supportive.

At *The New York Times*, I'm lucky to work with a great team of editors and journalists: business editor Ellen Pollock; finance editor David Enrich; my previous editor Bill Brink; deputy business editor Adrienne Carter; and from the masthead, executive editor Dean Baquet and deputy managing editor Matthew Purdy.

I can't imagine having finished this without my friends and family: my brother, Michael, his wife, Anna, and their children (my nephew Aidan worked for me one summer and did research on the origins of the "Deep State"); my sister, Jane Holden, her husband, John; and my fellow author and editor friends Jane Berentson, Sylvia Nasar, and Arthur Lubow. Steve Swartz was an especially valuable sounding board at our frequent lunches.

I've saved the most important for last: Benjamin Weil, my husband, who, among his many talents, is also an outstanding editor and writer. He not only provided sustained love and sustenance but did yeoman's work on the manuscript as first reader, editor, researcher, and organizer-in-chief. I will be hard-pressed to repay him.

NOTES

This book is the product of over two years of reporting, which included scores of interviews, the review of thousands of pages of transcripts, and research into published sources. These events have been the subject of numerous congressional hearings. Fortunately, many of those transcripts have been made public, including those from closed-door sessions, which provided a rich source of sworn testimony from which to draw.

Many of these events have also been the subject of outstanding reporting by my fellow journalists. I have cited their work in the notes that follow. The work of my *Times* colleagues Michael Schmidt and Adam Goldman, who were part of the team that won a Pulitzer Prize in 2018 for coverage of the Trump campaign's ties to Russia, has been exemplary. Reporters from *The Washington Post* also deserve recognition for their numerous scoops. The *Times*'s and *Post*'s coverage is cited disproportionately below.

Nearly all my interviews were on a not-for-attribution basis, which isn't surprising given the current political climate. Many people named either are the subject of ongoing investigations or fear they will be. Given Trump's vow to find and punish the "traitors" involved in investigating him, these fears appear to be only too well founded. To the extent sources are quoted by name directly in the text, other than from transcripts or published sources, they are from on-the-record interviews.

I have also used dialogue throughout. What words were spoken are facts like any others. Many are from transcripts or recordings. In those instances I have generally corrected grammatical errors and deleted repeated words and verbal tics. Others are based on the recollections of participants in the conversations. Some dialogue was included in official reports, such as the Mueller report.

I'm grateful to the many people who agreed to be interviewed, in some cases on many occasions and at great length. It took courage and trust on their part to speak to a reporter and author who, in most cases, they'd never met. I hope the day comes when they can reveal themselves without fear of retribution.

Introduction

1 **all white males**: "Directors, Then and Now," FBI.gov.
2 **the election made him "nauseous"**: Comey remarks at Senate Judiciary Committee, May 3, 2017.
3 **published a controversial "dossier"**: "These Reports Allege Trump Has Deep Ties to Russia," *BuzzFeed News*, January 10, 2017.
3 **formal FBI investigation into possible collusion**: House Intelligence Committee hearing on Russian interference in the 2016 U.S. election, March 20, 2017.
4 **new mission statement**: James Comey, *A Higher Loyalty: Truth, Lies, and Leadership* (New York: Flatiron Books, 2018), p. 263.
5 **"JAMES COMEY RESIGNS"**: "Did Fox News Report That James Comey Resigned?," Snopes, May 10, 2017.
5 **"TRUMP FIRES FBI DIRECTOR COMEY"**: CNN, May 9, 2017.
6 **As McCabe walked in**: Andrew McCabe, *The Threat: How the FBI Protects America in the Age of Terror and Trump* (New York: St. Martin's Press, 2019), 8.
7 **"No," Rosenstein interjected**: Ibid., 10.
7 **"Today, President Donald J. Trump informed"**: "Statement from the Press Secretary," May 9, 2017.
9 **Once outside, he fielded calls**: Comey, *Higher Loyalty*, 264–65.
11 **The two communicated constantly**: "Peter Strzok–Lisa Page Texts," FBI Archives.
12 **At 8:40 p.m., he texted Page**: Ibid.
14 **had sent a letter to Trump the prior year**: Memorandum, June 8, 2018.
14 **four-page letter to congressional leaders**: William Barr to Lindsey Graham et al., March 24, 2019.
14 **"complete and total exoneration"**: "Remarks by President Trump Before Air Force One Departure," Whitehouse.gov, March 24, 2019.
14 **"It was an illegal investigation"**: "Remarks by President Trump Before Marine One Departure," Whitehouse.gov, April 10, 2019.
15 **"I think spying did occur"**: "Justice Department Fiscal Year 2020 Budget Request," C-SPAN, April 10, 2019.

Chapter One: "Nobody Gets Out Alive"

19 **Obama said he'd seek**: "Obama Seeking Extension for Director of F.B.I.," *New York Times*, May 12, 2011.

19   **Comey wasn't exactly a clone of Mueller**: Comey, *Higher Loyalty*, 5–14.

19   **"You did not shade"**: Garrett M. Graff, *The Threat Matrix: The FBI at War in the Age of Terror* (New York: Little, Brown, 2011), 492.

19   **"standing for something. Making a difference"**: Comey, *Higher Loyalty*, 13.

20   **"Perhaps because I did survive"**: Graff, *Threat Matrix*, 290.

20   **As Mueller told graduates**: "Robert Mueller's 2013 Commencement Remarks," College of William & Mary, May 12, 2013.

21   **"I don't care about politics"**: Comey, *Higher Loyalty*, 94.

22   **"Like those before us"**: "American Civil Liberties Union 2003 Inaugural Membership Conference," June 13, 2003, FBI.gov.

22   **"whole life was about doing things"**: Comey, *Higher Loyalty*, 88.

22   **"Thousands of people are going to die"**: Ibid., 86.

23   **Comey reached Ashcroft's room**: U.S. Senate Judiciary Committee hearing on the U.S. attorney firings, May 15, 2007.

23   **Mueller arrived a few minutes later**: Robert Swan Mueller Program Log, March 10, 2004.

24   **"the law had held"**: Comey, *Higher Loyalty*, 91.

24   **"Here I stand"**: Ibid., 96.

26   **"some officials familiar with the continuing"**: "Bush Lets U.S. Spy on Caller Without Courts," *New York Times*, December 16, 2005.

27   **"contrary to Hollywood-style myth"**: Alberto R. Gonzales, *True Faith and Allegiance: A Story of Service and Sacrifice in War and Peace* (Nashville: Nelson Books, 2016).

27   **Gonzales never recovered politically**: "Embattled Attorney General Resigns," *New York Times*, August 27, 2007.

28   **"a near contempt for partisan politics"**: "Is James Comey Too Self-Righteous to Save Us from Terror?," *Newsweek*, June 5, 2013.

28   **"The biggest of Mr. Comey's misjudgments"**: "The Political Mr. Comey," *Wall Street Journal*, June 23, 2013.

28   **This time Eric Holder**: Comey, *Higher Loyalty*, 118–20.

29   **"I need to sleep at night"**: Ibid., 119.

30   **"Once you are director"**: Ibid., 120.

30   **"I know that everyone here joins me"**: "Remarks by the President at Nomination of James Comey as Director of the FBI," Whitehouse.gov, June 21, 2013.

32   **"there were only the two of you"**: McCabe, *Threat*, 166.

34   **after an "exhaustive" investigation**: "Investigative Report on the Terrorist Attacks on U.S. Facilities in Benghazi, Libya, September 11–12, 2012," U.S. House of Representatives Permanent Select Committee on Intelligence, November 21, 2014.

36   **Clinton answered reporters' questions**: "Hillary Clinton Tries to Quell Controversy over Private Email," *New York Times*, March 10, 2015.

36   **"It took eight days"**: "Hillary Clinton Formally Announces 2016 Run," *Politico*, April 12, 2015.

37   **"improbable quest"**: "Donald Trump, Pushing Someone Rich, Offers Himself," *New York Times*, June 16, 2015.

37   **"an uphill battle"**: "Donald Trump Announces Presidential Bid," *Washington Post*, June 16, 2015.

37   **honoring David Margolis's fifty years**: "Associate Deputy Attorney General David Margolis' 50th Anniversary at the Department of Justice—Part 2," U.S. Department of Justice, June 17, 2015.

38 **he made a formal referral**: "Clinton E-mail Investigation: Mishandling of Classified—Unknown Subject or Country (SIM)," U.S. Department of Justice, July 2016.

38 **"sensitive investigative matter"**: (U) Sensitive Investigative Matter/Academic Nexus, "Domestic Investigations and Operations Guide," Federal Bureau of Investigation.

38 **the FBI operating manual**: "Domestic Investigations and Operations Guide," Federal Bureau of Investigation, 10-1.

38 **"was considered one of, if not the foremost"**: Interview of Edward William Priestap, U.S. House of Representatives, Committee on the Judiciary, 31.

39 **"You know you are totally screwed"**: Comey, *Higher Loyalty*, 168.

Chapter Two: **"The Doors That Led to Hell"**

40 **Less than two weeks after the Clinton email referral**: "Inquiry Sought in Hillary Clinton's Use of Email," *New York Times*, July 23, 2015.

42 **the Espionage Act**: The Espionage Act of 1917, University of Houston Digital History.

43 **"gross negligence"**: Title 18-CRIMES AND CRIMINAL PROCEDURE, Office of the Law Revision Counsel: United States Code, 18 USC 793.

43 **what, exactly, constitutes "gross negligence"**: *A Review of Various Actions by the Federal Bureau of Investigation and Department of Justice in Advance of the 2016 Election*, U.S. Department of Justice, 26–34.

43 **Over the summer, the FBI team**: "Clinton E-mail Investigation: Mishandling of Classified—Unknown Subject of Country (SIM)," 18–22, Federal Bureau of Investigation.

44 **the comment made him "queasy"**: "Comey Says He Felt 'Queasy' After Lynch Directive on Email Probe," *Politico*, June 8, 2017.

44 **At the press roundtable**: "F.B.I. Chief Says Politics Won't Interfere with Inquiry on Hillary Clinton's Email," *New York Times*, October 1, 2015.

45 **"You know, she made a mistake"**: "President Obama," CBS News, October 11, 2015.

46 **Comey tapped McCabe**: "Andrew McCabe Named Deputy Director of the FBI," FBI National Press Office, January 29, 2016.

47 **running for statewide office**: McCabe, *Threat*, 168–73.

48 **Under the Hatch Act**: Political Activities, U.S. Department of Justice, updated March 22, 2016.

48 **He didn't vote**: "FBI Director Says He's No Longer a Registered Republican," *Politico*, July 7, 2016.

50 **"You guys are finally going to get that bitch"**: *Review of Various Actions by the Federal Bureau of Investigation and Department of Justice in Advance of the 2016 Election*, 199.

51 **"It is always a great honor"**: "Trump Says 'Great Honor' to Get Compliments from 'Highly Respected' Putin," ABC News, December 17, 2015.

51 **"I'm no prude"**: "Peter Strzok–Lisa Page Texts," FBI Archives.

52 **"because I was on the Clinton investigation"**: *Review of Various Actions by the Federal Bureau of Investigation and Department of Justice in Advance of the 2016 Election*, 401.

52 **"personal opinion talking to a friend"**: "FBI Agent Peter Strzok Faces Questions on Anti-Trump Texts," CNN Transcripts, July 12, 2018.

52 **"bright and inviolable line"**: *Review of Various Actions by the Federal Bureau of Investigation and Department of Justice in Advance of the 2016 Election*, 400.

52 **case against James J. Smith**: "F.B.I. Agent Pleads Guilty in Deal in Chinese Spy Case," *New York Times*, May 13, 2004.

52 **the gross negligence charges were never litigated**: Kelly J. Smith, "An Enemy of Freedom: *United States v. James J. Smith* and the Assault on the Fourth Amendment," *Loyola of Los Angeles Law Review* 39 (December 2006): 1424.

53 **Petraeus pleaded guilty to one**: "Criminal Prohibitions on Leaks and Other Disclosures of Classified Defense Information," Congressional Research Service, 24–25.

53 **"large volumes of highly classified information"**: "Improper Handling of Classified Information by John M. Deutch," Central Intelligence Agency, February 18, 2000.

54 **Such lack of provable intent**: Mary-Rose Papandrea, "National Security Information Disclosures and the Role of Intent," *William & Mary Law Review* 56, no. 4 (2015): 1426–33.

55 **"has to be so gross"**: *Review of Various Actions by the Federal Bureau of Investigation and Department of Justice in Advance of the 2016 Election*, 30–31.

55 **By the time McCabe became Comey's deputy**: "Why Intent, Not Gross Negligence, Is the Standard in Clinton Case," War on the Rocks, July 14, 2016.

55 **"Wasserman Schultz assured Benardo"**: Via Electronic Transmission, Senate Committee on the Judiciary, June 22, 2017.

60 **"In the Clinton situation"**: Ruth Marcus, "Why a No-Indictment for Hillary Clinton Would Still Be a Problem for America," *Washington Post*, March 29, 2016.

60 **"Things are fair not fixed"**: *Review of Various Actions by the Federal Bureau of Investigation and Department of Justice in Advance of the 2016 Election*, 186.

61 **"The both of us are just kind of like"**: Ibid.

61 **And there were some who felt the idea**: Ibid., 200–201.

62 **"very active and prominent role"**: Ibid., 177.

62 **"I wanted Comey up there"**: Ibid., 179.

62 **"Jim, I thought we had talked"**: Ibid., 175.

63 **The draft was tough on Clinton**: Ibid., 187–88.

64 **"While it is not noted specifically"**: Ibid., 182.

65 **An ongoing concern in discussions**: Ibid., 193–94.

65 **Comey said he just took the phrase**: Comey, *Higher Loyalty*, 181.

Chapter Three: A Sighting on the Tarmac

68 **That Lynch thought she could escape**: *Review of Various Actions by the Federal Bureau of Investigation and Department of Justice in Advance of the 2016 Election*, 202–9.

70 **Less than twenty-four hours later**: "Full Timeline & Breakdown of Uncovered Lynch-Clinton Emails," ACLJ, June 28, 2016.

70 **Later that day, Sign asked**: *Review of Various Actions by the Federal Bureau of Investigation and Department of Justice in Advance of the 2016 Election*, 213.

71 **"caused a cascading political storm"**: "Bill Clinton's Fondness for Tarmac Talk Gets Him into Trouble," *New York Times*, July 1, 2016.

71 **"doesn't take mistakes lightly"**: *Review of Various Actions by the Federal Bureau of Investigation and Department of Justice in Advance of the 2016 Election*, 217, 220.

73 **"reviewed by career supervisors"**: Ibid., 218.

73 **"I'll be briefed on it"**: Aspen Ideas Festival 2016: "Crime and Punishment: A Conversation on 21st Century Policing, Civil Rights, and Criminal Justice Reform," Aspen, Colorado, July 1, 2016.

74 **"Hey, you've surely already considered this"**: Ibid., 132.

75 **"technically illiterate"**: Ibid., 127.

75 **While she might have known little**: Hillary R. Clinton, FBI Records: The Vault, 1–33.

76 **"I can't sit here"**: *Review of Various Actions by the Federal Bureau of Investigation and Department of Justice in Advance of the 2016 Election*, 137.

77 **"I can't and I hope someday"**: Ibid., 224.

78 **"Good morning," Comey began**: "Statement by FBI Director James B. Comey on the

Investigation of Secretary Hillary Clinton's Use of a Personal E-mail System," FBI.gov, July 5, 2016.

78 **"short of dashing across the street"**: *Review of Various Actions by the Federal Bureau of Investigation and Department of Justice in Advance of the 2016 Election*, 226–27.

80 **"that was way out of order"**: Ibid., 228.

80 **"Today is the best evidence"**: "Coverage of Donald Trump's Speech in North Carolina; Trump Slams 'Crooked Hillary' Email Investigation; Trump on Clinton Email Decision: 'System Is Rigged,'" CNN, July 5, 2019.

Chapter Four: **"This Feels Momentous"**

82 **CNN ran a feature**: "FBI Boss Comey's 7 Most Damning Lines on Clinton," CNN, July 5, 2016.

82 **"Though he recommended no criminal charges"**: "FBI Recommends No Criminal Charges in Clinton Email Probe," *Washington Post*, July 5, 2016.

83 **"In just a few minutes of remarks"**: "F.B.I.'s Critique of Hillary Clinton Is a Ready-Made Attack Ad," *New York Times*, July 5, 2016.

83 **Not only had Comey emerged unscathed**: "12 Times Democrats Praised FBI Director James Comey as an American Hero," *The Federalist*, October 31, 2016.

85 **That night, just after Trump's formal nomination**: "Read Chris Christie's Convention Speech Attacking Hillary Clinton," *Time*, July 22, 2016.

86 **From the guilty cries emerged another refrain**: "How 'Lock Her Up!' Became a Mainstream GOP Rallying Cry," *Rolling Stone*, July 21, 2016.

86 **Others at the convention picked up the refrain**: "Michael Flynn Leads 'Lock Her Up' Chant at 2016 RNC," YouTube, December 1, 2017.

87 **"an energy and oil consultant, excellent guy"**: Transcript of Donald Trump's meeting with the *Washington Post*, washingtonpost.com, March 21, 2016.

87 **"said it would be damaging"**: "Alexander Downer, Signing Off," *Australian*, April 28, 2018.

87 **Even more intriguing**: *Report on the Investigation into Russian Interference in the 2016 Presidential Election*, U.S. Department of Justice, 2:89.

88 **The next day, at a press conference**: "Candidate Trump News Conference on July 27, 2016," C-SPAN, June 14, 2017.

89 **"Donald goes out of his way"**: "Michael Cohen Has Said He Would Take a Bullet for Trump. Maybe Not Anymore," *New York Times*, April 20, 2018.

89 **"lock and load"**: *Report on the Investigation into Russian Interference in the 2016 Presidential Election*, 2:137.

Chapter Five: **"The Band Is Back Together"**

98 **Comey explicitly refused to say**: "F.B.I. Director James Comey Testifies Before Congress," *New York Times*, July 7, 2016.

98 **Mercer Family contribution**: "'Clinton Cash' Book Got Most of Its Funding from One Hedge Fund Star," *Bloomberg News*, January 18, 2017.

98 **"When a source, no matter"**: "Don't Kill the Messenger," *U.S. News & World Report*, April 23, 2015.

99 **"The foundation should remove"**: "Clinton Foundation Should Stop Accepting Funds," *Boston Globe*, August 16, 2016.

100 **"One school of thought"**: Strzok testimony, Transcript of Peter Strzok House Judiciary Committee Interview, House Judiciary Committee, 269.

101 **"I want to believe the path"**: "What the Strzok-Page 'Insurance Policy' Text Was Actually About," *Washington Post*, March 14, 2019.

105 **"Anthony Weiner carried on a months-long"**: "EXCLUSIVE: Anthony Weiner Carried On a Months-Long Online Sexual Relationship with a Troubled 15-Year-Old Girl Telling Her She Made Him 'Hard,' Asking Her to Dress Up in 'School-Girl' Outfits, and Pressing Her to Engage in 'Rape Fantasies,'" *Daily Mail*, September 21, 2016.

105 **In just three paragraphs**: Article 235—NY Penal Law, New York State Law, Penal Law.

105 **"threatens to remind voters"**: "Anthony Weiner and Huma Abedin to Separate After His Latest Sexting Scandal," *New York Times*, August 29, 2016.

106 **Among the domain addresses**: FBI Communication on Discovery of Hillary Clinton E-mails on Anthony Weiner's Laptop Computer, FBI Records: The Vault, 2.

106 **"Just putting this on the record"**: JW v DOJ FBI Weiner production 02105, pg 34, October 17, 2018.

108 **"I don't even wait"**: "Trump Recorded Having Extremely Lewd Conversation about Women in 2005," *Washington Post*, October 7, 2016.

108 **Two days later, FBI agents**: "Clinton Campaign Chairman Ties Email Hack to Russians, Suggests Trump Had Early Warning," *Washington Post*, October 11, 2016.

110 **"We were consumed by these ever-increasing allegations"**: *Review of Various Actions by the Federal Bureau of Investigation and Department of Justice in Advance of the 2016 Election*, 298.

110 **"My focus wasn't on Midyear anymore"**: Ibid., 297.

112 **"FBI agents say the bureau"**: "Exclusive: FBI Agents Say Comey 'Stood in the Way' of Clinton Email Investigation," *Daily Caller*, October 17, 2016.

114 **"something had fallen through the cracks"**: *Review of Various Actions by the Federal Bureau of Investigation and Department of Justice in Advance of the 2016 Election*, 304.

114 **"I did the right thing"**: Ibid., 305.

114 **"Clinton Ally Aided Campaign"**: "Clinton Ally Aided Campaign of FBI Official's Wife," *Wall Street Journal*, October 24, 2016.

116 **"good news, in a bad news way"**: *Review of Various Actions by the Federal Bureau of Investigation and Department of Justice in Advance of the 2016 Election*, 317.

116 **Comey and McCabe wondered**: U.S. House of Representatives, Executive Session Committee on the Judiciary, Joint with the Committee on Government Reform and Oversight, 152–53.

118 **"We don't know with certainty"**: DOJ OIG Releases Report on Various Actions by the Federal Bureau of Investigation and Department of Justice in Advance of the 2016 Election, June 14, 2018, Office of the Inspector General.

Chapter Six: "To Speak or to Conceal"

123 **"I ought to be fired"**: *Review of Various Actions by the Federal Bureau of Investigation and Department of Justice in Advance of the 2016 Election*, 358.

124 **Axelrod was shocked and dismayed**: Ibid., 360–64.

126 **"This is BS"**: Ibid., 354–55.

128 **"FBI Dir just informed me"**: "FBI Dir just informed me, 'The FBI has learned of the existence of emails that appear to be pertinent to the investigation.' Case reopened," @jasoninthehouse, October 28, 2016, 11:57 A.M.

128 **"It sounds like Comey is being"**: "'This Changes Everything': Donald Trump Exults as Hillary Clinton's Team Scrambles," *New York Times*, October 28, 2016.

129 **"Comey made an independent decision"**: "Justice Officials Warned FBI That Comey's

Decision to Update Congress Was Not Consistent with Department Policy," *Washington Post*, October 29, 2016.

129 **"in love with my own righteousness"**: Comey, *Higher Loyalty*, 206.

130 **"FBI in Internal Feud"**: "FBI in Internal Feud over Hillary Clinton Probe," *Wall Street Journal*, October 30, 2016.

131 **A few days later, Comey asked**: McCabe, *Threat*, 196.

131 **"Comey had no choice"**: William Barr, "James Comey Did the Right Thing," *Washington Post*, October 31, 2016.

131 **"I have to tell you"**: "Presidential Candidate Donald Trump Rally in Phoenix, Arizona," C-SPAN, October 29, 2016.

131 **"Molotov cocktail"**: "Democrats' One-Word Answer to Their Horrible Night: Comey," *Washington Post*, September 11, 2016.

132 **"a former senior intelligence officer"**: David Corn, "A Veteran Spy Has Given the FBI Information Alleging a Russian Operation to Cultivate Donald Trump," *Mother Jones*, October 31, 2016.

134 **"swept away her largest and most immediate problem"**: "Emails Warrant No New Action Against Hillary Clinton, F.B.I. Director Says," *New York Times*, November 6, 2016.

135 **"A victory by Mr. Trump remains possible"**: "Who Will Be President," *New York Times*, November 8, 2016.

Chapter Seven: **"There Were No Prostitutes"**

139 **"We may find people of great technical talent"**: "Comey on FBI Hiring Cyber Talent," C-SPAN, August 30, 2016.

139 **In an interview on Fox News**: "Chris Wallace Hosts 'Fox News Sunday,' Interview with President-Elect Donald Trump," CQ Newsmaker Transcripts, December 11, 2016.

140 **The incoming White House chief of staff**: "Chris Wallace Hosts 'Fox News Sunday,' Interview with Incoming White House Chief of Staff Reince Priebus," Fox News, December 18, 2016; "Reince Priebus on War of Words with White House over Russia," Fox News, December 18, 2016.

140 **To the White House communications director**: *Report on the Investigation into Russian Interference in the 2016 Presidential Election*, 2:23.

145 **On January 6 a motorcade of black SUVs**: Comey, *Higher Loyalty*, 218–25.

145 **The focus would be Russian interference**: James Comey, memo, My notes from private session with PE on 1/6/17, January 7, 2017.

148 **"Classified documents presented last week"**: "Intel Chiefs Presented Trump with Claims of Russian Efforts to Compromise Him," CNN, January 12, 2017.

149 **Just one hour later, BuzzFeed News**: "These Reports Allege Trump Has Deep Ties to Russia."

149 **Michael Cohen, Trump's lawyer**: *Report on the Investigation into Russian Interference in the 2016 Presidential Election*, 2:27–28.

149 **"have been incalculable and will play"**: "How a Sensational, Unverified Dossier Became a Crisis for Donald Trump," *New York Times*, January 11, 2017.

150 **"if I could put out a statement"**: *Report on the Investigation into Russian Interference in the 2016 Presidential Election*, 2:28.

150 **"I'm a germophobe"**: Comey, *Higher Loyalty*, 226.

150 **"Something is rotten in the state of Denmark"**: David Ignatius, "Why Did Obama Dawdle on Russia's Hacking?," *Washington Post*, January 12, 2017.

152 **"We all have our personal lives"**: U.S. House of Representatives, Committee on the Judiciary, 45–46.

154 **On Sunday afternoon, January 22**: "Brief Remarks: Donald Trump Speaks to Inauguration Law Enforcement Officers—January 22, 2017," Factbase.

154 **When Comey described the encounter**: "What James Comey Told Me About Donald Trump," *Lawfare*, May 18, 2017.

155 **"You know what I said"**: Flynn quoted in McCabe, *Threat*, 200. (The comment doesn't appear in McCabe's contemporaneous notes.)

156 **The two agents arrived early**: Strzok's interview of Flynn, Case 1:17-cr-00232-EGS Document 62, U.S. Department of Justice, December 17, 2018.

156 **"relaxed and jocular,"**: *"United States of America v. Michael T. Flynn*, Defendant's Memorandum in Aid of Sentencing," United States District Court for the District of Columbia, December 11, 2018.

157 **"Not happy"**: Peter P. Strzok interview, Federal Bureau of Investigation, July 19, 2017.

158 **Trump didn't want to fire Flynn**: *Report on the Investigation into Russian Interference in the 2016 Presidential Election*, 2:41.

158 **"Not again, this guy, this stuff"**: Ibid., 32.

158 **Trump didn't waste any time**: Comey, *Higher Loyalty*, 235–44.

158 **The next day, Comey was lunching at his desk**: *Report on the Investigation into Russian Interference in the 2016 Presidential Election*, 2:35.

159 **"Don't talk about Russia"**: Ibid., 33.

161 **"I need loyalty," he said again**: Comey memo, My notes from private session with PE on 1/6/17, January 7, 2017.

Chapter Eight: "Where's My Roy Cohn?"
163 **The same day as Comey's dinner**: "Why Sally Yates Stood Up to Trump," *New Yorker*, May 22, 2017.

163 **About five hours later**: Sally Yates, U.S. Department of Justice, September 28, 2017.

164 **"a role model"**: "Read Rosenstein's Full Opening Statement on Comey to Congress," *PBS NewsHour*, May 19, 2017.

164 **"Rod is a survivor"**: "What James Comey Told Me About Donald Trump."

164 **On Sunday, February 5**: "President Trump Talks Travel Ban, Putin, Mexico; Could Trump Pull Federal Funds from California?; Trump Says There Could Be Tax Cut by End of 2017," CNN Transcripts, February 5, 2017.

165 **Three days later, on February 8**: Comey memo, My notes from private session with PE on 1/6/17, January 7, 2017; Comey, *Higher Loyalty*, 248–49.

168 **"privately discussed U.S. sanctions against Russia"**: "National Security Adviser Flynn Discussed Sanctions with Russian Ambassador, Despite Denials, Officials Say," *Washington Post*, February 9, 2017.

169 **"Oh, this is fine"**: Pence quoted in McCabe, *Threat*, 203.

170 **"Okay. That's fine. I got it"**: *Report on the Investigation into Russian Interference in the 2016 Presidential Election*, 2:37.

170 **"We'll give you a good recommendation"**: Ibid., 38.

170 **"Unfortunately, because of the fast pace of events"**: Michael Flynn, Whitehouse.gov, February 13, 2017.

170 **"The President was very concerned"**: Press Briefing by Press Secretary Sean Spicer, Whitehouse.gov, February 14, 2017.

171 **"Now that we fired Flynn"**: *Report on the Investigation into Russian Interference in the 2016 Presidential Election*, 2:38–39.

171 **"No way," he said**: Chris Christie, *Let Me Finish: Trump, the Kushners, Bannon, New Jersey, and the Power of In-Your-Face Politics*, with Ellis Henican (New York: Hachette Books, 2019), 329.

172 **The suggestion made Christie uncomfortable**: *Report on the Investigation into Russian Interference in the 2016 Presidential Election*, 2:39.

173 **"I want to talk about Mike Flynn"**: Ibid., 40.

174 **"I hope you can see your way"**: Ibid., 39–40.

174 **"unqualified contradiction to what the Bureau stood for"**: McCabe, *Threat*, 204.

175 **"General Flynn is a wonderful man"**: "Remarks by President Trump and Prime Minister Netanyahu of Israel in Joint Press Conference," Whitehouse.gov, February 15, 2017.

175 **"Phone records and intercepted calls"**: "Trump Aides Had Contact with Russian Intelligence," *New York Times*, February 15, 2017.

176 **"You're not being good partners"**: Priebus quoted in McCabe, *Threat*, 204.

176 **"acting like his own branch of government"**: *Report on the Investigation into Russian Interference in the 2016 Presidential Election*, 2:53.

176 **"fine man"**: "Remarks by President Trump in Press Conference," Whitehouse.gov, February 16, 2017.

177 **"violation of procedures"**: "FBI Refused White House Request to Knock Down Recent Trump-Russia Stories," CNN Politics, February 24, 2017.

179 **"I have decided to recuse myself"**: Attorney General Sessions Statement on Recusal, U.S. Department of Justice, March 2, 2017.

179 **meeting with McGahn and Priebus**: "Obstruction Inquiry Shows Trump's Struggle to Keep Grip on Russia Investigation," *New York Times*, January 4, 2018.

179 **"I don't have a lawyer"**: *Report on the Investigation into Russian Interference in the 2016 Presidential Election*, 2:50.

180 **"who to investigate"**: Ibid., 76.

180 **pulled Sessions aside to ask him to "unrecuse"**: Ibid., 51.

181 **Trump was in a "panic/chaos"**: Ibid., 52.

182 **On March 20, Comey gave a similar briefing**: Transcript of Comey testimony, March 20, 2017: Hearing on Russian Election Tampering Before the House Permanent Select Intelligence Committee, 15th Cong., 1st Sess.

183 **The next day, he was "beside himself"**: *Report on the Investigation into Russian Interference in the 2016 Presidential Election*, 2:54.

183 **The president was consumed with the issue**: Ibid., 55.

184 **At about 8:15 a.m. on March 30**: Comey, *Higher Loyalty*, 258–59.

184 **"lift the cloud"**: Comey memo, March 30, 2017.

185 **On April 7, Trump's nominee Neil M. Gorsuch**: "Neil Gorsuch Confirmed by Senate as Supreme Court Justice," *New York Times*, April 7, 2017.

186 **Just four days later**: Comey memo, April 11, 2017.

Chapter Nine: **"I Know You Told Me Not To"**

187 **A few hours after speaking to Comey**: "President Trump's Thoroughly Confusing Fox Business Interview, Annotated," *Washington Post*, April 11, 2017.

188 **"half vote-of-confidence"**: Ibid., annotation.

188 **"the last straw"**: *Report on the Investigation into Russian Interference in the 2016 Presidential Election*, 2:75.

189 "Hillary Clinton would probably be": Nate Silver, "The Comey Letter Probably Cost Clinton the Election," FiveThirtyEight, May 3, 2017.

189 While Silver didn't dismiss other factors: Ibid.

190 "Look, this is terrible": Oversight of the Federal Bureau of Investigation, Committee of the Judiciary, May 3, 2017.

192 "That ship had sailed": *Report on the Investigation into Russian Interference in the 2016 Presidential Election*, 2:64.

194 "I'm going to read you a letter": Ibid., 63–64.

194 At 5:00 p.m., the group met: Ibid., 67.

195 On the afternoon of May 9: *A Report of Investigation of Certain Allegations Relating to Former FBI Deputy Director Andrew McCabe*, Office of the Inspector General, 15.

196 Rosenstein's memo had duly landed: Restoring Public Confidence in the FBI, documentcloud, 1–3.

197 "not to see the light of day": *Report on the Investigation into Russian Interference in the 2016 Presidential Election*, 2:68.

198 "the only line the President cared about": Ibid., 69.

198 Fox News cheered the news: "Fox News Is Covering James Comey's Firing from an Alternate Reality," *Slate*, May 10, 2017.

198 The *Wall Street Journal* editorial page: "Comey's Deserved Dismissal," *Wall Street Journal*, May 9, 2017.

199 But they were exceptions: "Trump Fires FBI Director James Comey over Email Investigation," NBC News, May 9, 2017.

199 Evidently channel surfing: *Report on the Investigation into Russian Interference in the 2016 Presidential Election*, 2:70.

200 in which he was "screaming": Ibid.

200 "Just turn the lights off": "After Trump Fired Comey, White House Staff Scrambled to Explain Why," *Washington Post*, May 10, 2017.

200 Spicer told reporters: *Report on the Investigation into Russian Interference in the 2016 Presidential Election*, 2:70.

Chapter Ten: Seven Days in May

204 "I just fired the head of the FBI": "Trump Told Russians That Firing 'Nut Job' Comey Eased Pressure on Investigation," *New York Times*, May 19, 2017.

205 "Not only would it be an issue": Transcripts of Jim Baker Interview with House Judiciary and Oversight Committees, Lawfare, April 9, 2019.

210 The next morning, McCabe, Baker, and Lisa Page: McCabe's Senate testimony: Hearing on Worldwide Threats, U.S. Senate Select Committee on Intelligence, May 11, 2017.

213 "Never forget, no one speaks": "Behind the Scenes of Trump's Infamous Lester Holt Interview," *Axios*, April 21, 2019.

213 At the White House, Holt: "Lester Holt's Interview with Trump," NBC News, May 11, 2017.

214 "Something was needed": Comey, *Higher Loyalty*, 270.

215 The result was an explosive article: "In a Private Dinner, Trump Demanded Loyalty. Comey Demurred," *New York Times*, May 11, 2017.

217 In this highly charged environment: "Former Attorney General: Trump Made the Right Call on Comey," *Washington Post*, May 12, 2017.

217 On Friday morning McCabe had his first meeting: "Read the Full Transcript of

Former FBI Deputy Director Andrew McCabe's *60 Minutes* Interview," *Time*, February 18, 2019.

224 "have a heart attack": Ibid.

Chapter Eleven: "This Is the End of My Presidency"

227 "like feeding seagulls at the beach": James Comey testimony transcript on Trump and Russia, *Politico*, June 8, 2017.

229 "he did not come in looking for the job": *Report on the Investigation into Russian Interference in the 2016 Presidential Election*, 2:81.

230 "By virtue of the authority": Appointment of Special Counsel to Investigate Russian Interference with the 2016 Presidential Election and Related Matters, Office of the Deputy Attorney General, May 17, 2017.

231 "Oh my God. This is terrible": *Report on the Investigation into Russian Interference in the 2016 Presidential Election*, 2:78.

233 But Trump's was a solitary voice: "Special Counsel Appointment Gets Bipartisan Praise," *Hill*, May 17, 2017.

233 "a great deal of confidence": "Grassley Statement on the Appointment of Special Counsel in Russian Interference Probe," Chuck Grassley, May 17, 2017.

233 "has sterling credentials and is above reproach": "Senator Collins' Statement on Appointment of Former FBI Director Robert Mueller as Special Counsel," Susan Collins, May 17, 2017.

233 "The investigation will go on": "Robert Mueller: The Special Counsel America Needs," *New York Times*, May 17, 2017.

233 "part of the brotherhood of prosecutors": "The Mueller Caveat," *Wall Street Journal*, May 18, 2017.

235 The two debated the issue: "Strzok Page Text Messages 5-19-17," scribd, uploaded January 23, 2018.

237 "That did prompt some discussion": Peter Nicholas, Aruna Viswanatha, and Erica Orden, "Trump's Allies Urge Harder Line as Mueller Probe Heats Up," *Wall Street Journal*, December 8, 2017.

239 Bannon told Trump that his complaints: *Report on the Investigation into Russian Interference in the 2016 Presidential Election*, 2:81.

239 McGahn, too, told Trump: Ibid., 85.

240 Trump took his complaints about Mueller: Ibid., 81.

241 more than eighteen million viewers: "Nearly 20 Million Viewers Watched James Comey's Senate Testimony," *Fortune*, June 9, 2017.

244 "It rings in my ear": "Trump's Meddlesome Priest," *New York Times*, June 8, 2017.

244 Minutes after Comey finished testifying: "Donald Trump's Response to James Comey's Testimony: Read His Lawyer's Statement in Full," *Independent*, June 8, 2017.

245 The next day, at a press conference: "Remarks by President Trump and President Iohannis of Romania in a Joint Press Conference," Whitehouse.gov, June 9, 2017.

246 Ruddy appeared that evening: "Trump Confidant Christopher Ruddy Says Mueller Has 'Real Conflicts' as Special Counsel," *PBS NewsHour*, June 12, 2017.

246 "Spicer issued a bizarre late night press release": "Trump Friend Chris Ruddy Says Spicer's 'Bizarre' Statement Doesn't Deny Claim Trump Seeking Mueller Firing," ABC News, June 13, 2017.

247 "While the president has the right": *Report on the Investigation into Russian Interference in the 2016 Presidential Election*, 2:83.

247 Ruddy's comments prompted Senator Susan Collins: "Rosenstein Says He Wouldn't Fire Special Counsel Mueller Without Good Cause," NPR, June 13, 2017.

247 The president called Sessions at home: *Report on the Investigation into Russian Interference in the 2016 Presidential Election*, 2:107.

247 On June 14, *The Washington Post* disclosed: "Special Counsel Is Investigating Trump for Possible Obstruction of Justice, Officials Say," *Washington Post*, June 14, 2017.

249 "You gotta do this. You gotta call Rod": *Report on the Investigation into Russian Interference in the 2016 Presidential Election*, 2:85–86.

249 McGahn felt trapped: Ibid., 85.

249 "tired of it being portrayed": "Bork Irked by Emphasis on His Role in Watergate," *New York Times*, July 2, 1987.

Chapter Twelve: "The Worst Day of My Life"

251 The president's disdain for both men: "Sessions Told White House That Rosenstein's Firing Could Prompt His Departure, Too," *Washington Post*, April 20, 2018.

251 In the Oval Office on June 19: *Report on the Investigation into Russian Interference in the 2016 Presidential Election*, 2:90–93.

252 "What can I do? I'm not an employee": Ibid., 93.

252 Later that day, Trump and Hope Hicks: "Excerpts from the Times's Interview with Trump," *New York Times*, July 19, 2017.

254 Sunday meeting with Rosenstein and Mueller: "Rosenstein-McCabe Feud Dates Back to Angry Standoff in Front of Mueller," *Washington Post*, October 10, 2018.

255 To Hicks's dismay, the *Times* led: "Citing Recusal, Trump Says He Wouldn't Have Hired Sessions," *New York Times*, July 19, 2017.

255 there was an investigation before: *Report on the Investigation into Russian Interference in the 2016 Presidential Election*, 1:95.

257 The *Post* responded that: John Wagner, "Trump Levels False Attacks Against the Post and Amazon in a Pair of Tweets," *Washington Post*, July 23, 2017.

258 Priebus was soon ousted: Donald Trump (@realDonaldTrump), Twitter, July 28, 2017, 4:00 P.M.

260 McCabe later said he felt "disconnected": McCabe, *Threat*, 253.

264 On a late summer Friday: "Michael Cohen Would Take a Bullet for Donald Trump," *Vanity Fair*, September 6, 2017.

264 So it should have come as no surprise: "READ: Michael Cohen's Statement to the Senate Intelligence Committee," CNN, September 19, 2017.

265 He had his lawyer in the Russia investigation: "Text of Trump Team Memos to Special Counsel Assailing Comey," Associated Press, July 7, 2018.

266 but he had lied, too: *Report on the Investigation into Russian Interference in the 2016 Presidential Election*, 2:193.

268 "I'm sympathetic": Katelyn Polantz, "Transcript Released of Flynn Voicemail from Trump Lawyer Showing Possible Attempt to Obstruct," CNN, May 31, 2019.

268 The next day, the president tried to focus attention: "Remarks by President Trump Before Marine One Departure," Whitehouse.gov, December 15, 2017.

268 But reporters quickly asked about Flynn: "President Trump Remarks on Tax Reform and Michael Flynn Guilty Plea," C-SPAN, December 2, 2017.

268 Trump followed up with a series: "President Trump's Departure Remarks," C-SPAN, December 4, 2017.

270 **"those cheatin' FBI lovebirds"**: "FBI Lovebirds Might Be Getting Busy in Other Ways, Too," *New York Post*, April 10, 2018.

271 **The tirade prompted a rare response**: Eric Holder (@EricHolder), Twitter, December 3, 2017, 8:57 A.M.

274 **Wray said only that he**: "In Texts, FBI Officials in Russia Inquiry Said Clinton 'Just Has to Win,'" *New York Times*, December 12, 2017.

274 **Congressman Andy Biggs, Republican of Arizona**: "Rep. Biggs on Strzok-Page Texts: 'In Any Other Country We Would Call It a Coup,'" Fox News, April 26, 2019.

275 **"It's a shame what's happened"**: "Remarks by President Trump Before Marine One Departure," Whitehouse.gov, December 15, 2017.

275 **In this highly charged atmosphere**: U.S. House of Representatives, Executive Session Committee on the Judiciary, Joint with the Committee on Government Reform and Oversight, 16-258.

278 **Two days later, Trump did exactly that**: Donald Trump (@realDonaldTrump), Twitter, December 23, 2017, 2:27 P.M.

Chapter Thirteen: Deep State

279 **In an essay to accompany the Moyers interview**: "Essay: Anatomy of the Deep State," Moyers Archive, February 21, 2014.

280 **On January 12, *The Wall Street Journal***: "Trump Lawyer Arranged $130,000 Payment for Adult-Film Star's Silence," *Wall Street Journal*, January 12, 2018.

280 **When Cohen sought guidance**: *Report on the Investigation into Russian Interference in the 2016 Presidential Election*, 1:145.

281 **Trump said he wanted McGahn to write**: Ibid., 115, 116.

282 **The next day, in an Oval Office meeting**: Ibid., 116–17.

282 **Despite Trump's earlier public statements**: "The Trump Lawyers' Confidential Memo to Mueller, Explained," *New York Times*, June 2, 2018.

288 **McCabe was watching CNN**: "Ex–FBI Deputy Director Andrew McCabe Is Fired—and Fires Back," CNN, March 17, 2018.

288 **"Andrew McCabe FIRED"**: Donald Trump (@realDonaldTrump), Twitter, March 16, 2018, 11:08 P.M.

291 **A time-honored way**: *Report on the Investigation into Russian Interference in the 2016 Presidential Election*, 2:145–48.

291 **On April 24, at a press conference**: "'Stupid Question': Trump Curtly Dismisses a Reporter's Question About Pardoning Michael Cohen," *Washington Post*, April 24, 2018.

292 **"Much of the bad blood with Russia"**: Donald Trump (@realDonaldTrump), Twitter, April 11, 2018, 8:00 A.M.

293 **"DOJ just issued the McCabe report"**: Donald Trump (@realDonaldTrump), Twitter, April 13, 2018, 2:36 A.M.

293 **Trump had already taken to Twitter**: Donald Trump (@realDonaldTrump), Twitter, April 13, 2018, 7:01 A.M.

294 **Saying he was inspired by a video clip**: "Trump Touts Hannity's Show on 'Deep State Crime Families' Led by Mueller, Comey, and Clintons," *Washington Post*, April 12, 2018.

295 **Stephanopoulos and his producers were thorough**: "Transcript: James Comey's Interview with ABC News Chief Anchor George Stephanopoulos," ABC News, April 15, 2018.

296 **"The big questions in Comey's badly reviewed book"**: Donald Trump (@realDonaldTrump), Twitter, April 15, 2018, 6:57 A.M.

297 "James Comey's book is titled": Frank Bruni, "Comey Is Trump's Ultimate Victory," *New York Times*, April 16, 2018.

297 And Comey faced criticism: "Ex–FBI Agents Say Comey Is 'Damaging the Agency' as He Clashes with Trump," *Guardian*, April 17, 2018.

297 In the wake of Comey's ABC interview: President Trump Job Approval, RealClearPolitics, May 2018.

298 On June 8, 2018, William Barr: Memorandum, June 8, 2018.

298 On June 14, Michael Horowitz: DOJ OIG Releases Report on Various Actions by the Federal Bureau of Investigation and Department of Justice in Advance of the 2016 Election, Office of the Inspector General.

299 "Inspector General Blasts Comey": "Inspector General Blasts Comey and Also Says Others at FBI Showed 'Willingness to Take Official Action' to Hurt Trump," *Washington Post*, June 14, 2018.

299 "Comey's Actions 'Extraordinary and Insubordinate'": "Comey's Actions 'Extraordinary and Insubordinate,' Report Says," CNN, June 14, 2018.

299 "Those seven words are what Trump and his allies will seize on": "How 7 Words in the 500-Page IG Report Give Donald Trump All the 'Deep State' Ammo He Wanted," CNN, June 14, 2018.

301 Cohen turned to television: "EXCLUSIVE: Michael Cohen Says Family and Country, Not President Trump, Is His 'First Loyalty,'" ABC News, July 2, 2018.

302 Trump leaped on the disparity: "Trump: Cohen Payments Came from Me, Not the Campaign," Fox News, August 22, 2018.

302 In early September, the Justice Department: "Text Messages Between Former FBI Officials Capture Reactions to Stories on Russia Investigation," CNN, September 14, 2018.

303 A little more than a week later: "Rod Rosenstein Suggested Secretly Recording Trump and Discussed 25th Amendment," *New York Times*, September 21, 2018.

304 Rosenstein met with John Kelly: "Rod Rosenstein's Job Is Safe, for Now: Inside His Dramatic Day," *New York Times*, September 24, 2018.

304 "extended conversation": "At the request of Deputy Attorney General Rod Rosenstein, he and President Trump had an extended conversation to discuss the recent news stories. Because the President is at the United Nations General Assembly and has a full schedule with leaders from around the world, they will meet on Thursday when the President returns to Washington, D.C.," Sarah Sanders (@PressSec), Twitter, September 24, 2018, 11:48 A.M.

305 The next day, Trump was in: "Remarks by President Trump in Press Conference After Midterm Elections," Whitehouse.gov, November 7, 2018.

306 Just before his appointment to the Justice Department: "President Trump's Pick to Replace Jeff Sessions Suggested Cutting Off Robert Mueller's Funding," *Time*, November 7, 2018.

307 "He was my first choice from day one": "President Trump White House Departure," C-SPAN, December 7, 2018.

307 On November 20, Trump's lawyers finally submitted: "Full Text of Mueller's Questions and Trump's Answers," Associated Press, April 18, 2019.

307 "What I can tell you is": "Trump Submits Answers to Special Counsel Questions About Russian Interference," *Washington Post*, November 20, 2018.

308 Cohen was sentenced to three years: "'Dirty Deeds': Ex–Trump Lawyer Cohen Gets 3 Years in Prison," Associated Press, December 12, 2012.

309 "Attorney General Bill Barr is preparing": "Justice Department Preparing for Mueller Report as Early as Next Week," CNN, February 20, 2019.

309 "The special counsel's investigation has consumed": "Justice Department Preparing for Mueller Report in Coming Days," *Washington Post*, February 20, 2019.

309 "The great national psychodrama": "'Merely the End of Chapter One': The Mueller Report, Rumored to Drop Next Week, Is Only the Beginning," *Vanity Fair*, February 21, 2019.

309 A *New York Times* reporter spotted Giuliani: "Where's the Mueller Report? Washington Barely Handled the Anticipation," *New York Times*, March 22, 2019.

Conclusion

311 As he was boarding Air Force One: "Remarks by President Trump Before Air Force One Departure," Whitehouse.gov, March 24, 2019.

311 Rudy Giuliani and Jay Sekulow: Giuliani/Sekulow interview with Wolf Blitzer, "'Impossible to Obstruct Justice if There's No Underlying Crime,' No Collusion Means No Obstruction," RealClearPolitics, March 24, 2019.

312 The reality was far more complex: "Read: Letter from Special Counsel Robert Mueller to Attorney General William Barr," CNN, May 1, 2019; "Mueller Complained That Barr's Letter Did Not Capture 'Context' of Trump Probe," *Washington Post*, April 30, 2019; "Read Robert Mueller's Letter to William Barr Critiquing the Attorney General's Summary of His Report," *Time*, May 1, 2019.

314 Mueller demolished the notion: *Report on the Investigation into Russian Interference in the 2016 Presidential Election*, 2:157.

314 no underlying criminal activity: "Martha Stewart to Donald Trump: Can There Be Obstruction of Justice with No Underlying Crime?," PolitiFact, March 25, 2019.

315 "The only commitment I made": "I Can Land the Plane," Washington Post, April 28, 2019.

316 Mueller might not have concluded: *Report on the Investigation into Russian Interference in the 2016 Presidential Election*, 2:2.

318 He marked the occasion: "Full Transcript of Mueller's Statement on Russia Investigation," *New York Times*, May 29, 2019.

318 By then, it had dawned: "Remarks by President Trump Before Marine One Departure," Whitehouse.gov, May 30, 2019.

323 "maybe in modern political history": "The 48 Most Revealing Lines of Steve Bannon's '60 Minutes' Interview," CNN, September 12, 2017.

323 As the *New Yorker* editor David Remnick: "There Is No Deep State," *New Yorker*, March 11, 2017.

323 Even Mike Lofgren, whose essay: "Yes, There Is a Deep State—but Not the Right Wing's Caricature," Lobe Log, March 17, 2017.

325 For that he received no gratitude: Donald Trump (@realDonaldTrump), Twitter, May 11, 2019, 5:39 P.M.

325 Rod Rosenstein announced his resignation: "READ: Deputy AG Rod Rosenstein's Resignation Letter," CNN, April 29, 2019.

325 In a speech in New York on April 25: GBC 2019 Annual Meeting—Rod Rosenstein, Vimeo, May 17, 2019.

325 "We govern ourselves in accordance": "Deputy Attorney General Rod J. Rosenstein Delivers Remarks at the Armenian Bar Association's Public Servants Dinner," New York, April 25, 2019, U.S. Department of State.

325 **"Law Day recognizes that we govern"**: "President Donald J. Trump Proclaims May 1, 2018, as Law Day, U.S.A.," Whitehouse.gov, April 30, 2018.

326 **"The former director is a partisan pundit"**: Billy House and Chris Strohm, "Rod Rosenstein Attacks Comey, Defends Mueller Probe in Speech," *Bloomberg*, May 13, 2019.

327 **On May 28, in *The Washington Post***: "James Comey: No 'Treason.' No Coup. Just Lies—and Dumb Lies at That," *Washington Post*, May 28, 2019.

327 **McCabe also had a star turn**: "Andrew McCabe: The Full '60 Minutes' Interview," CBS News, February 17, 2019.

327 **McCabe has said he is constrained**: McCabe, *Threat*, 254–55, 259.

330 **In an interview on *60 Minutes***: "William Barr Interview: Read the Full Transcript," CBS News, May 31, 2019.

331 **"Sir, the Constitution says treason"**: "Remarks by President Trump on Supporting America's Farmers and Ranchers," Whitehouse.gov, May 23, 2019.

INDEX